SLAVONIC AND ROMANTIC
MUSIC

W9-AED-709

Slavonic and Romantic Music

Essays and Studies

by

GERALD ABRAHAM

WITHDRAWN
L. R. COLLEGE LIBRARY

ST. MARTIN'S PRESS
NEW YORK

CARL A. RUDISILL LIBRARY
LENOIR RHYNE COLLEGE

Printed in Great Britain

780
Ab8s
66889
August 1969

First published in the United States 1968
Library of Congress Catalogue Card Number:
68-13029

© *Gerald Abraham*
1968

CONTENTS

PREFACE

THE earliest of the essays reprinted here was probably written in 1928, the latest in 1966; however, since each bears the date of original publication, the reader can easily see whether he is confronted with the work of crabbed age or of youth. I have not tried to bring them up to date, though in the light of more recent information I have corrected a few errors of fact and—thanks to the generosity of the publishers—sometimes added further musical examples.

Chapters III, VIII, X, XVI, XXVI, XXVII, XXVIII and XXIX originally appeared in *Music and Letters*, VII, XI, XVII and XXIII in *Musical Times*, XIII, XIX, XX, XXI and XXIV in *The Monthly Musical Record*, XIV in *The Music Review*, XV in *Tempo*, XVIII and XXII in *The Musical Quarterly*, and I am grateful to the editors of these periodicals for permission to reprint. I was first printed in the *Proceedings of the Royal Musical Association* for 1960–61, II in the report of the Chopin Congress held at Warsaw in 1960. IV was a contribution to the Dvořák symposium edited by Viktor Fischl (Lindsay Drummond, 1943), IX a chapter in the similar Tchaïkovsky symposium edited by myself (Lindsay Drummond, 1945); the latter has been emended and enlarged by the insertion of passages from 'Tchaïkovsky's First Opera', a study written for the *Festschrift Karl Gustav Fellerer* (Bosse Verlag, Regensburg, 1962). XXV is a similar conflation of a contribution to Mr Herbert Van Thal's *Fanfare for Ernest Newman* (Arthur Barker, 1955) with an article on the original version of *The Flying Dutchman* which appeared in *Music and Letters*. XII was contributed to the *Festschrift Friedrich Blume* (Bärenreiter, Kassel, 1963). V and VI are published here for the first time.

London, 1967.   GERALD ABRAHAM

I—SLAVONIC MUSIC AND THE WESTERN WORLD

My title has nothing to do with the Iron Curtain and its effect on the world of music today. There is a much older curtain between Slavonic music and the Western world, which I should like to pull aside a little: a curtain woven by the group of languages spoken and written by the Slav peoples. It is true that a certain number of vocal works—mostly Russian operas of the period 1870–1910—have thrust their way through by sheer force of genius, and we have learned to enjoy Mussorgsky and Rimsky-Korsakov, Borodin and Tchaïkovsky in more or less unsatisfactory English or French translations, or even in Russian. (Sometimes at Covent Garden, in three languages simultaneously. But operatic audiences are accustomed to enjoying opera in languages they don't really understand.) But not more than three or four Czech operas have made any real impact on Western Europe, and not a single Polish one; even Russian opera is known only by a handful of works. In the field of solo song the position is much worse. We know Mussorgsky was a great song-composer, but we know that mainly because of intensive propaganda rather than from direct experience; it can hardly be otherwise so long as Western singers fight shy of Russian; we should still know Hugo Wolf by hearsay rather than by hearing if we had to rely on translations. Russian is at least as musical a language as German, and as subtle, and the best Russian song-composers—not only Mussorgsky—write vocal lines that reflect and intensify the sense of the words, that are moulded to a certain arrangement of vowels and consonants, like good song-composers in any other language. All this, the great corpus of Russian song, remains almost unknown—or known by its least fine and subtle examples. And not only Russian song; Poland has produced at least two remarkable song-writers, Moniuszko in the last century and Szymanowski in the present one, of whom Szymanowski is known only in German translations and Moniuszko not at all, for his songs have never been translated into English and the wretched French selection[1] is a hundred years old.

Instrumental music, of course, penetrates the curtain with no difficulty, with the result that we think of Russian and Polish music as mainly instrumental. This is a false picture. It is less false, I think, of Czech music. The Czechs (among whom I include the Moravians and Slovaks and Ruthenians, beside the Czechs proper) are an intensely musical people but, whether because they nearly lost their language as a culture-language under the Habsburg monarchy (so that even Smetana had to learn it as a

[1] *Mélodies de Moniuszko*. Traduction française d'Alfred des Essarts. Paris, n.d.

foreigner) or from deficiencies in the language itself (e.g. in vowel-sounds), for some reason their vocal literature is less rich than their instrumental.

The language-curtain obstructs much more than the free passage of Slavonic vocal music. It obstructs our knowledge of a great deal of music that would present no difficulty at all if we could only hear it: the older instrumental music of the Czechs and Poles, and their Latin church music. For—and here I come at last to the very heart of my subject—the Czechs and Poles have always shared the culture of Western Europe, including its music, whereas the Russians began to do so only in the second half of the eighteenth century. Not only were the Russians Christianised from Byzantium, either directly or through Bulgarian missionaries,[1] and left with a different alphabet, a different liturgy and a different liturgical language, for two centuries in the later Middle Ages they suffered under the 'Tatar yoke' and the Princes of Moscow were mere tributaries to Mongol khans. On the other hand, whatever the penetration of Central Europe by the old Slavonic liturgy, whatever the nature of the conflict there between Eastern and Western churches (and on this there are many important points on which the experts still disagree),[2] whatever the political vicissitudes of the Western Slav states, they were never detached in this way from the influences of Western Christendom; the Roman alphabet conquered the Cyrillic and in the church Latin conquered Old Slavonic. Polish and Czech chapter and monastery libraries at Gniezno and Vyšebrod possess Gregorian missals from the eleventh or early twelfth century, and although these no doubt came from the West—the Gniezno missal has St Gall-type neumes[3]—manuscripts of Polish and Czech origins were compiled before long. The Prague Troparium of 1235[4] is only the earliest of a number of Czech and Moravian musical codices of the thirteenth and fourteenth centuries[5] and the Poles claim the composition of a plainsong antiphon which can hardly be later than the twelfth century: 'Magna vox, laude sonora'[6] in honour of St Adalbert, who played such an important part in the Christianisation (or Romanisation) of both Poles and Czechs. And there is a significant parallelism in the appearance of the earliest religious songs with Czech or Polish words; both the Polish 'Bogurodzica' (Hymn to the Mother of God) and the Czech 'Hospodine, pomiluj ny'

[1] R. Palikarova Verdeil, *La musique chez les Bulgares et les Russes (du IXe au XIVe siècle)*, Copenhagen, 1953, pp. 66-7.

[2] See, for instance, Dimitrije Stefanovic, 'Einige Probleme zur Erforschung der slavischen Kirchenmusik', *Kirchenmusikalisches Jahrbuch*, XLIII (1959), p. 1.

[3] Zdzisław Jachimecki, *Historja muzyki polskiej*, Warsaw, 1920, p. 1.

[4] Prague, University Library, Cim 4.

[5] Listed by Jan Racek, *Středověká hudba*, Brno, 1946, p. 45, and *Česká hudba*, Prague, 1958, p. 23.

[6] Hieronim Feicht, 'Polskie średniowiecze', in *Z dziejów polskiej kultury muzycznej*, I (ed. Z. M. Szweykowski), Cracow, 1957, p. 16.

('Lord have mercy upon us', a vernacular *Kyrie*) are m
plainsong motives.[1] Moreover the earliest preserved s
for the same period; the oldest known manuscript o
dates from about 1407, that of 'Hospodine, pom
earlier, though the words are found without the mus

I have no intention of embarking on a potted
Slavonic music, beginning with the Middle Ages. I
only to drive home two points: the essential oneness of this musical culture
with that of Europe generally—and the differences. The Western Slavs
shared in the common stock but often drew from it elements which they
put to their own special uses. Standing on the outer edge of Western
culture, they developed all the fascinating peculiarities one expects to find
in peripheral cultures. One finds similar things in the music of Portugal
and at some periods of history in our own. Peripheral cultures naturally
tend to be 'backward'; even in a country the size of England, provincial
architecture has often been half-a-century or more behind the style
fashionable in London; as we all know, even Germany was very late in
developing polyphony. But there are wonderful compensations in the
variety, in the range of dialects (as it were). Sometimes political or other
non-musical factors play a part; the Hussite wars of the fifteenth century
gave a tremendous stimulus to vernacular Czech song[2] just as the two
centuries and more of Habsburg domination after the Battle of the White
Mountain overlaid and even seemed to extinguish the peculiarly Czech
elements in the music of Bohemia. But the Slavs were quite capable of
developing special musical characteristics without the help of extra-musical
circumstances. Even in the field of notation, Czech neumes evolved with
certain differences.[3] In the thirteenth century the Czechs were still using
non-diastematic neumes; in the fourteenth they progressed to the stave—
and their neumes began to assume peculiar rhomboid forms.[4] But things
were much *more* different in Russia, where liturgical melody had developed
—and developed quite a long way on its own lines—from Byzantine chant
but was stuck fast in a primitive notation which is still unreadable up to
the late fifteenth century, although comparative study with Byzantine
notation is now showing how it may be deciphered.[5] As for the five-line
stave, it reached the Ukraine only in the seventeenth century and Russia

[1] On the 'Bogurodzica', see Jachimecki, *Muzyka polska w rozwoju historycznym*, I.1
(Cracow, 1948), pp. 7–25; on 'Hospodine, pomiluj', see Racek, *Česká hudba*, p. 29, and the
facsimile facing p. 296.

[2] Zdeněk Nejedlý, *Dějiny husitského zpěvu* [six vols., Prague, 1954–6: a reissue of three
works published under different titles in 1904, 1907 and 1913].

[3] Josef Hutter, *Česká notace: I—Neumy* and *II—Nota choralis*, Prague, 1926 and 1930;
and *Notationis bohemicae antiquae specimina selecta*, Prague, 1931.

[4] See Hutter, *Notationis*, and the facsimiles in the appendix of Racek, *Středověká hudba*.

[5] Palikarova Verdeil, op. cit., Chap. VII.

...er in the eighteenth. Genuine polyphony was impossible though a ...ry primitive form of three-part polyphony—in the so-called *troestrochnoe* style, noted in three rows of neumes—begins to appear about the middle of the sixteenth century: the liturgical *cantus firmus* in the middle part is supported at first in unison or octaves by upper and lower voices which branch out from it and close in again to the unison in the manner of the *podgoloski* of Russian polyphonic folk-music. It is not until the mid-seventeenth century that one begins to find four-part polyphony, with the *cantus firmus* in the tenor and the added parts in note-against-note style producing common chords in root position:[1]

Ex. 1

(a) MID-SIXTEENTH CENTURY

Na verblïkh posrede eya o - be - si - kho - mo or - ga - - - - - - ní

(b) MID-SEVENTEENTH CENTURY

Ya - ko ta - - - mo vo - pro - si - sha - nï plen - shi - i nas......

At this period, when Russian liturgical polyphony was in its earliest infancy and Russian secular music reached no higher level than the songs and dance music of the *skomorokhi* (buffoons),[2] Poland and Bohemia were enjoying what modern Polish and Czech historians claim as a 'golden age of polyphony'. It may at first strike us as no more than a pale reflection of the golden age that was being enjoyed at the same time by all Europe, but that is not the whole truth. A great deal of this music deserves not only intensive study but performance.

Two difficulties confront the Western student of this music. One I have already mentioned: the language curtain. It does not conceal so much of the music itself, for a great deal of it is Latin church music, but it makes it difficult for most of us to get at the information about it, the existing stylistic research, and so on. Czech and Polish musicology have fairly long traditions and very high standards, as indeed has Soviet musicology, and the amount of study devoted to the Western Slav polyphonists—to say nothing of the instrumental composers of the seventeenth and eight-

[1] Examples of both three- and four-part chants in musical supplement to S. V. Smolensky, 'Znachenie XVII veka i evo "kantov" i "psalmov" . . .', *Muzïkalnaya starina*, V (1911), pp. 88–9.

[2] It is true that Ivan III had an Italian organist named Giovanni Salvatore and Elizabeth I astonished the court of Fyodor Ivanovich in 1586 with the gift of a clavichord, but these were only curiosities, like Boris Godunov's parrot and clock.

eenth centuries, and early Czech and Polish romantic piano music—is enormous. It exists in print, in books and monographs and learned periodicals, but it might be in Etruscan or Cretan Linear B for all that most of us can make of it and it would be well worth the while of some of the young musicologists now studying Russian to make Polish or Czech their second Slav language.

The second difficulty is that of actual scores. It has at times seemed as if Western Slav musicologists were more interested in studying their old masters than in getting their texts published. Józef Surzyński made an excellent start in 1885 with his Polish *Monumenta*[1] but succeeded in bringing out only four volumes; the later Polish series, *Wydawnictwo dawnej muzyki polskiej*, edited by Chybiński and begun in the 1930s, has produced nearly forty numbers but many of them are very slim, containing only a single work or a selection of short pieces. (The editorial prefaces were from the first provided with a French translation and the post-war numbers are translated into English, French, German and Russian.) The somewhat similar Czech series, *Musica Antiqua Bohemica*, has been devoted almost entirely to instrumental music of the late eighteenth and early nineteenth centuries; it is only in the last few years that the Czechs have begun to publish the work of their classic polyphonists—with trilingual *résumés* of the prefaces but not of the critical apparatus.

A third difficulty is the paucity of surviving material. Poland and the Czechoslovak lands have provided innumerable battlefields during the last four centuries; the Thirty Years War and the two World Wars were only the worst of a series, and the total destruction of music, both manuscript and printed, must have been enormous. (Incidentally, these countries began to print music quite early; a Czech-printed Catholic *Kancionál* appeared in 1529 and a Polish music-publisher, Łazarz Andrysowic, was active at Cracow from 1553 onward.) One reads of a Polish master such as Wacław z Szamotuł who was obviously a very considerable figure in the middle of the sixteenth century; two of his psalm-motets were published by Montanus and Neuber at Nuremberg in 1554 and 1564 in collections of works by the leading French and Netherland masters, and what survives of his music justifies the high esteem in which he was held. Yet one finds so little that does survive: these two motets, another preserved only in organ tablature, some songs with Polish words—a very small proportion of what he is known to have written. His eight-part Mass for the wedding of King Sigismund Augustus is lost; his office settings are lost; of his *Lamentationes*, printed at Cracow by Andrysowic, only the tenor part has been preserved. Another, rather later composer Tomasz Szadek—a member first of the king's private chapel and later of the royal chapel of the Rorantists at Cracow, the two chief centres of the Polish

[1] *Monumenta Musices Sacrae in Polonia*, Poznan, 1885-9.

'golden age'—survives in only two works, other than fragments, and of those two Masses one lacks the *Agnus*.

Technically these works are more or less in the 'late Netherland' style. What distinguishes them and gives them special interest is the infusion of Polish melodic elements, here a phrase from a Polish devotional song, there a pseudo-plainsong found only in Polish sources. Marcin Leopolita, composer and organist to the king in the early 1560s, composed a five-part *Missa pasehalis* or *Missa de resurrectione*,[1] the earliest complete setting of the Ordinary by a Polish composer that has come down to us, which is based on four Easter songs current in Poland and Germany.

The Polish 'golden age' was finally submerged by a flood of Italian musicians brought in by Sigismund III. There had of course been foreign musicians at the Polish court before; Heinrich Finck was a chorister in the royal chapel in his youth and returned there for fourteen years, perhaps as director, from 1492 to 1506. And there had been Italian musical influence.[2] But Sigismund III was a fanatic for the Counter-Reformation and for everything Italian; he moved his court from Cracow to Warsaw, enticed Marenzio to go there (but failed to keep him), invited Giovanni Gabrieli (also in vain) and appointed a whole series of Italians as directors of his chapel, including Asprilio Pacelli,[3] an ancestor of Pope Pius XII, and Giovanni Francesco Anerio. Sigismund evidently liked the brilliant Venetian polychoral style; Pacelli's work is in this style and so are the compositions by the Italian members of the court chapel collected by one of their number (Vincenzo Gigli) and published at Cracow in 1604. Seven years later a native Pole, Mikołaj Zieleński, organist to the Primate of Poland, published at Venice two great collections of Offertories and Communions for the whole year, which entitle him to high rank among the composers of early baroque church music. The Offertories are all for two choirs, with a *partitura pro organo* for each choir consisting of unfigured bass and the highest voice; in some numbers the use of trombones is indicated; the volume also contains a twelve-part *Magnificat* for three choirs.[4] On the other hand, the Communions are very varied in style: solos, duets for soprano and bass, and a great number of pieces in late sixteenth-century style, some with, some without instruments in addition to the organ.

I must repeat that I am not trying to give anything remotely like a

---

[1] Published by Surzyński, op. cit., III, and by Hieronim Feicht, *Wydawnictwo dawnej muzyki polskiej*, XXXV, Cracow, 1957. Feicht has published a study of it in *Kwartalnik muzyczny*, VI–VII (1930), p. 109.

[2] See especially Jachimecki, *Wpływy włoskie w muzyce polskiej—I: 1540–1640*, Cracow, 1911.

[3] Mateusz Gliński embarked on a complete edition of Pacelli's works at Rome in 1948.

[4] Reprinted by Chomiński and Lissa, but without the organ *partitura*, in *Music of the Polish Renaissance*, Cracow, 1955, p. 274.

complete account of Polish music at this period, but only to show the
kind of music that was being produced. Two other names must be mentioned: Adam Jarzębski, a man of many parts—violinist, poet and archi-
tect—and Marcin Mielczewski, both members of the royal chapel who
lived on till the middle of the seventeenth century. Jarzębski composed
only instrumental *canzoni* and *concerti*, such as the following:[1]

Ex. 2

Mielczewski wrote both *a cappella* church music and vocal solo *concerti*
and *motetti concertati* of which this passage from the concerto 'Deus in
nomine tuo'[2] gives a good idea:

Ex. 3

Bohemia suffered even more than Poland from the presence of brilliant
foreign composers at court. The Habsburg kings of Bohemia were either
Holy Roman Emperors or heirs to the Emperors, so that the court chapel
moved between Prague and Vienna; even when the monarch preferred

[1] *Wydawnictwo*, II. [2] *Wydawnictwo*, XV.

Prague, as Rudolf II did, this only resulted in the musical life of Prague being dominated by such foreign masters as Philip de Monte, Jacobus Kerle and Jacobus Gallus or Handl—of whom the last seems to have been of Southern Slav origin: a Slovene. The native Czech composers mostly devoted themselves to the service of the Protestant churches or the Bohemian Brethren, and even those—such as Jiří Rychnovský and Jan Trojan Turnovský—who wrote Latin church music often did so on Czech melodies as *canti fermi*:[1]

Ex. 4

But the most interesting figure, and perhaps the best Czech composer of late sixteenth-century polyphony, was a Catholic nobleman, Kryštof Harant z Polžic,[2] who took the patriotic side against Ferdinand II at the outset of the Thirty Years War and was one of the twenty-seven Czech leaders executed in 1621 after the Battle of the White Mountain. Harant was a rich man, who maintained a private chapel at his castle of Pecka; he visited the Holy Land and in 1608 published an account of his travels to which he appended a musical supplement, a six-part motet 'Qui confidunt in Domino' composed in Jerusalem ten years before under the inspiration (as he tells us) of the singing of the monks at a monastery near the holy places. His most important surviving composition is a five-part 'parody Mass' on Marenzio's 'Dolorosi martir', from which I quote the opening of the *Sanctus* (Ex. 5).

I have dealt at some length with Czech and Polish Catholic church music because this is perhaps the most important field of Slavonic music generally neglected by the Western world, though of course Western scholars from Wooldridge, in the second volume of the original *Oxford History of Music*, to Gustave Reèse, have not entirely overlooked it. But in other fields, too, the Western Slavs marched with the rest of Europe, not quite in step perhaps, but not so very far behind. Take, for instance, the setting of vernacular versions of the Psalms which one finds all over northern and central Europe in the middle of the sixteenth century—not only by Protestant musicians. Wacław z Szamotuł

---

[1] *Kyrie* 'Dunaj, voda hluboká' probably by Turnovský, printed in Jaroslav Pohanka, *Dějiny české hudby v příkladech*, Prague, 1958, p. 49.

[2] See Rudolf Quoika, 'Christoph Harant von Polschitz und seine Zeit', *Die Musikforschung*, VII (1954), 414. Harant's complete surviving musical works, small enough in bulk, have been published by Jiří Berkovec, Prague, 1956.

Ex. 5

spent the last years of his short life under the protection of the Protestant *wojewode* of Lithuania and made at least four four-part settings of Psalms in vernacular versions, with the popular melody in the tenor:[1]

Ex. 6
PSALM LXXXV

These must date from about 1555-60. Of course this is later than Sternhold and Louis Bourgeois but it is earlier than Goudimel. However, the complete setting of the Psalms in Polish, by Mikołaj Gomółka, which really challenges comparison with the big Western collections, did not appear until 1580:[2] Gomółka borrowed all sorts of *canti fermi*—plainsong, Protestant melodies, secular (even dance-like) tunes—and sometimes the settings appear to be entirely his own composition; his settings are all very simple, in little more than note-against-note counterpoint, but attractively varied in treatment:

Ex. 7
PSALM CXXXVII

As for other religious songs in the vernacular, these also flourished though not quite so much as in Germany and Bohemia; there was a great deal of

[1] Three of them are printed by Szweykowski, *Wydawnictwo*, XXVIII, Cracow, 1956; the fourth is lost.

[2] *Melodiae na Psalterz Polski, przez Mikoláiá Gomólke vczynioné* (Cracow, 1580); reprinted complete by J. W. Reiss, Cracow, 1923.

give-and-take musically in the song-books of the Lutherans, the Bohemian Brethren (and the Catholics too, for that matter). In at least one case a complete *Kancionál* of the Bohemian Brethren was translated into Polish.

Broadly speaking, then, in the sphere of vocal music it was Teutonic and Latin Europe that influenced Slavonic Europe, not the reverse. That, no doubt, is the real reason why we tend to ignore or dismiss the Slavonic achievement. It made no impact on us until the nineteenth century, and because we know that it was essentially an offshoot of Western music we assume that it has no great intrinsic value. This is as foolish as it would be to write off the English madrigal school as a mere offshoot of the Italian. But in one field of composition, although the Slavonic achievement may not have been given all the credit due to it, it has been given some credit. I mean instrumental music, which, as I have said, passes easily through the language curtain. Here the Poles in particular, at first, gave as well as took. The German lute and organ tablature books from Newsidler's in 1544 onward (Loeffelholtz's, Nörmiger's) contain 'Polish dances', Telemann wrote 'Sonates polonoises' and both J. S. Bach and, more notably, Wilhelm Friedemann composed 'polonaises'; the amount of genuine Polish influence varies considerably[1] but at least all this music indicates a constant awareness of a Polish music with special characteristics. And then, of course, there were not only Polish organ tablatures, beginning with Jan of Lublin's in the early sixteenth century[2] which doubtless remained unknown to Western musicians, but the works of the Polish lutenists which certainly were known. Besard published a number of delightful pieces by Wojciech Długoraj and Diomedes Cato (who was Venetian by birth but Polish by adoption and in style) in his *Thesaurus* in 1603 and Reys Jakub —better known as Jacob Polak or Polonois—was lutenist at the French court and had his work published in France, Germany and Holland.

Rather curiously, considering the later Czech pre-eminence in instrumental music, the Czechs can show no comparable flowering of lute music or early keyboard music. The oldest Czech lute tablature is a fragmentary collection now in the Národní Museum at Prague,[3] containing (among other things) transcriptions of songs by Jacob Regnart, Vice-*Kapellmeister* of the imperial chapel, which were apparently sung in Prague to Czech texts; it dates from the late sixteenth century and is in German tablature.

---

[1] See Alicja Simon, *Polnische Elemente in der deutschen Musik bis zur Zeit der Wiener Klassiker*, Zürich, 1916, and Chybiński, 'Polnische Musik und Musikkultur des 16. Jahrhunderts in ihren Beziehungen zu Deutschland', *Sammelbände der internationalen Musikgesellschaft*, XIII (1912), p. 463.

[2] 36 numbers printed by Chybiński, *Wydawnictwo*, XX, Cracow, 1948; complete facsimile, *Monumenta Musicae in Polonia*, seria B, I (Warsaw, 1964).

[3] XIII B 237. A Preambulum by Stephanus Laurentius Jacobides and a song transcription are printed in Pohanka, op. cit., p. 66. See also Pohanka's article, 'O nejstarších českých skaldbách pro loutnu', *Hudební rozhledy*, VIII (1955), p. 245.

The oldest Czech organ tablature is also in German notation; this is the České Budějovice fragment of about a hundred years earlier,[1] of historic rather than artistic value. The great period of Czech instrumental music and Czech musical influence on the West came later when religious and political persecution drove so many Czech musicians abroad and covered Europe with Dusíks and Bendas and Stamics and Myslivečeks.

The part played by these composers on the European scene, the fine piano music of Dussek and the eclogues and rhapsodies of Tomášek are fairly well known, but the Czech symphonic music of the early nineteenth century is less so. As an example I quote two passages from the scherzo of the symphony in D composed in 1821 by Jan Václav Voříšek, the opening of the scherzo proper and the trio.

The influence of Beethoven is less obvious than in his superb B flat minor Sonata for piano, but Voříšek's own mastery and his nationality are more marked in the Symphony.

[1] See Emilian Trolda's description in *Cyril*, LXXIII (1948), p. 25.

Nothing in Russian orchestral music of that period can compare in creative power with Voříšek's Symphony. The great days of Russian orchestral music were still to come. But it is worth remarking that they did not begin with Glinka; Alyabiev wrote in 1830 a strikingly scored Symphony in E minor of which the first movement survives.

1961

II—CHOPIN AND THE ORCHESTRA

Critical opinion on Chopin's handling of the orchestra is almost unanimous. The prevailing view was stated long ago by Berlioz, who said that 'in Chopin's composition all the interest is concentrated in the piano part; the orchestra of his concertos is nothing but a cold and almost useless accompaniment'. Writing of the first three works with orchestra—the '*Là ci darem*' *Variations*, the *Fantasia on Polish Airs*, and the *Krakowiak*—Niecks said that 'the orchestral accompaniments [. . .] show in every one of the three works [. . .] an ineptitude in writing for any other instrument than the piano that is quite surprising considering the great musical endowments of Chopin in other respects'; and he was equally cutting about the orchestra of the concertos. Much the same thing has been said by almost every critic down to our own day, when Arthur Hedley wrote that 'Chopin, who was entirely absorbed by the piano [. . .] had neither the gift for creating music in any other setting nor the inclination to master the art of writing for the orchestra'—though he did add that 'one ought not to imagine that Chopin was utterly incapable of writing for the orchestra. The accompaniment to the declamatory middle section of the *larghetto* of Op. 21 is quite a model of its kind.' I myself endorsed the conventional judgment twenty years ago in my book on *Chopin's Musical Style*, where I wrote of the concertos in which 'the inevitable long tuttis show up the inadequacy of the orchestration far more pitilessly than any of the short passages in the earlier works [. . .] It is significant that after this (i.e. after about 1830) Chopin never wrote for orchestra again.' Now and again a voice has been raised in dissent—notably Wojciech Sowiński's in the middle of the last century—but it is generally agreed that Chopin had neither a feeling for the poetry of the orchestra nor command of the technique of orchestration. Klindworth took it upon himself to re-orchestrate the F minor Concerto, Tausig and Balakirev, among others, not only re-scored but partly re-wrote the orchestral part of the E minor.

Only a lover of paradox for its own sake would assert that, on the contrary, Chopin was a master of the orchestra. But renewed study of those half-dozen scores—all dating from the period 1827–31—has convinced me that the generally accepted opinion of Chopin's treatment of the orchestra needs not to be reversed but to be considerably modified. To begin with, his orchestration must be seen in historical perspective. We do not compare Chopin's concertos, as total works, with Beethoven's: the complete difference in character is too obvious. But we do, I think, tend unconsciously to compare his scoring (to its disadvantage) with that of the glowing Romantic orchestra of a rather later period. If we put out of our minds the brilliant oil-painting of Berlioz, of Mendelssohn at his best, of Glinka, and think instead of the delicate water-colour orchestration of Hummel and Field—who were Chopin's real models—we shall at least hear his scoring in true perspective. If we compare it with that of his teacher, Józef Elsner—at least, with those examples of Elsner's orchestration I have been able to see—we shall at once be struck by Chopin's finer, more delicate, and more imaginative colouring. And it is greatly superior to Hummel's. It is true there is nothing in Chopin quite as striking as the *larghetto* of Hummel's B minor Concerto, Op. 89, where the orchestra is reduced to a quartet of horns—an outstandingly romantic effect—but on the other hand he is never as perfunctory as Hummel in his famous A minor Concerto, Op. 85, which obviously influenced Chopin's E minor thematically; here only Hummel's string parts are obbligato; the wind band can be dispensed with altogether. As we shall see, it is precisely in his treatment of the wind that Chopin is at his most poetic as an orchestrator.

The strings are naturally the basis of Chopin's orchestra, but in his most characteristic orchestral passages they are a basis in a quite special sense; they provide, as it were, a canvas on which solo woodwind—or of course the piano—embroiders a delicate melodic tracery. A typical instance is the opening of his very first work with orchestra, the '*Là ci darem*' *Variations*, Op. 2 (in which the handling of the instrumental force is throughout rather tentative): string phrases introduce a piano solo, which is accompanied by sustained string harmonies. But presently a solo flute echoes the last three notes of the piano melody, an octave higher (an effect common in the Italian opera scores of the period); and then solo bassoon and, later, solo clarinet also sound this little three-note motive. The effect is minute, yet characteristic. A little later, still in the *introduzione*, there is a highly important dialogue between first bassoon and first clarinet on the first four or five notes of the Mozart theme: the theme here appears for the first time in shorter note-values—it is beginning to emerge from the mist and take on its true shape (Ex. 1). Yet this passage is not shown at all in some important solo editions of the *Variations*; they print only the piano part which is merely the accompaniment to the thematic work. And here, as everywhere else, we must remember the relative lightness of Chopin's piano which would not have smothered delicate orchestral effects as our modern concert grands tend to do.

It is in the ordinary fuller combinations of strings and woodwind, still more in the tuttis, that Chopin's orchestration is most dull and conventional in the *Variations*—as in the later works generally. The thick, unimaginative scoring of the opening tuttis of the two concertos has done more harm than anything else to Chopin's reputation as an orchestrator.

Ex. 1

But such tuttis form only a small proportion of his scores, and we have the *Krakowiak*, Op. 14, and the finale of the E minor Concerto to show that he also could write effectively for the full orchestra.

On the whole, perhaps, the *Krakowiak*—though not Chopin's best work with orchestra—contains his best scoring. It certainly shows all the characteristics of his best scoring. The opening, with the melodic outline traced by the pianist's two hands, two octaves apart, over a sustained string chord, is as effective as it is simple. Later there is a very great deal of thematic dialogue for solo wind, including horn, against a background of glittering piano arpeggios and sustained string chords; high, light passages in simple octaves for the piano accompanied only by all the strings pizzicato—an effect which seems to anticipate things in Glinka; at one or two points (e.g. just at the very end) a Mozartean effect of flutes and bassoon two octaves apart.

Chopin's string-writing is generally sonorous enough, though not particularly enterprising—except in the finale of the F minor Concerto where, of course, he writes some very effective passages *col legno*, a device which he may have borrowed from Kurpiński's opera *Nowe Krakowiaki*. Another striking string effect occurs in the *larghetto* of the same Concerto on which I have already quoted Mr Hedley's comment: this is the accompaniment to the piano's dramatic recitative—string tremolo with pizzicato double-basses—of which Sir Donald Tovey has said: 'This is as fine a piece of instrumentation as Berlioz could have chosen to quote in his famous treatise.' Chopin's model here was probably Moscheles, who several times introduced such recitatives in the slow movements of his piano concertos; there is, for instance, just such a passage with string tremolo accompaniment in the *adagio* of Moscheles's G minor Concerto, Op. 68—but Chopin has far surpassed his model. And in the *larghetto* of the F minor Concerto by far the most Chopinesque touch in the orchestration is the bassoon solo after the return of the wonderful lyrical

25

theme, at first following the piano at a bar's distance (canon at the octave) and then (to quote Tovey once more) 'continuing in counterpoint of an adroit simplicity worthy of Bach or Mozart':

Ex. 2

Again a solo woodwind instrument has been used with poetic imagination to add a tiny, deft detail.

The F minor Concerto also offers Chopin's most striking brass effect: the fanfare for first horn, marked *cor de signal*, which heralds the coda. The theme itself has been built up thoroughly enough by the piano, but here its appearance on the horn—not easy on a natural horn—is none the less electrifying. Chopin's employment of brass is as follows:

	Horns	Trumpets	Bass Trombone
Variations, Op. 2	2	—	—
E minor Concerto, Op. 11	4	2	1
Fantasia, Op. 13	2	2	—
Krakowiak, Op. 14	2	2	—
F minor Concerto, Op. 21	2	2	1
Polonaise, Op. 22	2	—	1

(He invariably writes for woodwind—flutes, oboes, clarinets and bassoons—in pairs). It will be seen that the E minor Concerto, the later of the two in date of composition, is his most heavily scored work—not only with four horns but with three timpani instead of the pair used in all his other orchestral scores. The single bass trombone employed in both concertos and in the *Polonaise*, Op. 22, also deserves notice. This was probably a consequence of local conditions; quite a number of orchestras in the early nineteenth century possessed only one trombone instead of the normal three,[1] in which case the single instrument was probably a bass. And the evidence of a number of scores suggests that Warsaw was one of these cities. Elsner in his opera *Król Łokietek*, produced at Warsaw in 1818, writes for one bass trombone; Chopin's works date from ten

[1] See the tables in Adam Carse, *The Orchestra from Beethoven to Berlioz*, Cambridge, 1948, pp. 46–63.

or twelve years later; in 1848 Glinka wrote his *Night in Madrid* and *Kamarinskaya* in Warsaw (for the orchestra of the Governor, Prince Paskevitch) again with single bass trombone. This single bass trombone is always used simply to strengthen the bass line at certain points, almost like an extra bassoon; the part is therefore normally without much interest. But where—as in passages of the first movement of Chopin's E minor Concerto and the two Glinka works—the most important thematic line lies in the bass, the trombone comes into its own as a melodic instrument and is very necessary to bring out the main theme of the Concerto at several crucial points.

All Chopin's works with orchestra date from the period when he was on the eve of full artistic maturity but had not quite reached it. One may say that his orchestration exactly corresponds to such a stage in an artist's development. It is much more individual than is commonly assumed; it is markedly superior to that of his Polish predecessors or that of his Western models Field and Hummel. It is limited in scope, yet so far as it goes it is always adequate, except in the thick tuttis, and sometimes much more than adequate—bold or delicate and poetically imaginative (though always within the limits of what I have called 'water-colour' scoring). It is not the orchestration of an assured master but there is no reason to suppose that Chopin would not have widened the scope and tightened his grasp of his orchestra if he had gone on using it, just as his art widened and deepened in all other respects. That he did not do so is not necessarily proof of lack of *inclination* to write for the orchestra. He composed no more for orchestra partly because he no longer needed show-pieces in which to appear before the public, partly—and much more—because his art developed in the direction of shorter forms, or at least one-movement forms, and more subtle, more finely woven texture. The orchestra of the 1830 was still essentially the 'classical' orchestra; it was a totally unsuitable medium for a finely spun, harmonically complicated music such as Chopin's. Berlioz's innovations would not have helped in this direction, nor even Liszt's. A quarter of a century had to pass before Wagner reached the necessary standpoint with the orchestra of *Tristan*, and it was actually only the generation after Wagner—the generation of Szymanowski and Skryabin—which really discovered how to write Chopinesque music for the orchestra.

1960

27

III—THE GENESIS OF *THE BARTERED BRIDE*

Though a simple opera, *The Bartered Bride* has had a fairly complicated history. Not as complicated as that of *Boris Godunov*, certainly, nor as important as that of *Fidelio*, yet by no means without
interest. And its history all falls within the lifetime of its composer; it is
not a tale of posthumous re-hashing like the latter part of the eventful
story of *Boris* or, to take another comic opera (with a somewhat tragic
history), Cornelius's *Barbier von Bagdad*. As it happens, the histories of
the *Bride* and the *Barber* are slightly interwoven. Both were written
under the sign of Liszt, and it was actually at Weimar, in September
1857, that the first germ of the work—or of such a work—found its way
into Smetana's mind. There was a gathering of musicians and other
artists in connection with the Karl August centennial celebrations, and
Cornelius, always at Liszt's and the Princess Wittgenstein's beck and
call, his *Barber* held up largely on their account since early in the year,
was called upon to arrange a great deal of hospitality. Among the guests
was Smetana, making a détour on his way back to Sweden, and on one
of the two or three days he spent there the conversation turned on the
necessity of creating a modern type of comic opera as a complement to
Wagner's work. Can we doubt that Cornelius and his *Barber* were the
occasion for that turn in the conversation? And a little later the Viennese
Herbeck remarked somewhat tactlessly that, whereas the Czechs were
excellent performers, they seemed incapable of creating any music of
their own.[1] 'That evening,' Smetana said in later years, 'was decisive for
my whole life; I swore there and then that no other than I should beget
a native Czech music.' From that meeting at Weimar Cornelius fled,
without even taking leave of his friends at the Altenburg,[2] to finish
sketching out his *Barber* at Johannisberg; Smetana collected his sick wife
and family at Dresden to continue their journey to Sweden, but carrying
with him those two fruitful ideas of 'a modern type of comic opera' and
'a native Czech music'.

As it happened, when Smetana finally returned to settle in his native
land in May 1861, his first major composition—though Czech enough—
was not a comic opera but the historical and patriotic *Brandenburgers in*

[1] Some accounts date Herbeck's remark from a later meeting at Weimar, in June 1859,
but we know at any rate that Herbeck attended the Karl August Centenary.

[2] There was a new threat to his creative leisure: Liszt was again toying with his old idea
of an opera based on *Manfred*, and he wanted Cornelius to translate and adapt Byron.

Bohemia, written for a prize competition. But even before he put the finishing touches to the *Brandenburgers* on 23 April, 1863, he was noting down themes for a comic opera. As early as October 1862, for instance, he wrote in his note-book sixteen bars (4/4, *vivace*, G major) marked 'Chorus in comedy', which later became the theme of the opening chorus of the *Bride*, 'Proč bychom se netěšili' (in Mrs Newmarch's version: 'Come then, let us all be merry'). On 13 May, 1863 he noted eight bars (2/4, A major) marked 'In comic opera. Duetto!', afterwards used for the duet 'Věrné milováni' ('If our love is strong and true'). Again in September he recorded nineteen bars (2/4, *allegro*, A major) for the comic duet 'Milostné zvířátko' ('Now my dear Sir Bruin'). By that time he had at least got a libretto; his diary for 1863 contains an entry: '5 July. I've bought from Sabina the text for the comic operetta, which still has no name.' But this was probably not in the form he actually set, for we know that Sabina—who was also the librettist of the *Brandenburgers*—originally wrote the text in one act and that he expanded it to two at Smetana's request. We must not, therefore, blame Sabina if we find the action a little thin when spread, as it now is, over three acts; it is recorded that he said: 'If I had suspected what Smetana would make of my operetta, I should have taken more pains and written him a better and more solid libretto.'

The original *Bartered Bride* consisted of twenty numbers, including the overture, the dialogue being spoken:

Act I

(1) Introductory chorus (with the little interlude for Mařenka and Jeník, 'Proč jsi tak zasmušilá?'—'Why are you so sad today?').

(2) Mařenka's aria, 'Kdybych se cos takového' ('If I thought you would be faithless').

(3) Duet, 'Jako matka požehnáním' ('Though a mother is a blessing').

(4) Kecal's 'Jak vám pravím' ('As I said before, old crony').[1]

(5) Terzetto, 'Mladik slušný' ('Such a nice lad').

(6) The ensemble 'Tu ji máme' ('Here she comes').

(7) Vašek's 'Má matička povídala' ('Mama said to me').

(8) Duet, 'Známt' já jednu dívčinu' ('I know of one lonely maid').

(9) Duet, 'Nuže, milý chasníku' ('Just a word with you, my boy'), with Kecal's 'Každý jen tu svou' ('Ev'ry lover's girl') and the duet 'Známt' jednu dívku' ('I know a maiden').

(10) Jeník's aria, 'Až uzříš' ('How could he ever dream?').

(11) Finale, 'Pojd'te, lidičky' ('Come here, neighbours all').

---

[1] Kecal is never named in the composition sketch; he is always referred to simply as Dohazovač (the marriage-broker), usually abbreviated to 'Doh'.

ACT II

(1) Vašek's 'To mi v hlavě leží' ('With dread my wits are cumbered').
(2) Couplets for Esmeralda and the Manager.
(3) Duet, 'Milostné zvířátko' ('Now, my dear Sir Bruin').
(4) Ensemble, 'Jakže? Nechce jí?' ('What! What's this?'), with Mařenka's entry and the sextet.
(5) Mařenka's recitative, 'Ach, jaký žal' ('Ah! Bitterness!') and Jeník's entrance, with the duet 'Tak tvrdošíjnou, dívko, jsi' ('Now what a stubborn lass you are').
(6) Jeník's aria, 'Utiš se, dívko' ('Take comfort, my dearest') and the trio 'Teď přivedu sem rodiče' ('I'll summon back my people all').
(7) Ensemble, 'Jak si se, Mařenko, rozmyslila' ('Have you reflected?') as far as the entrance of the panic-stricken boys.
(8) Finale, beginning with Krušina's words, 'Pomněte, kmotře' ('Come now, neighbour').

Smetana appears not to have begun serious work on the composition for nearly a year—perhaps because of the desired recasting of the text in two acts—though he seems to have written the overture earlier; the musical paper *Slavoj* (1 December, 1863) reports the performance at the soirée of the Umělecká Beseda on 18 November of a 'comic overture by Smetana', presumably at the piano.[1] The composition of the actual libretto seems to have been begun about the end of August 1864. Smetana's note-book contains an entry for 1864:

This year I have been composing a comic opera in two acts by Sabina. I have tried to give it an entirely national character, as the action is from village life, where a bridegroom sells his sweetheart, but really for himself—which calls for national[2] music.

Writing to a Swedish friend on 12 October, 1865, the composer tells her he has finished the pencil sketch. The scoring took another five months, for the end of the score is dated 15 March, 1866. And the first version of *Prodaná nevěsta* (literally, 'The *Sold* Bride', which is of course

[1] Czech critics seem to agree in supposing that this 'comic overture' was that to *The Bartered Bride*. But may it not have been the overture to the puppet play, *Doktor Faust* (for two horns, bass trombone, triangle, bass drum, strings and piano) composed in December 1862? Another puppet overture, to Kopecky's *Oldřich a Božena*, for a similar collection of instruments, was written in December 1863 for the New Year's Eve celebration of the Umělecká Beseda. Both overtures were published in miniature score by the Umělecká Beseda in 1945.

[2] The word *národní*, which I have here twice translated as 'national', is ambiguous: it may mean 'national' or 'popular'.

more accurate[1]) was produced at the Provisional Theatre, Prague, on 30 May, only two months after its completion.

The times were unfavourable; it was the eve of the Seven Weeks' War, and the audience was small.[2] Smetana's friend Josef Srb-Debrnov did not go to the first performance, but he questioned the audience as they came out of the theatre:

> One praised it, another shook his head, and one well-known musician, a celebrated organist, said to me: 'That's no comic opera; it won't do. The opening chorus is fine, but I don't care for the rest.'

The second performance also had a poor audience and poor Thomé, the director of the Theatre, told the composer: 'Mit der *Prothana* ist nichts. You will be doing me the greatest pleasure if you cancel the contract for the performance of this opera; otherwise I shall have to pay you the 600 fl. out of my own pocket.' Yet the work had a good press and when it was revived after the war—the Emperor Franz Josef was present at the third performance (27 October)—its success was beyond all doubt.

But this was only the first version of the opera. Changes were made from the very beginning. The prose dialogue had been drastically cut even before the first performance and the couplets for Esmeralda and the Manager (No. 2 of Act II) were taken out. The need of a change of scene was also felt; for both acts were played with the same scenery: the village square. Librettist and composer took counsel and January 1869 saw the production of the second version of the *Bride*. The First Act was now divided, between Nos. 6 and 7, into two scenes of which the second was played inside the inn and opened by a new drinking chorus. The opening of the Second Act was enlivened by a polka—there were no dances in the first version—and after her recitative (No. 5) Mařenka was given a new aria, 'Ten lásky sen' ('Our dream of love'). A few months later further changes were made: the second part of Act I was made into a separate act, the polka was transferred from the beginning of the last act to the end of the First, the furiant—one of the few numbers based on actual folk-tunes—was inserted in Act II between the drinking-chorus and Vašek's first stuttering song, and a third dance, the skočna, was introduced in Act III. In this form—the third—*The Bartered Bride* was produced on June 1, 1869. Finally, in view of a forthcoming performance in Russian at the Maryinsky Theatre, St Petersburg, Smetana replaced

---

[1] Smetana's diary records that he himself gave it that name, 'as the poet didn't know what to call it'.

[2] When news came of the crushing Austrian defeat at Königgratz early in July, Smetana was thunderstruck. As composer of *The Brandenburgers in Bohemia* he expected to be shot when the Prussians entered Prague, or at best to be made to work with the rest of the inhabitants at demolition of the fortifications. So he fled to the country with his family.

the spoken dialogue by recitative, in which definitive form it was given in Prague on 25 September, 1870.

I have spoken above of the 'pencil sketch' of the original version, finished in October 1865. That sketch—in vocal score—was carefully preserved in the Bedřich Smetana Museum in Prague, and its publication in facsimile[1] allows us some interesting glimpses of Smetana's method of work. On the whole it is very clean, showing relatively few corrections, and there are hints here and there—not very decided ones—that Smetana composed at the piano. On that point the most reliable witnesses differ. According to Ferdinand Heller the *Bride* was composed at the piano, while Srb asserts that 'Smetana never used the piano while composing; only when the work was finished would he go to the piano and play it'. Obviously he did not *need* the piano, for three of his operas and all his best-known instrumental works were composed when he was completely deaf. One piece of evidence, for what it is worth, is a recollection of Smetana's eighty-four-year-old nephew sent to Mirko Očadlík, the editor of the facsimile edition, in 1941. The nephew, Alexander Kniesl, describes how as a six-year-old boy staying in the country in the summer of 1863 he often used to hear his uncle playing on 'an old black piano with a thin, hollow tone':

> He would call me, a six-year-old boy sitting on a little, low child's chair, to listen. 'Do you like it?' my uncle would ask in a kindly voice. . . . Naturally at six I had no critical judgment—but it was music and I would say, 'Yes, I love it!'—But without realizing it I had an opportunity of watching my uncle compose. On the desk lay manuscript paper partly written on and I saw how he would write the notes in pencil with the right hand while with the left he would turn what he had written into music. It often happened that my uncle would cross out a bar that did not please him and substitute another.—As a child I didn't pay much attention to all this, but years later I learned from my cousin Zdeňka Smetana that these sketches were the humble beginnings of *The Bartered Bride*.

If this really happened in the summer of 1863, the sketches must have related to Sabina's very first one-act version of the libretto, which Smetana found unsatisfactory.

The sketch begins directly with the opening chorus almost exactly as we have it now, though there is, for instance, no dominant seventh in bar 3: the tenors have D instead of C. After the first eight bars Smetana does not bother to write the piano (orchestral) part, which simply doubles the chorus, except in the interludes. These are always more abrupt than in the definitive version; for instance, in the little interlude before the

[1] By Melantrich and the Bedřich Smetana Society, Prague, 1944.

'Ouvej!' ('Heighho!') episode—rather different in the sketch—Smetana originally took only two bars instead of four to change from major to minor (there is an exact parallel in the transition after the sextet in the last act), while the transition back to the main theme is a perfunctory sketch of which only traces survive in the final sixteen-bar version. The other G minor episode, for the two lovers, is essentially the same in the sketch and the final version though the voice-parts, superimposed on the orchestral background, show considerable differences—a remark which applies to many other passages. Smetana naturally does not trouble to write out the main choral tune in full for the third time: he draws a wavy line and starts again with the *molto moderato* music of the coda, identical in substance with the long orchestral introduction to the First Act, though now with chorus parts added. But why did not Smetana sketch out his orchestral introduction first, instead of bringing in one of its themes as (apparently) an afterthought at the end of the chorus? The answer is that the essential part of the introduction had been written a good many years before *The Bartered Bride* was even thought of. In 1847 Smetana's pupil, the Countess Marie von Thun-Hohenstein, married; and as a wedding-present the composer dedicated to her a suite of three *Wedding Scenes* for piano: 'Wedding March', 'Bridegroom and Bride' and 'Wedding Festivities'. Now the middle part of the 'Wedding Festivities' is a *tempo di polka*, and it was this which Smetana fifteen years later used as a frame for the opening number of his opera. One interesting point is that the original key of the polka was F, the key of the overture to the *Bride*; but in the opera it had to be transposed to G, the key of the opening chorus, and was therefore provided with a ten-bar prelude modulating from F to G. The introduction as a whole therefore consists of:

10 bars on the chorus theme, modulating;
57 bars taken note for note (with a few one- and two-bar inserts) from the *Wedding Scenes*;
8 bars rounding off the polka;
22 bars of *allegro molto* on the chorus tune.

Mařenka's aria 'Kdybych se co takového' ('If I thought you would be faithless'), like most of the set numbers, lacks the orchestral introduction which in the finished product anticipates the vocal melody, but is otherwise identical except in unimportant details with the final version. But even the facsimile betrays a considerable amount of rubbing-out in the opening bars, and the editor has been able to decipher some twenty bars of the earlier sketch which he prints in the notes to the facsimile. I quote the opening (Ex. 1 on p. 34).

The ensuing duet differs entirely from that in the sketch: Smetana has scribbled at the head of the latter 'original; later re-composed'. Almost the only thing common to both settings of the words is that they fall into two sections, minor and relative major: in the sketch C minor and

Ex. 1

E flat major, in the published version G minor and B flat major. Now the odd point is that the lulling, rocking theme in B flat, of which the opening theme of the overture is perhaps a sparkling transformation, had been noted down long before (see *supra*) in A major and actually marked 'In comic opera. Duetto!'. ('In comic opera' may, of course, have meant 'in some comic opera', even though Smetana seems already at that time to have been at least discussing the *Bride* subject with Sabina; he often noted themes before he thought of the works in which to embody them; for instance, the note-books for 1863 also contain two themes afterwards used in *The Two Widows*, though he did not make the acquaintance of Mallefille's comedy, much less think of composing it, till 1868.) But in the composition sketch we find instead:

Ex. 2

And when, later in the First Act, Mařenka comments *sotto voce* 'Mám už jiného' ('I have a lover') the orchestra underlines the remark with Ex. 2 in the sketch, not with the B flat theme as in the published version. But there is one other passage in the published version where the orchestra refers back to the love-duet: just after Mařenka's agitated entry in the last act, when she is crushed by the apparent proof of her lover's baseness. And here in the sketch we find, not a corresponding allusion to Ex. 2, but a snatch of the B flat theme, incomplete and in 4/4 time, but in the right key and with the rather cloying orchestral sixths:

Ex. 3

It is worth noting that Smetana preserved the semiquaver accompaniment of Ex. 2 when he substituted the B flat tune and that *x* is echoed in one of the melodic cadences of the final version. On the other hand, if this feature already appears in the A major version of 1863, which I have not seen, we must put it that x is the echo; but it is a typical Smetana trait, familiar in *Vltava* and occurring in the closing bars of *The Bartered Bride* —to look no further.

I have already spoken of Smetana's alteration of voice-parts over an unchanged orchestral background. This is particularly true of declamatory passages, which he often re-writes completely, often for the sake of more comfortable range and tessitura, though in at least one case—Mařenka's passionate outburst in the last act, 'O jaky žal, když srdce oklamáno' ('Ah! bitterness! When hearts have trusted vainly')—a passage lying within a diminished fifth is expanded to cover a tenth. But it is also true of arias and ensembles, as in the trio 'Mladik slušny' ('Such a nice lad'):

Ex. 4

and the quartet from the next scene, from which I quote a typical passage for one voice:

Ex. 5

Incidentally, in the sketch the trio and scene 4 are separated by a ten-bar sketch for Vašek's first stuttering song—marked 'Scene VI—Vašek (dressed as bridegroom)'—in 3/4 time and quite different from the ultimate version; Smetana has drawn brackets round it and left it. The right version duly appears in its proper place in the score, though still incorrectly marked 'Scene VI' (instead of V), without its prelude and with its postlude shortened, but otherwise pretty much as we know it.

Both the duets for Mařenka and Vašek and for Jeník and Kecal appear in the sketch very much as we know them, not only in melody but in harmony and details of figuration; only the passage in the first duet, where Mařenka threatens Vašek with his fictitious admirer's suicide, is entirely different. Jeník's aria, 'Až uzříš' ('How could he ever dream?'),

35

shows more substantial changes. For once Smetana sketched a four-bar introduction—perhaps because it was *not* to anticipate the vocal melody —though it has practically nothing in common with the longer passage that replaced it. And the voice-part begins with quite a different melody, set to the words treated as recitative in the printed score:

Ex. 6

Aš už-říš komuš kou-pil nev-ěš - tu smutně nastou-píš smutně nastou-píš zpá-teč - ní ces-tu!

of which an echo remains in the final version at the words 'pro nějž mi neni nic obtižneho' ('No more shall that old huckster vex') for the sixteen bars beginning 'Drahou Mařenku' ('O lodestar of my soul') were taken over from twelve bars of the original sketch. A parallel case, also in the part of Jeník, occurs in the last act where in the duet 'Tak tvrdošíjnou, dívko, jsi'[1] ('Now what a stubborn lass you are') his melody originally began:

Ex. 7

Tak tvr-do - šíj - nou, dív-ko, jsi, že nechceš pravdu zvěd́t

continued for another six bars exactly as in the final version, and then diverged again.

The finale of Act I (that is, of Act II of the published score) originally began with four orchestral bars anticipating Kecal's call to the neighbours, instead of with seventeen bars more or less identical with the opening of the overture, and was written in 2/4 time instead of 4/4. The substance of the finale is generally the same, though there are the usual differences in the voice-parts and the original lacks the colourful modulation under-lining Jeník's significant reference to 'the son of Tobias Micha'. On the other hand, a little later at the reference to the 'three hundred crowns', Smetana softened his original modulation to A major (from the main key of F) into a simple dominant modulation to C.

The sketch for Act II (III in the published score) begins straight away with Vašek's first words, gives his lament pretty much as we know it, and then goes straight on to the ensemble, 'Aj! Jak že nechce ji?' ('What's this? You refuse?'), omitting not only the skočna—of course—but the music for the entry of the players, the lost couplets for Esmeralda and the Manager and their duet, 'Milostné zvířátko' ('Now, my dear Sir Bruin'), although the theme of the last-named number was one of the first Smetana noted down (see *supra*). We may conclude from this that originally neither Esmeralda nor the Manager was intended to be a singing part, and that although in September 1863 Smetana noted the theme

[1] Thus in Smetana's autograph; later emended to 'tvrdošijná'.

afterwards used for their duet he had at that time no definite idea how or where he was going to introduce it.

I have mentioned one instance—the two quotations of the love-duet—where the device of thematic reminiscence is used far more effectively in the final version than in the sketch. (I say 'thematic reminiscence' advisedly, for there are no *Leitmotive* in the true, Wagnerian sense in *The Bartered Bride*.) But there is one case of the reverse, of a theme having its outline so smoothed out in the printed score that two later references to it—perfectly obvious in the sketch—probably pass unnoticed by the audience, possibly even by students of the score. This is the theme, first heard in the ensemble 'Aj! Jakže, nechce ji?', as it appears in the sketch:

and this is the final form:

Bar 4 of Ex. 9, I should add, is anticipated in Háta's part in Ex. 8, which otherwise more or less doubles the orchestral part I have actually quoted. The words are 'Není v tom nikdo než ten pacholek sam' ('''Tis no other than the boy himself'—or, as Mrs Newmarch puts it, 'All this story of some pretty lady sounds like a stupid lie'). Now this is appropriately quoted in the next scene when Vašek notices Mařenka and cries 'A ta to byla' ('There's the very girl'): Ex. 8 in the sketch, Ex. 9 in the score. The theme is obviously associated with Mařenka. But when Smetana refers to it once again in the orchestral interjections to her recitative 'Oh jaký žal' ('Ah! bitterness'), he quotes in a form on the whole nearer to Ex. 8, which no one in the audience has heard, than to Ex. 9, which is not very distinctive anyhow.

It is impossible in the scope of a short study to mention a hundredth of the interesting points of detail that strike one in comparing sketch with score, but one other important number must at least be mentioned: the famous sextet. One fact revealed by the sketch is that Smetana originally intended it to be a quintet; the number is headed 'Quintetto—Micha, Háta, Vaš (tenor), Kruš, Doh'. Yet, although five singers are specified, the music is strictly in four parts until Mařenka's entry near the end; probably 'Micha' was a slip for 'Mařenka', especially as he—a bass—is mentioned first, otherwise the preponderance of men's voices would have been overwhelming. Ultimately Vašek was taken out and Ludmila, a soprano, substituted. The original version of the music was singularly flat and uninspired; I quote the opening:

Ex. 10

The final form of the sextet is also considerably expanded; bars 14–26, for instance—the repeat of the first thirteen bars with different distribution of the parts—were an afterthought.

The composition sketch breaks off rather oddly near the beginning of the opening chorus of the finale. Ten bars are written for sopranos and altos, with a blank stave for the tenor and bass parts; then another ten bars or so are indicated for sopranos only—and the rest is blank music-paper. The original form, erased but still legible, was:

Ex. 11

Jak si se, Ma-řen-ko, roz-mys-li - la   mluv, mluv,   rozmys-li - la,   by se věc dob-ře u -

-kon - či - la,   mluv, mluv

Smetana changed this to:

Ex. 12

But the printed version differs from both except in rhythm—an interesting sidelight on Smetana's approach to his text. Even the ultimate key, A major, for once differs from that in the sketch.

Does the sketch throw any penetrating light on Smetana's creative processes? To a limited extent only. After all, this is the sketch for only one work and a work of early rather than full maturity at that. But the rhythmic identity of Exs. 11 and 12, and their rhythmic identity with the final version, is typical. When Smetana alters a voice-part he is more likely, one observes, to change the melodic rise and fall than the rhythmic pattern. Alterations in the rhythmic pattern are more often modifications than complete changes. I have quoted instances (Exs. 4 and 5) of voice-parts rewritten over an unchanged instrumental passage, and the harmonic almost-identity of Exs. 8 and 9 will not have escaped the reader's notice. Can we conclude that Smetana's basic method of composition, at any rate in *The Bartered Bride*, was a species of piano improvisation to the words? I suggest that his first care was to get on to music-paper a continuous musical texture underlying the words; afterwards came the polishing of the vocal line. The always simple harmony usually came right the first time; sometimes even the figuration and quite often the part-writing. But only once in the whole sketch is there any indication of scoring: the word *Corno* marking the doubling of the voice-part an octave lower at the words 'Ni za tisíce' ('Not for a gold-mine') in Jeník's 'Až uzříš' aria.

1947

IV—DVOŘÁK'S MUSICAL PERSONALITY

It is of course true of a good many composers that, like the moon, they always keep half of themselves concealed from the public. The average music-lover, even the average professional musician—the two classes overlap, I admit—knows Handel's operas hardly at all, Haydn's symphonies and Schubert's songs only by roughly a ten-percentage and their work as a whole by a percentage much lower still. As for the Bizets and Liszts and Smetanas and Rimsky-Korsakovs, to say nothing of such older masters as Purcell and Domenico Scarlatti and C. P. E. Bach, most of us know them only through a little pile of scores that we could quite conveniently hold in one hand. But on the whole we do not inflict on them any serious injustice. It is very wrong to confine our interest to such narrow limits and it is much worse of conductors and performers and putters-up-of-money-for-opera-seasons not to dispel our ignorance, but we generally know these composers by their best works or at any rate by thoroughly representative works. We do not know them fully and intimately as the specialist student does; we see them in the flat like minor characters in Dickens, stamped in our minds by a few striking traits; he sees them in the round like characters in Tolstoy, knowing every side of them in living proportion. Yet what we see is generally characteristic enough, untrue only in the sense that a kindly caricature is untrue. A man has a heavy moustache and the caricaturist makes it a little heavier; Rimsky-Korsakov dabbled in pseudo-orientalism, and the pseudo-orientalism bulks a little too large in our conception of his musical personality. No more than that. But the case of Dvořák is rather different from these. Our conception of Dvořák's musical personality, if it is based mainly on, say, the *New World* and G major Symphonies, the F major Quartet, the *Slavonic Dances* and the *Carnival* Overture, is nearly as false as a caricature that makes a man *all* moustache. And even if we can correct that impression of a purely lyrical, childishly naïve musician, orchestrating in bright, simple, transparent colours, by an occasional hearing of the F minor Trio or the great D minor Symphony we shall still not have anything like a true picture. For Dvořák's musical personality, despite the naïveté of his everyday personality (perhaps, as I hope to show in a moment, *because* of his naïveté), was complex and many-sided.

When our grandfathers took Dvořák to their hearts in the 1880s, they knew him as he really was much better than we do, though they completed their picture of him with things that we have forgotten without losing much. In the background, behind the four symphonies and so on that they knew, they had *The Spectre's Bride* and the *Stabat Mater*—if indeed they did not put them in the foreground. (If they did, they were wrong, and they were still more wrong in badgering Dvořák to give them a *St. Ludmila*; but at any rate they could not put the works of Dvořák's American period in the front of the picture so as to conceal practically everything else.) It is easy to understand Dvořák's immediate success in Victorian England. As a writer in the *Athenaeum* put it in 1885: his music was 'equally interesting—and we must add equally pleasant—to the supporters of the conservative and of the progressive schools'. His musical ancestry could be traced back to Beethoven and Schubert—and, bar Handel and Mendelssohn, one could not have had more respectable ancestors; and he had recognizable affinities with all three of the principal musical tendencies of the period, with the conservatism of Brahms and his followers, with the modernism of the Liszt–Wagner school, and with the nationalism that was in almost every country but our own challenging the hegemony of German and Italian music in Europe. Above all he had a fresh and virile personality which made even the *Stabat Mater* and *The Spectre's Bride* sound brilliantly unconventional in the dreadfully decorous company of other Victorian oratorios and cantatas. 'Only those who were already in the prime of their concert-going days in the far-off eighties can realize the extraordinary enthusiasm which was evoked by these works', wrote Rosa Newmarch in 1928. 'But then, no one on the sunny side of middle age can remember the alternative novelties of the period: the flatulent, sophisticated simplicities of Gounod's musical "frescoes", or the insipidity of such an oratorio as Garrett's *Shunamite*. With each new work by Dvořák we could look forward to something joyous, and untouched by tedium.'

But these qualities have no necessary connection with the enduring value of Dvořák's music; this sort of liberal-conservatism has often carried mediocre composers to a high level of contemporary popularity, only to let them down a quarter of a century later. (When after a decade or so Dvořák himself was eclipsed by the novelty of Tchaïkovsky and the other Russians, a hasty and superficial English observer might almost have been pardoned for putting him too in that category.) All this only tells us what Dvořák was to our grandparents, which is interesting and (it is true) not unimportant; it helps us only a little in understanding what he *is*. It makes no difference to anyone but his contemporaries whether an artist is a progressive or a conservative; in the perspective of sixty years the two parties begin to draw closer, and their music neither continues a hallowed tradition of our fathers nor brings fresh and exciting elements into the art. Even Dvořák's claim to be considered a nationalist, a typically Czech musician, has been challenged—and by some of those who ought to know best: his compatriots. Nearly thirty years ago the Czech critic Josef Bartoš, in his book on Dvořák, asserted that 'our national style is something far deeper than his sonorous exoticism; therefore for the sake of this truth we must be prepared to renounce before future generations even so distinguished a musical personality as was Antonín Dvořák'. And there are distinguished Czech musicians today who will tell you that true Czechishness is to be found in the music of Smetana and Suk rather than in Dvořák's. (On the other hand, Smetana himself was frequently accused in his lifetime of being insufficiently Czech.) However paradoxical this may seem to us, we should remember that similar reservations have been made by Russians about Tchaïkovsky and by Englishmen about Elgar. There are in most countries composers whose work is so intimately and subtly national that it means very little to any but their compatriots, or at any rate means infinitely more to their compatriots than to foreigners: Bruckner in Germany, Fauré in France, Suk in Czechoslovakia. Foreigners naturally, and perhaps rightly, tend to consider them minor figures whose work is not for export; though if they wish to penetrate to the secrets of a country's feeling and thinking it is in these works that they have the best hope of surprising them. In art a personality counts for more than a representative national figure, though of course a man may happen to be both. Most non-Czech musicians, and doubtless many Czechs too, would say that Dvořák was both. So, dismissing the hopelessly dated appeal of his conservative-liberalism and setting on one side the appeal of his seriously disputed, though by no means disproved, nationalism, let us try to define his musical personality as it was and is; that 'essential Dvořák' which is one of the most attractive personalities in the whole history of music.

Before looking at it in detail, it will be just as well to stand back for a moment and remember the general impression one has of it, not only on the principle of putting the wood before the trees but because such a general impression is necessary to guide our approach to the details. Perhaps the first thing that strikes one about Dvořák's music as a whole is its 'purity'. In the whole of his large output the proportion that is linked with, and so (if ever so slightly) controlled by, words is comparatively small; and in that small proportion, even in the operas, the music always tends to keep the upper hand. Not only 'Songs my mother taught me' but several of the other *Gypsy Songs* would be almost equally effective as violin solos. And of the instrumental music, into which Dvořák put the best of himself, hardly any is programme-music of even the mildest kind; four overtures, the group of symphonic poems written in 1896, and a few odds and ends for piano, named only after they were composed, exhaust the list. Even the works behind which one suspects an emotional programme to be lurking are very few.

It is evident that Dvořák was often profoundly moved by personal experience, but though one senses passion and even tragedy in the background they are not clearly translated into musical terms but transmuted into musical emotion, that indeterminate emotion-*sui-generis* which is the quintessence of music. Almost the only definite labels one can venture to attach to Dvořák's expressions of more definite emotion are 'sad' and 'happy', the most naïve of all. That word 'naïve' is bound to keep creeping into any discussion of Dvořák. Naïveté was from the first an element of his musical personality, as it was (very much more markedly) of his everyday personality, but it was only in the last ten or twelve years of his life that he almost deliberately allowed this naïveté to become the predominant element. Despite his essential melodiousness, the lucidity of so much of his harmony, the brightness and transparency of his orchestral colours, despite all these peasant qualities, he is after all quite complex and many-sided. As Hadow pointed out long ago, his most ingenious melodies are often treated with remarkable technical sophistication—yet without incongruity or loss of charm. Moreover, his musical style is compounded of the most diverse elements—Beethoven, Schubert, Wagner, Brahms, Liszt, Smetana, Czech folk-song—and each one of these elements obviously corresponded to something real in the man himself, since he was able, in the melting-pot of his own creative mind, to fuse them into a quite individual style of his own.

It is arguable that this eclecticism is itself a Czech characteristic. Partly because of centuries of Teutonic cultural penetration, partly because Prague at any rate has always been in or near the main stream of European music, even Czech folk-music is not so peculiarly national as that of Russia, for instance. Again, the Czechs are a nation of what the Germans contemptuously call *Musikanten*, natural musicians who, even when they lack polish and musical culture, yet have the very essence of music in their blood. When a *Musikant* of genius composes, the music pours from him spontaneously, he is not concerned to be original; by his nature he will not be very self-critical. Even his musical learning, his high technical accomplishment, will only help him to keep the stream from running too thin; it will certainly not dam it in any way. Such a genius was Schubert; such—complicated by an intellect functioning mainly in non-musical directions—was Mahler; such, above all, was Dvořák. It may seem paradoxical to suggest that the spontaneous composer is likely to be less original, to be more open to influences, than his more sophisticated colleague. A moment's thought on the nature of musical idiom will show that it is not. Just as a child thinks and speaks in terms of the language it hears all round it, a musician naturally thinks and speaks music—that is, composes—in terms of the music that has come within his experience. Imagine a composer who had heard no music but Beethoven's; he would be unable to imagine music in any other than Beethovenian terms; if he were a completely naïve musician, however richly endowed with innate creative power, his own melodies and his treatment of them would be absolutely Beethovenian; only if he were intellectually self-conscious could he begin to conceive a non-Beethovenian music. Actually, of course, no composer is completely naïve and no composer derives his conception of music from only one of his predecessors. But he does derive it solely from the corpus of music actually known to him, and the more spontaneous he is the more openly will he derive it, the less will he be concerned with conscious originality.[1]

The corpus of music with which the young Dvořák was acquainted must have consisted at first of popular music—not necessarily folk-music in the true sense, but village dance-music and songs—and later of the classics: Mozart, Beethoven, Schubert, and Heaven knows what minor figures. And so, as one would expect, his earliest compositions—the A minor Quintet of 1861 and the A major Quartet of 1862—were (we are told) written under the influence of Mozart, Beethoven and Schubert. That word 'influence' is necessarily very commonly used in this connection, but its significance is equally commonly misunderstood. And it is used to describe two different things: natural, unconscious picking up of something of an older master's idiom (particularly of those elements in it that correspond to something in oneself and so specially appeal to one), and deliberate technical modelling on the methods of the older master (a process to which every composer must submit while learning his craft). Beethoven and Schubert formed an important part of the corpus of music from which Dvořák naturally acquired the beginnings of his own idiom, but they also served at first—and from time to time in later years—as his conscious models. And throughout his life he continued in the same way, always unconsciously drawing new elements into his musical make-up, often consciously studying new models. This might have been disastrous. In the case of a lesser man it would have been disastrous. But creative imagination shows itself in this very point: what it can do with the absorbed elements. Without that mysterious power, a musician, however technically gifted, will only absorb a mixture of elements and regurgitate them—as a mixture. With it, he will by some mysterious chemistry of the mind transmute them into something quite new—a compound. The pages of musical history are littered with innumerable composers of the former class, the eclectics with feeble powers of digestion. On the other hand, there has never been a composer of great eminence who was not an eclectic of the other kind. The perhaps greatest of all, Mozart, was almost certainly the most eclectic of all; Wyzewa and Saint-Foix in their masterly account of his *vie musicale* have been able to distinguish no

[1] The idea here baldly and crudely stated has been worked out at great length in two fascinating books by Julius Bahle, *Der musikalische Schaffensprozess* and *Eingebung und Tat im musikalischen Schaffen*, Leipzig, 1936 and 1939.

fewer than thirty-four periods each marked by some change of style in most cases produced by the impact of some fresh influence. Even Dvořák was hardly as susceptible as this, though of course his digestive power, the transmuting potency of his creative imagination, was far inferior to Mozart's.

Nevertheless there is a rough parallel between his development and Mozart's. Wyzewa and Saint-Foix carried their classification to an extreme; I should not care to have to distinguish more than half-a-dozen such periods in Dvořák's career and I shall not attempt even that here. For the drawing of firm lines to mark the stages of an artist's evolution, though convenient for critical purposes, is often misleading; one can sometimes note precisely the impact of a new influence but never the stages of the 'digestion' of an old one. And in Dvořák's case such a classification is not even very convenient, for the influences not only ebb and flow but overlap or run parallel in the most confusing way, and ultimately one would find oneself having to trace Dvořák's course work by work, almost month by month, as the two French critics have done with Mozart, and to distinguish a score of more of 'periods'. I content myself here with indicating the general tendencies of Dvořák's work.

First of all, then, comes the already mentioned period of apprenticeship, the period when his gods were Mozart, Beethoven and Schubert, particularly the two latter, but throughout which the magic of Wagner and the advanced Romantic school exercised an ever growing fascination on him; its products include a couple of symphonies, in C minor and B flat, and a Cello Concerto in A, none of which was published in the composer's lifetime. By 1870 the influence of Liszt and Wagner had more or less completely eclipsed that of the classics, reaching its apogee that year in two string quartets, in D major and E minor, and the opera *Alfred*; it is still strongly marked in the unpublished or posthumously published works, such as the E flat Symphony and the A minor String Quartet, of 1873, but the posthumously published Quartet in F minor, written in the interval between these two works, shows that—apart from the strong dash of Chopin in the third movement (*tempo di valse*)— Dvořák had already advanced some way in the process of digesting the basic material of classics and romantics into a personal idiom of his own. From this point onward there is always a real, essential Dvořák—who continues, it is true, to absorb fresh raw materials for his imagination to work on but who is never in the third-rate composer's difficulty of having chewed more than he can digest. So when we speak of a return to classical models, particularly those of Beethoven and Schubert, in the works of 1873–6—the earlier of Dvořák's two symphonies in D minor (Op. 13), the G minor Trio, the E major Quartet (Op. 80), the *Theme and Variations* for piano (Op. 36), and others—we do not mean that the composer

45

began to imitate the processes of their technique again, still less that there was any important re-fertilisation of his idiom by Beethoven's or Schubert's. There was, I think, some re-fertilisation; it is said that at this period one of Dvořák's favourite works was Beethoven's Quartet in C sharp minor. But all these works remain unmistakably Dvořákian; one can only say that Dvořák must have experienced a spiritual swing back toward classicism. Technically, Dvořák did not go back to school; he took a refresher course, particularly (I suspect) in classical variation-writing. The results are to be found not only in the A flat *Variations* for piano, but in the variation-movements of the String Sextet and the D major Piano Quartet, and above all in the *Symphonic Variations*, all written in the period 1875–8.

All the same, one cannot label these years simply 'Period of Classical Reaction', for simultaneously Dvořák was becoming increasingly conscious both of the artistic personality of Smetana and of the value of Czech national music in general. To those who remember that Smetana was eighteen years older than Dvořák and in some respects his forerunner, this recognition may seem a little belated. But in the sixties Smetana had produced little beyond three operas: *The Bartered Bride*, *The Brandenburgers in Bohemia* and *Dalibor*; *The Two Widows* and *The Kiss* came only in the early seventies; *Libuše*, though written then, was not produced till 1881. As for Smetana's major instrumental works, *Vyšehrad* and *Vltava* were composed at the end of 1874, the Quartet *From my Life* in 1876; *From Bohemia's Woods and Fields* and *Šárka* were first performed in December 1876, and May 1877, respectively; the last two of the cycle of symphonic poems, though written a year or so earlier, were not heard till 1880. If Dvořák did not recognise Smetana's talent earlier, it was because there was not much to recognise. The real impact of Smetana on him was that of a contemporary, not of a predecessor. Without attempting to minimise the direct effect of that impact, I think it may be said that its most important consequence was to turn Dvořák's conscious attention to that heritage of national music which he had hitherto drawn upon only naturally and spontaneously as one breathes the air about one. The *Moravian Duets*, the second version of *King and Collier*,[1] *The Peasant a Rogue*, all date from 1874–6, the height of the 'period of classical reaction'. Dvořák continues, then, to be a dual musical personality, though the Hyde behind the classical Jekyll is no longer Wagnerian but nationalist.

The nationalist Hyde triumphs in the compositions of 1878–80: the String Sextet, the *Slavonic Rhapsodies*, the first set of *Slavonic Dances*, the E flat Quartet and the *Gypsy Songs*. But at this very moment Jekyll

---

[1] This was long the accepted English title, but the young *uhlir* Jeník was really a charcoal burner.

himself enters upon a fresh incarnation—as Johannes Brahms. There had been traces of Brahms—or are they only of the Beethovenian and Schubertian elements in Brahms?—in the D minor Quartet of 1877, which is dedicated to him. In the Violin Concerto and the so-called 'First' Symphony (in D, Op. 60), in 1880, Jekyll and Hyde struggle for the mastery; and Jekyll seems to win in the C major Quartet of 1881. But the metaphor really breaks down at this point. Throughout the eighties, when Dvořák was probably at the height of his powers, one becomes less and less conscious of a struggle between opposing elements and increasingly aware of an equilibrium between them. It is true that sometimes one seems to have slightly the upper hand, sometimes the other. But such ripe and splendid compositions as the F minor Trio, the great D minor Symphony (the so-called Second), the *Scherzo Capriccioso* for orchestra and the Piano Quintet (all dating from 1883–7) are the results not of a struggle but of a synthesis. The Piano Quintet contains the first symptoms of a fresh phase, continued through the E flat Piano Quartet, the G major Symphony, the *Dumky* Trio, and the *Carnival* Overture, which may be described as a mellowing of that synthesis. One hesitates to apply the word 'overripe' to such delightful works as these; it would be untrue to say that in them Dvořák is not taking pains or that he is exploiting the spontaneity that the English found so attractive. But he does seem to be taking things a little more easily; he is a big enough master to be able to do it and there is a peculiar charm in the ease of his relaxation.

Then came the American visits of 1892–5, with the new and unexpected interest in Negro and Indian music that they aroused. I shall try to show in a moment that these new influences were not so new as many people, including perhaps Dvořák himself, have thought; that they attracted him because they were closely related to something already present in him, something which they helped to clarify and crystallise. But it would be foolish to assert that they did nothing to him, and what they did is manifest in the *New World* Symphony, the F major Quartet, the E flat Quintet and the little Violin Sonatina, works which, among other things, heighten that impression of the master taking his ease in the later afternoon of his life. Nor is there very much in the last group of compositions of all to modify that impression. Some of them—the Quartets in A flat and G, the Cello Concerto, *The Devil and Kate*, and *Rusalka*—are technically superior to the little group of more specifically 'American' works; the symphonic poems of 1896–7, curious products of a still more curious belief that the forms of absolute instrumental music were exhausted, are inferior except in orchestration. All these works are melodically charming; all have a delicious translucency of texture and colour that Dvořák had only partially and occasionally attained in earlier days. But, except perhaps the operas, they are the products almost of slippered ease, not of high artistic endeavour. Oddly enough, the operas show a reawakened interest in Wagner, and the crossing of Wagner with nationalism produced results very like those of the similar crossing in the Rimsky-Korsakov operas of the same period.

Only one thing remains to be said to correct this account of a rather complicated personal evolution; that it would not be difficult to find in any of these periods at least one or two compositions that are at variance with the predominant tendency of the moment. But it is necessary to make it a little clearer what these influences amount to, digested or undigested or half-digested, in the music of Dvořák's maturity. I must, for instance, show what I mean by the assertion that Negro music corresponded to something already latent in Dvořák's musical make-up. The Negro traits in Dvořák's music are partly rhythmic—mainly a type of syncopation so unspecifically Negro that it has long been popularly known as the 'Scottish snap'—partly melodic, or rather modal: a tendency to flatten the seventh degree of the scale and a love of pentatonic melodies or pentatonic segments of ordinary major or minor melodies, particularly of what I venture to call the melodic 'knight's move': the permutations and combinations of the first, fifth and sixth, or second, third and fifth degrees of the major scale (the two groups together forming the complete pentatonic scale). That the *New World* Symphony, and to an even greater extent the F major Quartet and the E flat Quintet, are stamped all over with these traits no one will deny; that these obsessions, for they amount to that, were due to Dvořák's interest in the music of the American Negroes is highly probable. But each one of these traits may be found in Dvořák's music long before he crossed the Atlantic, even if they did not yet amount to obsessions. Dvořák had written a major melody with the flattened seventh in No. 6 of the *Gypsy Songs* of 1880. The wistful rising third in syncopated rhythm that one finds in the *New World* Symphony, the F major Quartet, and the middle section of the popular G flat *Humoreske* for piano, occurs in at least two quite different passages of the slow movement of the G major Symphony, to look no further: in the curiously interjected little passages for clarinets in thirds near the beginning (which sound more like anticipations of Sibelius than echoes of Negro song—which, the Symphony having been written in 1889, they could not have been) and in the melody quoted as Ex. 13*b* below. Of the two motives which the alleged 'Swing low, sweet chariot' theme in the *New World* has in common with its 'original', one is the pentatonic knight's move, the other may be found (in the minor) in the Czech folk-song, 'Pod tím našim okenečkem'; moreover the motive in the latter has the characteristic syncopated rhythm of the *first* motive of the symphonic theme. That gives us the clue; these melodic and rhythmic traits are not uncommon in the music of many countries and many composers, but if

Dvořák picked them up from any particular sources it was from Smetana and the folk-music of his native land. Consider these two fragments of melody:

Ex. 1

They are quoted not from some work of Dvořák's 'Negro' period but from Smetana's Trio in G minor, written in 1855. And the pentatonic knight's move may be found in the opening bars of *The Bartered Bride* overture, in the first theme of *Vyšehrad*, in Martinka's song in the First Act of *The Kiss*, and doubtless in many other characteristic pages of Smetana.

Smetana's influence on Dvořák was, of course, not limited to these particular traits, though it is less wide or deep than one might expect. And it is not easy for a non-Czech critic to make up his mind in some instances whether Dvořák is reflecting Smetana or both are reflecting Czech folk-idiom. On some technical points and in one or two cases of something like reminiscence one can speak more confidently. Reminiscences are the least important aspect of influence, worth noting only because they show what the influenced composer has failed to digest quite completely; so I only observe by the way that the introduction to *The Spectre's Bride* and the theme which suggests the 'rapid gait' of the demon-lover would probably not have turned out quite as they did if Smetana had not written *Vltava* and *Šárka*. And I draw attention to the similarity of the introduction to the last of the *Biblical Songs* to the love-duet in the First Act of *The Bartered Bride* only to show what a very, very naïve old man that naïve old man could be. There are, however, more interesting relationships between them than these. Oddest of all is Dvořák's trick of modelling the lay-out of the opening of a work on that of one of Smetana's compositions. The harp-passage that introduces the *Slavonic Rhapsody* in A flat can hardly fail to remind anyone who knows Smetana's *Vyšehrad* of the harp-solo which opens that work. A subtler parallel—between the openings of Dvořák's F major Quartet and Smetana's E minor (*From my Life*)—has been pointed out by Dunhill in his book on chamber-music: 'We have in the first few bars of each the same *pianissimo* movement in sixths by the two violins, giving the key chord; the same holding note on the cello, forming a pedal-bass; a similar space of silence for the viola, and a similar trumpet-like entry at the end of the rest.' ('But here,' adds Dunhill, 'the similarity ends,' and he goes on to show how favourably Dvořák's pure chamber-style compares with Smetana's quasi-orchestral writing.) There is a similar rough parallel between the brilliant opening tuttis of Dvořák's *Carnival* Overture and that to Smetana's *Kiss*, though here again closer examination soon shows how the young composer refined on the older.

When we come to those naïve repetitions of a motive, perhaps a single bar of melody, perhaps a figure in a cadential or transitional passage, we touch on something more fundamental in the musical thought of both —and we can say with some confidence that both were indebted for it to a habit of Czech folk-song. One notices it in Smetana's G minor Trio, in the overture to *Libuše* and above all (as one would expect) in his *Czech Dances* for piano, which, unlike Dvořák's *Slavonic Dances*, are arrangements of actual folk-tunes (cf. in particular the 'Cibulička', where motive-repetition is not only characteristic of the chief melody but used in the manner made familiar by Dvořák to produce points of repose). How profoundly the habit pervaded and affected Dvořák's musical thought I shall try to show later. Another trick common to both the Czech masters is quick alternation of major and minor, immediate repetition of a major phrase or chord-progression in the minor, or vice versa. This *may* be a folk-trait, but it is quite certainly one of the hall-marks of nineteenth-century romanticism; its origins lie back beyond Schubert, though it was Schubert who first exploited it to the full—so fully as almost to make it his personal property. When the rest of the musical material is utterly un-Schubertian, as in Smetana's 'Furiant' for piano (from the *Czech Dances*), one does not think of him; but it is the almost imperceptible swings from minor to major and back again, even more than the nonchalant rhythm and the half-gay, half-melancholy, altogether sweet melody, that make one inwardly cry 'Schubert!' when one hears the second movement of the *Dumky* Trio.

Though the likeness is not often so obvious as here, one often does think of Schubert when listening to Dvořák. We know that the Czech master deliberately took Schubert as one of his models, even in orchestration; he was apt to remember rather disconcertingly, not any specific Schubertian theme, but Schubert's style in general, perhaps melodically (e.g., the second subject of the first movement of the Quartet in E major), perhaps harmonically (e.g., the cadence that concludes the cello-clarinet-bassoon-and-horn melody at the beginning of the Fourth Symphony); but deeper than all this is a true spiritual affinity. Dvořák was not such a great composer as Schubert, but if anyone were competent to play Elisha to Schubert's Elijah it was he. No one else since Schubert has had quite such a well of rich, spontaneous, endlessly singing melody, others have— unfortunately—caught Schubert's discursiveness, none but Dvořák the secret of the long-drawn sweetness that can make such discursiveness delightful. He himself fails to do it in a comparatively early work like the F minor String Quartet, where in the first movement, trying to fill a big space with inadequate material, he falls back on the typical Schubertian device of erecting chord-edifices to which he tries to give the appearance of 'thematic working-out' by stamping each harmonic brick with a pattern of theme. He imitates Schubert's syncopated-chord accompaniments even in such a mature work as the D major Symphony, but when in the slow movement of the same work he catches the very essence of Schubert's rustic sweetness he does it not by imitation but by natural affinity. More than one commentator has heard in the coda of that slow movement echoes of the corresponding passages in Beethoven's Ninth Symphony; indeed one would have to be deaf or a serious sufferer from loss of memory not to hear them; but although we know that Dvořák also took the greater master as a model, there is much less of Beethoven in him than of Schubert. There was not the same affinity of spirit or of musical nature and capability. Anyone can hear that Dvořák had carefully studied Beethoven's style, his methods of structure and working-out, the *durch-brochene Arbeit* of his texture; sometimes we can even catch him at work on a definite model, as in the fourth variation of the finale of the String Sextet which is obviously referable to the sixth variation of the finale of Beethoven's Quartet, Op. 74. But even in the most Beethovenian of all Dvořák's compositions—the A flat *Variations* for piano, related (though more distantly than the case just quoted) to the A flat variations of the C minor Symphony, Beethovenian even in the piano-writing—even this work is closer to Schubert than to Beethoven. One might accurately put it that Dvořák was influenced less by Beethoven than by the Beethovenian element in Schubert.

In the same way he was especially influenced by the Schubertian element in Brahms. H. C. Colles has shown[1] how the opening of Dvořák's D major Symphony is modelled on the parallel passage in Brahms's Symphony in the same key, which had appeared two or three years earlier: 'Though the idea is all Dvořák's own, it will be seen that the constructional plan is very close to that of Brahms even to the point of an identity in the harmonic sequence. . . . Look further on after the double bar to the way in which Dvořák approaches his development of this idea, and the impression must be confirmed that not merely Brahms's general method of structure but the example of the Second Symphony in particular is acting as his unconscious guide.' This is the same sort of 'modelling' that we have already noticed in connection with Smetana and I am tempted to put a question-mark after Colles's 'unconscious', as well as to remark parenthetically that the harmonic

[1] *Oxford History of Music*, Vol. VII, London, 1934.

trends show that both composers had learned the rules of musical behaviour from Beethoven; but the less instructed listener, hearing the
naïve *Ländler*-like melody and the syncopated horn- and viola-chords,
will be more likely to think of Schubert than of Brahms. Even the
D minor String Quartet, which is actually dedicated to Brahms and does
here and there appropriately touch its hat to him, is both spiritually and
technically nearer to Schubert than to the recipient of the dedication.
Dvořák does sometimes draw near to Brahms in melodic feeling (cf. the
chief melody of the slow movement of the Dvořák Violin Concerto
which is a distant cousin of typically Brahmsian melodies in the first
movement of the Clarinet Quintet, the slow movement of the Fourth
Symphony, and 'Von ewiger Liebe'), just as he sometimes sounds the
depths of his solemn harmonies (e.g. in the sixth of the piano *Variations*)
or even, more surprisingly, picks up an orchestral trick from him (e.g.,
the essentially pianistic arpeggios drawn across the score in bar 10 of the
poco adagio of the D minor Symphony). But it is worth pointing out that
in the one case where Dvořák does lapse into direct reminiscence of
Brahms—the second subject of the first movement of the D minor Symphony, of which the first two bars are note for note the same even in key
as the slow-movement melody of Brahms's B flat Piano Concerto—the
essentially Brahmsian feature of Dvořák's melody is not this coincidence
of notes, which is only an amusing case of failure to digest something
acquired by the unconscious, but the continuation, which reflects one of
Brahms's most purely individual traits: the uninterrupted extension of a
'tuneful', songlike phrase into what can only be described as 'thematic
line'. We hear the beginning of what sounds like a stanzaic song-melody,
but at the point where one expects a more or less commonplace cadence
and an answering phrase it throws out tendrils consisting of motives that
can be, and invariably are, developed in the classical symphonic manner.
Dvořák follows this pattern also in the first theme of the same movement
and in that of the *allegro non troppo* of his F minor Trio. It is in such
points as this rather than in mere melodic reminiscences that one detects
the real impact of one composer's mind on another's.

The impact of Liszt and Wagner is less evident than Brahms's, perhaps because it occurred at an earlier period of Dvořák's life and produced the most obvious results in immature works that Dvořák suppressed
or even destroyed, whereas that of Brahms happened in his maturity and
is specially apparent in such masterpieces as the Symphony and Trio just
mentioned. Neither Liszt nor Wagner affected his style as they did Smetana's. Of Liszt one can only say that Dvořák probably learned from him
the technique of theme-transformation—though he might have learned
it just as easily from Schubert's *Wanderer* Fantasia. (Similarly there is
little doubt that Dvořák acquired the continuous texture of his operas

and his somewhat rudimentary *Leitmotiv* technique from Wagner, though it is more than likely that he and his contemporaries would have arrived where they did by a process of evolution from the operas of Spohr, Weber, Marschner and Schumann even if these two tendencies, continuous texture and use of *Leitmotive*, had never been crystallised in the work of a single genius like Wagner; indeed Dvořák, except perhaps in his last operas, and most of the other post-Wagnerians are nearer to the pre-Wagnerians than to Wagner himself.) Many of Dvořák's theme-transformations must be familiar to almost every music-lover: the basing of the finale of the Fourth Symphony on a theme expanded from the principal idea of the first movement, the coda of the *allegretto* of the same Symphony based on a transformation of the trio melody, the slow and quick sections of the dumka of the E flat String Quartet, the transformations in the *New World* Symphony, the metamorphoses of the motto-theme of 'death' in the Requiem and of the theme common to the *Carnival, Nature* and *Othello* overtures. There is a beautiful half-reference in the scherzo of the G major String Quartet to part of the theme of the preceding *adagio*, the motive quoted in Ex. 16 below. But I choose for quotation two examples from less-known quartets, both because they are subtler and because they are more typical of Dvořák's musical thinking at its best than the cruder, more Lisztian metamorphoses in the Fourth and Fifth Symphonies. The second subject of the first *allegro* of the D minor Quartet:

Ex. 2

is itself evolved from the first subject:

Ex. 3

Now at the very end of the slow movement this second subject of the *allegro* steals in almost imperceptibly on second violin and viola, unwinds in a new direction, and most beautifully puts its seal on the piece:

Ex. 4

But its introduction here, far from sounding forced or mechanical, like the similar quotations in the *New World* Symphony, is perfectly natural because it grows out of a movement which from its opening bars (Ex. 5) has dwelt on another, very similar but not identical, semiquaver motive.

Ex. 5
Adagio

Ex. 5 is not naturally related to Exs. 2 and 3, but Ex. 4 affects their marriage. Something very similar happens in the C major Quartet; the opening theme of the scherzo:

Ex. 6
Allegro vivo

hints at a relationship with that of the first movement:

Ex. 7
Allegro

but it is not till later in the scherzo that the relationship is frankly acknowledged:

Ex. 8

There is a whiff, the faintest possible whiff, of Wagner in Ex. 7; it is Wagner almost completely dissolved in Dvořák's melting-pot. But there is seldom even so much as this of *le fantôme du vieux Klingsor* in Dvořák's music. The 'essential turn' in melody, if not Wagner's personal property, is such an essential part of his style that one can hardly help greeting it as a Wagnerism when one meets it near the end of the exposition of the first movement of Dvořák's String Sextet, or in the well-known horn solo in the *poco adagio* of his D minor Symphony, or in the slow movement of his G major String Quartet. Siegfried's *Waldvogel* sings most unexpectedly in Dvořák's *Nature* overture—being evidently a Sudeten bird. But there are few other traces of that early enthusiasm; the Wagnerian crystals of thought were almost all completely dissolved in the solution of other elements that constituted Dvořák's musical fluid, until another handful of them was thrown into *The Devil and Kate* and *Rusalka*. Only to some extent in the sphere of harmony (for example, the free use of accented chromatic appoggiaturas) have they perceptibly coloured the solution. And just here and there, as in this passage from *The Spectre's Bride*:

and in the already mentioned motto-theme of the Requiem, one does find a not wholly dissolved crystal.

I must have given a very crude and imperfect idea of my theory of the formation of a creative personality if I have left any reader with the impression that I believe Dvořák, or any other composer with true creative power, to be little more than the sum of a number of influences. To trace all the elements that have contributed something to a man's musical make-up is a by no means useless pastime; to spot the undissolved particles of these elements is at any rate an amusing one. But when we have strained away these particles, these impurities, we are still left with the pure solution of the man's own musical thought—not a mere mixture of elements but a magical brew which by the chemistry of a living mind has been changed into a new element. To analyse this element, define its peculiarities and describe its properties is a much more difficult operation than to fish out the bits of undissolved ingredient, but it must be attempted.

The most striking property of Dvořák's music is its abundant melody, and study of his melodic style takes one at once to the very heart of his genius—though not, if I may play with a rather unsatisfactory metaphor, to its mind. Let me admit at once that to analyse melody, especially melody of the spontaneous Dvořákian type, bears some resemblance to the often mentioned, though extremely improbable, process of breaking a butterfly on the wheel. But a critic can no more sit back and merely enjoy tunes than an entomologist can lie in the grass and merely enjoy the play and colour of butterflies. Those enjoyments are enormously important to both of them, and they must come first; but after that both critic and entomologist begin to query and study and classify. They not only enjoy the process of study; when they go back from it to purely aesthetic enjoyment, they find that that too has become both finer and richer in consequence. The man who has learned to distinguish various types of melodic formation in a composer can much more easily distinguish the finer examples of each type. Every point is enriched by the overtones of association. It is only when you have noticed that the vast majority of Dvořák's melodies begin on a strong down-beat that you detect any special significance in the exceptions (e.g. the three-note up-beat which plays such an important part in the slow movement of the G major Symphony, which is indeed one of the two factors that nearly succeed in holding that charming, but oddly loose and incoherent movement together).

It is arguable, though I should not care to have to defend the thesis, that down-beat openings are marks of melodic inspiration in its crudest—or, if you prefer, its most naïve—form, that a tune which just 'comes into a man's head' is most likely to begin on a down-beat. I merely remark here in passing that in Beethoven's sketch-books 'there are a large number of instances in which melodies, *originally without up-beats*, are given one later on'.[1] A very characteristic opening of Dvořák's is a down-beat, usually on the dominant of the scale, followed by an upward swing, most frequently of a sixth, and a gradual descent. This melody from the finale of the posthumously published String Quartet in F minor, written in 1873, is very typical:

Ex. 10

Each four-bar phrase begins with an upward swing from the dominant of a sixth, a fourth or an octave, and it is only the octave leap that generates enough power for the melody's free continuation. Another instance of the upward swing of a sixth from the dominant degree, followed by a gradual descent, is the main theme of the *Slavonic Dance* in E minor, Op. 46, No. 2. Everyone must remember the violin build-up from this basic material in the finale of the *New World* Symphony; and the second subject of the first movement of the F minor Trio is yet another case, though here the melody proper is prefaced by an up-beat so elaborate that one feels it must have been, like so many of Beethoven's up-beats, an afterthought. Nearly as common is the octave leap from the dominant as in the ninth bar of Ex. 10; one thinks at once of the middle section of the first *Slavonic Dance* and the trio of that movement which runs so oddly parallel to the *Dance*: the furiant of the String Sextet. In the principal theme of the finale of the D minor Symphony the descent after the octave-swing is more complicated and long-breathed; it belongs to the same family as the *Dance* and Sextet melodies but has reached a higher stage of evolution.

The upward leap is not always from the dominant, nor does it always

[1] Paul Mies, *Beethoven's Sketches*, English translation, London, 1929.

consist of a sixth or octave. The deliciously lazy motive that punctuates the polka-theme of the *Slavonic Dance* in A flat, Op. 46, No. 6, swings upward only a fourth (cf. bars 5–6 of Ex. 10). And the first and last movements of the String Quintet in G major are marked by a number of themes springing upward a sixth or an octave from down-beats not always on the dominant. Also closely related to this type of melody are a large group of more tender, wistful motives that begin with a rise of only a third and then turn back on themselves. The prototype will be found embedded in the slow movement of the so-called Third Symphony (in F), but a better example is this melody from the slow movement of the Violin Concerto:

Ex. 11

where the rising sixth, too, though not the *gradual* descent from it, re-appears in the third bar. The opening of the *poco adagio e molto cantabile* of the String Quartet in C, written a year or two later, one of Dvořák's most 'classical' works, subtilises the same basic idea:

Ex. 12

and is very obviously a more polished form, or even a variation (in the classical sense), of a more crude original inspiration. To show both the frequency of some of these unconscious basic elements in Dvořák's melodic thought and the infinite variety of the changes he (equally unconsciously) rings on them, I quote three melodies from the finale of the so-called Second Symphony, the slow movement of the Fourth, and the second movement of the *Dumky* Trio, respectively:

Ex. 13
(*a*) Allegro

(*b*) Adagio

(*c*) Poco adagio

and ask the reader to compare the motives marked *x*, *y* and *z* with those in Ex. 11; the comparison will emphasise the very different aesthetic values of these snatches of melody, particularly the shapelessness of Ex. 13*b*. The reader will hardly fail to notice that *y* is also the basis of the chief second-subject theme of the first movement of the *New World* Symphony.

Again related to the *x* motive is a common form of the triplet kink that Dvořák loves to insert in melodies in duple or quadruple time. The examples in the cello melodies that open both the Piano Quintet and the G major Symphony are too familiar to need quotation. But an even more characteristic form of this triplet kink begins with a rising fourth instead of a third. My examples:

are taken respectively from the first of the *Gypsy Songs*, the first movement of the *Dumky* Trio, and the Princess's Song at the end of Act II of *Rusalka*. Another type of kink, even more suggestive of a possible gypsy origin (at any rate to such as I, whose knowledge of gypsy music is lamentably superficial) may be illustrated by these examples from the 'Virgo, virginum præclara' of the *Stabat Mater*, from the fifteenth movement of *The Spectre's Bride*, and from the Prelude to *Rusalka*:

Here again there is no question of Dvořák's simply repeating a formula; his thought unconsciously tends to follow certain curves but the curves are never, or very seldom, quite the same.

Another of the curve-marks of Dvořák's melody, the 'pentatonic knight's move', has already been mentioned. It would not be quite true to say that it is ubiquitous in his music, but it would be very nearly true. In addition to the Fourth and Fifth Symphonies, the F major Quartet and the E flat String Quintet—where it becomes quite wearisome—it marks the slow movements of the D major and D minor Symphonies, much of the *Peasant a Rogue*, *Carnival* and *Nature* overtures, and dozens of other typical themes and melodies. (Two of the triplet motives in Exs. 14*a* and *b* are 'knight's moves'.) Then again there is that curious little mannerism, the rise and fall of a perfect fourth (cf. the dumka of the E flat Quartet, the King's song in Act I, scene 7, of *King and Collier*, a prominent *Leitmotiv* in *The Jacobin*, the first theme of the D major *Slavonic Rhapsody* and a theme in the G minor, the trio of the D major Symphony, the *Slavonic Dance* in F, Op. 46, No. 4, the slow movement of the Cello Concerto), which has left important marks on the *adagio* of the G major Symphony. And there is the penchant for descending chromatic, or partly chromatic, lines, as in the opening of the *Stabat Mater*, the theme of the piano *Variations*, the second theme of the second *Slavonic Dance*, the *grandioso* theme in the first movement of the F major Symphony, the subsidiary theme in the *allegretto* of the Fourth Symphony. In one of the subsidiary themes of the finale of the Violin Concerto a decorated chromatic line suddenly generates one of the familiar rising-sixth-and-gradually-descending motives.

Yet I have so far spoken only of the curve-marks of Dvořák's melody, saying nothing of its rhythmic and metrical and modal peculiarities. I can touch only on a few salient points. Perhaps the most striking of all is the variety in the length of Dvořák's phrases. He can write long-breathed continuous tunes like the opening themes of the first and last movements of the G major Symphony and he will be equally happy with brief, square cut, symmetrically balancing fragments of two bars, or even one bar, as in the *Slavonic Dances*. He thinks usually in the conventional four- or eight-bar units, but that opening tune of the G major Symphony begins with a six-bar phrase and answers it with one of five bars. Ex. 12 is a three-bar idea. The dumka of the String Sextet is written almost entirely in five-bar phrases. The melody of the male-voice chorus, 'Guslar', on which Dvořák afterwards wrote his *Symphonic Variations*, begins with a seven-bar phrase. Another peculiarity of Dvořák's is his tendency to cross a prevailing 3/4 with phrases or whole passages of 2/4, as in the first movement of the F minor String Quartet, the *allegro scherzando* of the E major String Quartet, the first movement of the D major Symphony, and the finale of the F minor Trio. Here we can see the direct influence of the characteristic rhythm of the furiant—though, as it happens, the movements so called in the String Sextet and Piano Quintet lack this characteristic.[1] (Conversely, the chief theme of the finale of the Violin Concerto, though not so labelled, is a perfect example of a furiant tune; so are the first and eighth *Slavonic Dances*, in C major and G minor.) In the fifth movement of the *Dumky* Trio 6/8 is similarly crossed by 3/4.

[1] So do some of Dvořák's other furiants, a fact which possibly accounts for Tovey's typically perverse refusal to see anything characteristic in the furiant at all.

Dvořák must also have picked up from folk-music his habit, sometimes delightful, sometimes rather irritating, of naïvely repeating a short phrase or a mere motive like a child crooning to itself. But here we pass from purely melodic characteristics to one that marks Dvořák's musical thought in general. And, since this is a folk-trait, we shall see how 'folk-song influence' can go much deeper than the melodic surface. It is naturally most prominent in such works as the *Slavonic Dances* where Dvořák is more or less deliberately copying the folk-idiom, but it is more interesting to trace it in his chamber-music and symphonies. Sometimes, of course, in these too it is introduced quite naïvely, almost as a method of getting up melodic steam; in this respect the second subject of the first movement of the C major String Quartet is essentially the same as 'Songs my mother taught me'. But the repetition does not always occur in the first member of the melody; consider for instance the *poco andante* of the G major String Quintet or Ex. 13*b* from the Fourth Symphony. In these two instances the harmony, too, is repeated unchanged; this frequently happens, but there are also a number of cases of repeated phrases or motives with delicately changing harmonic support (cf. the flute-and-oboe melody near the beginning of the *adagio* of the Fourth Symphony). Near the end of the *adagio* of the late G major String Quartet Dvořák produces an enchanting effect simply by repeating a motive four times but dividing the repetitions between the first and second violins:

Ex. 16

And in the exactly parallel place in the *adagio* of the G major Symphony he produces an equally enchanting effect by repeating a mere three-note motive four times (but the fourth time altered and extended) and dividing the repetitions between oboe, horn and first violins. In these two cases the repetitions provide major points of repose, such as Dvořák loved to introduce towards the ends of his slow movements (see, for another example, the *adagio* of the D minor Quartet), but, as Smetana had done before him, he uses similar but simpler repetitions—often of the most primitive two-note motives—to create minor points of repose at cadential and transitional passages. This trait, like most of his 'naïve' mannerisms, is particularly prominent in his later works, from the *Carnival* Overture onward—above all in the 'American' compositions and the Cello Concerto—but it is also noticeable in many earlier ones: the Quartets in F minor, D minor and C major, the *Dumky* Trio and various others. But none of these is so inwardly conditioned by the habit of singing each strain twice over as the Quartet in E flat; only careful listening or a close examination of the score will fully reveal how the whole structure of the work depends on it, but a glance at the first page will suffice to show how overpowering this obsession could be.

Yet another rustic trait—for I think it is rustic rather than Italian or Brahmsian or Lisztian in origin (and certainly is so in effect)—is Dvořák's affection for melodies doubled in thirds. Even when they do not run wholly or almost wholly in simple thirds as in the second subject of the first movement of the E major Quartet, the scherzo of the Second Symphony, the opening of the *Nature* Overture and dozens of passages in the *New World* alone,[1] his part-writing very easily drops into thirds in passing (as in Ex. 5), or the thirds are lightly decorated, or both (as in the F sharp major section of the dumka of the String Sextet). The same 'third' feeling is equally present in Ex. 12, only there the fine craftsman that Dvořák could always be when he liked has disguised the crude original conception by suspensions and ornamentation. (Whether you prefer your Dvořák at his ease and in all his rustic crudity, or fully exerting both his creative and his technical power, is literally a matter of taste.)

Suspensions such as these and a free use of appoggiaturas, particularly *Tristan*esque chromatic appoggiaturas, account for most of the peculiarities of Dvořák's harmony. And I should say that his love of free and constant, and frequently enharmonic, modulation accounts for the rest; the habit is an outward and audible token of that loss or extreme weakening of the classical feeling for tonality which he shared with so many nineteenth-century composers. Dvořák's contemporaries thought otherwise about his harmony and contemporary judgments on points like this are never to be despised; they may be hopelessly wrong but they will help us to get our own judgments right—or more nearly right. It seems fantastic to regard Dvořák as even a forerunner of the atonalists and polytonalists, yet in his lifetime one of the greatest of all English critics, Hadow, regarded him as both an occasional atonalist and an occasional polytonalist.[2] (He naturally modified his view in the perspective of later years.) Writing his *Studies in Modern Music* in 1894, Hadow asserted that 'Dvořák is the one solitary instance of a composer who adopts the chromatic scale as unit, who regards all notes as equally related. His method is totally different from that of chromatic writers like Grieg and Chopin, for Grieg uses the effects as isolated points of colour, and Chopin embroiders them, mainly as appoggiaturas, on a basis of diatonic harmony.

---

[1] Dvořák particularly loves clarinets in thirds: e.g., first movement of the D minor Symphony, slow movement of the G major.

[2] Dvořák did actually write a short passage in the whole-tone mode in the prelude to Act II of *The Devil and Kate* (1898-9), depicting a scene in Hell.

His "equal temperament" is totally different from that of Bach, for Bach only showed that all keys could be employed, not that they could be arranged in any chance order or sequence. But to Dvořák the chromatic passages are part of the essential texture, and the most extreme modulations follow as simply and easily as the most obvious. In a word, his work from this standpoint, is truly a *nuova musica*. . . . We rather lose our bearings when, in the second of the *Legenden*, we find a phrase which has its treble in G and its tenor in D flat; or when, as in the fifth number of *The Spectre's Bride*, the music passes from one remote key to another with a continuous and facile display of resource that is apparently inexhaustible.' But if Dvořák played his part in undermining the average musician's sense of key, or rather perhaps of reducing tonal procedure to a thing known and familiar rather than directly and keenly felt, we can see now that he was only extending and elaborating one of the practices of the great classic composer to whom he is most nearly related. Schubert's sudden and romantic key-changes, his enharmonic ambiguities, are the seeds of most of the things in Dvořák that puzzled Hadow. And, heard in the perspective of half-a-century, Dvořák's harmonic innovations do not seem very much more advanced than some of Schubert's. If the reader will take down the score of Schubert's best-known quartet, the D minor (*Death and the Maiden*), and look at the passage beginning eighteen bars before the double-bar at the end of the exposition of the first movement, he will find in four or five bars the key to Dvořák's most complicated harmonic puzzles.

His harmonic idiom was also enriched to some extent, as I have said, by the idiom of Liszt and Wagner, particularly the chromatic appoggiatura. And sometimes, as in the scene between Rusalka and the witch:

Ex. 17
Vivace

his quite logical use of this device produces sounds that must have struck our grandfathers as very 'modern' in the unpleasant sense. Dvořák never shrank from a harmonic clash if his logic demanded it. (See, for instance, those produced by the treble and bass patterns in the piano passages at the end of each stanza of the song, 'Silent Woods', Op. 55, No. 3.) The passage that made Hadow lose his bearings near the end of the *Legend*, Op. 59, No. 2 (Ex. 18, on facing page), is another case in point. (Observe, incidentally, the similarity of bars 1, 3 and 5 to the last bar of Ex. 15c.)

There is no question at all of polytonality here; the harmonic basis of the passage is simply:

The F sharp in the second bar, the B naturals in the fourth, and the B flat and B natural in the sixth, are appoggiaturas, and the general effect is slightly crabbed. But generally Dvořák's part-writing is quite remarkable for its smoothness and euphony, which is one of the main reasons why his orchestration always sounds so transparent and his chamber-music so sonorous. His mind was of that order which finds it easy, too, to devise slick, natural-sounding bits of canon or imitation (cf. the *stringendo* passage nine or ten bars later in this same *Legend*) or to invent simple, melodious counter-melodies (such as the bassoon solo towards the end of the finale of the *New World* Symphony). It is an order of minds, I should add, that can be entered even by the most gifted only after a fairly severe training; if Dvořák admittedly works with very plastic material, he works with it like a master; it nearly always remains firm in his hands. It is very seldom that he goes beyond the limits of bearable naïveté, as he does in the descending scales in sixths of the *adagio* of the Fourth Symphony.

To modern ears, for which Dvořák's chromaticism has lost the charm of whatever novelty it possessed for our grandfathers, perhaps the most striking, certainly the most attractive, feature of his harmony is his skilful employment of common chords and inversions. Colles said that Brahms 'reaches to the sublime by his use of common chords'. The sublime was not up Dvořák's street, but he does manage to give a surprising amount of colour to the most sober diatonic harmony by the free use of the mediant and submediant triads and the first inversion of the subdominant. Ex. 5 is thoroughly characteristic of his clear, diatonic harmony, his natural-sounding use of contrapuntal device, and his transparent but beautifully sonorous texture—though it must be admitted that, owing to all the double-stopping, this particular passage is apt to sound less transparent than it looks on paper.

Indeed these two factors that constitute musical texture—harmony and its expression through part-writing and figuration; instrumentation (that is, the technique of writing for instruments or voices singly and in combination)—though separable in theory for convenience of discussion, are not so in practice. Or if the composer does separate them, it is always at his peril and generally to his disaster. Apart altogether from those musicians, of whom Sibelius is an outstanding example, with whom theme, elaborating texture and orchestration seem to be only different aspects of the same idea, every composer must obviously allow his thought to be controlled to some extent by the medium. The necessity would seem too obvious to need mentioning if almost every page of musical history had not to tell of musicians, and real masters at that, who have written instrumentally for the voice or pianistically for the orchestra or orchestrally for the string quartet. Dvořák does not belong to that class; I can think of only one or two really bad cases of music miscast for the medium of all the works of his that I know: the brief *fff grandioso* outburst in the slow movement of the String Quartet in G, Op. 106, and some passages in the first and last movements of the much earlier String Quintet in the same key. It is true that most of his short piano pieces are not specially suited to their medium, but unimportant compositions of that sort, a great man's odds and ends, are seldom remarkable for a keen sense of style. Dvořák's comparative failure in his more important piano compositions, the A flat *Variations* and the Concerto, is of a rather different kind; he does not write the wrong sort of music for the piano; he writes the right sort in the wrong way. The stuff is pianistic in essence, and the figuration and layout, carefully modelled on the piano-writing of Beethoven and Schubert and (occasionally) Brahms, look all right on paper; it is only when one sits down to play it that one finds how little direct sense he had of hand on keyboard. His Piano Concerto is comparable with what the Brahms and Elgar violin concertos would probably have been if their composers had not had a Joachim and a W. H. Reed to look over their solo parts. Dvořák was himself a string-player (and how many times, particularly in his chamber-music, does he take care to provide a bit of what is technically known as 'fat' for his own instrument, the viola) and his string-parts are always beautifully and most effectively written. Even with the piano he is happy enough when it is no longer the leading lady but only an ordinary member of his repertory company. Though a pianist, as Elgar was a violinist, he was not a good enough pianist to be able to write star parts for the piano, but he understood it, as he understood the orchestral wind, well enough to make highly effective use of its timbre in an ensemble. His figuration always remains conventional, yet the effects he produces with the piano in the *allegro grazioso* of the F minor Trio, the dumka and furiant of the Piano Quintet, and several passages of the *Dumky* Trio, are quite delicious.

While Dvořák seldom falls into incongruity of means and ends, he is admittedly not of the tribe of Berlioz and Sibelius. There are passages in his music where one feels that the whole idea, melody, harmony and instrumental colouring, must have come to him at one blow; one instance is the delightfully naïve opening of the *andantino con moto* episode in the otherwise rather too gaudy *Carnival* Overture, the passage with the crooning cor anglais ostinato; but these are exceptions. Generally one feels that Dvořák's music is, if I may invent a word, post-orchestrated—though almost always quite superbly orchestrated. He is equally happy with the instruments as individuals, in groups and in masses. I have already spoken of his singing string-parts; his flutes spread sweetness and light over many pages of his scores and the low flute-writing in the first movement of the *New World* is a model of its kind; the cor anglais was a real person to him and he cast it for some of the most memorable roles in its whole repertoire, not only the passage just mentioned and the *largo* of the *New World* but such brief yet unforgettable character-parts as the re-entry of the main theme at the beginning of the recapitulation in the first movement of the G major Symphony. His treatment of the horns, especially in his later works, is in its much simpler way as individual as Brahms's or even Wagner's; broadly speaking, it is a modern extension of Schubert's practice (cf. the opening of Schubert's great C major Symphony and the horn-passages near the beginnings of the first and fourth movements of the *New World*). But Dvořák's orchestration in general is what one would be tempted to call 'of the school of Schubert' if one did not suspect that it had its roots further back in the baroque church music of eighteenth-century Austria. That his palette is brighter than Schubert's is mainly due to some influence from Liszt. (And his scoring also seems to have been breathed upon at times by the spirits of Wagner and Smetana and even Brahms.) Dvořák is not a subtle orchestrator; you find few effects of fine shading in his scores; a melodic line or an accompaniment pattern is always carried right through by the instrument or instruments that began it. There is little, even in the D minor Symphony, of the rich, sonorous weaving of German scores; Dvořák prefers primary colours or simple, but always brightly effective mixtures for both thematic line and background—and the latter is always transparent, always kept in its place. 'Sometimes too much in its place', growls the devil's advocate, and it must be admitted that Dvořák's noisier tuttis are sometimes shrill and top-heavy,[1] with in one or two cases even the trumpets used to bring out a lyrical melody. On the other hand, he evolved from classical, and particularly Schubertian, practice an (I think) entirely novel treatment of the same instruments in the tutti. Everyone will remember the *pp* trumpet 'signals' in the *allegretto* of Schubert's C major Symphony (pp. 124–9 of the Eulenburg miniature score); such 'signals'—for they are more like

---

[1] Though hardly, as Hugo Wolf wrote of the scoring of *The Peasant a Rogue*, 'abscheulich, brutal, abgeschmackt'.

military calls than ordinary orchestral figures or fanfares—are characteristic of Austrian orchestration: Mahler's, for instance. But, so far as I
know, Dvorak's method of further enlivening a *fortissimo* tutti by introducing 'signal' figures, independent of the rest of the orchestral texture,
on both trumpets in *ff* unison, is quite peculiar to him. There are instances
in almost all his mature orchestral works: e.g., pp. 22 and 67 of the miniature score of the D minor Symphony, p. 176 of the G major Symphony,
pp. 73–4 of the *Carnival* Overture, p. 119 of the *New World* Symphony,
pp. 21–2 and 31–2 of the Cello Concerto.

Dvořák's orchestral writing increased in brilliance towards the end of
his life. I know *The Devil and Kate* and *Rusalka* only from the vocal
scores and *Armida* not at all, but the symphonic poems, weak enough in
other respects, are masterpieces of orchestration. Compare the almost
classical scores of the *Symphonic Variations,* the Violin Concerto and the
Symphonies in D major and D minor with those of the last two symphonies, the Cello Concerto, and the cycles of overtures and symphonic
poems. The increase of virtuosity is remarkable in the later works; they
are written with superb slickness and assurance, and if orchestral colouring were all that mattered they would be what the concert-going public
too often assumes them to be: Dvořák's masterpieces. But considered as
musical organisms they are generally inferior; not only is the melodic and
thematic material poorer, the thought is looser and the forms are less
organic. At his best—even in the slow movement of his greatest work, the
D minor Symphony—Dvořák was a discursive thinker, but his digres-
sions are the outpourings of a rich and overflowing mind; in some of the
later and most popular works, above all in the G major Symphony, they
are often little better than delightful garrulousness. Tovey, whose analytical essays on Dvořák contain some of his most penetrating criticism
embedded in some of his most irritating writing, has shown at length and
in detail—which is the only possible way to show such things—how
closely reasoned, how highly organised is the great tragic first movement
of the D minor Symphony. (And if he had been dealing with the chamber
works he might easily have found parallels in the best of those.) He has
also, though one of Dvořák's warmest and most intelligent English admirers since Hadow, pointed out the weaknesses that oblige us to class
some of the later works as lower organic types: the 'flat reiterations', the
too strong magnetism of the tonic, the tendency to improvise that reveals
itself in those 'series of short phrases, each of which comes in the manner
of an afterthought suggested by the one before'. The G major Symphony,
which exhibits most of Dvořák's weaknesses of structure, Tovey does
not discuss at all. But for those very reasons, and because it contains so
much charming if rambling and ill-connected music, it is worth discussing
for a moment.

The form of both first and last movements is, of course, experimental; and we may as well charitably conclude that the form of the *adagio* is experimental too, though it is not so easy to see what Dvořák was trying to do in it. Dvořák always had a mild tendency to indulge in structural experiments, and the broad pattern of the first movement of the G major Symphony is in some respects an elaboration of that of the *Peasant a Rogue* overture. The latter has a long *andante* introduction which returns in the dominant in the middle of the *allegro* and again in the tonic at the end just before the brilliant coda, which is also partly based on one of its themes. In the Symphony the place of the *andante* in this scheme is to some extent taken by the long-breathed melody, unconnected with the rest of the thematic material, which is heard at the beginning and end of the exposition and again between the development and the recapitulation. But what one accepts easily enough in a comedy overture can be quite puzzling when it is inserted in a symphonic movement in sonata form (which the *allegro* of the overture is not). One asks what its meaning or function is, and one gets no answer from the music. The corresponding feature in the *Peasant* overture holds the whole thing together; this is, if anything, a disintegrating factor. Yet—and this is the real weakness of the movement—one can hardly speak of the disintegration of something that never shows any signs of being integrated. One idea after another is put forward—I say nothing of the actual quality of the ideas—only to be abandoned or mislaid among passages of transitional padding. There are neat points, of course, such as the opening of the development in the tonic key and with the same scoring (solo flute over tremolo strings) as the opening of the exposition proper, suggesting that we are to have a full repeat in the classical manner and then happily disappointing us; Beethoven had done the same thing in the first of his *Razumovsky* Quartets. There are pleasant tunes and charming orchestral noises; it is easy to love the thing, with all its shortcomings. But if the word 'symphonic' means anything at all, this is not a symphonic movement. Dvořák's defence would be no doubt that he was not trying to write a movement as closely knit as the first movement of the D minor or even that of the D major, that he was aiming at a new kind of symphonic first movement, in which lyrical expansiveness should take the place of logical development. But to aim is not necessarily to hit, and he himself four years later produced a far finer example of such a lyrical, only slightly 'developed' first movement in the *New World*. And if one can speak of 'development by lyrical expansion', he had already done that superbly in the finale of the D minor Symphony, as may be seen by comparing Ex. 13*a* with the form in which this melody first appears:

Ex. 20

mf espressivo

Of the other 'experimental' movements of the G major—the delightful *allegretto grazioso* is quite conventional, except for its important coda—the slow movement is even less successful than the first, the finale rather more so. For one thing, it is based on a gorgeously long-breathed tune. For another, Dvořák can generally be relied upon to produce something worthwhile when he writes a set of variations, whether a large set for a large orchestra (the *Symphonic Variations*) or a tiny set for a tiny ensemble (those which round off the masterly little Terzetto for two violins and viola); the variations in the String Sextet and in the early Piano Quartet, Op. 23, are by far the best movements in those works. He was not a great master of variation-writing like Beethoven or Brahms, but his fertile imagination showed him endless *minor* possibilities in a theme, and he usually chose a rather odd one (cf. particularly the *Symphonic Variations*, the A flat *Variations* for piano and the finale of the Terzetto); and the necessity of keeping more or less to a given topic curbed his dangerous tendency to digress. In other words, he digresses to just that extent which makes a musical variation, or a literary essay, delightful. In the finale of the G major Symphony, by perverse contrast with his procedure in the first two movements, he hardly digresses enough. As on so many other pages of this score, his imagination seems to be functioning at only half-pressure. But the theme itself is so compelling that one can easily enjoy the movement in uncritical heedlessness of its failure to combine variation-form satisfactorily with sonata-form.

The *Dumky* Trio is, I feel, another of Dvořák's failures in structural experimentation, however attractive in other respects; six separate movements can hardly be made into a single whole by loose key-relationship and by building each on the same formal pattern. Actually they hold together less firmly than the three overtures of the *Nature, Life and Love* cycle—*Nature, Carnival* and *Othello*—which are at least thematically connected and would actually gain by being played consecutively, as Dvořák intended; one does not grasp the real significance of the *andantino con moto* in the *Carnival* Overture unless one recognises the 'nature' theme in it.[1] Dvořák's liberties with the conventions of sonata-form also vary in success. Most of these are concerned with the recapitulation and generally with its curtailment, though in one very familiar example, the return of the *allegro molto* second subject of the *New World* Symphony, the unorthodoxy lies in the surprising choice of key. The most drastic of all these curtailments occurs in the *allegro ma non troppo* of the Violin Concerto, a very free and rhapsodic movement in every aspect, where only the first subject is brought back quite briefly and the music then works round

---

[1] The liberal use of the 'nature' theme in *Othello* calls for some explanation—which Dvořák has accordingly given in the score: 'Scene: in the open air!' Nothing could be more characteristic of his naïveté.

without a break into the *adagio*. One may have one's doubts about the success of this, but the handling of the reprise in the first movement of the D minor Symphony is masterly beyond all question. Only the end of the first-subject material, corresponding to the passage on page 11 of the miniature score, is brought back; but it returns as the crown of a great climax that has been built up from this material almost throughout the development section. To have said any more on this topic at this point would have been first-rate crassitude, though many a lesser composer has fallen into such a trap; as it is, Dvořák reserves most of the *structural*, as contrasted with the dramatic, weight of this theme's return for the long and important coda. The fusion of conventional form into organic form in this movement is complete. And it only remains to be added that Dvořák then proceeds to do the same thing all over again, except as regards the coda, in the finale of the same symphony. Less subtle, more audacious and equally successful is the complete dropping of the first-subject material in the first movement of the Cello Concerto and the opening of the recapitulation—after a chromatic scale in octaves for the soloist, which even quite eminent cellists have been known to play without the octaves—with the second subject, tutti and *fortissimo*; but for that Dvořák had a precedent in Chopin—the Sonata in B flat minor.

Nevertheless Dvořák was in by far the greater number of his works content to adopt the well-tried formal conventions of his great classical and romantic predecessors with only minor adjustments, very much as he adopted and adapted their harmonic language. Even in opera he found as early as the second version of *King and Collier* the convention that satisfied him for the rest of his life, a simple convention of lyrical passages, thinly disguised or undisguised 'numbers' embedded in a mock-Wagnerian continuous texture; within that convention he developed very different musical tendencies, but he never altered the convention itself in any essential. Ultimately it matters very little what conventions of form or idiom an artist adopts to express himself through, provided he remains true to them and provided they are adequate vehicles for what he has to say. Dvořák is seldom untrue to his conventions, seldom uses an Eliza Doolittle harmonic adjective or sews a patch of symphonic purple on to a simple lyrical opera; and his conventions never let him down. But to say that is not in the least to accuse him of being 'conventional' in the everyday, pejorative sense of the word. A conventional person is one lacking in personality; I have failed most miserably if I have given an impression that Dvořák's creative personality is not one of the most clearly defined—I do not say 'one of the strongest'—in musical history.

1943

V—AN EROTIC DIARY FOR PIANO

It is common knowledge that Zdeněk[1] Fibich composed 376 short piano-pieces which he published under the title *Nálady, Dojmy a Upomínky* (Moods, Impressions and Memories), of which no. 139 was arranged by Jan Kubelík as a violin piece with the title *Poème* and in that form (and various derangements) enjoyed vast popularity during the rlier part of the present century. This so-called 'poem' is probably the only composition by Fibich that has ever become well known outside his native land, although he was unquestionably one of the best Czech symphonists of the last century. As for the other 375 *Nálady, Dojmy a Upomínky*, even the English champions of Czech music seem to be not very well informed about them. The author of the very sympathetic article on Fibich in the fifth edition of *Grove*[2] says only that they 'are, with the exception of Op. 44, mainly preparatory studies for larger works printed on two staves and owe their charm to their musical value rather than to any exploitation of pianoforte technique', on which one must comment that although some are preparatory studies for, or were used again in, larger works—more, certainly, than are so described in the published version—such studies are nevertheless only a small minority of the pieces. Moreover, many of the supposed 'studies' are really quotations from major works already completed. Rosa Newmarch does better,[3] though she speaks of 'about 350 separate pieces':

> None of these is as perfect as the best of Schumann's short pieces, or the emotional epitomes of Chopin's Preludes, but they are on a far higher level than the lilliputian swarms which were published in Germany from the pen of a Reinecke, a Scharwenka, or a Theodore Kirchner about the eighties of last century. Fibich jots down in music what others may do in a written diary, and the result is a kind of musical daybook in which we may read with considerable entertainment. Here are marches, dances, such as polkas, furiants, valses; reminiscences of some modal tune; experiments in rhythm and harmony; folk-melodies real or evolved from a long familiarity; obvious parodies; quotations from other composers, as a painter might preserve the memory of another artist's masterpiece in his own sketch-book. A heterogeneous collection, delightful and amusing as a bric-à-brac shop, in which we may at any moment light upon a small gem.

[1] He commonly wrote his Christian name 'Zdenko'.
[2] The 'Fibich' article in *Die Musik in Geschichte und Gegenwart* does not even mention them, except 'das vielgespielte *Poem*'.
[3] *The Music of Czechoslovakia*, London, 1942, p. 106.

This is a very fair assessment. The pieces differ very considerably in value, in length (from eight bars to nine pages), and in difficulty from the very easy to the quite difficult. Broadly speaking, those which are most nearly suitable for public performance are the weakest. And 'diary' is absolutely right, though Mrs Newmarch forgets to tell us that almost every piece is precisely—but, as we shall see, sometimes incorrectly—dated. Although she goes on to mention that 'some of the short pieces are the seeds from which larger works have germinated', she has failed to notice the very numerous thematic inter-relationships and cross-references of the pieces themselves.

The *Nálady, Dojmy a Upomínky* were published by Fr. A. Urbánek of Prague in four series, each with a separate opus-number: Opps. 41, 44 and 47 in 1896–7, Op. 57 posthumously. (Fibich died in 1900.) Although each opus has its 'internal' numbering, the whole collection is also numbered from beginning to end—and this is the most convenient way of referring to the pieces to avoid confusion. Three of the four series (*řady*) consist of several 'books' (*sešity*). Thus Op. 41 is made up of one book of 'moods' (nos. 1–44), two of 'impressions' (45–85 and 86–125) and one of 'memories' (126–71), Op. 47 of four books of 'moods' (205–30, 231–48, 249–59, 260–71), four of 'impressions' (272–84, 285–302, 303–13, 314–30), and two of 'memories' (331–9 and 340–52). The posthumous Op. 57 contains three books, unclassified (333–9, 360–9, 370–6). Op. 44 is entitled *Novella* and consists of preface (172), introduction (173), four chapters (174–81, 182–7, 188–94, 195–203), and epilogue (204). We are left to guess what the 'novel' is about.

The few hints scattered here and there also provoke guesses. In the very first book we find no. 40 marked 'Studie k opeře *Hedy*' (i.e. the opera based on the Haidée episode of Byron's *Don Juan*) and no. 44, 'Studie k opeře *Bouře*' (i.e. on Shakespeare's *Tempest*), and we are satisfied. But why does no. 15, another 'study for *Hedy*' (its first bar identical with that of no. 8) suddenly break into a *ff* quotation from Mendelssohn's wedding march? And why the expressly marked quotation from a *Song without Words* (Op. 62, no. 1) in no. 331? The pianist browsing through these pieces—which is the right approach to them—often finds himself asking 'Why . . .?' Yet the answers—and it is precisely the answers that make the *Nálady, Dojmy a Upomínky* not merely interesting but fascinating, indeed unique—have been available ever since Zdeněk Nejedlý published his *Zdeňka Fibicha Milostný Deník* in 1948. The book seems to have attracted little attention—Fibich's reputation was then at its nadir in his native land and, in any case, Czechs and Slovaks had other preoccupations in 1948—though naturally the more recent Fibich literature in Czech[1] takes full account of it.

[1] For instance, Jaroslav Jiránek's *Zdeněk Fibich*, Prague, 1963.

But before we can use the key Nejedlý has put in our hands, we need to know a few details of Fibich's biography. He was married twice: first in February 1873 to a girl, Ružena Hanušová, who died in October of the following year, leaving him with a nine-month-old daughter. Unfortunately, on her death-bed, she begged her older sister Betty to take her place as wife and mother—which after a year she did. Betty Hanušová was a year older than Fibich himself, already a well-known dramatic contralto—indeed better known in Prague than he was at that time—who during the next few years was to sing the leading contralto roles in, among other things, most of Smetana's operas as they appeared. As she sang Radmila in *Libuše*, her voice (she proudly remembered) was the first to be heard in the National Theatre when it was opened in 1881. Fibich wrote the parts of the White Lady in his *Blaník* and Isabella in his *Bride of Messina* for her. But, however happy as an artistic and domestic companionship, the marriage was foredoomed as a marriage and during the 1890s it was subjected to an intolerable strain which led to a final break in 1897. The cause of the strain was a girl more than seventeen years Fibich's junior, Anežka Schulzová, daughter of Professor Ferdinand Schulz, a then well-known historian and critic of Czech literature. In 1885 or 1886 Anežka, then 17 or 18, had for a short time had piano lessons from Fibich but she seems to have made no impression on him, musical or otherwise. When she came back in the spring of 1892, asking for lessons in composition, it was a different matter. She was now a beautiful, passionate blue-stocking, very much the 'emancipated woman' of the day. Her main interest was literature; she was intensely attracted by contemporary French writers, above all Anatole France, later by Russian literature; and she practised as a dramatic critic. She was to provide Fibich with the libretti of his last three operas, *Hedy*, *Šárka* and *The Fall of Arkun*. But she also acquired enough musical knowledge to make the published four-hand arrangement of Fibich's Quintet and, after his death, to publish pseudonymously the monograph which was for a long time the only available book on his music: *Zdenko Fibich: eine musikalische Silhouette* by 'Carl Ludwig Richter'.[1]

The real fascination of the *Nálady, Dojmy a Upomínky* lies in the fact that they are a record, written in the first place for Anežka only and comprehensible to no one but her, of Fibich's love for her. They indeed constitute a 'love-diary' (*milostný deník*) as Nejedlý calls it, though the dates are not necessarily those of composition—they often refer to the event recorded or commemorated in the piece. Moreover the printed dates sometimes differ from those in the autographs; there are various corrections by Fibich himself or by Anežka. The autographs are more important still in that they are inscribed with the titles or, often, mere hints (initials)

[1] Prague, 1900.

which enabled Nejedlý to begin his decipherment. In addition he found partial lists made on separate pieces of paper, by Anežka or Fibich himself.

Instead of trying to sort the pieces into chronological order of events or composition, it will probably be more helpful to browse through them more or less in the order Fibich printed them. We begin with a disappointment; there are hardly any clues to the first eighteen numbers. The beautiful *adagio* no. 1 is marked only 'thema symfonie'; in no. 3 we may notice a brief reference to no. 27; we can identify no. 15 as Haidée's death-song but can only guess that the Mendelssohn quotation is a burst of savage irony. No. 19, fiery and virile, is a self-portrait. It is only with no. 20 that we can begin to read an autobiographical meaning. It is another 'study for *Hedy*', the beginning of the introduction to the last Act, with the theme of Lambro's inexorable cruelty; but it originated, as did most of the pieces dated 16–29 September, 1894, in Fibich's jealousy of the Danish critic Georg Brandes, who was visiting Prague and to whom Anežka was drawn by common literary interests. No. 25, which also reappears in the last Act of *Hedy*, reflects on 'how I caused Anežka pain' and no. 26 is a prayer for forgiveness. Nos. 22 and 23 also reflect jealousy, as does no. 54 ('Meeting in the street'); but no. 24 was marked 'Dreams, when jealousy was forgotten' and the love-theme from *Hedy* (which had already appeared in *The Tempest* and in no. 123, written nearly a year before) appears, *dolce*, in a slightly altered form. No. 6, bearing the same date—a much more striking little piece which might almost be by Janáček—marks the end of this fit of jealousy. The remainder of this first set of 'moods' consist mostly of character-studies and portraits of Anežka: in playful mood (27), the spoiled darling (28), 'Good night!' (29), 'How Anežka sleeps' (30), 'How Anežka struggles in the night' (31), 'Good morning!' (32) which ends with the theme of 'question-and-answer', first set down (chronologically) in no. 130, with the real 'answer' concealed in an unstressed inner part:

Ex. 1

and a number of times elsewhere, 'How Anežka works' (33), 'Our harmony' (36), and a series of portraits (37–44) of Anežka in homely clothes, in a white dress, in black, in green, in pale blue, in a blue evening-dress, in pale brown, and in purple. No. 40 ('green') was to go into the Act III ballet of *Hedy* as an entry of hunters, and no. 44 ('purple') was translated into Ferdinand's passionate arioso at the beginning of Act II of *The Tempest*. Its climactic phrase, 'My queen, there is your home!'

Ex. 2

is based on a motive already associated with Anežka in no. 45 (January 27, 1893), the first of the 'impressions' (cf. Ex. 3).

These two books of 'impressions' are devoted almost entirely to the physical description of Anežka, detail by detail. They begin with an exquisitely tender dedication (45):

Ex. 3
Lento

marked 'Da capo senza Fine!!!' and ending with another form of the 'answer' motive (cf. no. 32). Even the occasion is noted: 'po Debože', i.e. after the first performance of J. B. Foerster's opera *Debora*. This is followed by poems on her head (46), her forehead (47), her brain (the fugal no. 48), her nerves (49, which ends with the 'queen' motive and the assurance of love), her temples (50) and her hair (51, which also served for Miranda's hair in *The Tempest*). In no. 52 she smoothes her hair, so her hand (no. 74) naturally appears as well. No. 53, her mouth, is one of the most beautiful of all the pieces:

Ex. 4
Lento

It is not only referred to a number of times in other pieces but provides the central portion of Fibich's Third Symphony, in E minor (where it is preceded by no. 208, 'When I was, with every right, reprimanded', written more than two years later); yet one prefers it in its original form, a perfect 32-bar miniature, ending with the 'answer'. So Fibich continues with her tongue (54), her teeth (55, a brilliant and amusing jest—and Anežka clearly bites just before the end), her eyes (56, which 'must be played twice' and which reappears in Act II of *The Tempest* when Ferdinand speaks of 'the sweet magic' of Miranda's eyes), her lashes (57), her eyebrows (outlined in two melodic curves of four bars each, 58), her nose (59), her face 'with a blissful expression' (60), her dimples (61), the down on her cheeks (62), her chin (63) and her ears (64). The autograph of no. 65 is enigmatically marked 'L.+S.U.' Fibich then continues with her neck (66), two marks on her neck (67 and 68), her shoulders (69), 'P.p.' (i.e. 'Pod paží', 'under the arms', 70), her arm (71), her elbow (72), her knuckles (73), her hand (74), her palm (75, which again 'must be played twice'), her fingers (76) and her nails (77)—the last two prefaced by references to her hand. As for the rest of the book (79–85), Nejedlý becomes a little mysterious, describing them as a 'glorification of the female breast'; no. 80 is certainly marked 'N' (for 'ňadra') and the music is recalled when Don Juan mentions Haidée's breast in the Second Act of *Hedy*.

The next book of impressions continues with a description of Anežka's physical charms, though the very first piece was apparently intended to suggest her heart. According to Nejedlý, nos. 87–92 'depict the *body* itself' over which he modestly leaves a veil—though he does tell us that no. 87 is a playful description of Anežka's hips 'evidently as she walks'. No. 91 turns up in *The Tempest*, where it is associated with Miranda's neck. Indeed a number of pieces from this book are connected with *The Tempest*: no. 94, marked 'Č', is based mostly on the Ariel theme but with a middle section on 'Miranda's white fingers' during a game of chess. No. 95 is a conflation of two pieces, originally separate—one in D major marked 'M.p.', the other in D minor, 'M.z.'—and full of references to other numbers: 104, 108, 111, 117 and 344. No. 98 is connected with Miranda, 99 and 100 with Ferdinand (no. 100 is marked 'F crescendo'), 102 and 106 with Ariel, 104 with Prospero's magic power—though Nejedlý says this is the first of a series of pieces, 104–16, inspired by Anežka's legs. It is quoted again and again, for instance in 105 (which, like 95, is a whole network of quotations telling a tale that only the lovers can have understood) and 109. No. 108 appears in *The Tempest* in connection with the words 'further and further, ever further, o thought; one kiss on it . . .', applied here to Miranda's neck but obviously in the composer's mind to her leg.[1] No. 107 is definitely Anežka's knees, 110 her ankles, 111 (quoted by Don Juan when he thinks of Haidée's 'gentle little foot') her feet—and is therefore appropriately prefixed to 112 (her toes) and 113 (her toe nails). In no. 114 Fibich mocks her scuffling walk and 'the monotonous movement of her heels'. With 117 and 119 we are back in the world of *The*

---

[1] The facsimile in *Zdenko Fibich: eine musikalische Silhouette*, facing p. 36, shows that it was prefixed with an 'L', which could stand for 'lýtko' (calf) and was followed (as usual when pairs are concerned) with the direction 'Must be played twice'.

Tempest, with Caliban, who also throws his shadow over no. 120 (a conflation like no. 95), where the second half contains a disguised reference to Miranda. The book ends with a series of enigmas: 'Z.' (121), 'Š!!!' (122), 'Z.' (but Anežka's copy has 'B.') (123), 'J.b.' (124), and 'A.Z.' (125). But they are not entirely insoluble. 'Z.' must be 'Zdeněk'; 123 and 124 are based almost entirely on the love-theme from *Hedy*, already mentioned for its appearance in no. 24, though one can only guess at the meaning of the *misterioso* interruptions in 124; and the little piece bearing the initials of both their Christian names, which plays an important part in the D major Piano Quintet and E flat Symphony, is unmistakably a solemn hymn to their love.

The distinction between 'moods', 'impressions' and 'memories' was very clear to Fibich; the book of 'memories' which completes the first series of pieces is quite different in subject-matter from the others. It records memories of the first two or three years of his association with Anežka, and the descriptive—even narrative—element becomes more noticeable. The very first 'memory', no. 126, goes back to March 1892 and Anežka's composition lessons; this is 'how Anežka learned' and the melody and bass of the opening are actually hers. The next three pieces, with their significant dates, recall 'how we talked together', 'how we went along the street together for the first time', and 'how we sat on Žofín', the island in the Vltava at Prague, now renamed Slovanský Ostrov, on which Anežka lived with her parents. No. 130 is marked simply '1/7 92!!'; it was the day they confessed their love for each other and the piece ends with the first version of the question-and-answer (Ex. 1). (This date, like Anežka's name-day, January 21, and birthday, March 24, was commemorated each year by a new composition.) Another version of the question-and-answer ends no. 131, 'First meeting after the first holidays', i.e. after the first parting. A third version ends no. 132, entitled 'Love song', afterwards embodied in the finale of the Second Symphony, in E flat.

No. 133 is cautiously entitled 'První J.', 'First . . .'; 'J.' could stand for 'jednota' (union), though Nejedlý does not suggest this. It begins quietly and in bars 8–9 is heard the rhythmic-harmonic idea often associated with Miranda or Anežka-as-Miranda combined with Ferdinand's chief theme. Then it rises to a triumphant climax—'Not triumphant in the customary erotic sense', Nejedlý hastens to comment—crowned by repeated *ff* chords in the rhythm which came to signify 'our goal', i.e. working together.

Ex. 5

(It recurs frequently and no. 169, referring to their collaboration on *Hedy*, is actually so headed.) On New Year's Day 1893 Fibich paid his first visit to Anežka's parents; no. 134 suggests ceremonial bows and general stiffness—interspersed with secret *ppp* laughter. No. 135 is a straightforward polka. Anežka marked no. 136 'Jealousy without cause' and 137 commemorates 'how we lunched alone together'. As for the quotations from *Tannhäuser*, *Dalibor* and *Walküre* in no. 138, which must have puzzled every browser in these pages, the explanation is very simple: Fibich was now (April 1894)[1] quite at home in the Schulz household and he had been playing excerpts from these operas to her father. No. 139, the by no means deservedly famous *Poème*, was originally entitled 'Evenings on Žofín' and reflects the composer's happiness in this domestic circle. Fibich himself made it the central section of an orchestral idyll, *V podvečer* (In the evening), where it is lusciously scored, worked up to an overdone climax, surrounded with bird-calls, and framed in music associated mainly with Anežka's mother but also introducing the motives of her father (*a*) and her young sister Dagmar ('Daška') (*b*):

Just before the end of the orchestral piece there is a hardly noticeable reference to the E flat Symphony, which had been given its first performance not long before.

Nos. 140 and 141, which are to be played without a break, record 'danger to our love' and 'rescue'. (141 became part of the music of Prospero's farewell.) They are followed by a sequence of thirteen numbers, 142–54, forming a continuous narrative. On 1 July, 1893 (no. 142, anniversary of the first confession of love: cf. no. 130, which also preceded a parting), the Schulzes went on holiday to Ústí nad Orlicí and Fibich was unable to set off to visit them there until 20 August. No. 143 depicts his 'impatience on the journey to Ústí, no. 144 'the night journey to Česká Třebová'. Nos. 145–52 relate the happenings on the 21st: Fibich's reunion with Anežka (145), her family coming to greet him, with Daška *scherzando* and a recollection of the evenings at home (146), a visit to a hermit who lived near Ústí (birds sing—their music was used again when Vlasta hears them sing in the First Act of *Šárka*—and the quotations from no. 53 tell us that the lovers kissed) (147). In no. 148 they go on into the murmuring forest and Anežka marked no. 149 'The Way by Řetová'. The latter is a curious piece; as they walked among the quiet woods, the pair seem to have talked of Anežka's composition-lessons (no. 126), *The Tempest*, which Fibich had now finished, and Anežka's father—and they

---

[1] Indeed the date should probably be 1893; most of the pieces here date from 1893 and at least one (140) is known to be wrongly dated 1894.

certainly kissed. Then follow mood-impressions: 'On the little green place' (150), 'Evening' (151), and 'Parting' (152). On the next day Fibich left Ústí with a heavy heart (153) though at the end of the piece his thoughts dwell on the immutability of their love (cf. no. 125). And on 13 September (154) came the joyous reunion, with triumphant fragments from the Second Symphony near the end.

The other 'memories' of this book are disconnected. There are visits to the theatre: to the first performance of *Meistersinger* at the National Theatre (as for once the published version tells us) (155), to *Mr. Brouček's Excursion from the Moon to the Exhibition* (a piece—probably a skit—by Ferdinand Šamberk,[1] for which Karel Kovařovic wrote incidental music) (166), a play by Sudermann (168). No. 156 tells 'how the Quintet was practised'; a transformed theme from the first movement opens it, a snatch of the finale appears at bar 21, the scherzo is quoted in the bass seven bars before the end. Anežka's birthday and name-day in 1894 are commemorated in nos. 157 and 171. Nos. 159–64 seem to be connected with a trip to Zell in the Salzkammergut which Anežka made in June 1894. 159 and 160 mourn her approaching departure or absence; 136, which was used for part of the reapers' dance in Act III of *Hedy*, is headed 'Journey to the Alps'; 162, the 'second anniversary' piece, was presumably sent to her; 163 marks her return to Prague on 22 July and 164 their meeting next day. As I have already mentioned, no. 169 is headed 'our goal', referring here to their work together on *Hedy*, and no. 170, three days later, records the opening of the opera—but solemnly, *pp lento*, instead of *f allegro* as in the opera. (It is, however, antedated by other 'studies' for the opera.) 158 is entitled 'How the Vltava separates us'—no tragic situation, since Anežka lived on Žofín and Fibich at no. 1, Ostrovní ulice, just behind the National Theatre and conveniently near a bridge leading across a very narrow arm of the river to the island. 165, which records 'a little steamer trip', was used for the entry of the fishers in the Act III ballet in *Hedy*. And no. 167 tells 'how Ivan [Anežka's elder brother] joined the army'.

Op. 41, composed for the most part during 1893–4 and relating to the emotions and events of those years, with a few earlier recollections, contains the best of the *Nálady, Dojmy a Upomínky*, the freshest, the most individual and the most highly polished miniatures. But the second series, Op. 44, the *Novella*, while it has nothing as beautiful as the best pieces in the first, is full of interest. Essentially it is a carrying-out on a more extended scale of what Fibich had already done in nos. 142–54. In 1895 the Schulzes spent their summer holiday at Karlsbad (renamed Karlovy Vary in 1918) and Fibich was allowed to spend with them not one day as at Ústí but four. The four 'chapters' of the 'novel' narrate the events of those

---

[1] Svatopluk Čech's hero was popular in his own country before Janáček gave him world fame. *Mr. Brouček at the Exhibition* is the last of the Brouček stories.

four days. But they are preceded by both a preface and an introduction. The preface (172, dated 31 July) marks the day when both Fibich and Anežka left Prague, she to go to Karlsbad with her father, he for Hallstatt in the Salzkammergut where he stayed from 1 August to 20 August and where his mood is reflected in the Introduction (173).

Chapter I (22 August): no. 174 is 'the journey to Anežka'—the engine whistles, the station bell rings, the train puffs slowly out of the station and gradually gathers speed. Fibich is lost in happy thoughts and at the end the love-theme from *Hedy* (cf. no. 124) sings out triumphantly in the left hand. With no. 175 he is at Karlsbad; this is 'the coach-ride'. He meets Anežka (177) but she is not alone; real joy comes with 'the first walk' together. 178 is quiet 'Afternoon', 179 the early-evening stroll in the Holzplatz, 180 the walk back, during which they evidently talked about *Hedy*, and 181 'Evening in the park'.

Chapter II (23 August): no. 182 is 'the first morning' with a variety of moods—and a warm embrace when Ex. 4 is heard—and 183 is said to be a portrait of Anežka, evidently in a very lively mood. In 184 we have one of Fibich's essays in naïve programme-music: 'At the spring, breakfast at Pupp's[1]—a well-known café—and stroll'. When they get to the spring, there is a quotation from *Hedy*, 'Man must drink,' but it appears here *lento*, in the minor, as there is only water; and Professor Schulz's theme indicates that the lovers are not alone. 185 and 186 are concerned with the afternoon, the first quiet, the second, *molto agitato*, to which Fibich supplied an adjective which is unreadable since Anežka wrote over it 'bouřlivé' (stormy, passionate); 187 is 'evening in front of the house'.

Chapter III (24 August) begins with 188, in which Fibich describes himself waiting for a letter by the first post, first patiently, then impatiently (*allegro con fuoco*), with a reminiscence of the music to which Ferdinand had awaited Miranda; then the post-horn is heard in the distance, *ppp*, and the letter evidently brings the message hoped for. At the beginning of 189 a clock strikes eight, and then they all walk to the pump-room again; a band plays a waltz, an opera-selection (a parody of Meyerbeer), and another waltz. Then comes an afternoon sequence on the lines of nos. 147–150. In 190 the lovers walk to St Leonard's Chapel in the woods; Ariel's theme suggests that it is he who has brought them there; they kiss (Ex. 4) and test the famous echo. In 191 they return to the Jägerhaus (the Myslivna café) where Professor Schulz is waiting for them, apparently in rather a bad temper; but Ex. 4 suggests that Anežka pacifies him with a kiss and they evidently tell him about their visit to the chapel. They go back to the town and in 192 Fibich, in his room, awaits a visit from his mistress; twice he imagines he hears her knock. The real knock comes *marcato*; we hear the familiar love-theme from *Hedy*—and the rest of the

[1] Pupp's Hotel is now the Grand Hotel Moskva.

piece is as explicit as the introduction to *Rosenkavalier*. In 193 Anežka, back at her hotel, is getting ready for the evening walk; near the end her father comes, *serioso*, to tell her to hurry up. 194 is again 'evening in front of the house'.

Chapter IV (25 August): the last day is more sober; even the weather has turned bad. 195 is 'morning', 196 'breakfast at the spring' (with the ceaseless patter of rain; instead of the usual walk, they then take a droshky (197) and we hear the clop of hooves against the incessant semiquaver rain. In 198 Fibich visits the Schulzes; the conversation appears to be rather sticky. The subdued mood predominates in 199 (lunch together), 200 (afternoon), 201 (supper together, with an unsuccessful attempt— *scherzando*—to cheer themselves up), and 202 (the walk home). 203 tells of the parting; Professor Schulz is taking his daughter back to Prague, while Fibich has to stay behind in Karlsbad for a day or two. A horse clops realistically again as they drive to the station; the moment of parting comes suddenly; Anežka twice calls goodbye ('Na shledanou!'), *quasi recitativo*; the train disappears into the night and Fibich drives back in the cab, recalling at the very end the last tragic bars of *Hedy*.

The epilogue (204) celebrates the composer's joyful return to Prague on the 27th. Part of it is identical with 174, for he is again hurrying toward Anežka; he recalls no. 198 (one can hardly guess why) and the *Novella* ends *adagio* with the love-theme from *Hedy* and the theme of the 'common goal'.

Many of the 'moods' of Op. 47 relate to dates earlier in 1895. They record, for instance, 'Anežka in the rain on a warm, dark evening' in June (206), 'great longing for Anežka' (207), the receipt of 'a very beautiful letter' from her (210), thanks 'for a morning letter' (214), 'memory of a very sweet day' (216). One feels that the musical diary-keeping was becoming a habit. There is less spontaneous emotion; the pieces lack focus and sense of occasion. Only here and there, as when 'Anežka smokes' in the summer of 1896 (230), does some of the original freshness reappear. No. 219 ('How Zdeněk is *mine*', wrote Anežka—September 16, 1895) was to be used later for Přemysl's song, 'Větve dvě', in the First Act of *Šárka*. In the second and third books of Op. 47 Fibich is so gravelled for ideas that he once again paints Anežka in various dresses, or the articles of her dress: mantilla (239), cloak (240), light coat (241), shawl (242) and so on. Most of the pieces even lack point, though no. 246 (her little shoes) effectively transforms—by diminution—the theme of her feet (no. 111). In the fourth book (260–71) he is even reduced to drawing generalised female portraits, perhaps mocking Anežka, perhaps unconnected with her: lady, woman, sweetheart, wench, mistress, 'little animal', bride, odalisque, 'S . . . ě' which, to judge from the realistic grunting, must be 'svině' (sow). We have no clues at all to the 'impressions' 272–302, except that no. 295 later became Ctirad's impassioned 'Moje, moje jsi' (You are mine and no one shall tear you from me) in Act II of *Šárka*. Nos. 303–13, however, return to the theme of Anežka's toes. Most of the other 'impressions' of Op. 47 remain unsolved enigmas to which the only clues are musical—e.g. no. 314 ends with Ferdinand's 'My queen' (Ex. 2) and no. 318 must have something to do with Anežka's feet—or incomprehensible initials: 'l.B.', 'l.u.', 'J. na z.', and the like. However, the polka no. 319 is 'Mademoiselle Pimpernelle'.

Some of the 'memories' of Op. 47 go back to earlier days. Thus 331 recalls Anežka as a piano student in the 1880s (hence the Mendelssohn quotation) and 332 an incident in September 1891 when Anežka was made much of by the French delegates to the Jubilee Exhibition in Prague. (Her 'girl' theme, taken over from the preceding piece, is broken into by a snatch of the 'Marseillaise' and the 'Iago' theme from Fibich's symphonic poem *Othello*[1]. Fibich always disliked the French and he was already at this time a little jealous of men around Anežka.) No. 333 commemorates the first kissing of her hand (hence the quotation of no. 111), two months later; this is an instance of the printed date, 28 November, differing from that in the manuscript, 9 November. No. 334 is a reminiscence of the first performance of Jaroslav Vrchlický's comedy *Pietro Aretino*, for which Fibich had composed incidental music, on 30 April (not 3 as in the published version), 1892. And no. 335 tells of a more significant theatre visit a month or so later, when Fibich's 'melodrama' *Námluvy Pelopovy* (Pelops's wooing), the first part of his *Hippodamia* trilogy, was performed on 3 June at an international musical and theatrical exhibition in Vienna; naturally there are quotations from the work—notably the *adagio* music of the Delphic oracle—and the *Blue Danube* (bars 10 ff.) sets the scene, while the motive of Anežka's feet (no. 111) suggests a walk to the theatre before the performance. She had been sent to the exhibition as a dramatic critic and this visit to Vienna brought them closer together; a month later (cf. no. 130) they confessed their love to each other. However diverting such pieces may be when one can decode them, their musical value, like that of the similar things in the *Novella*, is very slight. Perhaps the most naïve of all these essays in cryptic programme-music is no. 340, which describes a visit to the Ethnographic Exhibition in Prague in June 1895. It is held together only by recurrence of the opening music, which presumably suggests happy laughter; a quotation from the *adagio* of the Second Symphony indicates Anežka's presence and the drinking song from *Hedy* appears soon after (*meno mosso*), this time in its original major, not in the minor as at Karlsbad. Then we get bagpipe music, a suggestion of ecclesiastical art, a polka—and, *adagio lamentoso*, a minor version of a

---

[1] Nejedlý, op. cit., p. 56, calls it 'the motive of jealousy'; Fibich had in mind Iago's 'O beware, my lord, of jealousy'.

popular song, 'Ó Velvary', which in its original form goes:

Ex. 7

Ó Vel-va-ry, ó Vel-va-ry! kde jsou me to - la - ry?

('Where are my dollars? I've eaten, I've drunk, I've feasted, I've loved pretty girls . . .'). We deduce that Fibich's money has run out. More ingenious hotch-potches are the 'First Greeting for the Fourth Year' (no. 341; 1 July, 1895), which packs into a short piece quotations from the Second Symphony, the love theme from *V podvečer* (no. 139), the second movement of the Piano Quintet, Miranda's avowal of her love, love-themes from *Hedy*, 'our goal' and 'question and answer'; and no. 348 (for Anežka's name-day, 1896) which is entirely based on themes from *Šárka*.

The posthumous gathering in Op. 57 is even more disappointing. The birthday pieces for Anežka in 1897 and 1898 (358 and 359), the former a set of fourteen variations on an eight-bar theme, with coda, are both oddly impersonal. Some of the pieces are not even dated. Familiar motives, such as 'our goal', appear perfunctorily. According to Nejedlý, some of the pieces record another visit to the Salzkammergut, this time to the Attersee, in the summer of 1896; 368 paints a storm on the lake, 369 peace after the storm, 371 a search for mushrooms in the woods, 375 an old, moss-grown mill beside the lake. Nos. 360–3 were all written in April 1898 when, according to Anežka, Fibich was contemplating an opera on a contemporary, realistic subject—possibly Ibsen's *Lady from the Sea*—and these are apparently attempts to catch a light, 'conversational' style. The last dated number is 364 (5 February, 1899), a wistful little piece marked by extra-ordinary juxtaposition of very ordinary chords:

Ex. 8
Moderato

p

1965

VI—REALISM IN JANÁČEK'S OPERAS

A specious claim might be made for Janáček that he came nearer and with more sustained success to the realisation of Mussorgsky's ideals—approximation of opera to real life and integration of ordinary speech with music—than Mussorgsky did himself. This would by no means be the same as claiming that he was a 'greater' composer than Mussorgsky (as if such things were measurable), that the ideals are susceptible of full realisation, or even that the ideals are generally valid. An ideal is no more than a guiding-star for a creative artist; it may be quite wrong for the next man, whose gifts and inclinations point him in a different direction. Janáček's case is made all the more fascinating by inclinations—we shall have to enquire later whether they were really 'gifts'—which sometimes led him to turn his back on his guiding-star. The similarity of his ideals to Mussorgsky's, despite the deep differences between their musical styles, inevitably tempts one to compare them and to consider the possibility of some direct influence. Leoš Firkušný recorded a typical utterance to an interviewer:

> *The reality behind phenomena* (*bytnost jevů*). That's the justification of opera . . . I show things *through truth*. Truth to the extreme . . . Truth doesn't exclude beauty; on the contrary, truth and beauty, the more of one, the more of the other. The main thing is life.[1]

This has the very ring of Mussorgsky; compare it, for instance, with the often quoted passage in a letter to Stasov (August 7, 1875):

> *Life*, wherever it shows itself; *truth*, no matter how bitter; bold sincere speech with people *à bout portant*, that's what I'm after . . .

Or compare Janáček's celebrated 'speech-melodies' with Mussorgsky's much earlier aspiration (expressed to Lyudmila Shestakova, 30 July, 1868):

> I'll tell you what I'd like to do: to make my characters speak on the stage as living people really speak, but also so that the character and power of intonation of the actors, supported by the orchestra which constitutes the musical groundwork of their speech, directly effect their purpose, i.e. my music must be an artistic reproduction of human speech in all its finest shades, i.e. *the sounds of human speech*, as outward manifestations of thought and feeling, must, without exaggeration and forcing, become *music* that is truthful, precise, *but* artistic, high-artistic.

---

[1] *Odkaz Leoše Janáčka české opeře*, Brno, 1939, p. 13.

That's the ideal I'm striving toward ('Savishna', 'The Orphan', 'Eremushka', 'Child and Nurse').

Janáček's preference for prose texts adapted directly from the literary originals seems to reflect Mussorgsky's attempt to set Gogol's prose-comedy *Marriage* just as it stood and the passages of prose-setting in his other works, such as the inn-scene in *Boris*. Janáček studied Russian at two periods in his life, 1872–5 and 1883–4, and, according to Racek, 'mastered it later almost like his mother-tongue'[1]; he visited Russia twice, in 1896 and 1902, paying due attention to Russian folklore and Russian 'speech-melody'; his library contained numerous Russian books; one of his earliest compositions, the orchestral melodrama *Smrt* (Death) (1876), was a setting of Lermontov, and in 1889 he planned a *Slavonic Symphony* on Russian themes; two of his finest operas were inspired by Ostrovsky and Dostoevsky, and two of his best instrumental works by Tolstoy and Gogol. It seems impossible that he should not have been interested in and affected by Russian music in general and the work of Mussorgsky in particular. Yet there is a great deal of evidence for the seemingly impossible. One Russian composer did make a deep impression on him in his early days—Rubinstein! The impression, not merely of his pianistic mastery, was deepened when he heard him play in Leipzig in November 1879. But the library that contained so many Russian books included only a few Russian scores: Rubinstein's G minor Piano Quintet, a piano score of *Nutcracker*, the suite from *L'Histoire du soldat*, and the more or less complete piano works of Mussorgsky.[2] At one time Janáček also possessed a vocal score of *Boris* (naturally in the Rimsky-Korsakov version), but, alas, this score—which he apparently acquired about 1909—is said to have had only adverse criticisms scribbled in the margins,[3] and it has now disappeared. Writing to Artuš Rektorys, he asserted that 'Mussorgsky went from Wagnerian motives to speech-motives, but *didn't recognise their beauties*. If he had, he would have gone on with them.' And he told Loewenbach that 'Mussorgsky didn't interest him and he hadn't followed him'. Composers—for instance, Wagner—have been known to denigrate colleagues and predecessors by whom they have been unquestionably influenced, but Janáček seems to have been shatteringly truthful in most things and the remarks in the score of *Boris* can have been intended for no one but himself. The case against Mussorgskian influences does appear fairly strong.

There is not even any justification for picking on Mussorgsky as the particular precursor in setting prose libretti. Janáček may, of course, have

[1] Jan Racek, *Leoš Janáček*, Leipzig, 1962, p. 77.
[2] I am indebted to Dr Theodora Straková for this information.
[3] Josef Loewenbach, 'Dramatický princip Leoše Janáčka a M.P. Musorgského' in the volume *Leoš Janáček a soudobá hudba* (Prague, 1963), p. 211.

heard of Mussorgsky's essays even though he did not know them at first hand. But we have to remember that composition of prose, in the interest of 'truth', was a not unpopular exercise during the last three decades of the nineteenth century. Everyone knows about Mussorgsky; few people know that in February 1873, when the definitive version of *Boris* was finished though not yet performed, Gounod—of all people—embarked on 'une tentative d'innovation dans le domaine de la musique dramatique', nothing less than a setting of Molière's *George Dandin*. He completed only a few numbers, including settings of Act II, scenes 7 and 9. But he wrote a preface, printed two years later with his so-called *Autobiographie* (London, 1875), in which he explains that in setting verse to music,

'la vérité de l'expression musicale disparaît sous l'entraînement banal et irréfléchi de la formule et de la routine'. [In prose, on the contrary:] 'Quelle mine féconde, inépuisable, de variété dans l'intonation chantée ou déclamée, dans la durée et dans l'intensité de l'accent, dans la proportion et le développement de la période musicale, développement qui, dès lors, ne repose plus sur le continuel rabâchage des redites, mais sur la progression logique et sur le crescendo de l'idée-mère qui domine et conduit le morceau!'

The music itself has never been published, so far as I know, but a letter to Mrs Weldon written at the time suggests that he was not really on the right track: 'C'est quelquefois difficile de donner à la prose une construction musicale qui ait de la symétrie et de la régularité rhythmique.' All the same, this was an attempt to set realistic, prosaic prose like Gogol's in *The Marriage* or Pushkin's in *Boris*, not heightened, poetic prose like that of *Salome* and *Pelléas*. Even Zola's prose libretti for Bruneau's *Messidor* (1897) and *L'Ouragan* (1901) are not exactly naturalistic, while the one that Charpentier concocted, with or without the help of friends, for *Louise* (1900) staggers all over the road between the naturalistic and the high-falutin'.

Prose libretti were undeniably fashionable, then, at the period when Janáček was composing *Její pastorkyňa* (*Jenůfa*) to a 'book' which he himself carved out of Gabriela Preissová's prose 'drama of Moravian village life'. It is real prose but Janáček not only cut but modified it, and reduced its naturalism by verbal repetitions.[1] A short article in the Brno programme of the first performance of *Pastorkyňa* (1904)—anonymous but probably by the composer himself—mentions Bruneau but claims that Janáček had hit on the idea of setting prose independently: 'the

[1] Compare the opening of Act I, scene 5, as it stands, with the facsimile of the corresponding printed page of the play, with Janáček's cuts in the text and musical sketches, reproduced as pl. 21 in Jaroslav Vogel, *Leoš Janáček*, Prague, 1963 (English edition, London, 1962).

score of *Její Pastorkyňa* already existed in fair copy in 1897'. But as Vogel points out, if this is true, it can be true only of Act I since the Second Act was not composed till the winter of 1901–2. There is no need to look in *Pastorkyňa* for the element of symbolism that stains the naturalism of the Zola-Bruneau and Charpentier operas and sets them apart from Puccini and Italian *verismo* in general; the *kostelnička* (sexton's wife) who commits murder for the sake of 'her stepdaughter' (*její pastor-kyňa*) is no more a symbol than Carmen is. Yet Janáček was undoubtedly attracted to the subject through his fascination by the theme of tragic womanhood—comparable with, but essentially different from, Puccini's. (It is genuinely compassionate; he never gloats sadistically.) And the element of symbolism was to enter in full force later; indeed it had already done so in his very first, entirely romantic opera *Šárka* (1888) where the heroine certainly is a symbol of oppressed womanhood, as Katya Kaban-ova was to be thirty years later.

While in these respects Janáček was very much a man of the period, in another he was perhaps unique. The peculiar importance of his prose-texts lies in their inspiration of a type of music that pervades and con-ditions so much of his musical fabric, and thus keeps them on a realistic plane whereas such equally true-to-life, and not so very much more melodramatic, dramas as *Cavalleria* and *Pagliacci* are tunefully removed from it. Anyone who knows anything at all about him knows something of his *nápěvky mluvy*, the musical intonations of everyday speech which he began to note down at about the time when he was composing the First Act of *Pastorkyňa*:

> At the time I was composing *Její pastorkyňa*, I was also concerning myself with the melody of the spoken word—not after the manner of my distinguished predecessors. I listened to the speech of passers-by; I read in their facial expression; my eyes followed every movement; I observed the speakers' surroundings, the company, the time, the light and the darkness, the cold and the warmth. I felt the reflection of all this in the notes of the speech-motive. How many variations of the speech-motive of one and and the same word became apparent! Now it shone and melted, now it became stern and inflexible. Yet I divined in the speech-motive something deeper still, something that was not manifest, not displayed openly; I felt that in the speech-motive lay the consequences of inner, secret happenings. I perceived in it sorrow and the light of joy, decision and doubt . . . In short, in the speech-motive I felt the enigmas of the soul.[1]

Verbally inspired instrumental themes, with or without intervening vocal forms, exist almost everywhere in music; they are particularly common

[1] 'Okolo Její pastorkyně', *Hudební revue*, IX, 1916, p. 245.

in nineteenth-century music from Beethoven to Schumann, Brahms and Dvořák; but usually they are essentially melodic themes inspired by metrical words, by verse. Jaroslav Vogel has shown how, as early as 1891 in *Počátek románu*, which has a verse libretto, Janáček derived the Count's motive:

Ex. 1

from his prosaic 'I've lost my monocle!'

Ex. 2

Mo-no-kl jsem ztra-til!

But the last scene of Act II of *Pastorkyňa* provides a classical example of Janáček's use of two speech-motives on an extended scale. Jenůfa consents at last to marry Laca, while the wretched stepmother is torn between joy in their happiness and guilt for the crime which has made their happiness possible. First comes a short passage of recitative through which sounds a tiny three-note motive on the clarinet, the very yearning of Laca's heart, and no more able to express his love than he is, until both it and he find release with his cry 'Jenůfka!' And then Jenůfa begins meekly

Ex. 3

Moderato

Dě-ku-ji ti, La - co, za vše-cko dob - ré co

'Thank you, Laca, for all the good things you thought of me at that time when I was out of your sight!' This little motive in voice or orchestra dominates the first part of the scene, nearly five pages of vocal score. Then for seven or eight bars the voices of the lovers join *dolce* in a caressing, almost Smetana-like duet while the stepmother pulls herself together with the conviction that 'all the same, I did well'. She blesses them

Ex. 4

Moderato

at' vas Pán-bůh... vzdy - vy-trh-ne...

and again a tiny motive provides the musical material for four pages of vocal score until her horror reaches a climax and the curtain falls quickly.

The most striking feature of the motives themselves, particularly Ex. 4, is their musical insignificance. They are both short-breathed and short in note-value. The shortness of breath is perhaps a personal characteristic of Janáček's; the long-arched melodic phrase is the exception rather than the rule with him and even then it is usually achieved by the building up of single short phrases, rather than by balancing, answering phrases. He normally works with little melodic tesserae laid side by side in a way that corresponds strikingly with his lapidary prose-style, scornful of normal transitions, and conveying a sense of tension by their very shortness of breath. The motives hammer or bore into the mind. But the shortness of note-values is conditioned by the very nature of the Czech language, with its poverty in vowels on which the voice can develop tone. A language in which it is possible for stressed syllables or monosyllabic nouns to have no defined vowel-sound—*Vl*tava, *Br*no, *srd*ce (heart), trh (market), prst (finger)—is hardly a language of song. Hence perhaps the relative neglect of the art-song by Czech composers, and hence no doubt the continued cultivation of the full-length melodrama beside opera in the hands of Fibich and J. B. Foerster. The intense musicality of the Czechs is fundamentally instrumental; Czech folk-melody is fundamentally instrumental. (I have heard very ordinary vocal bawling in a Czech inn miraculously transfigured when instrumental support was added—by a piano-accordionist and a much more than half-drunk trumpeter.) The beautiful tunes of Smetana's and Dvořák's operas are essentially independent melodies stretched over the words without undue regard for 'just note and accent'—neither Smetana nor Dvořák, nor (very surprisingly) Janáček for that matter, was very accurate in declamation —and rarely seem to be truly born from the words except in a general, metrical sense. A music inspired as directly as Janáček's by non-metrical Czech speech was bound to be not only short-breathed but inclined to shortness of note-values.

Nothing is more fascinating in Janáček's technique than the way in which he applies his totally non-instrumental motives—except in so far as the suggested harmonic element in Ex. 3 is instrumental—to construct long stretches of instrumental fabric. Admittedly Jenůfa's little motive has not only this harmonic property, which is never developed, but a faint expressive quality (the tenderness of the falling seventh) which dramatically justifies its protracted use in this scene. But it is not a *Leitmotiv*; it has a verbal origin but no verbal significance. (One can hardly argue that it is 'the theme of Jenůfa's gratitude', though Janáček asserted that the musically still less significant, chromatically descending four-note motive, when the stepmother is about to commit her crime—

'Vidíte ji, *Kostelničku!*', near the end of Act II, scene 5—was the theme of 'the stepmother as murderer'.) It is just a melodic fragment thrown up by the words, used again and again to other words, echoed in the orchestra, generating little instrumental suffixes. And the same thing happens even more remarkably with Ex. 4, which is even less significant both expressively and in musical content; after a few repetitions in the voice-part it becomes a purely instrumental motive and the basis of the otherwise conventional chromatic storm corresponding to the physical storm arising outside the house (and of course the emotional storm in the stepmother's breast). The brief storm is as near Janáček ever gets to 'rhetoric'. It is the general musical understatement, which rests so firmly on its basis of prose-inspired motives, filled with idiosyncratic vitality but secure against inflation, which makes Janáček's dramatic treatment seem so naturalistic, so far from *verismo*—despite the purely 'veristic' character of the *Pastorkyňa* subject.

It is also very far from Mussorgsky. The Russian would keep a (modified) one-bar speech-motive going throughout a short song, as in the famous 'Savishna', but generally his vocal line is continuously generated by the text, rises into more songlike passages, and is supported by a more independent orchestral fabric which may have its own themes and figures. I suppose that this is what Janáček meant when he spoke of Mussorgsky's failure to 'recognise the beauties' of speech-motives.

The technique evolved in *Pastorkyňa* served Janáček superbly in his later works, though his next operatic essay, *Osud* (Fate) (1904) was a failure. It is a failure that repays examination, however: a real-life subject, based on a real contemporary happening (like the Piano Sonata of 1905 and *The Diary of one who vanished*) and real people—in fact an odd mixture of autobiography and autobiography-at-second-hand. A few years before, a young Czech conductor and composer, L. V. Čelanský, had avenged himself on a faithless sweetheart (like Berlioz on Henrietta Smithson) by putting her into his *Kamilla*, an interesting attempt to fuse opera and melodrama produced in Prague in October 1897. The girl's name actually was Kamila—Kamila Urválková—and in August 1903 Janáček, mourning the recent loss of his daughter Olga, met her at the spa of Luhačovice where years later he was to spend hot August days with another Kamila: Kamila Stösslová. Kamila Urválková, 'touched by his sadness and loneliness', sent the three red roses she was wearing to his table, and a spa-romance developed; in his seventies he still remembered her as 'one of the most beautiful of women. Her voice was like a viola d'amore.' That was no doubt why in 1928, writing the String Quartet (*Intimate Letters*) which commemorates his love for the second Kamila, he thought of introducing the viola d'amore[1]—since it secretly recalled

[1] Already used in *Katya Kabanova* in association with Katya (Kamila): see Ex. 8*b*.

to him the first. But at the time he composed the first Kamila, not into a quartet but into an opera, first named *The Red Rose*, then *The Star of Luhačovice, Mamma, do you know what love is?*, *Blind Fate* and finally *Fate: fragments of a novel from Life*. Easily persuaded that Čelanský's *Kamilla* had cruelly misrepresented her, he conceived a sort of sequel in which Kamila is called Míla (actually Míla Válková in the first place) and meets her old lover, the composer Živný (Čelanský continued as Janáček), who is writing an autobiographical opera about a composer named Lenský . . . (We should remember that this was twenty years before Gide wrote *Les Fauxmonnayeurs*.) The name Lenský is clearly an echo of Čelanský but it also reminds us how much the conception of the 'opera-novel' owes to *Eugene Onegin*[1] as well as to that other so-called *roman musical, Louise*.

But the importance of *Osud* in Janáček's operatic development surely lies in the crossing of extreme realism with symbolism—which Vogel discusses at length in his admirable book—with melodrama (Míla's mother kills herself—and Míla), and with a contrived, unreal idea: not merely the opera about an opera about an opera, but the mystification about Živný's opera being 'without a last act'. During a run-through by his students at the Conservatoire, he is struck by lightning, falls and imagines he hears the dead Míla weeping. 'Perhaps it's music, perhaps from the last act!' comments one of the students helpfully. But the dying man suddenly sits up to deny this: 'From the last act? That is in God's hands and will stay there!' *Osud* was a total failure, never performed in Janáček's lifetime, but from that time onward we find him again and again attracted by rather contrived fantastic ideas which he endeavours now with more, now with less success to combine with simple realism; I emphasise the 'contrivance' of these ideas, for they are very different from, say, the folk-comic magic elements in the various Russian operas on Gogol subjects; they are essentially mechanical—above all in his penultimate opera, *The Makropulos Affair*. And in these operas, the *Brouček* 'bilogie' (as he called it), the *Vixen* and *Makropulos*, the fantastic element is not introduced by way of contrast to the realism; it is central, and the realistic element is merely inserted to support it or frame it.

After *Osud* Janáček contemplated several opera subjects—including *Anna Karenina*, which he began to compose in Russian—before he decided in 1908 on one of Svatopluk Čech's *Mr. Brouček* stories, *Mr. Brouček's Excursion to the Moon*. (There was at first some difficulty about the rights, which had been granted to another composer, Karel Moor, whose operetta was produced in 1910, long before Janáček finished his

---

[1] See Theodora Straková, 'Janáčkova opera *Osud*', *Acta Musei Moraviae*, XLII, 1957 Kamila Urválková signed her letters to Janáček 'Tatyana', presumably his nickname for her.

score.) There were endless difficulties with libretto and librettists, and the score was finished only in 1917, after the Prague production of *Její pastorkyňa* with which the real success of that work began. It was then, also, that Janáček decided to compose another *Brouček* story, *Mr. Brouček's Excursion to the Fifteenth Century*. This he proceeded to do in seven months, though the sequel was not perhaps the happiest of ideas, for the first *Excursion* is a satisfactory self-contained whole, except that the 'bilogie' makes up a full evening's programme.

The *Excursions* are, of course, satires. But they are also dreams, the drunken dreams of a character who was, as Janáček said himself, 'to our people what [Goncharov's] Oblomov was to the Russian people ... Only don't let's put up with Brouček's nature as one puts up with Oblomov's.'[1] Brouček is of the earth and both his adventures begin and end[2] outside the Vikárka, a well-known tavern in the Hradčany at Prague much frequented by Svatopluk Čech himself. (Near the beginning of the second *Excursion* Janáček introduces an apparition of the author in person 'in a greenish light' to deliver a lengthy monologue—another unhappy idea.) These 'framing' scenes are realistic enough, though the one at the beginning of the second *Excursion* is only heard, not seen. And Janáček, in the article just quoted from, insisted that the moon-people and the fifteenth-century Hussites 'are *genuine* people ... The moon-people are only in dream-exaggeration dissolved, so to speak, into cobweb-like beings. The pioneers of divine truths in the fifteenth century are exact.' Indeed all these characters are only dream-transformations of Brouček's cronies and acquaintances in nineteenth-century Prague: the Cathedral sacristan becomes Lunobor on the moon and the sexton of the Týn Church, the sacristan's daughter Málinka appears as Etherea and Kunka but is always his daughter, Würfl the innkeeper of the Vikárka becomes Čaroskvouci ('the magic-shining one'), the ruler of the moon, and the fifteenth-century town councillor. The trouble is that none of these characters, even in their 'real' forms, exists in the round; they are hardly more than cut-outs. To say that is not to condemn *Brouček* for not being a different kind of opera; 'flat' characters can be brought to musical life by some composers—for instance, the Rimsky-Korsakov of *Tsar Saltan* and the *Cockerel* (to say nothing of Wagner or the Mozart of *Così fan tutte*). But Janáček needed full, rounded characters not only to excite his musical imagination but to give inner substance to his dramatic music. Despite the humour, the poetry of the tone-picture of starry space, the epic effect of the entry of Žižka's victorious army, *Mr. Brouček* is not one of Janáček's best operas. It is the gimmicks that help to make Janáček

[1] Janáček, *Fejetony z 'Lidových Novin'* (second, enlarged edition), Brno, 1958, p. 52.
[2] In the authentic version, not in the vocal score with German words only—which should be ignored.

such a fascinating composer, but the farther he pursues gimmicks at the expense of the reality that is 'the justification of opera' the less successful he is.

With his next opera after *Brouček*, *Katya Kabanova* (1919–21), he turned his back on gimmicks altogether and produced a masterpiece. But in *The Experiences of the little vixen Sharp-Ears* (1923)[1] and *The Makropulos Affair* (1925) realism has to contend—with more or less success—with a basic fantastic idea. Paradoxically, the *Vixen*—with its animal heroine and its shadowy parallels between human and animal characters (forester's wife/owl, mayor/gnat, parson/badger; even Bystrouška herself has a parallel in the gypsy girl Terynka, who never appears but who marries Harašta after he has shot Bystrouška)—is more real than *The Makropulos Affair* with its modern setting, its lawyer's office and telephone conversations, its theatre backstage, and its—with one exception—everyday characters. It is more real because 'nature' was very real to Janáček; he knew and loved the woods and their inhabitants. He felt a strange, profound compassion for his three-hundred-year-old heroine[2]—mainly, of course, because he contrived to identify her, like Katya Kabanova and Bystrouška, with Kamila Stösslová: '*You* are poor Elina Makropulos,' he told her (8 June, 1927)—but the other characters of *The Makropulos Affair* can have meant nothing to him. He certainly failed to create them in musical terms, though the score does mark a new stage in his style: an almost complete abandonment of the lyrical phrase and a further refinement of his mosaic technique, which is so striking in his last opera, *From a House of the Dead* (1928).

Janáček's two 'Russian' operas, both masterpieces of realism uncomplicated by gimmicks and only slightly poeticised by symbols (the eagle in one, the storm and the river in the other), differ profoundly. Not only in musical style—for there is still a great deal of lyrical music in *Katya Kabanova*—but in dramatic substance. *A House of the Dead* is based on a book that is not even a novel but a thinly disguised account of Dostoevsky's four years in the convict-prison at Omsk, a book that offered characters and incidents rather than 'action' for dramatic treatment. Ostrovsky's *Storm*—which happens to be exactly contemporary with

---

[1] *Příhody lišky Bystroušky:* 'Bystro-uška' means 'Quick-Ears', not 'cunning' as it is commonly translated. Her literary creator, Rudolf Tešnohlidek, who was commissioned by the editor of *Lidové noviny* to provide texts for a series of drawings of fox-life in the forest, originally called her Bystronožka (Quick-Foot): 'they changed her to Bystrouška at the printers', he said.

[2] 'She is taken for a liar, a swindler, a hysterical woman—and she is finally so unhappy! I wanted everyone to like her . . . Poor three-hundred-year-old beauty! People thought her a thief, a liar, a feelingless beast. They'd have liked to strangle her—and her guilt? That she had to live so long. I feel such compassion for her!' (letters to Kamila Stösslová, 3 and 5 March, 1925).

the book: both date from 1859–60—provided a superb drama ready-made; an action curiously parallel with that of Shostakovich's *The Lady Macbeth of Mtsensk*, except that Katerina Kabanova is essentially a good woman while Katerina Ismaylova is essentially a bad one; real, solid characters—even the minor ones; and a setting—a pleasant little Volga town in summer—which could easily have seduced another composer into overmuch background scene-painting. Ostrovsky indeed offered such a fine basis that Janáček needed only to pare away inessentials, as Boito did with Shakespeare; these changes are discussed by Vogel. But some, if trivial, are a little puzzling. Why in the opening scene where Ostrovsky has Kuligin admiring the view and Kudryash prosaically unmoved (I retain the Russian forms of the names) has Janáček made Kudryash admire the view and brought in the maid Glasha as the voice of prose? And why in the Third Act, where Dikoy and Kuligin are talking about lightning-conductors, has Janáček again substituted Kudryash for Kuligin? The obvious answer—'to get rid of the character of Kuligin' —is not the right one, for he has not got rid of Kuligin. But one often notices in Janáček a certain strain of sheer wilfulness.

It is in *Katya Kabanova*, more than in any other of Janáček's operas, that one is reminded of Mussorgsky. Partly, of course, because of the Russian subject and the occasional Russian flavour of the music, but also in such passages as that in the second scene of Act II when Katya has come to Boris at their first rendezvous, a truly realistic, unromanticised declaration of love:

or in the conversation about the lightning-conductor just mentioned, where the matter-of-fact orchestral figure gradually shapes into a premonition:

of the choral 'sigh of the Volga' which sounds so unforgettably through the final scene:

(This effect had, of course, been anticipated in the 'voice of the forest' in

93

the *Vixen* and Janáček returned to it in the wordless choruses of the convicts in *A House of the Dead*.) It should not be forgotten that Janáček had become interested in a later, much less significant Russian composer, Rebikov, whose short 'musical-psychological drama' *Alfa i Omega* he made his opera-class in 1914–15 study beside *Tristan* and *The Bartered Bride*; the increased asperity of Janáček's harmony from *Mr. Brouček's Excursion to the Fifteenth Century* onward may owe something to Rebikov. Rebikov's harmony tends to be schematic, as does Janáček's in his later works. Earlier, Janáček's, like Mussorgsky's, often seems to be empirical; he taught harmony, but often found it impossible to convey his meaning to his students. In *Katya*, as in *Boris*, one gets alternations of such purely 'expressionist' harmony and declamation with normal diatonic melody and harmony, not in a sense of contrast but as the natural reflection of changing emotional temperature. And Katya herself is distinguished from the other characters by her more lyrical melodic ambience, e.g. at her first appearance (*a*); near the beginning of Act III, scene 2 ('to see him, part, and then die') (*b*); and the wonderful passage just before she throws herself into the river when she foresees how 'birds will fly over the grave, bringing up their young, and flowers will bloom —red and blue and golden . . .' (*c*),[1] evoking with the fewest possible notes at once a visual image and a poignant emotion:

[1] A characteristic example of Janáček's 'top and bottom' orchestral lay-out.

The affinity of her themes with those of the Second Quartet has often been pointed out; it is natural, for as Janáček composed Katya it was always with Kamila Stösslová's image in his mind, and the Second Quartet consists of 'intimate letters' addressed to her.

From a House of the Dead lacks any such central character to precipitate lyrical ideas; in fact it lacks any central character at all. Goryanchikov, the 'I' of Dostoevsky's books, a flimsy mask for Dostoevsky himself, is a perceptive and accurate observer rather than a character. And the young Tatar, Aley, is no substitute for a Kamila figure; Janáček conceived the part as a mezzo role—despite Dostoevsky's description of him as 'no more than twenty-two'—obviously because he needed more relief from male voices than is given by the prostitute's dozen bars near the end of Act II; and he extended it far beyond Dostoevsky's four-page description plus a couple of later references, but still without making him anything more than the devoted object of Goryanchikov's affection. This typifies one of the major difficulties of turning the book into an opera; its value is documentary rather than artistic, despite the power of some of the passages as prose (for instance, the bath-house scene which reminded Turgenev of Dante). Each convict is described (as Aley is), brought to life by an incident or a dialogue, and then dropped—though he may reappear from time to time later. Not only is there no drama; there is no story. And in his attempt to create some sort of narrative, Janáček contrived to confuse and blur what Dostoevsky gives us in plenty: the characters. With that passionate immediate reaction to a book, an idea or an event that is so typical of the man, and in a manner that reminds one of the way some of the greatest Russian composers set about writing operas —Glinka with *Ruslan*, Mussorgsky, Borodin, even Tchaïkovsky with *Onegin*—he read Dostoevsky, in Russian, and made notes for a scenario, also mainly in Russian though with lapses into Czech or the Roman alphabet. Thus for Act I:

> Arrival, p. 361
> —— eagle, p. 326
> Aleya, p. 87
> Orlov, p. 78
> Isay Fomich, p. 92
> Sushilov, p. 102
> A—v, p. 105 (without a soul)
> Skuratov, pp. 117–19 (singer)
> Petrov, p. 140
> Luchka, p. 153
> Baklushin, p. 175 [comment illegible]
> Songs, p. 185

Varlamov, p. 190[1]
'lies! lies!'

Having thus made a first selection of outstanding characters and incidents, he proceeded to discard and rearrange and condense in a way that was almost inevitable if a practicable scenario was to be arrived at. But in the process both characters and incidents were conflated and transposed and sometimes falsified in a way that Hollywood itself could hardly surpass. Consider Act III. The first scene is in the prison-hospital, where Goryanchikov is sitting at Aley's bedside. (There is no mention of Aley's illness in the book, but Janáček attached a curious importance to it: 'Aleya in his white hospital robe remains as a symbol of *the divine spark* in man', he wrote at the end of the sketch of the last scene.) The first snatch of conversation about Jesus is taken directly from the book (Part I, Chap. 5), though the miracle of the clay bird is told not by Aley but by one of his brothers. Chekunov brings tea as in II, 1, but the consumptive patient in the book is not Luka but quite a different character, Ustyantsev. The long-eared Shapkin's story comes from II, 3, but 'the maniac Skuratov' does not interrupt it in Dostoevsky by calling out, 'O Luise!', and dancing. And for a very good reason: his story about Luise in Act II really belongs to another man, Baklushin (I, 10), and Dostoevsky's Skuratov remains from first to last a cheerful character who enjoys singing and playing the fool. The beautiful scene where all are sleeping except the Old Believer sitting on the stove, who breaks into a passionate cry for the children he will never see again, is borrowed from I, 4. Shishkov's long account of his marriage to the wretched Akulka—overlong, 35 pages of vocal score, despite Cherevin's interruptions, and the cries of the feverish Aley and the dying Luka interjected by the composer—is condensed from II, 4, where it is *not* terminated by Ustyantsev—Luka's death and that preposterous invention, Shishkov's belated discovery that the dead man is none other than the villain of his story. (The after-death scene is borrowed from another death, II, 1, where the Old Believer's touching remark, 'He, too, had a mother!', is made by Chekunov.) The second scene of Act III is an even more ingenious compilation. The dialogue between Goryanchikov and the brutal Major is borrowed (*a*) from one between the Major and an elderly Polish professor whom he has had wrongly flogged, II, 8 (in the book Goryanchikov was never flogged), (*b*) from one, also in II, 8, between the kindly Governor and another Pole who is to be prematurely released (Goryanchikov served his full term). The touching farewell with Aley is, of course, purely

---

[1] I am not sure whether this is a slip, of a kind to which Janáček was even more addicted than most of us, for Vermalov—a convict who sings a song on the evening of Christmas Day—or whether Janáček meant that the song was by Varlamov, the composer of the famous 'Red Sarafan'.

Janáček's invention; Aley is never mentioned in the Second Part of the book at all. And the freeing of the eagle, that symbolic eagle which is the bane of all producers, is not associated in the book with any convict's release nor does it happen in quite the same way. The broken wing has not mended—'but let him die in freedom', say the convicts. 'The eagle's the tsar of the forests,' comments Skuratov, but 'nobody took any notice of him'. So they throw the poor thing over the ramparts and watch it make off, fluttering the wing—a more true and touching symbol of a released convict than the soaring eagle of the opera. And then they tramp off back to work, as in Janáček's own ending. (The triumphant ending printed in the vocal score was cooked up after Janáček's death by the conductor Břetislav Bakala and the composer Osvald Chlubna at the request of Ota Zítek who 'revised' the libretto.)

Dostoevsky's *From a House of the Dead* is as grim a piece of realism as one can find in nineteenth-century literature. And, despite the sentimental and idealistic elements Janáček injected, the total effect of the opera does not fall so very far short of the original. The falsification was necessary in order to bring the subject within the field of possible music, and the power of the music compensates for the falsification. But the nature of Janáček's musical realism in this last opera demands closer attention. It is essentially prosaic, of course, more prosaic than in *Katya Kabanova*, much more than in *Pastorkyňa*. Such more lyrical passages as there are remind one of Mussorgsky; for instance, this passage in Shishkov's story when he begins to describe his prosperous father-in-law's 'big farm with plenty of labourers':

But generally the quasi-Russian idioms are modified by Janáček's astringent harmony, which is much more schematic than Mussorgsky's. He never, I think, borrows a Russian tune either here or in *Katya*, even when the libretto offers a pretext; he deliberately avoids 'Kamarinskaya' in the prison-entertainment, although Dostoevsky actually specifies it.

Considered from a little distance, *A House of the Dead* does seem rather Mussorgskian: the total effect produced by the building up of disconnected scenes, the 'collective hero', the prose realism. Yet directly one examines that prose realism closely, one sees the profound difference. Mussorgsky's vocal writing is usually directly generated by the text, freely following its course, even though there are plenty of instances where it flows between the harmonic banks of a preconceived orchestral basis. Janáček's process is more sophisticated. His motivic *données* very often come from the text, the *nápěvky mluvy*, and a fascinating, peculiarly coloured orchestral fabric is developed from them and from those endlessly subtle modifications and transformations of them which enable Czech critics to speak with some justice of his monothematicism. But the voice parts that rest on this fabric, particularly in his two last operas, are apt to be dry and recitative-like.

The real was Janáček's primary motive-force. Immediacy was immensely important to him: the shooting of a workman in a riot in Brno, an emotional experience of his own, a happening revealed by poems in a local newspaper, the reading of a book, the intonations of the human voices—and the bird-song—around him, all produced immediate reactions which might be as small as a tiny melodic motive or as large as a big instrumental composition or an opera. But the working out was another matter. Much of the unique fascination of Janáček's music is, I suspect, due to the contrast of the naïve immediacy of the basic conceptions with the gnomic sophistication of the final forms.

1966

VII—ANTON RUBINSTEIN: RUSSIAN COMPOSER

'Rubinstein is not a Russian composer,' declared César Cui. 'He is only a Russian who composes.' And the distinction has been generally accepted, although Cui was the last person who ought to have made it. When Calvocoressi and I were planning our *Masters of Russian Music* we had little difficulty in persuading each other that whatever Rubinstein might have been a master of, it was not Russian music. Indeed by far the greater proportion of that great dead bulk of symphonies and sonatas and 'sacred operas' is Russian music only in the sense that it was composed by a subject of the Tsar. (Like Mendelssohn's and Meyerbeer's, it is Jewish in that it belongs to no particular country.) As a song-writer Rubinstein set German words far more often, and far more successfully, than Russian ones; even the best things he ever did, the *Zwölf Lieder des Mirza Schaffy, aus dem persischen von F. Bodenstedt,* Op. 34, were settings of German words, the Russian text having been added later—and by no less distinguished a translator than Tchaïkovsky. And yet . . . every now and again the student of Russian music comes across something of Rubinstein's that shows him influencing—or, much more oddly, being influenced by—his almost lifelong antagonists, the deliberate nationalists. Oddest of all, one finds him at one period, round about 1879–80, actually trying to set up as a nationalist composer himself and producing at least one work, almost completely unknown, which might well be worth a conductor's while to rescue from limbo.

Rubinstein actually began his operatic career with a Russian libretto and a Russian historical subject, the subject treated many years later by the Soviet composer, Shaporin: *Dmitry Donskoy: or The Battle of Kulikovo* (1852). The only part of the music that survives is the overture, which is completely devoid of Russian characteristics although the second subject of the *allegro*:

Ex. 1
Moderato assai
mf con espressione

has a marked affinity with the weaker sort of love-theme one finds later in the operas of Rimsky-Korsakov (e.g. *Sadko, Tsar Saltan*). But a certain party, including the critic of the *St. Peterburgskiya Vedomosti,* praised Rubinstein's opera at the expense of Glinka's *Ruslan* and *Life for the Tsar,* and a fierce newspaper battle developed. Matters were made worse when the next year, at the request of his patroness the Grand Duchess Helena Pavlovna, Rubinstein produced three little one-act operas 'depicting the different peoples of Russia': *Hadji Abrek* (to a poem by Lermontov), *The Siberian Hunters* and *Fomka the Fool*. As Yury Arnold puts it in his reminiscences:[1]

In 1853 Rubinstein again appeared on the Russian stage with a one-act comic opera *Fomka the Fool*, in which he evidently wished to express himself as a nationally-Russian composer. In this 'dramatic' composition *the pot-house* and *vodka* play an important rôle; this circumstance gave Glinka's antagonists an opportunity to draw attention to the 'real' (in their opinion) significance of the Russian tendency in music. But this 'attempt' by no means pleased the Russian public, Mr Rubinstein's 'comic opera' was unwittingly taken by the patriotic party as a deliberate parody on Glinka's operas, and it suffered complete disaster.

Doubtless these little pleasantries account for a good deal of Rubinstein's bitterness in later years against the group who claimed to be the heirs of Glinka, just as the 'complete disaster' accounts for his almost complete abandonment even of Russian libretti; of his fifteen later operas, only four are Russian, the remaining eleven—including the 'sacred operas' which are in intention and effect oratorios in costume—being German.

A year or two after the unlucky *Fomka* Rubinstein composed in its original four-movement form (which was therefore only four-sevenths as bad as the final one) his best-known orchestral work, the *Ocean* Symphony. Nothing could be less Russian, yet we are indebted to it indirectly for one of the best Russian operas, Korsakov's *Sadko*. We learn from a letter from Stasov to Balakirev in 1861 that the latter had been 'strongly attracted by Anton's *Sea* Symphony. From a recent conversation with you I saw that the subject had not merely fired you temporarily but was firmly fixed in your mind.' But if Balakirev wants to write a sea-piece, too, let it be something new and Russian, not 'common-European' music; and Stasov puts forward the subject of the old verse-legend, which he has just come across, of the Novgorod merchant Sadko. Like so much else that Balakirev projected, the sea-piece was passed to someone else to write; in this case, the sailor Rimsky-Korsakov, who thirty years later used the subject and musical themes of his orchestral 'picture' for his much-better-known opera.

But this is by the way. Rubinstein's own first essay in 'Russian' orchestral music was the musical character-picture *Ivan the Terrible* (1868). This is really a concert-overture based on themes presumably intended

<hr/>

[1] *Vospominaniya*, III, Moscow, 1893, p. 103.

CARL A. RUDISILL LIBRARY
LENOIR RHYNE COLLEGE

to suggest Ivan's might, military prowess, cruelty and religious tendencies (sincere or hypocritical). It is not a very remarkable work, but even Rubinstein's adversaries admired it in its day. Balakirev gave its first performance at one of his Free School concerts in 1869 and Borodin was moved to write to his wife that he was

> ... surprised to find a great deal of good stuff in it; you simply wouldn't recognise it as A. Rubinstein. No Mendelssohnism; nothing like his earlier things. There is real power in some passages.

The opening of the *allegro*, or rather *moderato*, is of the forcible-feeble order, but I quote the rather pallidly Russian second subject (presumably the musical symbol of the Tsaritsa Anastasia who was a restraining influence in Ivan's younger days):

the military theme

and the opening of one of those passages which Borodin probably means when he speaks of 'real power':

Rubinstein also seems to have expected his opera *The Demon* to appeal to the Mighty Handful and their friends. It was on a Caucasian subject and had a Russian libretto based on a poem by Lermontov, though bearing pretty much the same relation to it as Ambroise Thomas's *Hamlet* and Gounod's *Roméo et Juliette* do to Shakespeare. Ever since *Ruslan* Russian composers with nationalist tendencies had shown an interest in the recently conquered Caucasian peoples and their native music, and Rubinstein invited Stasov, Rimsky-Korsakov, Mussorgsky, Cui and others of their circle to hear him play and sing *The Demon* privately, in September, 1871, soon after its completion. Unfortunately his audience seems to have been unimpressed and it is not difficult to understand why. The orientalism of the Handful was not very genuine, being largely a

CARL A. RUDISILL LIBRARY
LENOIR RHYNE COLLEGE

matter of convention; but Rubinstein's was even less genuine and in a less convincing convention. For his earlier essay in oriental opera, *Feramors* (1863), he had gone to the India of Tom Moore and presented it in terms of the musical orientalism of David's *Le Désert*, Meyerbeer's *L'Africaine* and Bizet's *Djamileh* and *Pêcheurs de perles*. But in *The Demon* he had at least got his orientalism from *Ruslan* and he doubtless felt that his Prince Gudal:

Ex. 5

was near enough to Glinka's Ratmir to win the sympathy of Glinka's admirers. But one has only to compare his oriental dances:

Ex. 6

with, say, Borodin's or the Persian dances in *Khovanshchina* to hear how they lack savour, quite charming though they are. His Caucasian lezginka is even weaker by comparison with Glinka's in *Ruslan* and on later occasions when he needed a lezginka Rubinstein, as we shall see, unashamedly helped himself to the native tune used by Glinka.

Yet one passage in *The Demon*, though not oriental, seems to have been carried away in the mind of one of the listeners on that occasion. For this phrase of the Demon's, heard several times in Act III:

Ex. 7

was to reappear almost note for note, and in the same key, in the Prelude to *Khovanschchina*. Similarly Tamara's phrase:

Ex. 8

surely recurred, spiritually if not literally, when Tchaïkovsky wrote one of the finest pages of *Onegin*.

Yet, whatever the merits of *The Demon*—and it is far better than most of Rubinstein's music—its main claim to be considered Russian music is the somewhat flimsy one that, like other Russian music, it contains a lot of attractive but spurious exoticism. Rubinstein's real 'Russian' period came several years later: about 1879–82 to be precise. I have not been able to find a score of his *Russian Capriccio* for piano and orchestra, Op. 102, which Tchaïkovsky admired 'not only as a piano piece but as an orchestral one'; but the other compositions of this time—the really striking Fifth Symphony in G minor, Op 107, the opera *The Merchant Kalashnikov*, and the orchestral piece *Russia*—are well worth looking at and the Symphony is even worth a performance or two. *Russia*, a noisy and shoddy occasional piece, has no artistic value; but even that has some amusing features to which I shall return in a moment.

The G minor Symphony is the most completely and unmistakably Russian of all Rubinstein's works, practically every theme being cast in the mould of folk-song. (Whether any of them are actual folk-tunes I cannot say.) The very opening melody:

Ex. 9

Moderato assai

mp espressivo

might well be a peasant *protyazhnaya* ('long-drawn' song); its family likeness to the opening theme of *Boris Godunov* is striking. And not only the theme but the scoring announces the debut of quite a new Rubinstein. The melody is heard on solo flute, solo clarinet and solo bassoon in three octaves, entirely unsupported; Rubinstein must have remembered the opening of his pupil Tchaïkovsky's First Symphony in the same key, and decided to take a step further in the same direction. The second subject:

Ex. 10

p

is first played by a solo oboe, accompanied by dancing woodwind chords. Like every composer who sets out to construct a symphonic movement from this sort of material, Rubinstein finds himself confronted with some nearly insoluble problems. But he does not get round them as one would have expected, by taking fragments of his themes and trying to 'work' them according to respectable academic prescriptions; at least, there is very little of this. The bridge-passages and development and so on are mainly constructed from subsidiary scraps of material which act as cement holding the main thematic blocks in position. Much of the scoring is charmingly bright and transparent and if Rubinstein could only have found modal or quasi-modal alternatives to his nine-teenth-century text-book harmonies he would have turned out a movement as Russian as anything in the repertory.

The second movement is based on a pentatonic pattern:

played first by a solo clarinet against the lightest pizzicato background. It is a humorous scherzo, of the same type as the buffoons' dances that occur in so many Russian operas, with a fugato middle section based on another piece of unmistakably Russian cantilena:

The slow movement is less attractive, more heavily weighted by conventional harmonisation. But the last movement is delightfully racy. I quote both the main subjects to show how Rubinstein just managed to take the bloom off attractive tunes in one case by insisting on a proper leading-note, in the other by unimaginative harmony. Rubinstein was incapable of recognising any modes other than major and minor:

The Merchant Kalashnikov written at nearly the same time as the Fifth Symphony is an equally determined attempt to compose a thoroughly Russian opera. Like *The Demon* it is based on one of Lermontov's finest poems: *The Song of Tsar Ivan Vasilevich, the Young Oprichnik and the Brave Merchant Kalashnikov*, written in the style of the old Russian epic-ballads. (Incidentally, a German version of Lermontov's poem had been made by that same Bodenstedt who provided Rubinstein with the texts for his *Persian Songs*; it created a considerable sensation in its day.) The cruelties of Ivan the Terrible and his infamous bodyguard, the oprichniks, were a favourite subject of Russian historical opera; Rimsky-Korsakov and Tchaïkovsky had already depicted them in *The Maid of Pskov* and *The Oprichnik*, and Korsakov was to return to them in his *Tsar's Bride*. In Lermontov's poem Rubinstein found all the necessary ingredients. Kalashnikov, a young Muscovite merchant has his wife abducted by an oprichnik, challenges the villain to a fight with bare fists, kills him, and is condemned to death by the Tsar in spite of his wife's intercession. (According to Mrs Newmarch's *Russian Opera*, the Tsar finally relents and pardons him, but in the German score published by Senff, the only one I have been able to consult, Kalashnikov is led off to execution; possibly the happy ending was an attempt to make the opera more acceptable to the censor, who insisted on its withdrawal almost immediately after the first performance and again after the revival in 1889.)

Rubinstein's score, like the plot, contains all the familiar elements of Russian historical opera: folk-songs for the Court jester, ecclesiastical chants for the oprichniks (who were accustomed to dress as monks), dances of buffoons, even a chorus of greeting to the Tsar, based on the famous melody used in the second *Razumovsky* Quartet, the coronation scene of *Boris*, and *The Tsar's Bride*. A good deal of it is mediocre, colourless music of the type we commonly associate with Rubinstein; the more definitely Russian melody sometimes tends to watery lyricism or else is weakened by conventional harmonisation; the buffoons' dance unashamedly echoes the lezginka in *The Demon*. But mixed with all this is much beautiful, colourful and expressive music, music that one might easily take to be from some unknown work of Borodin or Rimsky-Korsakov, e.g. the drinking chorus of the oprichniks in the First Act, the pleading of Kalashnikov's wife in the Second, the entry of his brothers a little later and his reply to them. I quote two other passages, the truly Russian recitative of the heralds before the fight scene in the last act:

Ex. 14
Lento

He, wo seid Ihr, tap - fe re Leu - te Ihr? Un - ter - halt - ung schaffet dem Czar, ihm den Mächtigen,

and part of a little eight-bar chorus of Kalashnikov's neighbours consoling him when he first learns what has happened to his wife. Here, for once, the harmony is as Russian as the melody:

Ex. 15
Moderato assai

Hal - te ein mit Klag-en, uns zer - reisst's das Herz, Blick zu Gott, ver - trau - e ihm in Not und Schmerz

The orchestral piece *Russia* is in quite a different class from the Fifth Symphony and *Kalashnikov*. Like Tchaïkovsky's *1812*, it was written for the Moscow Exhibition of 1882; in fact, it was used to open the

Exhibition concerts. After a short introduction on a liturgical melody, Rubinstein writes a more or less conventional sonata movement with a definitely Russian main theme

Ex. 16

Moderato

f risoluto

but breaks off in the recapitulation for a series of short passages symbolising the non-Russian subjects of the Russian Empire: the Poles, Caucasians, Germans, Letts, Estonians, Tatars, Finns, Little-Russians, Jews and—Gypsies! Finally he combines these contrapuntally in a sort of quodlibet, returns for a moment to Ex. 16 and winds up with a very noisy coda which allows for the *ad lib.* interpolation of the national anthem, 'God preserve the Tsar.' Tchaïkovsky's comment on this quaint production (in a letter to his, and Rubinstein's, publisher Jurgenson) is worth quoting:

> *Russia* doesn't please me at all. Only a limited, not to say stupid, man could have written such nonsense. Why all these Estonians and Jews and all this procession of foreigners? Why has Rubinstein's muse illustrated the melancholy ethnographic fact that Russia is rather a patchy affair and has not yet welded itself into something whole and strong? Is he glorifying this fact or deploring it? I don't believe he knows himself!

But two figures in the 'procession of foreigners' attract attention as they pass. The Caucasians are represented by the melody of the lezginka from *Ruslan,* which Rubinstein had already used in his *Album of Popular Dances of the Different Nations* for piano, Op. 82. (Russia proper is represented in the Album by a 'Russkaya i Trepak' in which the national colouring is not particularly bright.) And the Tatars are most oddly depicted by the languorous 6/8 melody from Balakirev's *Islamey,* which is (I believe) of *Armenian* origin. Curiouser and curiouser: Rubinstein borrowed not only Balakirev's melody but Balakirev's harmony.

Rubinstein's changed attitude to conscious nationalism was not a mere passing fancy, though it produced nothing else comparable with the Fifth Symphony and *Kalashnikov.* He told the publisher Bessel on one occasion, later in the eighties, that he now felt differently about the so-called 'new Russian school' and proposed to give it generous representation in his programmes. And during his second term as Director of the St Petersburg Conservatoire he did actively champion Russian opera and Russian music in general.

1945

VIII—TCHAÏKOVSKY: SOME CENTENNIAL
REFLECTIONS

Maurice Baring has said that 'if you take as ingredients Peter the Great, Dostoevsky's Myshkin—the idiot, the pure fool who is wiser than the wise—and the hero of Gogol's *Revizor*, Khlestakov the liar and windbag, you can, I think, out of these elements, reconstitute any Russian who has ever lived. That is to say, you will find that every single Russian is compounded either of one or more of these elements.'

Pausing only to commend this very acute observation to the attention of those who are specially interested in Tchaïkovsky's personal character, I pass on to make another generalisation, less acute but equally dogmatic: 'If you take as ingredients Russian folk-music, Italian opera, French ballet music and Western romanticism (the music of Berlioz, Schumann, Liszt and one or two minor figures such as Henry Litolff, who impressed both Borodin and Tchaïkovsky), you can reconstitute any Russian music written before 1910 and most of the Russian music written since.'

One of the two most obvious differences between Tchaïkovsky and his most important contemporaries in his own country—Borodin, Balakirev, Mussorgsky and Rimsky-Korsakov—lay in the unusually large proportion of the third element, French ballet music, no doubt a consequence of his partly French blood. (His maternal grandfather was a Frenchman.) The other is the fact that his sound professional training at the St Petersburg Conservatoire gave him a special facility in handling his material and a regrettable facility in the art of spinning something out of nothing. Yet even the most insensitive listener must feel that Tchaïkovsky's music, at any rate his later music, that by which he is generally known to the average musician, differs in some deeper ways from that of the Mighty Handful.

Perhaps we can define this difference most clearly by comparing two remarkably similar passages in the slow movements of Borodin's Second and Tchaïkovsky's Fifth Symphonies, at nearly the same structural point in each: in Borodin the reappearance of the principal theme, *forte*, in Tchaïkovsky the return of the very important subsidiary theme, *fff*, in both cases at a slightly quicker pace than in the first part of the movement. At each point a warm, lyrical melody is sung out in octaves by all the strings, except double basses, and some woodwind, against a harmonic background supplied by the remaining woodwind and horns; in each case the complex of material is completed by the later entry of a more or less *cantabile* middle-part counter-subject on solo trumpet and trombone in octaves. Indeed, the general lay-out of the two passages is so similar that it is impossible to believe that Tchaïkovsky was not consciously or unconsciously recollecting Borodin when he wrote his own Symphony ten years later. But there the similarity ends. In essence the two passages are profoundly different; the underlying feeling in Tchaïkovsky has nothing in common with Borodin's except emotional expansiveness. And the differences are revealed both in the melodic lines and in the way the composers wish them to be treated. The Borodin tune is very subtly articulated rhythmically: two bars of 3/4—really one of 6/8 and one of genuine 3/4—four of 4/4, four of 3/4, and so on; but it sings simply on its way without a single mark of expression beyond the initial *cantabile*. The justification for its existence lies solely in its lovely, slightly arabesque outline, so unlike the outline of Western European melodies. It may or may not have been originally conceived as a bard's song in praise of Russian valour in the projected epilogue to *Prince Igor*; no one would dream of reading any extra-musical meaning into it, though it probably gives off certain spiritual overtones, akin to those of much of Lermontov's poetry, which our Western ears cannot catch, just as foreigners cannot hear all that Austrians hear in Bruckner or all that we hear in, say, Elgar's *Introduction and Allegro*. It is intensely individual in that no one but Borodin wrote just that type of tune, but it is completely impersonal; it tells us nothing about Borodin except that he had a gift for writing lovely tunes. And in all these respects it is thoroughly typical of the best of Russian lyrical music—other than Tchaïkovsky's.

Now consider the Tchaïkovsky melody in the parallel passage. Rhythmically it is very simple, with no other complications than an occasional three-against-four within the beat; but the tempo is modified at least every two bars—*animando, riten., tempo primo, animando un poco*, and then a pace slightly quicker than the *tempo primo*, all within half-a-dozen bars; and the theme is marked first *con anima*, then *con desiderio e passione*, and three bars later *con tutta forza* (notwithstanding which, the composer still expects his strings to have something in reserve for the *ffff*, four bars later still). Yet there is nothing unfamiliar or exotic about it. In fact it is more than a little reminiscent of a phrase in a work very dear to Tchaïkovsky: Escamillo's 'Si tu m'aimes, Carmen, *tu pourras, tout à l'heure*, être fière de moi!' Its justification lies not in its slightly banal and reminiscent self, but in its extra-musical meaning. I remember reading somewhere, but cannot verify the reference, that Tchaïkovsky wrote over the horn solo that opens this movement the words, 'O, que je t'aime! O, mon amie!' (Or more probably 'ami'.) 'O, how I love. . . . If you love me. . . . With desire and passion. . . .': even without these clues the music itself tells us unmistakably that it is straining, almost to breaking-point, to express *something* not implicit in the musical substance alone. And this something is a dramatic personal outcry about a keenly felt emotion, a cry so nearly articulate that it seems to need words to complete it and make its message clear beyond all doubt, and so dramatic that one feels it would be more in place at the climax of an opera scene than in a movement of a symphony. Borodin, then, is individual but impersonal (like Glinka and Balakirev and Mussorgsky and Rimsky-Korsakov and Stravinsky); Tchaïkovsky, at any rate in this particular instance with its echo of Bizet, is not particularly individual but intensely personal. And his personal emotion is expressed in terms of a melody which, far from being peculiarly Russian, might appear without incongruity in an Italian opera or a French ballet.

The frequent employment of that sort of melody was not, of course, the sole basis of the charge—first made by S. I. Taneyev and often repeated, notably by Tovey in the final volume of *Essays in Musical Analysis*—that Tchaïkovsky was essentially a composer of ballet music or 'light music'. There is also his tendency to drop into dance-rhythms, particularly waltz-rhythms, at any moment, even in the most incongruous circumstances. Consider, for instance, the second-subject material for the first movement of the Fourth Symphony. This is the point where, according to the often quoted letter of Nadezhda von Meck of 17 February, 1878, he turns from the 'hopeless, disconsolate feeling' of the opening of the *moderato* (itself expressed in music that hovers dangerously on the brink of the dance-like and is actually marked *In movimento di valse*) and reflects: 'Is it not better to turn away from reality and bury oneself in dreams? . . . O joy! A sweet and tender dream appears. A blissful, radiant human form floats beckoning by.' Now it is disconcerting enough to find the second-subject material of a symphonic movement consisting, first, of a quaint piquant little clarinet tune, surrounded by little chromatic runs on flute and bassoon,[1] which would not seem at all strange if connected with the Reed-Pipes and the Sugar-Plum Fairy of *Nutcracker*, and, second, of a delicious waltz. But it is all the more curious when one finds that these charming musical toys symbolise the radiant visions that console a great artist bowed hopelessly beneath the power of destiny.

Yet this sheds a certain amount of light on Tchaïkovsky's in many respects naïve character. He *could* console himself with radiant visions in waltz time. And, as is shown by his letter of 27 March, 1878, in reply to Taneyev's criticism of this very Symphony, he would have been unmoved by—he would not even have understood—the complaint that

[1] Very similar flutings surround the melancholy oboe melody in the slow movement ('Dreary land, misty land') of the First Symphony (*Winter Daydreams*) written ten years earlier. Here is a close similarity of mood to the passage in the Fourth Symphony. But Tchaïkovsky loved such woodwind trimmings; one finds them throughout his music. Do they not also betray what one must, for want of a better term, call 'the ballet mind'?

such music was out of place in a symphony. To his mind music was simply music, whether one used it for a symphony, an opera, a ballet or a piano concerto. If he wrote ballet music in a symphony, he was also capable, as in parts of *The Sleeping Beauty*, of writing symphonic music in a ballet. His opera music differs in no essential respect from his symphonic music[1] and is really successful only when he can completely identify himself with one or more of his characters (Hermann in *The Queen of Spades*, Tatyana and Lensky and Onegin in turn in *Eugene Onegin*). The *Pathétique* Symphony is, in a sense, an opera with one character, no singing and no stage-action. And the only way to enjoy Tchaïkovsky to the full is to smother very firmly all one's notions of the artistic fitness of things in symphonies and concertos, and to listen to his music in the same naïve way that he conceived it.

What was Tchaïkovsky's conception of music, then? First and last, the spontaneous, lyrical idea—whether embodied in a short theme or, as was more often the case with his own compositions, in a fairly long-breathed melody. The art of composition was to him the craft of dressing up and fitting together such ideas in the most effective way. He disliked music that lacked this inward lyrical feeling or in which it was, in his view, smothered by elaborate technical treatment. He disliked genuine programme-music—that is to say, music with a literary or pictorial as distinguished from a merely emotional programme—probably because the impulse to it came from outside, as it were. He sometimes wrote it himself, but as he told Balakirev (letter of 12 November, 1882) he considered both *Francesca da Rimini* and *The Tempest* 'extremely cold, false and weak' and even in *Romeo and Juliet* ('which, God knows why, people praise as exaggeratedly as they depreciate my other works') he painfully acknowledged 'the complete lack of connection between Shakespeare's representation of the youthful passion of the Italian Romeo and my own bitter-sweet moanings'. Attacked from the other side by Taneyev, who actually reproached him for writing programme music in the Fourth Symphony, he defended himself on what is really the same ground: 'I shouldn't like symphonic compositions to come from my pen expressing nothing and consisting of an empty play of chords, tempos, modulations. . . .' And in a letter of later date to the same correspondent he protests vigorously against his younger friend's wish that he should 'turn himself into a Josquin des Prés'. Actually he was no mean contrapuntist; the first movements of the D major Quartet and the Serenade for strings and several of the variations in the third orchestral Suite (to take only a few of the examples that occur to one immediately) show him as a complete

---

[1] The march in the Second Symphony was originally written for the opera *Undine*; conversely, the *alla tedesca* of the Third Symphony was afterwards used in the incidental music to *Hamlet*.

master of the art of fluent, effective part-writing. One of his favourite
devices is to add a counter-subject, usually in a different instrumental
colour, to a given melody. But the object is simply to enhance the original
idea, to show it in a new light; there is very little genuine polyphonic
thinking in his music. As the reference to Josquin suggests, he tended to
think of true polyphony as cold, brain-spun tissue.[1]

Tchaïkovsky disliked the music of his two greatest German contemporaries[2] mainly because it was too complicated, because he missed
in it the clear-cut melodic phrases which to him were the essence of music.
He found Wagner's harmony 'too involved, too far-fetched'. As for his
melody:

> I cannot call this music, these kaleidoscopic, motley musical frag-
> ments which follow each other incessantly, never leading to anything
> and not once giving you a chance to relax on some easily perceptible
> musical form. Not one broad, complete melody, no scope at all for
> the singer.

As for Brahms:

> The Russian heart finds this master's music somewhat dry, cold,
> cloudy and repellent; from our point of view Brahms is completely
> lacking in melodic invention. His musical thought is never quite
> fully expressed; a melodic phrase is no sooner hinted at than it is
> smothered in all sorts of harmonic ingenuities, as if the composer had
> set himself the task of being incomprehensible and profound; he
> actually irritates our musical feeling by his failure to satisfy its needs
> and speak to us in the tones that go to the heart.

Such criticisms may not have much value as judgments on Wagner
and Brahms, but they shed valuable light on their author. A composer
who attaches so much importance to 'complete melody', the sort of
melody that consists of clear-cut, balancing phrases, cannot hope to reach
the first rank in the large classical instrumental forms. To develop this
sort of melody, or a part of it, is to ruin it. And where each idea is so
complete, so well-defined, the business of transition from one to another
becomes so nearly impossible that it can be managed only with perfunctory artlessness. Whereas the two despised German masters brought this
art of subtle, almost imperceptible transition wellnigh to perfection,
Tchaïkovsky was obliged to admit that 'my seams always showed, and

---

[1] Tchaïkovsky's view of Josquin was, of course, the false nineteenth-century view.
[2] Though he admitted the influence of the *Ring* on *Francesca*, particularly the introduction. 'Isn't it remarkable that I was unable to escape the influence of a work that is very
antipathetic to me?' he remarked to Taneyev.

there was no organic union between the separate episodes'. In this particular case, it is true, he was speaking of his earlier works, but only four years before his death he confessed to the Grand Duke Konstantin: 'There is frequently padding in my works; to an experienced eye the stitches show in my seams, but I can't help it.'

This overwhelming respect for the rights of the clear-cut, spontaneous melodic phrase 'speaking in tones that go to the heart', also seriously limited Tchaïkovsky as a variation-writer. He either repeats the theme unchanged melodically but with fresh harmonies, counterpoints and instrumental colour-schemes, as in the folksong finale of the Second Symphony (which owes so much to Glinka's *Kamarinskaya*), the first variation in the finale of the Trio, the first and third variations in the third orchestral Suite, and the fifth of the *Variations on a Rococo Theme*; or he surrounds the theme with ornamentation that hardly does more than lightly veil its original form (first *Rococo* variation); or, his favourite method, he subjects the theme to a Lisztian metamorphosis into a mazurka or chorale or polonaise and writes a little genre-piece on it in this new form, as in so many of the Suite and Trio variations—to say nothing of the curious and little-known set of six piano pieces, Op. 21: Prelude, Fugue, Impromptu, Funeral March, Mazurka and Scherzo, all based on the same theme. These limitations in the art of variation-writing naturally also limit Tchaïkovsky's handling of his material in symphonies and concertos.

Loving well-defined lyrical melody as he did, Tchaïkovsky's preference for the music of such composers as Bizet, Delibes, Massenet and Grieg, among his contemporaries, is easily comprehensible. So too is his love of Mozart and the age of rococo in general, a love reflected on many pages of his own scores. The decidedly un-Mozartian orchestration of *Mozartiana* and the Wardour-Street-rococo theme of the cello Variations are by no means his best tributes to the late eighteenth century. For those one must turn to the 'Faithful Shepherdess' interlude in *The Queen of Spades*, the duet for Liza and Polina in the first act of the same opera (in the finale of the Second Act Tchaïkovsky actually introduces an air from Grétry's *Richard Cœur de Lion*), Triquet's couplets in *Onegin* and the sarabande in the last act of *The Sleeping Beauty*.

Equally natural was Tchaïkovsky's love of Russian (and Italian) folksong. He dissembled it more successfully than some of his contemporaries, but the proportion of actual folk-melodies, as distinguished from original themes showing folk influence, in his total output is probably higher than Borodin's. The works written about the period 1871–3, when he was more or less allied with the Mighty Handful—the operas *The Oprichnik* and *Vakula the Smith*, the First String Quartet and the Second Symphony —are particularly full of such borrowings from 'the people'. But throughout his life he was always willing to use a folk-tune if it served his purpose.

With regard to the Russian *element* in my compositions, I can tell you that it has not infrequently happened that I have sat down to compose, with the deliberate intention of employing some folk-song or other that has taken my fancy. Sometimes (as, for instance, in the finale of our Symphony [the Fourth]) this happened of its own accord, quite unexpectedly. As regards the Russian element in general in my music, *i.e.* the instances of melody and harmony originating in folk-song, this is the result of the facts that I grew up in the backwoods, filling myself from earliest childhood with the inexplicable beauty of the characteristic traits of Russian folk-music, and that I passionately love the Russian element in all its manifestations, that, in short, I am *Russian* in the fullest sense of the word.[1]

Without denying the considerable quantity of Tchaïkovsky's music that does show the influence of folk-song traits (e.g. in *Onegin* the reapers' music, the nurse's song, the shepherd's pipe at dawn—always supposing that these are not genuine folk-tunes that I have failed to identify), I feel that Tchaïkovsky here exaggerates this influence. The folk-song idiom never really permeated his own musical thought; the second subject of the finale of the Third Symphony—a quite characterless tune with just one bar based on a characteristic folk-motive—is typical. Consequently, when he quotes an actual folk-melody the quotation rather draws attention to itself as such; it does not quite match his own natural melodic style.

What *are* the characteristics of his own melodic style, then? They are important, for, as we have seen, they must contain the essence of Tchaïkovsky's art: this warm, spontaneous, clear-cut lyrical melody that to him was almost the be-all and end-all of music. Think of a few typical Tchaïkovsky melodies: the horn tune near the end of Tatyana's letter song in *Onegin*, the opening of the B flat minor Piano Concerto, the love theme in *Romeo and Juliet*, the *piangendo* melody in G flat major in the slow movement of the E flat minor Quartet. Besides their warm spontaneity of feeling—they are all obviously genuine *Einfälle*, as the Germans call it—and their clear definition, they have something else in common: they are decidedly convolute in outline, marked by leaps rather than steps, moving boldly up and down like handwriting full of character. There is nothing quite like those particular melodies, and the dozens of others like them that occur throughout Tchaïkovsky's work, in the rest of music. They are, I suggest, the secret of his musical individuality, his real contribution to our art. One finds other recurrent types of melody in his work, of course. Compare, for instance, two themes from *Onegin* (*a*) and

[1] Letter to Nadezhda von Meck, 5 March, 1878.

The Queen of Spades (*b*) with the opening of the finale of the Sixth
Symphony (*c*):

But they are not peculiar to Tchaïkovsky; the melodies just quoted, for
instance, would not sound out of place in many of the French operas
of the 1860s, 70s and 80s.

In each case this rather weak and sentimental melodic shape is associated with nothing less than the idea of death. The 'coming day' brings
death to Lensky—and he feels forebodings. The complete words of the
passage from *The Queen of Spades* are as follows in Rosa Newmarch's
translation:

> Thou shalt die when a third man, impell'd by despair,
> Shall strive from thy bosom the secret to tear
> Of three cards!

And recent research has shown beyond reasonable doubt that 'death' was
the secret programmatic idea at the back of the finale of the *Pathétique*.

The fact is that, wonderful as his flow of melodic inspiration was,
Tchaïkovsky over-tapped it by his habit of 'working like a cobbler, day
in, day out, and often to order', as he put it. Every period of his career is
marked by a quantity of work inferior in inspiration though seldom perfunctory in craftsmanship. And towards the end of his life he began to
subject his melodic inspiration to yet another strain: that of more definite emotional expressiveness, the almost extra-musical expressiveness—
struggling for the precision of words—which I have pointed out in the
passage in the slow movement of the Fifth Symphony. Up to 1877, the
year of *Onegin* and the Fourth Symphony (and that disastrous marriage
which was surely the real turning-point in Tchaïkovsky's inner life), his
melodies are no more precisely expressive than, say, Borodin's; they
spring from the impulse to sing rather than from the desire to write
musical autobiography. Side by side with this striving for emotional
precision came a falling-off in the purely musical quality of the invention.
The Bizet-like melody in the Fifth Symphony (1888) is far more commonplace and less individual than the love theme of *Romeo and Juliet* (1870).

The second subject of the first movement of the *Pathétique* (1893) is banal by comparison with the opening of the B flat minor Concerto (1875) or the G flat melody from the Third Quartet (1876).

The skill with which Tchaïkovsky dressed up his melodic ideas is as striking as his failure to build them into large-scale instrumental forms. Except when he writes for the piano, his *facture* is usually irreproachable. Of the easy assurance of his part-writing I have already spoken; of his mastery of orchestration, garish though it is at times, there is no need to speak. But something must be said of his harmony, which was often commonplace, sometimes spicy, as in *Francesca*, and not without individual traits. He himself told Mme. von Meck that 'every melodic idea brings its own inevitable harmony', and it is quite true that with him melody and harmony play into each other's hands more frequently than with most Russian composers. (With the Mighty Handful harmony always seems inessential to the original idea, a mere support or decoration.) The pull of appoggiaturas and suspensions, for instance, is frequently felt in Tchaïkovsky's melody. But his harmonic thinking is curiously limited. He feels the great tidal pulls of the tonal system as little as the members of the Handful. He is conscious only of the more limited forces of gravitation within the key. Typical Tchaïkovskian harmony more often than not consists of a comparatively short progression of apparently complicated chords gravitating towards tonic or dominant, more often the latter (introduction to *Onegin*, opening of the finale of the *Pathétique* Symphony.) A favourite harmonic device of his was the simple alternation of two chords. The ninth variation in the Trio is almost entirely based on two chords; everyone will remember the poetic effects Tchaïkovsky produces in this way in *Romeo and Juliet* and the first movement of the B flat minor Concerto; and it is hardly an exaggeration to say that the harmonic germ of the whole of the first movement of the Fifth Symphony consists of the alternation of the minor tonic chord with the subdominant. This last, a peculiarly 'weary' effect, frequently occurs in Tchaïkovsky, the subdominant chord being sometimes the simple triad or inversion, as in Hermann's despairing song in the finale of Act I of *The Queen of Spades*, sometimes with the added sixth (introduction to scene 6 of *The Queen of Spades*, in which Liza commits suicide, and introduction to the duel scene in *Onegin*).

It would be easy to continue the catalogue of Tchaïkovsky's peculiarities of harmony and melody to much greater length; but my object here has been, not a full technical discussion of Tchaïkovsky's style—which would need a book rather than an essay—but a rationalisation and statement in precise terms of my own very mixed feelings about Tchaïkovsky's music. For where music is concerned 'precise' terms usually mean technical terms.   1940

IX—TCHAÏKOVSKY'S OPERAS

It would certainly be inaccurate to speak of Tchaïkovsky as an operatic composer who wrote symphonies and other instrumental music in his spare time. Yet that view of his work as a whole would be no more badly out of focus than the popular one: that he was an instrumental composer who composed an opera or two. Tchaïkovsky wrote six symphonies—seven if you count *Manfred*—but ten operas, and if the non-symphonic instrumental works are thrown into one of the scales we can still put the incidental music for Ostrovsky's *Snow Maiden* and for *Hamlet* (to say nothing of the three ballets) into the other. Even some of the instrumental works, e.g. *Francesca da Rimini*, originated in opera-projects. 'To refrain from writing operas is, in its way, heroism,' wrote Tchaïkovsky in 1885. 'I don't possess this heroism, and the stage with all its tawdry brilliance none the less attracts me.' From July 1854, when, barely fourteen, he wrote to the now almost forgotten poet, V. I. Olkhovsky, about a libretto for a one-act comic-lyric opera, *Hyperbole*—a work which he was certainly quite incapable of composing at that age[1]—to his death nearly forty years later, when he was considering the operatic possibilities of one of George Eliot's *Scenes of Clerical Life* (*The Sad Fortunes of the Rev. Amos Barton*), the spell of the stage was never broken, the longing to succeed on it never stilled. In addition to the ten libretti which he actually set, he began or at least considered no fewer than twenty others. And although of the ten operas he completed some failed to satisfy even himself and only two have won much success in the world, they embody an enormous mass of music far too beautiful and too interesting to be passed heedlessly by. Moreover, Tchaïkovsky's search for subjects, his views on their nature and treatment, his work on libretti, throw penetrating light on his creative personality.

The early fascination of the stage is easily accounted for. In the years of Tchaïkovsky's impressionable boyhood opera—and Italian opera at that —was the only kind of music that flourished in St Petersburg. The sole chance of hearing symphonic music was at the Sunday afternoon University concerts, where a mainly amateur band sight-read its way through classical scores. Even the Russian Opera was in a poor state, and the boy went there only to hear his favourite *Life for the Tsar*, itself more Italian than some of our history-book accounts would lead us to believe. But it was the Italian Opera that fascinated him; it was only there, his brother

[1] There is extant a letter in which the would-be composer tells the poet that his libretto 'completely corresponds to his wishes: there is only one thing—there are too many arias and recitatives, but very few doets [*sic*], trios, etc.'

Modest tells us, that he could hear 'a good orchestra, good choral singing and first-rate soloists'; it was there that he deepened his early love for *Don Giovanni* and *Der Freischütz* and made the exciting acquaintance of Meyerbeer, Rossini, Donizetti, Bellini and Verdi. And these Italian sympathies were considerably strengthened by the influence of the Neapolitan singing-master Piccioli, who acknowledged no music but that of the last four of those masters and held Beethoven and Glinka in equal contempt. Modest does his best to minimise Piccioli's influence but has to admit it as one of the reasons why 'Peter Ilyich at that time preferred operatic music to symphonic and not only took little interest in the latter but even regarded it somewhat disdainfully.' In considering Tchaïkovsky's career as an opera-composer all this must be kept well in mind. He began it— and ended it—as a follower of the traditions of Verdi and Meyerbeer and Glinka. Though more than a quarter of a century younger than Wagner, he was—apart from his general dislike of Wagner's music—not interested in 'music drama' or operatic reform. Though a contemporary and companion of Dargomïzhsky and Mussorgsky, he had no use for operatic realism: 'If the quest for realism in opera is carried to its ultimate conclusion, then you will inevitably arrive at a complete negation of opera,' he said, apropos of Dargomïzhsky's *Stone Guest*. He was content to take, and leave, the conventions of Victorian opera as he found them.

He once stated his very simple aesthetics of opera to Nadezhda von Meck (letter of 27 November, 1879):

> In composing an opera, the author must constantly think of the stage, i.e., not forget that the theatre needs not only melodies and harmonies but action to hold the attention of the theatre-goer who has come to hear *and see*—finally, that the style of theatre music must correspond to the style of scene-painting: simple, clear and colourful. Just as a picture by Meissonier would lose all its charm if it were put on the stage, so would rich music, full of harmonic subtleties, lose a great deal in the theatre, for there the listener needs sharply drawn melodies against a transparent harmonic background. In my *Voevoda*, however, I was mainly concerned with filigree-work and quite forgot the stage and all its conditions.

And he went on to state yet another reason for his persistent pursuit of operatic success:

> The stage often paralyses the composer's musical inspiration, so that symphonic and chamber music stand far higher than operatic music. A symphony or sonata imposes on me no limitations; on the other hand opera possesses the advantage that it gives the possibility to speak in the musical language of the masses. An opera may be given forty times in one season, a symphony perhaps once in ten years.

At the same time, 'despite all the seductions of opera, I write a symphony, sonata or quartet with infinitely greater pleasure'. Again, writing on the same theme to the same correspondent six years later (letter of 27 September, 1885), he says:

I am *pleased* by your supercilious attitude to opera. You are right in disapproving this really *false type of art*. But there is something irrepressible that attracts all composers to opera: it is that it alone gives you the means to communicate with the *masses* of the public. My *Manfred* will be played once or twice, then laid aside for Heaven knows how long, and no one but the handful of connoisseurs who go to symphony concerts will know it. Opera, and opera alone, makes you friends with people, makes your music familiar to the real public, makes you the property not merely of separate little circles but—with luck—of the whole nation. I don't think there is anything reprehensible in striving for this, i.e., it wasn't vanity that guided Schumann when he wrote *Genoveva* or Beethoven when he composed his *Fidelio*, but a natural impulse to broaden the circle of their hearers, to act on the hearts of the greatest possible number of people. It isn't just a matter of pursuing external effects, but of choosing subjects of artistic value, interesting and touching the quick.

'Touching the quick': that was Tchaïkovsky's vital test for an opera subject. It must be concerned with strong human emotions. Twice in his early days (1869) he toyed with fantastic subjects, *Undine* and a *Mandragora* of which we know very little, but he never returned to them. In the summer of 1891 he was offered a fantastic and exotic libretto, *Vatanabe*, by Karl Waltz, the principal machinist and scene-painter of the Bolshoy Theatre, Moscow,[1] and a letter to Waltz expresses his views on a genre that has been cultivated with great success by other Russian masters:

I have read *Vatanabe* with the liveliest satisfaction. The subject is charming, in the highest degree poetic, and at the same time effective. I am ready to write music for it with the greatest pleasure, but on the following conditions. *Vatanabe* will be a *fairy ballet*, not an *opera ballet*.[2] I absolutely refuse to acknowledge that indefinite and unsympathetic form of art known as *opera ballet*. For one thing: either my characters will *sing* or they will *mime*. That they should do both is absolutely unthinkable. As an opera *Vatanabe* is not a suitable subject for me, since I tolerate a fantastic element in opera only in so far as it

[1] Author of a fascinating book of reminiscences, *Sixty-five Years in the Theatre*, Moscow and Leningrad, 1928.

[2] A hybrid genre, of which Rimsky-Korsakov's *Mlada*, which in 1891 had been finished but not yet produced, is the outstanding example.

doesn't get in the way of the doings of real, simple people with their simple human sufferings and feelings. But make the *Sun Prince* sing I emphatically cannot. Only human beings can sing—or, if you like, angels and demons mixing with humans on the human plane. Moreover, *Vatanabe and Ga-tani and Nao-Shik* are for me essentially beings outside the real world, and I should find it decidedly difficult to depict them properly by other than *symphonic* means. However, I regard *Vatanabe* as an excellent *ballet* subject and I am prepared to write music for this unusually well-chosen idea to the best of my ability. . . .

Again, to A. F. Fedotov, who offered him a *Prisoner of Chillon* libretto in February 1892, he wrote:

I cannot write music with love and enthusiasm for any subject, however effective, if the characters do not compel my lively sympathy, if I do not love them, *pity* them, as living people love and *pity*. . . .

And one other interesting point:

Finally, it is no slight objection that in general I avoid foreign subjects, since I know and embrace only the Russian man, the Russian girl or woman. Medieval dukes and knights and ladies captivate my imagination but not my *heart*, and where the heart is not touched—there can't be any music.[1]

Hence his rejection of such subjects as S. A. Rachinsky's *Raimond Lully*, de Vigny's *Cinq-Mars* and Konstantin Shilovsky's *Ephraim*; hence his failure with *Die Jungfrau von Orleans*.

Deep human emotion, then, was the first requisite, and *Romeo and Juliet* delighted him, 'for in it is love, love, love. . . .' Not that love was the only emotion he recognised as suitable: 'I need', he wrote to Stasov rejecting the latter's suggestion of an opera based on *Cinq-Mars*, 'a subject in which a single dramatic motive predominates, for example, love (whether maternal or sexual makes no difference), jealousy, ambition, patriotism . . .' (letter of 8 April, 1877). At the same time he recognised that, while operatic subjects and characters must be broad and simple in conception, the simplicity must not be extreme. Among his reasons for turning down the idea of an opera on Pushkin's short novel, *The Captain's Daughter*, was that 'the heroine, Mariya Ivanovna, is lacking in interest and character; she is a faultlessly good and honest girl and nothing else, and that isn't enough for music'. Again: 'I was tempted above all

[1] Compare his judgments on *Aïda* and *Parsifal* respectively: 'I must have people, not dolls. The feelings of an Egyptian princess, a Pharaoh and some crazy Nubian girl are outside my knowledge and comprehension' (letter to S. I. Taneyev, 2 January, 1878). 'Lord, how boring and—despite the genius and mastery—how false—*nonsens*—all this miraculous stuff is!' (letter to his brother Modest, 11 September, 1884).

by the last-century setting and by the contrast between the gentry in European costumes on one side and Pugachev and his wild rabble on the other. But a single contrast isn't much for an opera subject: one must have living characters, touching situations.' On the other hand, he found the subject as a whole 'too broken up and demanding too many conversations, explanations and actions unsuited to musical treatment'.

Operatic action must be not only clear-cut but strong and swift. 'In the ordinary drama it is always possible to keep the interest alive by little scenes of social habits (*bĭtovĭmi stsenkami*) or by brilliant dialogue—in opera (where this holds good only to a certain extent) speed and conciseness of action are indispensable, or the composer will never have the power to write—or the audience to listen to the end', he wrote to Shpazhinsky, the librettist of his *Sorceress*. Musset's *Lorenzaccio, André del Sarto* and *Les Caprices de Marianne*, though the subjects had attracted him, were finally turned down on the grounds of 'absence of dramatic action' and 'profusion of philosophising'. One must go straight into action. He asks Stasov, who was rather unwillingly preparing an *Othello* libretto for him (Stasov considered the subject 'decidedly unsuited' to Tchaïkovsky's talents and character), to cut out the first two street scenes and start the action straight away in the council-chamber: 'Brabantio rushes in and announces Desdemona's disappearance.' Again: 'It seems to me that the mutual relations of the characters must be made clear to the spectator down to the smallest details in the very first act, in Venice.' Superfluous characters must be done away with and essential points in the action simplified and underlined: 'Cannot Bianca be dispensed with in Act IV and the handkerchief scene be arranged without her; for instance, couldn't Iago bring in the handkerchief? Is such a departure from Shakespeare possible? . . . I should be glad if Bianca didn't exist.' And the whole business of the handkerchief 'ought to be made much more noticeable and in stronger relief'. In the case of Shpazhinsky's *Sorceress* Tchaïkovsky had peculiar difficulties, for Shpazhinsky was not merely the librettist but the author of the original drama and tended to cling rather determinedly to inessential lines and scenes. The composer has to tell him, for instance, that 'after the Third Act, i.e. the scene of "Kuma" and the young Prince, where the drama has reached its culminating point and is ripe for the catastrophe, it is impossible to drag out two more whole vast acts, at any rate it's impossible in opera.' Considering that Tchaïkovsky was such a sound theorist on operatic technique, it is surprising—though a cynic might say it is not surprising—that he was not more successful in its practice.

It is possible that Tchaïkovsky's first essay in opera was inspired by Pushkin's *Boris Godunov*; at any rate we know from a letter of Laroche's, written in January 1866, that he had composed a 'scene from *Boris*'.

(It was the scene between the Pretender and Marina by the fountain.) But his first completed operatic score was based on *The Voevoda* by A. N. Ostrovsky (1823–86), the founder of Russian realistic drama. Ostrovsky's *Storm* was Tchaïkovsky's favourite Russian play; it inspired one of his earliest orchestral overtures and roused the desire to write an opera on it. *The Voevoda* was published in January 1865 and produced in St Petersburg on 28 April (10 May) of the same year, when Tchaïkovsky probably saw it and Mussorgsky set the lullaby from it. (It was not very successful and Ostrovsky withdrew it; twenty years later he remodelled it as *Dream on the Volga* in which form it provided the subject of an opera by Arensky.) In January 1866 Tchaïkovsky moved to Moscow; he seems very soon to have made Ostrovsky's acquaintance there, for on 8/20 November he informed his brother Anatol that 'there is hope that Ostrovsky himself will write me a libretto on *The Voevoda*'. Ostrovsky actually did so, the composer received the First Act, and promptly set to work. Then by some extraordinary mischance he mislaid the libretto and, after a vain search, had to ask Ostrovsky to write it out again and to send him the remaining acts. (The five acts, and prologue, of the original play were reduced to four, and later to three, acts.) This Ostrovsky goodnaturedly agreed to do, but he was busy with other matters.

He reconstructed the First Act from memory, and three months later sent the first scene of Act II—but nothing more, except the words of Marya's song in Act II, scene 2, the melody of which Tchaïkovsky noted down from the singing of a peasant woman at Kuntsevo, near Moscow. The composer had to write the rest of the libretto himself and condensed the Third and Fourth Acts into the present Third. He completed the music of the Third Act (as originally planned) by the end of November, began the orchestration of the Third Act in February 1868, and finished the whole score in Paris in June. Rehearsals in the Moscow theatre began in September, with a view to production in October, but the visit of an Italian company necessitated a postponement until early in the next year.

At the first performance (30 January/11 February) *The Voevoda* 'went very satisfactorily', Tchaïkovsky told his brother Modest, 'despite the very banal libretto, it had a most brilliant success'. But the critics were not altogether enthusiastic and Tchaïkovsky was deeply wounded by his friend Laroche's article in the *Sovremennaya letopis* (February 9): 'Mr. Tchaïkovsky's music, oscillating between the German (predominant) and the Italian styles, is completely lacking in any Russian quality . . . Tchaïkovsky's opera is rich in separate musical beauties. But in the general course of the drama it reveals the composer's limited ability to adapt himself to the different problems of word and situation, the absence of any Russian national element and inability or, rather, unwillingness to subordinate the orchestra to the voices and to use the latter not for egoistic, virtuosic aims but in accordance with the demands of the poetic sense.' However much Tchaïkovsky may have resented all this at the time, he himself criticised the work much more severely in later years and at some time destroyed the score.[1]

Laroche's accusation of non-Russianness was directed solely at Tchaïkovsky's melodic invention: 'From time to time in *The Voevoda* Russian folk-songs appear, which the composer takes as themes for broad development and treats with indubitable taste. But these songs reveal all the more the non-national nature of all the remaining numbers.' It is indeed possible that the number of folk-songs introduced in Ostrovsky's original play (arranged for the Petersburg production by Vladimir Kashperov, who also based on opera on Ostrovsky's *Storm*) may have played a part in attracting Tchaïkovsky to it as an operatic subject. Ostrovsky was an enthusiast for Russian folk-music, which he knew very well and he actually gave Tchaïkovsky the song 'Na more utushka' on which the opening chorus of the opera is based. 'I remember that I did not substantially change it,' Tchaïkovsky told Rimsky-Korsakov years afterwards,[2] 'but only monotonised it, since I very well remember that he had beautified it with a sharp leading-note. Where Ostrovsky himself noted down "Utushka" I don't know. I suppose he remembered it from childhood.'

Unfortunately, too many of these essentially Russian features—folk-songs and folk-customs, the depiction of a whole way of life—which are the life-breath of Ostrovsky's plays, had to be excised from *The Voevoda* in the process of cutting it down to a libretto, and when these essential 'inessentials' had been removed, nothing was left but a conventional melodrama about the misdeeds of a voevoda (provincial governor) in an unspecified town on the Volga in the middle of the seventeenth century. He is betrothed to Praskovya, the elder daughter of a rich merchant, Vlas Dyuzhoy; the younger daughter, Marya, is in love with a young noble named Bastryukov. In Act I the voevoda, Shaligin, visiting Dyuzhoy

---

[1] In the 1920s S. S. Popov, searching in the archives of the Bolshoy Theatre, discovered the orchestral parts (except that for the harp), the chorus parts and five of the solo parts; and with the aid of further materials he reconstructed the score. Yet this score was apparently never published. The reconstruction, from the same sources, which was produced at the Little Opera Theatre, Leningrad, on 28 September, 1949, was said to be the work of Paul Lamm—with the gaps in the vocal parts filled by Lamm himself, Asafiev (who was said to have had a hand in the Popov reconstruction) and Shebalin. In 1953 this Lamm score was published (full score in three volumes, and vocal score) in the complete edition of Tchaïkovsky's works.

[2] Letter of 7 September, 1876 (*Literaturnïe proizvedeniya*, VI, p. 67). Rimsky-Korsakov wished to include the song in his *Sbornik russkikh narodnïkh pesen*, Op. 24, where it appears (with Tchaïkovsky's harmonisation) as No. 89; its first bar is echoed in one of the themes of *Tsar Saltan*. It appears as No. 23 in Tchaïkovsky's own *50 russkikh narodnïkh pesen*, for piano duet, on which he was working in 1868.

happens to see Marya, prefers her to her sister, and carries her off by force. The first scene of Act II is laid in Bastryukov's house; to him comes a young townsman, Roman Dubrovin, with a tale of another of the voevoda's misdeeds—two years before Shaligin had ruined and outlawed him and carried off his beautiful wife Olyona. The next day the voevoda and his servants are going on a pilgrimage and Dubrovin suggests that they should take advantage of his absence to rescue the girls. The second scene shows Olyona bringing the instructions for the escape to Marya. Act III shows the escape. The girls descend the ladder safely, but the reunited lovers delay too long; the voevoda returns unexpectedly with his servants and seizes them. All seems lost. But a *deus ex machina* appears: a new voevoda sent from Moscow to supersede Shaligin. A parallel with *Entführung* is succeeded by a parallel with *Fidelio*.

Tchaïkovsky's music is only conventionally dramatic; it embodies very little genuine characterisation. But Laroche's criticism that it is non-Russian is astonishing; while only three identifiable folk-songs are introduced, a great deal of Tchaïkovsky's own music is saturated in the folk-idiom and could easily be mistaken for genuine folk-music—as perhaps Laroche did mistake it. And however severe Tchaïkovsky's criticism may have been in later years, he cannot have thought too ill of his score, seeing that he used so much of it again in later works: mainly in *The Oprichnik* (1872) but also in the ballet *Swan Lake* (1876) and the *Overture 1812* (1880).

Act I begins with the already mentioned folksong chorus 'Na more utushka', which was transferred bodily to Act I of *The Oprichnik*; even the little dialogue between Marya and her maid Nedviga, which interrupts it, became a dialogue between Natalya and her maid Zakharevna. In the next number the passage from page 48, bar 2[1] to the end was similarly transferred to the later opera (pp. 44–53), and even No. 3, for Bastryukov, his attendant Rezvy and his chorus of servants was used *in toto* for No. 4 of *The Oprichnik*—Andrey, his friend Basmanov and chorus of oprichniks (imperial bodyguards)—with merely octave transposition of Rezvy's bass part for Basmanov (alto). The latter section, *andante non troppo*, of the love duet (No. 5) was itself a borrowing from Tchaïkovsky's leaving exercise from the Petersburg Conservatoire in 1865, a setting of parts of a Russian translation of Schiller's 'An die Freude': the duet in G flat was adapted from a quartet setting of 'Deine Zauber binden wieder' in G. In No. 6 an agitated two-bar passage, used again on p. 131, was thought worth using again in *The Oprichnik* (p. 71), and the opening of No. 7—a conversation between the voevoda and Dyuzhoy over a very folksong-like orchestral background—became the opening scene of the later opera

[1] References are to the vocal scores of *The Voevoda* and *The Oprichnik* in the *Polnoe sobranie sochineniy*, Vols. 1 (supp.) and 34.

(conversation between Zhemchuzhny and Molchan Mitkov) though the music necessarily takes a different course later. The orchestral part of No. 7, from page 111, bar 17, to page 116, bar 10, is taken from a Concert Overture in C minor composed in 1866,[1] the autograph of which shows Tchaïkovsky's pencil sketches for the added voice-parts. In the finale of Act I the outstanding passage is a beautiful folksong-like *adagio* sung by Bastryukov and partly accompanied by a male voice chorus of his servants; this was transferred with different words to Act IV of *The Oprichnik*, where it is sung by Andrey and repeated—not accompanied—by a chorus of oprichniks (see Ex. 7, *infra*); the orchestration was, as usual, unchanged.

The music of the Introduction to Act II is taken from the opening of the Concert Overture in C minor—the first 14 bars note for note; indeed, the same music, in E minor, had originally opened the still earlier overture to Ostrovsky's *Storm*. But this *andante* is followed by a *moderato* on yet another folksong-like theme, heard a number of times later in association with Dubrovin. Bastryukov's melody of unhappy love in this scene (p. 192) served with different words, for Andrey's melody of unhappy love in Act II of *The Oprichnik* (p. 110), and Bastryukov's dialogue with Dubrovin (p. 206), at the end of the first scene of the Act was easily transformed into the end of Andrey's duet with his mother (p. 116) by octave transposition of Dubrovin's baritone part to the mezzo-soprano register, changes in the note-values of the recitative to fit the new words, and replacement of the Dubrovin theme in the orchestral part (first flute and first oboe in octaves) by another theme played by the same instruments. The second scene of Act II opens with an orchestral 'Entr'acte and Dances of the Serving-Maids', a re-scored version of the *Characteristic Dances* of 1865, with which Tchaïkovsky had achieved his earliest public success. Marya's song in No. 5 is based on the already mentioned folk-melody which Tchaïkovsky had noted at Kuntsevo in September 1867:

Ex. 1

Cantabile

So - lo - vush-ka v dub - ro - vush-ke grom - ko——— svi - shchet, tak grom-ko svi - shchet.

though this provided only the first 12 bars; Tchaïkovsky composed the continuation—and a remarkably inappropropriate coloratura cadenza. All this, with the orchestral substance of the preceding recitative, was given to Natalya in the First Act of *The Oprichnik*. No. 7, a duet for Marya and Olyona, is based on a theme used again in the entr'acte before Act III, a composition which a few years later—with no change except the substitution of F trumpets for B flat trumpets—became the entr'acte before Act IV of *Swan Lake* (1876). No. 8, in which the duet is continued,

[1] *Polnoe sobranie*, Vol. 21.

brings a still more familiar melody: the second subject of the *allegro* of the *1812 Overture*:

The last of the *Oprichnik* borrowings from *The Voevoda* was made from the finale of this Second Act: the folk-song khorovod of the girls, which is given a more effective ending in the later work (end of Act I), and the 19-bar passage preceding it—in which Nedviga (Zakharevna) urges them to sing and dance in accents

curiously like those of the Nurse in the earliest version of the Second Act of Mussorgsky's *Boris* (written a little later: April 1869). This passage is the only instance of transference from *The Voevoda* to *The Oprichnik* in which Tchaïkovsky felt it necessary to revise the original scoring: Nedviga's part is underlined by first violins and violas, Zakharevna's by solo clarinet and bassoon; the lay-out of the wind chords accompanying the girls' reply is altered and a triangle silenced.

Nothing from the Third Act of *The Voevoda* was transferred to *The Oprichnik*. Indeed the only passage from it—other than the already mentioned entr'acte—which Tchaïkovsky thought worth rescuing in another score was the orchestral *andante* (p. 283) to which the two pairs of re-united lovers throw themselves into each others' arms; this was transferred in its entirety, except for the final transition, to *Swan Lake* where it opens the last scene (No. 29): the Prince rushes in to embrace his true love, Odette (a close dramatic parallel). Tchaïkovsky did make one characteristic change in the scoring of the first seven bars for *Swan Lake*: whereas in *The Voevoda* the melody was played only by the violins, while violas and cellos had pizzicato arpeggios, in *Swan Lake* the melody is given to all the strings except double-basses, in octaves, and the pizzicato is replaced by powerful harp chords. In the same passage the oboe and clarinet parts in the repeated woodwind chords are readjusted for three bars, and B flat clarinets are substituted for A clarinets throughout. Otherwise the two scores are identical. It is difficult to believe that Tchaïkovsky remembered every detail of this passage and of the preceding entr'acte; hence we may assume with some confidence that the full score of *The Voevoda* was not destroyed until after 1876—perhaps not until after 1880, when *1812* was composed.

If *The Voevoda* had bad luck[1] its successor *Undine* had worse; for it never even reached the stage. After toying for a while with a Græco-Babylonian subject from the time of Alexander the Great, offered him by Ostrovsky, Tchaïkovsky came across a ready-made libretto on the subject of La Motte Fouqué's *Undine*. Zhukovsky's beautiful translation of Fouqué's story had long been a favourite with Tchaïkovsky, and it was long believed that this libretto, made by Count F. A. Sollogub for Lvov, the composer of the Tsarist national anthem, was based on Zhukovsky; according to Alfred Loewenberg, however, Sollogub's version is a translation of a French text by the well-known libretto-monger Vernoy de Saint-Georges.[2] The action differs in some details from that of the *Undine* operas of E. T. A. Hoffmann and Albert Lortzing; for instance the striking figure of the water-spirit Kühleborn has disappeared:

Act I. Undine's foster-parents, the fisherman and his wife, in their hut. Enter the knight, Huldbrand (tenor), who tells them of his adventures in the wood. Enter Undine (soprano), with whom he falls in love, forgetting his betrothed, Berthalda. The lovers embrace and go out together into the stormy night.

Act II. The Duke, Berthalda's father, is naturally enraged with Huldbrand, but the knight has now returned to his first love and appears at her birthday festivities. Undine also appears and, having interrupted the rejoicings with a ballad revealing that Berthalda is really the daughter of the fisherfolk, leaps into the Danube.

Act III. Huldbrand, once more in love with Undine, bewails her loss as he waits before his marriage to Berthalda. The bridal procession is interrupted first by the Duke, then by the fisherman, each of whom has been visited by Undine's spirit and persuaded to forbid the marriage. Berthalda insists on going on with it, but Undine herself rises from a well and effectually disperses the procession. Final love-duet for Undine and the knight, after which he dies and she is transformed into a spring.

[1] Tchaïkovsky returned to Ostrovsky's play many years later when at the dramatist's request he wrote an orchestral 'melodrama' to accompany the monologue of the Domovoy (or 'house-goblin'), a character he had excluded from his operatic version, at the end of Act II. The music was used for a production of the play at the Maly Theatre, Moscow, on 19/31 January, 1886, but was long believed lost. In 1932 it was discovered in the Central Music Library of the State Academic Theatres in Leningrad; it consists of 45 bars of lyrical music in G minor, scored for two flutes, oboe, clarinet, bassoon, harp and strings (*Polnoe sobranie sochineniy*, Vol. 14).

[2] *Annals of Opera*, Cambridge, 1943. Lvov's *Undine* was produced in St Petersburg in 1848.

Tchaïkovsky set this farrago of romantic nonsense with tremendous enthusiasm; he began the composition in January 1869, finished it in April and completed the orchestration in July of the same year. The score was hurriedly despatched to St Petersburg, where it was shelved for nearly a year on one pretext after another and then rejected by the opera committee of the Imperial Theatre, the same committee which a few months later also rejected the original version of Mussorgsky's *Boris*. As with *The Voevoda*, Tchaïkovsky afterwards used some of the best numbers in other works—thus the fateful bridal procession of Act III became the *andantino marziale* of the Second Symphony, while one of the love-duets for Undine and Huldbrand (probably that in the last Act) is now familiar to everyone as Odette's *adagio* in Act II of *Swan Lake*—and then burned the score. Thanks to the circumstance that five numbers from Act I were given a concert performance in Moscow in March 1870, and so were preserved in the archives of the Bolshoy Theatre, we still know something of the *Undine* music in its original form. These five numbers were:

(1) Introduction to the opera;
(2) Undine's song, 'Streamlet, my brother';
(3) Mixed chorus (*allegro*): 'Help, help! Our stream is raging';
(4) Duet for Undine and Huldbrand: 'O happiness, O blessed moment';
(5) Finale for soloists and mixed chorus: 'O hours of death.'[1]

The last three had been forgotten till Popov unearthed them in 1920; he also found that the Introduction had been used unchanged as the Introduction to Ostrovsky's *Snow Maiden* when Tchaïkovsky wrote his incidental music to that play and that Undine's song, re-orchestrated and somewhat altered, had been turned to account for Lel's first song in the same play. (In *Undine* Tchaïkovsky had made novel and effective use of the piano as an orchestral instrument in the accompaniment to this aria.)

Undiscouraged by this failure with a fantastic-romantic subject, Tchaïkovsky turned to a curiously parallel one in S. A. Rachinsky's *Mandragora*, a story of a knight who finds the magic plant in his castle garden, uproots it and finds it transformed into a lovely girl. She follows him, dressed as a page; he falls in love with another woman; and Mandragora is changed back again into a flower. Again a knight who falls in love with a faëry being, is unfaithful to her, and drives her back to her native element! Indeed, the parallel is so close that one wonders whether Tchaïkovsky was not already playing with the idea of putting some of the *Undine* music to fresh use. But the only fresh music composed for *Mandragora* was a 'chorus of flowers and insects' bearing the date '27 Decem-

[1] Undine's song and the finale in the *Polnoe sobranie sochineniy*, 2, Moscow and Leningrad, 1950.

ber, 1869', and orchestrated during the first fortnight of 1870; this chorus was afterwards performed several times as a concert-piece[1] and won the praise of critics as opposed as Balakirev and Laroche. Long before this, however, Tchaïkovsky had, on Kashkin's advice, abandoned the idea of the opera. In January 1870 Rachinsky began another libretto for him, *Raimond Lully*, but by February his choice had definitely fallen on a tragedy, *The Oprichnik*, by a well-known historical novelist, Ivan Ivanovich Lazhechnikov (1792–1868), and he proceeded to work out his own libretto. Yet, the choice once made, little further was done for a whole year; the non-performance of *Undine* seems to have damped Tchaïkovsky's interest in his new opera and he does not appear to have worked at it much till nearly the end of 1870; it was not finished till April 1872.

The Oprichnik was luckier than *Undine*. After seven months' delay it was unanimously accepted by the opera committee and produced at the Maryinsky Theatre, St Petersburg, on 12/24 April, 1874. And although the composer at once felt a profound dislike for the work and would gladly have suppressed it,[2] it is by no means as bad as one might therefore suppose.

The 'oprichniks' were the dreaded bodyguard of Ioann IV, popularly known as Ivan the Terrible—aristocratic rakes and ruffians in the dress of monks—and Lazhechnikov's play is just such another drama of the reign of that unpleasant monarch as Mey's *Maid of Pskov* which Rimsky-Korsakov had just turned into an opera (produced in 1873) and his *Tsar's Bride* which attracted the same composer a quarter of a century later:

Act I. Prince Zhemchuzhny (bass) is in his garden, entertaining his friend, the elderly Molchan Mitkov (bass), to whom he promises his daughter Natalya in marriage: exeunt. Enter Natalya (soprano) with the old nurse Zakharyevna (soprano) and maids; she bemoans her fate; exeunt. Enter, roughly breaking down the fence, Natalya's true love, Andrey Morozov (tenor) and his friend, the Tsar's favourite, Basmanov (alto) with oprichniks. It appears that Zhemchuzhny has robbed Andrey and his mother of their fortune and driven them from their home; Andrey decides to join the ranks of the oprichniks in order to get his revenge; exeunt. Re-enter Natalya, mourning for her lost lover. Re-enter Zakharyevna with the maids, who sing and dance to distract her.

[1] The full score was then lost, though Glazunov made an orchestral version from the piano score in 1898, but the original full score was discovered among Nikolay Rubinstein's papers in the Moscow Conservatoire in 1912 and published nearly forty years later in the second volume of the *Sobranie sochineniy*.

[2] In later years he tried to forbid its performance but was unable to do so, having parted with all his rights to the publisher Bessel. At the time of his death he was thinking of 're-composing two-thirds of *The Oprichnik*'.

Act II. *Scene* 1. Andrey's mother, the Boyarïnya Morozova (mezzo-soprano), alone, brooding over her wrongs. Her heart is not lightened when Andrey enters and tells her of his friendship with Basmanov, whom she regards as his evil genius.

Scene 2: Andrey, before the assembled oprichniks, takes the most solemn oath to become one of their number, renouncing everything else in the world, however dear. As he does so, he sheds bitter tears—to the joy of Prince Vyazminsky (baritone), his father's old enemy.[1]

Act III. A square in Moscow; the populace complain of the doings of the oprichniks, and the old Boyarïnya is hooted after by boys who call her 'bitch' and 'she-oprichnik'. In rushes Natalya, who has run away from father and bridegroom, and throws herself into the old lady's arms. Enter Zhemchuzhny with servants in pursuit; he is about to carry off his daughter when Andrey and Basmanov appear, with a band of oprichniks. The women are rescued but are horrified to find Andrey has become an oprichnik; his mother disowns him; Basmanov suggests that the Tsar may release him from his oath.

Act IV. Wedding festivities in the Tsar's palace. Andrey is to be released from his oath and to marry Natalya; but till midnight he is still an oprichnik. Vyazminsky interrupts the festivities, with malicious joy, with the announcement that the Tsar wishes to see the bride—alone. Andrey is beside himself; in trying to save Natalya he breaks his oath. The oprichniks lead Natalya to the Tsar and Andrey to execution. The stage is empty for some time. Vyazminsky leads in the old Boyarïnya, who demands to be taken to her son; from the window the Prince shows her the scene of execution; she falls dead.

In justice to Lazhechnikov it should be said that his play, however melodramatic, is marked not only by subtler character-drawing—for instance, Molchan Mitkov is shown as a noble and sympathetic figure, who renounces Natalya and even pleads for Andrey—but by a more clearly motivated action. For the weaknesses of the libretto Tchaïkovsky was himself to blame, for (as we have seen) he had the extraordinary idea of transferring to *The Oprichnik* not only a good deal of the music of *The Voevoda* but its original text as well. Up to a point there was little harm in this. One heroine lamenting her fate is very like another, one chorus of servants trying to cheer up their mistress with song and dance is like any other chorus of servants trying to cheer up their mistress with song and dance. But because Tchaïkovsky wanted to use the music of

---

[1] Vyazminsky had to be introduced in the opera in place of the Tsar himself, whose representation was forbidden by the censor. (The censor also took out some lines from Basmanov's part in Act I, describing the oprichniks' nocturnal amusements.) Oddly enough, Ivan had been allowed to appear and sing the year before in *The Maid of Pskov*; in *The Tsar's Bride* he was allowed to appear, but only as a mute character.

Bastryukov's entrance in Act I again for Andrey's entrance in Act I (the parallel being that each is a young lover breaking into a garden to see his sweetheart), Andrey is made to break in violently with his violent friends instead of creeping in alone and unobtrusively as in Lazhechnikov's play. Of the sixty-two pages of Act I in the vocal score of *The Oprichnik* only thirteen were new music: Basmanov's recitative and arioso, with Andrey's reply, and Natalya's fine arioso in G flat, 'O wild wind, carry to my love the tale of my bitter sorrow', one of those rich, passionately singing melodies that bear the unmistakable mark of Tchaïkovsky's invention:

Ex. 4

Yet if unmistakably Tchaïkovskian, it is not altogether unrelated to a famous passage in the same key in the Fourth Act of *Les Huguenots*, Raoul's 'Tu l'as dit; oui, tu m'aimes'. That places *The Oprichnik* pretty accurately; it is Meyerbeer translated into Russian. The subject—the crude drama with one 'strong' situation after another—would have delighted Meyerbeer. And the operatic convention that Tchaïkovsky adopted to clothe it in music is not very different from the convention of, say, *Le Prophète*: a 'number' opera with the numbers partly broken down and linked with ariosos and the like, and the whole texture given a semblance of unity by the use of one or two reminiscence-themes (more than in Meyerbeer but hardly enough to claim comparison with Wagnerian *Leitmotive*). The two most important of these recurring themes are contrasted in the short orchestral introduction which takes the place of an overture; one is the menacing theme of the oprichniks:

Ex. 5

the other the melody in which the old Boyarïnya pleads, 'Dear son, thou wilt not leave me lonely in my bitter lot,' in the first scene of Act II:

Ex. 6

(The introduction is laid out sectionally: (*a*) conventional stormy figures and 'oprichniks' theme, D minor, (*b*) Ex. 6 in A major, with Ex. 5 breaking in, pizzicato, (*c*) the aria from the second scene of Act II, in which Andrey tells the assembled oprichniks why he wishes to become one of them, F major, (*d*) Ex. 6 in F, with Ex. 5 breaking in as before, (*e*) the music of the execution scene, Ex. 6 distorted and in diminution, (*f*) Ex. 5 transformed into D major and thundered out triumphantly.) The 'oprichniks' theme in both its minor and its major forms, and in various transformations, plays an important part throughout the last three acts. In the dramatic pause while the stage remains empty before the final catastrophe Exs. 5 and 6 are effectively combined.[1]

I have said that *The Oprichnik* is Meyerbeer translated into Russian. I must emphasise that it is very thoroughly translated. Not only are the passages transferred from *The Voevoda* almost entirely folkish;[2] not only are a number of actual folk-melodies introduced;[3] but many pages of the score are saturated with Russian folk and ecclesiastical idioms (e.g. the old Boyarïnya's great monologue at the beginning of Act II, which emphatically deserves rescue from oblivion, the various choruses of the oprichniks,[4] the wedding chorus that opens Act IV). Sometimes Tchaïkovsky spoils the intensely national flavour of his melodic line by commonplace or text-book harmonisation, at others—for instance, the beautiful B flat minor passage for Andrey, echoed by the chorus,[5] in the scene immediately following the oprichniks' dance in the last Act—the matching of Russian melody with Russian harmony is perfect and any expert might be pardoned for attributing the music to Rimsky-Korsakov or Mussorgsky-processed-by-Rimsky-Korsakov (Ex 7 on p. 132).

In *The Voevoda* and *The Oprichnik*, indeed, Tchaïkovsky stands very close to his colleagues of the Mighty Handful. Some of the girls' choruses in Act I might easily be transferred to Korsakov's *May Night*; the passage just before the end of the Act where Zakharyevna tells the girls to sing

[1] Perhaps this is the place to mention that the short orchestral prelude to Act II was composed and orchestrated by Tchaïkovsky's pupil, Vladimir Shilovsky.

[2] Mrs Newmarch's remark in *The Russian Opera* about Tchaïkovsky's 'grafting upon *The Oprichnik*, with its crying need for national colour and special treatment, a portion of the pretty Italianised music of *The Voevoda*' is so preposterous that I can only suppose she had never seen the score; as I have shown, two of these 'almost Italian' graftings were based on Russian folk-melodies.

[3] Those in the 'Dance of the Oprichniks and Women' in the last Act include Nos. 10, 17, 29, 32 and 34 of the *Fifty Russian Folk-Songs* for piano duet.

[4] Their first devout modal chorus in Act II, scene 2, has a close affinity with the introduction to the *Romeo and Juliet* overture, an affinity that is emphasised when the theme is taken up by the orchestra with a pizzicato bass moving in quavers.

[5] A passage, already used in *The Voevoda*, that Tchaïkovsky recalled almost note for note and in the same key, not only in the accompaniment to Frost's monologue in his *Snow Maiden* music but, very slightly altered and still in B flat minor, in the 'Cygnets' Dance' in Act IV of *Swan Lake*.

and dance has already been quoted in Ex. 3; as in the finale of the Second Symphony, written at about the same time, there are experiments with

Ex. 7

the whole-tone scale (cf. the passage some forty bars before the end of Act III); orchestral motives, sometimes from a previous number, are used to hold together recitative dialogue or even a vocal solo (cf. the scene between Andrey and his mother, following her monologue in Act II, and Natalya's arioso when she pleads with her father in Act III). Even the long stretches of rather watery and colourless lyricism do not finally stamp the opera as something that could not possibly have been written by one of the Handful. It is in Tchaïkovsky's conventional handling of the chorus that one feels the difference most: particularly in the choral crowd-scene that opens Act III, which stands immeasurably below not only Mussorgsky in dramatic quality but Rimsky-Korsakov in colour and raciness. The last part, *cantabile e con grandezza*, of the penultimate scene of the opera is hopelessly weak, and uncharacteristic—particularly Vyazminsky's part.

On the other hand the 'watery and colourless lyricism' is always liable to colour and thicken into that type of cantilena which is absolutely and peculiarly Tchaïkovskian. I have already quoted from Natalya's first arioso (Ex. 4). Andrey's aria in the second scene of Act II, used in the introduction to the opera, is similar but less striking. And unfortunately most of these patches of lyrical charm occur in contexts from which they could hardly be detached for concert performance, the outstanding case being the crown of the love-duet in the last Act, 'Thou art my life and light, my joy and rest,' where Tchaïkovsky salvages a theme from the (temporarily) destroyed symphonic poem *Fate*:

Ex. 8

In the same way, the G minor *andante* portion of the already mentioned penultimate scene stands out as truly Tchaïkovskian; and even such a comparatively weak passage as the *andante espressivo* of Natalya's arioso in the Third Act foreshadows one of the most memorable melodies in *Eugene Onegin* (cf. Ex. 16).

Tchaïkovsky's next stage work was not an opera but the already mentioned incidental music to his favourite Ostrovsky's 'spring tale' *Snegurochka* (*Snow Maiden*), familiar to every lover of Russian music through Rimsky-Korsakov's operatic setting (composed 1880–1 and produced early in 1882). This poetic play, packed with symbolism and Slavonic mythology and folk-lore, concerned with characters some of whom are human, some personified forces of nature, and set in the fantastic never-never kingdom of the Berendeys, is strikingly different from the prose dramas of the Moscow bourgeoisie with which Ostrovsky's name is generally associated—though there were fantastic elements in the original *Voevoda* play. For the third time Tchaïkovsky had as his subject the unhappy love of a non-mortal girl for a mortal and her final dissolution into her native element. *Snow Maiden* was a commissioned work for both poet and composer; the Bolshoy Theatre urgently needed a 'show'—a spectacle combining opera, play and ballet—just as the Maryinsky Theatre in Petersburg had needed a 'show' the previous year and thus given birth (or, rather, miscarriage) to the famous collective *Mlada* of Cui, Mussorgsky, Rimsky-Korsakov and Borodin. According to Kashkin, the whole score—nineteen numbers—was completed in three weeks during March and April 1873 (for the production on 11/23 May).

Now nineteen real numbers, not mere fanfares and the like, represent a considerable quantity of music for one play, and although the only singing characters are the shepherd Lel and the chorus (plus a monologue that is almost a monotone for Frost, and a song for the young peasant Brusilo, who has disappeared altogether from Korsakov's version) it would not have needed an enormous amount of extra work to turn the whole thing into an opera, and, according to his brother, Tchaïkovsky had some idea of doing this but was forestalled, to his intense annoyance, by Rimsky-Korsakov. But the circumstance that the same subject was set by these two masters at so nearly the same period does give the critic a chance to make some piquantly odious comparisons, the more easily as Korsakov's prologue and four acts correspond exactly to Ostrovsky's, his alterations being limited to simplifications and cuts (such as the excision of 'the fair Helen' who appears as Bermyata's wife.)

Of the five numbers Tchaïkovsky provided for the Prologue, the introduction is (as I have already told) simply the not very interesting introduction to *Undine*. But the dances and chorus of the shivering birds, Frost's monologue, the chorus of Berendeys dragging in the *maslyanitsa* (the carnival effigy), and the melodrama accompanying the *maslyanitsa's* lines, are well worth looking at—and hearing. One is almost at once plunged into the same folk-melodic ambience as in Korsakov's opera: the bird chorus, the accompaniment to the monologue, and the melodies of the carnival chorus (one of which also provides the basis of the melodrama) are all either directly borrowed or closely imitated from folk-music; the composer enumerates them with their sources in the letter to Rimsky-Korsakov already quoted on p. 122, adding 'as you see, I've altered them slightly'. And one also notes with amusement that Rimsky-Korsakov in the accompaniment to *his* bird chorus saw fit to adopt precisely the same acciaccatura 'twittering' effect as that with which Tchaïkovsky had begun his dances, that he likewise cast his bird music in naïve 2/4 rhythms, and that his *maslyanitsa* monotones pretty much as Tchaïkovsky's Frost does. And if Rimsky-Korsakov's seven-bar patterns (2 + 2 + 3) have a peculiar charm, Tchaïkovsky's bird dances are not altogether conventional either; I quote his melody beside its folk-original from Prokunin's collection:

Tchaïkovsky then opens the First Act with a delicious little pastoral duet, still folkish in flavour, for two clarinets over quiet string chords; Korsakov opens it with pastoral calls for solo horn and solo oboe. As regards Lel's first two songs the honours are even, for if Tchaïkovsky's adaptation of the rather feeble aria from *Undine* cannot compare with his rival's beautiful, almost unaccompanied, modal setting of the berry-gathering song, his treatment of the second song, 'The shepherd sings as the forest murmurs', is decidedly the more attractive. It is again modelled on a folk-song and is orchestrated in the bright, transparent, primary colours, that one associates with Rimsky-Korsakov:

It seems to have exercised some slight influence on Korsakov's A major bird chorus in the Prologue.

Neglecting Tchaïkovsky's not very interesting prelude to Act II and the melodrama for muted strings accompanying Kupava's complaint to the Tsar, based on part of the same music, we reach a particularly interesting series of parallels. First the chorus of blind gusli-players in praise of Tsar Berendey that opens the Second Act: Tchaïkovsky wrote this[1] in E minor, Aeolian, and Rimsky-Korsakov was content to do the same, though his melody has a finer spread and his use of Glinka's harp-and-piano convention to represent the guslis is more picturesque than Tchaïkovsky's simple pizzicato chords:

Tchaïkovsky's chorus of people and courtiers, though not without folkish touches, sounds square-cut and conventional beside Rimsky-Korsakov's striking unaccompanied version, but it is difficult to choose between the two introductions and opening choruses of Act III although the music is in both cases founded, in accordance with Ostrovsky's direction, on the folk-tune, 'Ay, vo pole lipon'ka' ('In the fields stands a lime tree'). It is perhaps characteristic of the two musicians that Tchaïkovsky chose a version of the tune in normal A major and harmonised it with modal cadences, while Korsakov's version is in A Mixolydian (i.e., A major with G natural). But it would be a nice point to determine which is the more authentic—and which the more 'Russian' treatment of it.

The dance of the *skomorokhi* (clowns or tumblers) presents no such problem; Rimsky-Korsakov's familiar piece has won general popularity, while Tchaïkovsky's—noisy and commonplace—has been not unjustly forgotten. Nor can either of Tchaïkovsky's settings of Lel's third song (an entirely new one was published posthumously) seriously challenge Rimsky-Korsakov's, though here again the latter has taken a hint from his predecessor in introducing the song with some capers on a solo clarinet. Brusilo's song about the beaver,[2] which Korsakov transferred to the old peasant Bakula and placed earlier in the act, does not amount to much, and the short orchestral piece which Tchaïkovsky wrote for the scene where Mizgir in the enchanted wood is led astray by the Wood Spirit, though adequate, demonstrates his marked inferiority to Rimsky-Korsakov in grotesque and fantastic conceptions. But the purely lyrical music for the Spring Fairy's granting of her daughter's wish and the chorus of flowers—Tchaïkovsky uses the same music for the prelude to Act IV—restores the balance; this is Tchaïkovsky's ground rather than

---

[1] Extending it from a nine-note folk-fragment, the original of which will be found in his *Fifty Russian Folk-Songs* (No. 14).

[2] Yet another tune from Prokunin's collection, where it appears as No. 25.

his rival's; indeed, his rival's music (9/8, A major, *andante*) seems to be slightly indebted to his own (6/8, A major, *andantino*) and one of the motives of Korsakov's Spring Fairy is a modified echo of a little bass motive in Tchaïkovsky.

The two remaining numbers of Tchaïkovsky's *Snow Maiden* music are 'Tsar Berendey's March and Chorus' and the final hymn to the sun-god Yarilo. The march corresponds not to Korsakov's 'Tsar Berendey's March' (which belongs to the Second Act) but to the opening of his finale, one of his most striking and charming pages; Tchaïkovsky's music has its own, if less original, piquancy and his tiny folk-tune trio[1] is deliciously naïve. In both cases the processional music leads without a break into the millet-sowing ritual and both composers have necessarily based their choruses on the traditional tunes associated with the words;[2] both settings are extremely effective. The two settings of the hymn to Yarilo, however, are completely different in conception; Tchaïkovsky took yet another folk-tune, 'Vo gornitse, vo svetlitse',[3] which happened to fit Ostrovsky's words, and evolved from it a most brilliant finale which has nothing in common with Rimsky-Korsakov's novel setting in 11/4 time.

To sum up: if Tchaïkovsky's *Snow Maiden* music is inferior to Rimsky-Korsakov's delightful opera, it still by no means deserves oblivion. Few of his early works are more deserving of resuscitation, and though it will obviously never be heard again in the theatre nothing would be easier than to prepare a concert suite of the best numbers.

Oddly enough, Tchaïkovsky's next opera, *Vakula the Smith*, was also challenged by a later Rimsky-Korsakov work on the same subject, though in this case the younger man, aware of the other's feelings on the subject of *Snow Maiden*, tactfully waited for his death to 'release' the subject (Gogol's story *Christmas Eve*). But the parallels between *Vakula* and Korsakov's *Christmas Eve*, though interesting, are less so than the *Snow Maiden* parallels since Korsakov wrote his own libretto while Tchaïkovsky's opera was a setting of a 'book' prepared by the poet Polonsky for Alexander Serov and then made the subject of a competition in which Tchaïkovsky, after (though not as the result of) some discreditable manœuvring, was successful. The original version of Tchaïkovsky's opera was composed and orchestrated in less than three months (early June to 21 August/2 September, 1874) and produced on the Maryinsky stage, Petersburg, on 24 November/6 December, 1876. I say 'the original version' for although *Vakula* was a favourite work of Tchaïkovsky's he recognised its shortcomings; it was 'overfilled with details, too thick in

---

[1] The tune is No. 24 in Balakirev's collection, No. 36 in Tchaïkovsky's.

[2] Rimsky-Korsakov introduces both the variants given by Balakirev (Nos. 8 and 9 of his collection; Tchaïkovsky uses No. 8 only and in a slightly altered form: cf. also No. 26 of his *Fifty Russian Folk-Songs*.

[3] Cf. No. 96 of Rimsky-Korsakov's *Hundred Russian Folk-Songs*.

scoring, insufficiently effective from the point of view of the singers . . . too musical and not theatrical enough, the harmony too chromatic. *C'est un menu surchargé de mets épicés . . . too symphonic, or even like chamber-music'*. Accordingly in February and March 1885 he undertook a drastic revision of the score—'writing completely new scenes, taking out the bad, leaving in the good, lightening the weight of the harmony', as he wrote to the singer Emiliya Pavlovskaya—and the new version was produced at the Bolshoy Theatre, Moscow, on 19/31 January, 1887, with a new title, *Cherevichki* (*The Slippers*), so odd to Western ears and so unpromising in translation that it is generally known outside Russia as *Les Caprices d'Oxane* or *Die goldene Schuhe*. The original 'comic opera in three acts' had become a 'comic-fantastic opera in four acts'—though the new Fourth Act is simply the last scene of the original Third Act; of the 484 pages of the new full score, 112 were fresh music.[1]

The action is as follows:

Act I. *Scene* 1. Moonlit, snow-covered Ukrainian village. Comic love scene between the witch Solokha (mezzo-soprano) and a devil (baritone), who has a grudge against Solokha's son, the smith Vakula (tenor). As he flies off with Solokha the devil causes a snowstorm and steals the moon so as to interfere with the young man's courtship of Oksana (soprano), daughter of the old Cossack, Chub (bass). Chub and his crony Panas (tenor) are seen blundering about in the dark.

Scene 2: Chub's hut. The coquettish Oksana mocks at Vakula's love-making. Enter Chub, so covered with snow that Vakula doesn't recognise him and throws him out. Oksana in turn drives Vakula away—and then regrets him. Enter village girls singing Christmas carols.

Act II *Scene* 1. Solokha's hut. She and the devil flirting and dancing.

---

[1] The passages inserted or completely re-written in 1885 are:

In the overture: 7 bars in the *allegro giusto*.

In Act I: The last four pages (in the vocal score) of the duet for Solokha and the devil; the dialogue of Chub and Panas in the snowstorm scene (some 25 bars were cut from the snowstorm music itself); the 45-bar *allegro non troppo* leading to Vakula's arioso; and the greater part of the music following this ariosos (i.e. practically the whole of Nos. 5, 6 and 7).

In Act II: The schoolmaster's little song, with the recitative passages preceding and following it; all but the first 24 bars of Solokha's scene with Chub; the quintet; 26 bars in the chorus at the beginning of the second scene (from the entry of the first group of youths and maids, bearing a star); the last 21 bars of this chorus; the 21-bar dialogue before Oksana's song (Ex. 13*b*) in the next number; 14 bars of choral exclamations and recitative for Vakula a little later, and minor interpolations in Oksana's part (including the brief *molto più lento* with its coloratura cadenza, and the trills at the very end of the number).

In Act III: Vakula's recitative (with echo) when he first appears with the devil in the sack; His Highness's couplets; all the music after exit of the Master of Ceremonies.

In Act IV: The *allegro vivace* chorus of peasant lads (except the first 8 bars).

A knock; the devil hides in a sack; enter another of Solokha's lovers, the *golova* or headman (bass). Another knock; the *golova* hides in another sack. The scene is repeated with the schoolmaster (tenor) and with Chub. Last of all enters Vakula, who carries the sacks away to his smithy to make more room in the hut for the Christmas festivities.

Scene 2: Carollers, among them Oksana who mockingly tells Vakula she will marry him—if he will give her the Tsaritsa's slippers. He goes off absent-mindedly with only one of the sacks, the one with the devil inside. The carollers find the other sacks—and their contents.

Act III. *Scene* 1. River-bank. The rusalkas (water-spirits) tempt the melancholy Vakula to leap into the water. The devil creeps out of the sack and nearly gets Vakula in his power, but the smith gets the better of him, leaps on his back and orders him to fly to the Tsaritsa.

Scene 2. Antechamber of a palace. Vakula flies in on the devil's back. His appearance coincides with the entrance of a band of Zaporozhtsy Cossacks who are to have audience of the Tsaritsa.

Scene 3. The throne-room, Vakula and the Zaporozhtsy are received by 'His Serene Highness' (bass).[1] Vakula plucks up courage to ask for the Empress's shoes; the boon is granted; amid the general festivities (dances by the Cossacks and ladies of the Court) Vakula summons the devil and rides away on his back unnoticed.

Act IV. Christmas morning in the village. Solokha and Oksana are bewailing the supposed loss of son and lover. Vakula appears with the slippers; Oksana admits that she wants him more than the slippers. General rejoicing.

The music with which Tchaïkovsky clothed this typically Gogolian tale ranks among the best he ever wrote.[2] In fineness of workmanship the score ranks high above that of *The Oprichnik* and its lyrical inspiration is purer and far less uneven. Melodically *Vakula* is saturated with the characteristics of Ukrainian folk-music; I have not been able to identify a number of complete folk-tunes as in *The Oprichnik*—my acquaintance with Ukrainian folk-melodies is a good deal more limited than with Russian ones—but I can testify that the score is full of typical Ukrainian and Russian folk-motives. Perhaps the most obvious, and least attractive, Ukrainian feature is the short-breathed hopak-type tune in 2/4 time, of which there are numerous examples in *Vakula*: Solokha's sparkling duet

---

[1] The censorship would not tolerate the representation of even an anonymous Tsaritsa on the opera stage. (Through Gogol's story she could be identified as Catherine the Great.) Rimsky-Korsakov got permission for a 'Tsaritsa' and wrote the part for a mezzo, but members of the Imperial family raised a storm at the *répétition générale* and a baritone 'Highness' had to be substituted at the first performance, as in Tchaïkovsky's opera.

[2] That was also his own opinion. As late as 1890 he told Jurgenson that he 'considered it, so far as the music is concerned, almost my best opera' (letter of 2/14 July).

with the devil in the first scene (which also provides the music for Vakula's aerial ride), her dance with him in Act II, most of the scene with the *golova* in Act II, the song for the schoolmaster inserted in the revised score, the Russian dance and the dance of the Zaporozhtsy in the court scene, the 'drink' chorus of the young peasants in the final scene, among others. Even the recitative is often nationally coloured, as in the passage where Oksana laments that her father has gone out and left her alone on Christmas Eve:

Ex. 12

And I can give no better indication of the charm of Oksana's musical portrait than by quoting first the opening of the aria which immediately follows that ('An apple-tree bloomed in the garden') and then the melody to which she proposes the bargain with the Empress's slippers:

Ex. 13

Rimsky-Korsakov's Oksana is colder and harder; the big 'mirror aria,' which corresponds in his *Christmas Eve* to the scene in which Exs. 12 and 13*a* occur, more successfully hits off the character of Gogol's coquette. But Tchaïkovsky's Oksana is easier to fall in love with.

There is an interesting parallel a little later when Vakula enters, thanks to the fact that both librettists kept closely to an actual phase of Gogol's:

Ex. 14

Tchaikovsky's setting has the more lyrical impetus and the almost-identity of the second bars of each melody suggests that some dim—and doubtless unconscious—recollection of it helped to control Korsakov's inspiration twenty years later. Otherwise the score of *Vakula* had little or no influence on that of *Christmas Eve*, though oddly enough I suspect that it may have had some on Korsakov's already mentioned *Snow Maiden*. Such passages as the accompaniment to the devil's whisperings just before he creeps into the sack and the scene where Oksana is drawn on in a sledge towards the end of Act II are thoroughly characteristic of Rimsky-Korsakov's *Snow Maiden* style; and the Russian and Zaporozhtsy dances in the court scene have something more in common with the popular dance of the *skomorokhi* in Korsakov's *Snow Maiden* than a slight common debt to Dargomïzhsky's *Kazachok*. As Rimsky-Korsakov himself freely admitted, he was always extremely susceptible to influences. Yet period and environment—and common indebtedness to Glinka, in particular—account for much. Tchaïkovsky harmonises Exs. 13 and 14*b* with transparent, diatonic chords absolutely in Glinka's style, that same 'Glinka's style' which we recognise so often in Borodin and the more lyrical pages of Mussorgsky and Rimsky-Korsakov. The simple variations on the theme of the Zaporozhtsy, when they first appear in the second scene of Act III, are pure Glinka (cf. Finn's ballad in *Ruslan*). As one turns the pages of the score of *Vakula* one is struck, even more forcibly than in *The Oprichnik*, by the younger Tchaïkovsky's affinity with the Handful. The magnificent broad melody in B major in which the devil evokes the snowstorm in the First Act might have been written by Borodin, and though the snowstorm is musically rather conventional

there are some novel harmonic effects of seconds and ninths[1] as Chub and
Panas stumble about in the dark, and the scene concludes not only with
descending whole-tone passages in the bass but with whole-tone harmonies[2] that are hardly perceptibly resolved on the last bass crotchet:

The augmented and diminished intervals of the music that follows the
first knock which interrupts the devil's dance with Solokha, the entire
texture of the music to which the disconsolate Vakula appears on the
river-bank, carrying the devil in the sack, the chorus of rusalkas just
before, with its alternation of 3/4 and 5/4 measures: all these stand in the
direct line which stretches from the fantastic and supernatural music of
Glinka's *Ruslan* to the fantastic and supernatural music that Rimsky-
Korsakov was writing more than half a century after *Ruslan*. The opening
of the choral scene at the beginning of the second scene of Act II, with its
double pedals, is pure Glinka—though, as usual with Tchaïkovsky, the
Glinka of *Life for the Tsar* rather than the Glinka of *Ruslan and Lyudmila*.
(With the Mighty Handful, it was the reverse: on the whole *Ruslan* meant
more to them than the earlier opera.) Not that Tchaïkovsky's own musical
personality fails to manifest itself, of course. Sometimes it makes itself felt
through academic *gaucheries*, as when later in that same choral scene, at
the words 'Tikhaya nochen'ka', he cannot resist the temptation to sharpen
the leading note in the accompaniment to a melody in the Aeolian mode;
sometimes through that unmistakable kind of cantilena, that species of
Bellini-with-a-Russian-accent, to which Tchaïkovsky alone has ever had
the real secret, though Rakhmaninov and Glazunov and many others
have produced clever imitations (cf. Vakula's arioso at the end of the first
scene of Act II, or the melody in G flat which dominates the finale of that
act). The polonaise of the Court scene is one of those conventional
Russian polonaises that crop up wherever festive, ceremonial music is
required; it is less brilliant than the corresponding one in Korsakov's
Christmas Eve, less tuneful than that in *Onegin*. But the minuet is graceful
and pretty, and also noteworthy as the first of a whole series of rococo
insets in Tchaïkovsky's stage-works. Again, in the course of Chub's

[1] They occur in one of the additions of 1885.

[2] Tchaïkovsky also used descending whole-tone scales, though not whole-tone harmonies, many years later in scenes 5 and 7 of *The Queen of Spades* to mark the appearances
of the old Countess's avenging ghost to Hermann. Its employment here was probably
suggested by the recollection of Dargomïzhsky's use of whole-tone music in *The Stone
Guest* to mark the appearance of the Commander's avenging ghost to Don Juan.

hospitable invitation in the finale of the last act, the grazioso 'ballet' element in Tchaïkovsky's musical make-up peeps out rather incongruously.

Broadly speaking, the operatic convention adopted in *Vakula* is the same as that of *The Oprichnik*—or the average Western opera of the same period: the convention of set numbers embedded in a more or less continuous texture. In the original *Vakula* the pudding in which these plums are set consists of quasi-melodic arioso; in the *Cherevichki* version this is replaced by recitative in order to speed up the action. Thematic reminiscence is used even more sparingly than in *The Oprichnik*; indeed, the only theme with any claim to be considered a *Leitmotiv* in even the loosest sense of the word is Ex. 14*b*, which is referred to three or four times later: in the finale of Act I, when Vakula enters his mother's hut in the next scene, and in the final scene of the opera. (As it happens, Ex. 14*a* is a form of the 'Vakula' theme of *Christmas Eve*.) The overture to the opera is sectional, like that to *The Oprichnik*, but considerably longer, and as there are no dramatic elements to be opposed to each other the piece is a purely musical composition on themes from the opera:

Introduction (*andante con moto*).
Song of the kobza players from the final scene (*andante*).
Allegro giusto in sonata form, based on a new version of the devil-and-
    Solokha hopak for first subject and a new version of the Vakula
    theme for second.
Song of the kobza-players.
Coda (*più mosso* and *allegro vivace*), based on the final chorus.

After *Vakula* Tchaïkovsky was attracted in turn by *Ephraim*, a libretto by his friend K. S. Shilovsky, about happenings at the court of Pharaoh in the time of Moses (obviously inspired by *Aïda*, which had been produced in Petersburg two or three months earlier), by a *Francesca da Rimini* by K. I. Zvantsev (of which the only result was the well-known symphonic fantasia), and the already-mentioned *Othello* libretto by Stasov. In May 1877 his brother Modest sent him the scenario of an opera based on Charles Nodier's *Ines de Las-Sierras*, but in the very letter in which the composer rejects *Ines* as 'too episodic and too little poetic' he tells the story of Elizaveta Lavrovskaya's suggestion that he should compose a *Eugene Onegin*. On the face of it, it seems rather a crazy idea; Pushkin's poem is a 'novel in verse', not a drama, and it lacks most of the elements of drama; most of its charm lies in the tone and the poetry of the narrative.[1] 'It struck me as wild, and I made no reply,' says Tchaïkovsky himself. But after a time he thought it 'possible'; bought a

[1] The English or American reader is referred to Professor Oliver Elton's translation, London, 1943, that by Babette Deutsch in a volume of Pushkin translations edited by A. Yarmolinsky, London, 1940, or—best of all—Vladimir Nabokov's, New York, 1965.

Pushkin with some difficulty—it was Vol. I of the 1838 edition, for the copy has been preserved—spent a sleepless night and produced a scenario corresponding very closely to the action of the opera as we know it and which I quote in place of a synopsis:

First Act. Scene 1: Mme. Larina and the nurse are sitting in the garden, making preserves. Duet. A song is heard from the house: Tatyana and Olga sing a duet with harp-accompaniment. Enter reapers (with the last sheaf); they sing and dance. Suddenly the servant announces guests. Enter Eugene and Lensky. Ceremony of introduction and entertainment (bilberry wine). Eugene exchanges impressions with Lensky and Tatyana with Olga: quintet *à la Mozart*. The older women go away to prepare dinner. The young people stay and walk in the garden in pairs (as in *Faust*). Tatyana is reserved at first, then falls in love.
Scene 2: Tatyana's letter.
Scene 3: Scene between Onegin and Tatyana.
Second Act. Scene I: Tatyana's name-day. Ball. Lensky's jealousy. He insults Onegin and challenges him. General confusion.
Scene 2: Lensky's aria and the duel.
Third Act. Scene 1: Moscow. Ball in the Nobles' Hall. Tatyana meets a whole string of aunts and cousins. They sing a chorus. Appearance of the general. He falls in love with Tatyana. She tells him her story and agrees to marry him.
Scene 2: Petersburg. Tatyana awaits Onegin. He appears. Big duet. Tatyana still loves him and fights a hard inner battle with herself. Her husband comes. Duty triumphs. Onegin rushes off in despair.[1]

In the definitive form of the opera the principal changes were these:

In Act I, scene 1, there is no 'ceremony of entertainment' and no 'quintet *à la Mozart*'; the nurse Filipyevna disappears before the young men enter and Mme. Larina leaves her daughters alone with the visitors almost immediately. Then follows a *quartet* which might be charitably regarded as *à la Mozart*.
Act III, scene 1, was entirely abandoned in favour of a different ball scene, in Petersburg. Instead of a shy debutante, Tatyana is already a polished woman of the world and already married to 'the general', now christened 'Prince Gremin'. Onegin sees her at this ball.

The very end of the opera gave Tchaïkovsky considerable trouble. Tatyana repulses the man who had once repulsed her. ('But now, to-day,

---

[1] Unlike the earlier operas I have discussed, the story of *Onegin* must be well enough known to every reader to make further elucidation of this scenario unnecessary.

my turn has come.') And in Pushkin the scene ends with her quiet, firm avowal (I quote from Professor Elton's admirable version):

> '. . . I love you (why sophisticate it?),
> But am another's, pledged; and I
> To him stay constant, till I die.'
>
> .   .   .   .   .   .
>
> So she departed: and Evgeny
> Like a man thunderstricken stood

till the sound of the husband's approach breaks the spell. In his own copy of the poem Tchaïkovsky first of all underlined the words 'So she departed', as if he had intended to follow the poet closely, then crossed out the underlining, allowed Tatyana 'overcome with emotion' to 'sink on Onegin's breast' and added six pages (in vocal score) of passionate love-duet before she finally nerves herself to dismiss her lover. (There is no final appearance of the husband, as in the poem and the first draft of the scenario.) Even so, the definitive version of the end (made before the first professional performance of the opera at the Bolshoy Theatre, Moscow, on 11/23 January, 1881) is said to be closer to Pushkin than the version given at the actual first performance (by students of the Moscow Conservatoire in the Maly Theatre on 17/29 March, 1879). One curious point: in the original libretto Onegin's final words were 'O death, O death, I go to seek thee!'; according to N. Rukavishnikov[1] 'the composer apparently did not care much for this phrase and made no protest when it was changed'. But no one knows who was responsible for the substituted line, 'Anguish! Dishonour! How pitiful my fate!'

But, broadly speaking, the libretto is Tchaïkovsky's own.[2] He preserved Pushkin's own verses wherever possible and imitated his style to the best of his ability in the necessarily numerous interpolations, though these changes and interpolations in a passionately loved classic—almost as much as the lack of conventional drama and the not so very long out-of-date costume of the 1830's—were probably a principal cause of *Onegin's* slow success in its early days.[3] Thanks to the preservation of Tchaïkovsky's own copy of the poem, we can even trace in his underlinings and

---

[1] In a fascinating study of 'Pushkin in Tchaïkovsky's Library', *Sovetskaya Muzïka*, January 1937, to which I am indebted for a number of particulars concerning Tchaïkovsky's work on his three Pushkin libretti.

[2] The French and Russian texts of the couplets sung by the French guest, Triquet, in Act II, scene 1, were written by K. S. Shilovsky, who also had some hand in the expansion of the original draft scenario. Judging from Tchaïkovsky's letter to his brother-in-law of 19/31 May, 1877, and other statements, Shilovsky embarked on the whole libretto, but nothing came of this.

[3] Having seen a vocal score of the opera, Turgenev wrote to Leo Tolstoy (15/27 November, 1878): 'Undoubtedly notable music. The lyrical, melodic passages are particularly good. But what a libretto!'

crossings-out, not only his shaping of the libretto from most unpromising material, but (as Rukavishnikov says) his 'deep sympathy for Tatyana and Lensky and a certain coldness towards Onegin'. For instance, in the margin of stanza xxiii of Chapter I, describing Onegin's fashionable room, the composer has scribbled: 'unpleasant'. But Chapter IV, stanza xi, where Onegin is touched by Tatyana's letter, is marked and there are signs that Tchaïkovsky at first had some thought of setting the five following stanzas—Onegin's 'sermonising'—more or less as they stand; he has scribbled a more singable alternative for one line; but the final text of Onegin's aria in Act I, scene 3, though it still embodies a number of Pushkin's lines, was practically written afresh. The poem written by Lensky during the night before the duel (VI, xxi and xxii) was used in its entirety, though with some expansion at the end, as the text of his famous aria in Act II, scene 2; before the line 'Will come, fair maiden', Tchaïkovsky has noted in the margin: 'ret. of I theme' (the first theme does actually return here), and he ringed round the last two lines of the twenty-second stanza, marking them 'conclusion' (they provide the basis of the *andante mosso* coda), showing that the musical form of the aria had begun to take shape in his mind at a very early stage—possibly even at the first reading. Similarly stanzas xx and xxi of Chapter II were adapted—the third person being changed to first—for Lensky's arioso in the first scene.

But the majority of Tchaïkovsky's marginal markings, and the majority of his more wholesale borrowings from the original text, relate to Tatyana, with whom he was from the first 'absolutely in love'. It was Tatyana who aroused that 'love and pity, as for a real person' which he needed if he was to be genuinely inspired. He told Kashkin many years afterwards: 'I had so familiarised myself with the figure of Tatyana that she had become for me a living person in living surroundings. I loved Tatyana and was terribly indignant with Onegin, who seemed to me a cold, heartless coxcomb.'[1] He began to set Tatyana's famous letter even before he prepared his libretto.[2] Indeed, two-thirds of the whole opera was written or at least roughed out in short score by 23 June/5 July, 1877—that is, in little more than five weeks after Mme Lavrovskaya's suggestion; the non-completion of the score till January of the following year was due partly to work on the Fourth Symphony, another favourite work which was composed side by side with *Onegin*, but mainly to the composer's catastrophic marriage and the illness that followed it.

The best way to approach the music of *Onegin* is by beginning where

[1] For his account to Kashkin of the manner in which this illusion of Tatyana's reality, and the parallel between her behaviour and Antonina Milyukova's, became a factor—or so he alleged—in his decision to marry Antonina, I must refer the reader to the chapter on 'Eugene Onegin and Tchaïkovsky's Marriage' in my book *On Russian Music*, London, 1939.

[2] According to Kashkin, he had thought long before of setting the letter as a solo song.

Tchaïkovsky began: with Tatyana's letter. Though, as it was composed before the libretto existed, we should remember that this could not have been the whole letter scene as we now know it, but only the letter itself, beginning with the words 'I write to you without reflection' (in H. G. Chapman's English version of the libretto) or rather with the orchestral passage, *moderato assai, quasi andante*, leading up to them and continuing under them with the voice part as purely incidental as in any of the Wagner passages to which Tchaïkovsky objected. (One notices the same thing at Tatyana's entrance in the ball scene in Act III, where all the essential music lies in the orchestra—the charming and characteristic clarinet melody—and the vocal parts are simply patched on; Tchaïkovsky had been at Bayreuth the year before he wrote *Onegin* and, however un-Wagnerian the stuff of his music, he was not altogether unaffected by Wagner's methods.) But the orchestral conception is masterly; the simple oboe line crossed by the dropping fourths and fifths of flute, clarinet and horn and the light splash of the harp magically not only conveys the naïve character and romantic mood of the writer but suggests, almost pantomimically, the act of writing in a way comparable with, though not like, the 'writing' passages in *Boris* and *Khovanshchina* (the scene in Pimen's cell and the scene of the public scribe). This fusion of emotional expression with graphic tone-painting is sustained throughout the letter, even through the less successful 'No, never any other' passage, and towards the end, as Tatyana's passion approaches its climax, the dual quality of the music also touches a new level in a horn phrase of melting warmth:

Ex. 16

which contains the purest essence of Tchaïkovskian melody while the harmony of the second bar touches the very nerve centre of Russian romantic harmony (the flattened sixth). As I have pointed out elsewhere,[1] that horn phrase, or rather its first few notes, became a sort of motto-theme for the whole opera, though doubtless an unconscious one. (To have used it deliberately as it is used would have been pointless.)

We hear it first in the duet behind the scenes which opens the First Act. It occurs in a little phrase piped out by flute and oboe at the end of the quartet when Onegin first looks at the shy girl 'rather familiarly' and then goes up to her. We hear it again in the viola phrases which close the love scene between Olga and Lensky, and once more (in the

[1] *On Russian Music*, p. 233.

orchestra) near the beginning of the second scene, when Tatyana says to her old nurse: 'Amuse me; and tell me some tale of long ago.' In the letter scene itself it occurs quite early in a different musical context. It assumes two different forms in Gremin's aria in Act III, and it occurs again in Tatyana's sweeping phrase which dominates the last passionate scene of the opera.

Indeed, the whole score—from the short monothematic introduction to the final avowal—is saturated with the spirit, if not the letter, of that warm, lyrical motto-theme. Although he gives his name to the work, Onegin himself is not the principal figure as he is in Pushkin's poem. It is Tatyana who takes the centre of the stage, as indeed she nearly does in Pushkin; Tchaïkovsky could identify himself with her shy, affectionate, quintessentially feminine character more completely than with any male character in his operas, more even than with Hermann in *The Queen of Spades*; and to paint her musical portrait he only had to pour out freely the peculiar kind of lyrical melody which constitutes the most individual element in his musical make-up. So, like Mozart's heroines, she is not merely a character set to appropriate music; she exists *as* music. To a less extent, that is true of Lensky also. He too is a piece of musical self-projection on Tchaïkovsky's part; though, being a less definite and less intensely sympathetic figure than Tatyana, even the best of his music—his arioso in Act I and the famous aria before the duel—has less warmth and less character than hers. But the titular hero comes to life musically only when he echoes Tatyana's music—as he does with superbly ironic effect in the penultimate scene: discovering his passion for the transformed Tatyana in the very music of the opening of the letter scene, here beautifully led up to. Or in his 'sermonising' aria (Act I, scene 3) where once again the 'motto' from Ex. 16 steals into the vocal line ('You *are* what *I do most admire*').

The rest of the music is 'background'. Not 'background music' in the common sense of the phrase, but music painting the background of the novel; for, just as Pushkin called his poem a 'novel in verse', it remains a musico-poetic novel—rather than a drama—when transferred to the stage.[1] In the First Act it paints the country setting with liberal quantities of attractive folk-music (or folkish music): the chorus and dance of the reapers, the scene of Tatyana and the nurse, the oboe-pipe of the shepherd sounding so magically cool and fresh after the passion of the letter scene, the Glinka-like chorus of girls gathering berries (taken direct from Pushkin) which so effectively and ironically frames the Tatyana–Onegin scene in the garden. Throughout a great deal of the Second and Third Acts it has to paint ball settings, the country 'hop' at the Larins and the

---

[1] There is a more modern parallel in Delius's *Fennimore and Gerda*, based on Jens Peter Jacobsen's novel, *Niels Lyhne*.

fashionable assembly in St Petersburg, and there too Tchaïkovsky was in his element with valse and mazurka and polonaise.[1] Everything in *Onegin* seems specially made for Tchaïkovsky: even Triquet's pseudo-rococo couplets were not arbitrarily inserted by him like the couplets in Act III of *Cherevichki*; they are justified by the poem (V, xxvii).[2] That is why *Onegin* is his operatic masterpiece. From a purely musical point of view, *Vakula* is perhaps more beautiful. It is, as Tchaïkovsky recognised, more finely wrought, *too* finely wrought; *Onegin*, besides possessing a heroine equally attractive musically as Oksana and twenty times more attractive dramatically, has more of that broad simplicity, that human warmth, without which no opera—however fine musically—can hope to keep the stage.

Yet Tchaïkovsky himself feared that even *Onegin* would be ineffective. On 30 August/11 September, 1877, 'when the first fire had passed off' and he could 'consider the composition objectively', he confided to Nadezhda von Meck his fear that it was 'condemned to fail and to be ignored by the mass of the public. Its content is very unsophisticated, there are no scenic effects, the music lacks brilliance and rhetorical effectiveness.' It is true there may be some chosen spirits who 'hearing this music, will be touched by those emotions which agitated me when I wrote it'. But 'on the stage *Onegin* won't be *interesting*. For it won't satisfy the first requirement of opera—*scenic movement*.' His only hope is that it will please those who are capable of appreciating in opera 'the simple, everyday feelings common to all mankind'. Later, writing to Taneyev in more pugnacious mood, he could 'spit on all stage effect'. But he was always sure that *Onegin* could have no future in the theatre. And he almost rejoiced in the fact, for he dreaded to see these ideal characters reduced to the painful realities of the opera stage.

In a letter to Nadezhda von Meck of 16/28 December, 1877, he writes:

> Where shall I find the *Tatyana* whom Pushkin imagined and whom I've tried to illustrate musically? Where is the artist who can even approach the ideal Onegin, that cold dandy penetrated to the marrow with worldly *bon ton*? Where is there a Lensky, an eighteen-year-old

[1] The écossaise in the last act was added in August 1885 at the request of Vsevolozhsky, Director of the Imperial Theatres, and there is extant an amusing letter of Tchaïkovsky's to his publisher in which he admits that, after a long discussion with Vsevolozhsky of the kind of dance to be inserted he agreed on an écossaise without in the least knowing what an écossaise was like: 'I believe Schubert wrote écossaises. If not, perhaps you can tell me where I can find one for a model. . . . I *must* have an écossaise.' The one he actually wrote, Modest tells us, was composed, orchestrated and sent to Petersburg in one day; it sounds like it.

[2] A few months before taking up *Onegin* Tchaïkovsky had set Almaviva's couplets 'Vous l'ordonnez' in *Le Barbier de Séville* for a student performance in the Maly Theatre, Moscow; the setting is printed in the *Polnoe sobranie*, Vol. 14.

youth with the thick curls and the impetuous and original ways of a young poet *à la* Schiller? How Pushkin's charming picture will be vulgarised when it's transferred to the stage with its routine, its senseless traditions, its veterans of both sexes who—like Alexandrova and Kommisarzhevsky *i tutti quanti*—shamelessly take on the rôles of sixteen-year-old girls and beardless youths!

The whole thing was not so much an opera as 'lyrical scenes' conceived for 'limited resources and a small stage'. It is very odd that, having found the subject which perfectly satisfied his demands for real and sympathetic characters, for strong, simple human emotions, Tchaïkovsky should ever have felt so doubtful about it—after the first overpowering burst of enthusiasm—and that he should never have returned to anything like it, except partially in *The Queen of Spades*.

In one respect the music of *Onegin* accidentally, though strikingly, symbolises the change that came over Tchaïkovsky's music at about this period: the folk-music is all in Act I, there is none in the rest of the work. In most of the works we have discussed up to this point—*The Voevoda, The Oprichnik, Snow Maiden, Vakula the Smith*, in fact all except *Undine* —there has been a strong national flavour in much of the music, a flavour that has never failed to heighten its charm. After *Onegin*—or rather, after the First Act of *Onegin*—that flavour suddenly becomes much fainter and except in the First Acts of *Mazeppa* and *The Sorceress*, almost disappears.[1] For a time Tchaïkovsky turns abruptly away from Russian subjects. He even returns to the old *Undine* theme, having come across Zhukovsky's translation of the tale again in his sister's library at Kamenka, and commissions his brother Modest to prepare a scenario; only to discover, as a result of re-reading *Romeo and Juliet*, that 'Undine, Berthalda, Huldbrand and the rest are childish nonsense'. He will 'of course write a *Romeo and Juliet*'; it will be 'my supreme masterpiece'; and one can only regret that he allowed himself to be frightened away from the subject by its 'awful difficulty' and the fact that Gounod had already used it. The fact that Verdi had written a *Giovanna d'Arco* did *not*, however, deter him from essaying a *Maid of Orleans*.

This idea first came to Tchaïkovsky in April 1878, at the same time as the revival of interest in *Undine* and in the same way: among Zhukovsky's works he came across his superb translation of Schiller's *Jungfrau von Orleans*. But nothing came of this till seven months later. Then at the end of November he tells Madame von Meck that he is 'seriously attracted' to this subject for his next opera. He wants to get hold of the libretto of

[1] On the other hand, even in *The Maid of Orleans*, where Tchaïkovsky was naturally trying to be non-Russian, the French king lapses into an unmistakably Russian accent (his first recitative in the finale of Act III), and the opening chorus of girls is Glinka-like in texture.

Auguste Mermet's *Jeanne d'Arc* produced in Paris a couple of years before; he has already bought Verdi's 'extremely bad' work and thinks it will be useful to compare the libretto with Mermet's, which he had heard highly praised;[1] in Paris he must also buy some books on Joan of Arc. And Nadezhda von Meck promptly makes him a present of a very expensive one, Henri-Alexandre Wallon's *Jeanne d'Arc*, reading which he 'wept a great deal over the passage describing her execution (when she was led to the stake she screamed and begged to be beheaded instead of burned). I felt infinite sorrow for all mankind . . .' (letter to Modest, 10/22 December, 1878). But he was still puzzling over the libretto and had not yet settled on a definite plan. 'A great deal in Schiller pleases me, but I must confess his contempt for historical truth somewhat discourages me.'

He wished to keep to Schiller's—or, rather, Zhukovsky's—text as closely as possible, but there were, of course 'too many characters and too many secondary episodes'. And there were other points:

> For example, Schiller has a scene where Joan fights with Lionel. For various considerations, I should like to substitute Montgomery for Lionel. Is this possible? Are these historical characters? To know all this, I shall have to read a few books. Meanwhile I've taken direct from Zhukovsky one scene which, in any case, I shall have to have, even if I don't find it in Mermet: the scene where the King, archbishop and knights recognise Joan as an ambassador from on high.

Finally he came to the conclusion that 'although Schiller's tragedy doesn't conform to historical truth, it surpasses all other artistic portrayals of Joan in deep psychological truth'. Even before this, without a libretto, without even a scenario, he had begun the music of that essential scene of Joan's recognition on 5/17 December and had finished it (i.e., all the second part of Act II) in five days. Then, at Clarens, on the last day of the old year (12 January, 1879, new style) Tchaïkovsky wrote the chorus of girls that opens the First Act—and completed the whole work, words and music, on 21 February/5 March, though the scoring was not finished till the following August. The music came easily enough, but the libretto cost him endless trouble and he gave Nadezhda von Meck an amusing account of the number of penholders gnawed away in the effort to compose a few lines. He had particular difficulty with the rhymes and lamented the non-existence of a Russian rhyming dictionary. The final scenario was based mainly on Schiller–Zhukovsky (the text 'preserving many of Zhukovsky's verses' as the title-page of the opera reassures us) but with one or two additions or modifications from Wallon's book, Jules Barbier's

---

[1] When he did get Mermet's libretto, he found 'his scenario very bad, though with two or three effective scenes which I may be able to use'.

tragedy *Jeanne d'Arc* (final scene) and the Mermet libretto (beginning of Act I):

Act I. Joan (soprano)[1] and village-girls are decorating the Druids' oak. Enter her father Thibaut (bass) and her lover Raimond (tenor); Thibaut presses Joan to marry. She says she is destined for 'another fate'; Thibaut reproaches her for commerce with evil spirits. Distant fires are seen. Enter fugitive villagers, one of whom, the aged Bertrand (bass), describes the wretched state of France. Joan prophesies the expulsion of the English and says Salisbury[2] is already killed; she is disbelieved but her second-sight is immediately confirmed by a soldier (bass) who has just come from Orleans. The people are convinced. Left alone, Joan realises that 'her hour is come' and takes a passionate farewell of her home—strengthened and comforted by a chorus of angels.

Act II. The castle of Chinon. The King (tenor), with Agnes Sorel (soprano) and Dunois (baritone), is being entertained by the songs of minstrels and the dances of gypsies and buffoons. Dunois tries to nerve the King to action, but he cannot bring himself to leave Agnes. A wounded warrior, Lauret (bass), is brought in with news of another defeat and dies at the King's feet. Agnes consoles the King. Short love-duet. Enter a chorus of people hailing 'the Saviour Maid'; Dunois announces the victory; the Archbishop (bass) tells how an unknown girl has turned the tide of battle. Enter Joan, who picks out the King from among the courtiers, tells him his secret prayers, and relates the story of her life; all present recognise her as an emissary of Heaven.

Act III. *Scene* 1. Near a battlefield and the burning English camp. Enter Lionel, a Burgundian knight (baritone), pursued by Joan. They fight, but when she has him at her mercy, she sees his face—and spares him. Unwillingly they fall in love. Dunois appears with a detachment. Instead of fleeing Lionel surrenders to him and offers to join the King's party; Dunois joyfully accepts him.

Scene 2. The Square before Rheims Cathedral. As the Coronation procession leaves the Cathedral, Thibaut denounces Joan as an agent of Hell, and when he and the Archbishop ask Joan if she 'considers herself pure and holy' she remains silent because of her guilty love for Lionel. Lionel comes forward as the champion of her innocence but

---

[1] In Russian she becomes 'Ioanna' after Schiller's 'Johanna'. Though written for a soprano the part was taken at the first performance (Maryinsky Theatre, St Petersburg, February 13/25, 1881) by a mezzo, Mme Kamenskaya, and various transpositions and adjustments had to be made. For the sake of the same fine exponent of the part, further temporary changes were made in 1882, but the definitive form of the opera remains the same as the original form.

[2] Which Tchaïkovsky sets as a four-syllable word: 'Sa-lis-bou-ry.'

his challenge is answered by thunder. 'It is the voice of Heaven!' say the people. 'She is guilty!' The King banishes her from Rheims. When Lionel tries to accompany her, she repulses him as 'her foe and the ruin of her soul'.

Act IV. *Scene* 1. Joan is sitting in a wood, deep in thought. She admits the reality of her love for Lionel—who promptly appears. They embrace. Their love-duet is interrupted first by the angelic voices who tell Joan she will atone for her sin by suffering and death, then by the advent of 'British' soldiers who kill Lionel and take Joan prisoner.

Scene 2. Rouen. Joan is led to the stake and the fire is lit.

Absurd and distasteful as this romantic manipulation of historic facts undeniably is, Tchaïkovsky could at least plead that he had kept nearer the truth than Schiller, who allowed Joan to escape from her captors, rescue the wretched Charles VII (who had got captured too) and die on the battlefield, standard in hand, surrounded by her friends. Just before his death, however, Tchaïkovsky—plagued by his brother Modest—was contemplating the substitution of Schiller's 'rose-coloured death scene', as Schlegel called it, for his own gloomily veracious one. He might also have contended that the ridiculous Joan–Lionel fight and love-affair had the respectable operatic precedent of Tancred and Clorinda, and pointed out that his transformation of Schiller's Lionel from an English general into a Burgundian knight had the very faintest justification in the fact that the historic Joan surrendered at Compiègne to a Burgundian named Lionel. But Tchaïkovsky's Lionel has very little in common with Schiller. Schiller's Lionel does not surrender to Dunois or change sides; indeed, he sees Joan only once more, when she is a prisoner; their love remains on a purely ideal and abstract plane. The Lionel at the end of Act III, scene 2, is essentially Schiller's Dunois; the Lionel of Act IV, scene 1, is purely a creation of Tchaïkovsky's own. But there is little point in discussing the origin or behaviour of a baritone in fancy dress. And in saying that, we put our finger on the crippling weakness of the whole opera.

As we have seen from his remarks to Fedotov, 'medieval dukes and knights and ladies captivate my imagination but not my *heart*, and where the heart is not touched there can't be any music'. Not only Lionel but Charles VII and Dunois and Agnes and even the grim old peasant father are merely characters in fancy dress; they never touched Tchaïkovsky's heart and never evoked from him any real music. But Joan herself? We know at least that he was deeply moved by her martyrdom, though even this was ultimately portrayed simply by a gloomily effective funeral march which emphasises only the pitiless cruelty of her captors, expresses neither Joan's courage and nobility nor her human weakness, and reflects none of that 'infinite sorrow for all mankind' aroused by the reading of

Wallon's description. On the whole, Joan too remains only a lay figure—except in one passage: her 'narrative' in the Second Act and her recognition as the emissary of Heaven. That passage, as we have seen, was written first as Tatyana's letter scene was written first and it rises even higher above the rest of the opera than the letter scene does in *Onegin*. Even the cello melody to which she enters—it recurs again at the end of the Act, and in the Coronation scene when the King points to Joan as 'the ambassadress of Heaven'—though simple 'processional' music, has a quiet dignity that saves it from the banal; Joan's snatch of recitative, 'I saw thee, but only where none but God saw thee,' has the exquisite sweetness of nineteenth-century French opera at its best; and the King's outburst, 'I believe, I believe: this cannot be by man alone,' oddly reminds one of the opening of Elgar's A flat Symphony (perhaps because both were evidently written under the influence of the A flat passage of Chopin's F minor Fantaisie). But all this is only the prelude to Joan's narration proper, which is so beautiful that its neglect in favour of the far inferior 'farewell' aria in Act I is quite incomprehensible. I quote the opening: 'Holy father, they call me Joan; I am the daughter of a simple shepherd,' or as Schiller has it:

> Ehrwürd'ger Herr, Johanna nennt man mich.
> Ich bin nur eines Hirten niedre Tochter

for Tchaïkovsky has set Zhukovsky's version quite straightforwardly:

Ex. 17

And the phrase a little later to which Joan sings the words of the heavenly apparition, 'Rise up and leave your flock' ('Ich bin's. Steh auf, Johanna. Lass die Herde'), was used throughout the opera—though generally sung elsewhere by an invisible choir of angels—as the motive of the 'heavenly voices'. (There are one or two other cases of thematic reminiscence in the score—notably the ironic use of the melody to which the Archbishop has acclaimed Joan in the finale of Act II, when he is challenging her innocence in the finale of Act III—but nothing approaching a Wagnerian *Leitmotiv*.)[1] Here in this narration, and here alone, is Joan herself adequately characterised in the music; having written it Tchaïkovsky seems to have been deserted by his inspiration.

There is very little in the rest of the score that even bears the stamp of Tchaïkovsky's musical personality. Perhaps the most Tchaïkovskian

---

[1] A reminiscence of a different kind is prominent in the King's music in Act II, where Tchaïkovsky did not realise that he was remembering the opening of the *Jupiter* Symphony.

things, both melodically and orchestrally, are Joan's familiar 'farewell' aria and her two duets with Lionel, but all three are weak Tchaïkovsky. And the G flat coda of the duettino for Agnes and the King, though recognisably from the same hand, also helps one to recognise the general influence on Tchaïkovsky's style of the famous duet in the same key in the Fourth Act of *Les Huguenots*. But if Tchaïkovsky had always been conscious of Meyerbeer, he had never been so much so as in *The Maid of Orleans*. The whole work is so deliberately French, so completely conceived in terms of the Paris Grand Opera and its great crowd effects, that it is not unkind to assume that the secret motive controlling its inception and execution was the hope of a great operatic triumph in Western Europe. And one must admit the success, the stagey effectiveness, of some of the music conceived in these terms: for instance, the finale of Act II, the Coronation music, the final scene. Nor do we need the testimony of Tchaïkovsky's letters to gather that at this period he was particularly interested in contemporary French opera, the post-Meyerbeerian and more lyrical stage-works of Massenet and the rest; many pages of *The Maid* reflect their palest and most sugary melodiousness, while Agnes' arioso in Act II might have been written by Gounod[1] in one of his happier moments. Yet another French symptom is the long ballet—twenty-one pages of piano score—forcibly inserted in the Second Act. A couple of lines in Schiller do offer a slight pretext for the chorus of minstrels, but this ballet, lacking even the slight dramatic justification for the dances in *The Oprichnik* and *Vakula* (to say nothing of *Onegin*, where the ballet is essential), simply holds up the action. However, as music the ballet is by no means the worst part of the score, and the final buffoons' dance with its angular syncopations to which piquantly scored counter-

Ex. 18
Allegro molto

points are added later, might well be included in the orchestral repertoire. That can hardly he said of the introduction to the opera, much longer than the brief monothematic prelude to *Onegin* but less well organised than the overture to *Vakula*; it begins promisingly with a beautiful little flute theme treated somewhat like the descent of the Grail, with increasingly full scoring, breaks off into the alarm music of the first scene, builds up to Joan's song in the finale of Act I, returns to the opening music—and

---

[1] 'Gounod is a first-rate master, if not a first-rate creative genius,' Tchaïkovsky had written a year or two before (8/20 April, 1877). 'In the sphere of opera, I consider that, with the exception of Wagner, there is no living composer to whom it would not be an honour to enter into rivalry with Gounod. So far as I am concerned I should consider myself a happy man if I could write an opera half as beautiful as *Faust*.' Tchaïkovsky's admiration for Gounod was really limited to that one work.

then peters out in a long and quite incredibly empty and showy flute cadenza.

In less than four months after the production of *The Maid of Orleans* Tchaïkovsky informed his publisher that he was contemplating yet another opera: 'This is now the only form of composition capable of arousing my enthusiasm. I've got hold of a very decent libretto, given me by K. Y. Davïdov, who had himself begun to write an opera on it but gave it up for want of time. The libretto is based on Pushkin's *Poltava* and has been put together by Burenin.[1] So you can take it that if I write anything big it will be an opera' (letter of 4/16 June, 1881). During the next two or three months he wrote four numbers—though which four I do not know —for this new opera, afterwards named *Mazeppa* after its villain-hero, but he wrote with no enthusiasm; he had at this period lost all taste for composition, everything seemed '*remplissage*, routine and hackneyed technical devices'. (A decade or so later Rimsky-Korsakov was to pass through a precisely similar phase.) By October *Mazeppa* was abandoned; Tchaïkovsky had returned to 'the old yet ever new subject of *Romeo and Juliet*' and it was probably at this time that he began to sketch out the love-duet, partly based on material from his overture-fantasia, which was posthumously completed and scored by Taneyev. But before the month was out, he was clamouring for a copy of Luka Antropov's play *Vanka the Steward*, based on a story by D. V. Averkiev. The subject was 'very sympathetic'—mainly, it appears, because it centred on a love scene in a garden at night, 'more or less on the lines of *Romeo and Juliet*'. And sure enough, at the end of November he began to compose a love scene in a room with doors open on a garden at night; but it was the scene between Mariya and Mazeppa. 'One fine day,' he told Nadezhda von Meck (29 May/ 10 June, 1882):

> I re-read the libretto and skimmed over Pushkin's poem, was touched by several scenes and verses—and began with the scene between Mariya and Mazeppa, which had been transferred unchanged from the poem to the libretto. Although up to now I have not experienced the profound joy that I felt in composing *Eugene Onegin*, for example, and although on the whole the composition progresses quietly and I don't feel particularly attracted by the characters—still I'm writing and I've already achieved something.

Actually the bulk of the composition was done between the date of that letter and 15/27 September, and the orchestration was finished by 28 April/10 May, 1883. The first performance was given in the Bolshoy Theatre, Moscow, on 3/15 February of the following year.

[1] Viktor Petrovich Burenin, a poet and critic who died as recently as 1926 at the age of eighty-five.

While Tchaïkovsky preserved Burenin's scenario, he made considerable cuts and changes in the actual libretto, inserting or adapting Pushkin's
own verses where possible. This was not often, for *Poltava* is a narrative
poem of which only the first two cantos are concerned with Mazeppa's
love and treason (the subject of the opera) while the third and most
important, the crown of the whole, is devoted to a marvellous description
of the Battle of Poltava and to the glorification of Peter the Great and the
triumph of the new Russian state over both foreign invaders and Ukrainian
separatists. But it is interesting to the Russian if not to the English reader
to trace how the composer takes, for instance, the words in which
Pushkin addresses Mariya and adapts them to be sung by Mariya herself;
the two copies of *Poltava* in which he made his marginal notes and
scribbled new bits of libretto are still preserved (or were until the last
war), and in one instance he has begun to sketch a musical idea beside
the passage that suggested it:

Ex. 19

Po - slushay

which is interesting as evidence of the way in which musical germs
occurred to him, though the equivalent passage in the finished opera bears
no relation to it; even the word 'Poslushay' ('Listen!'), is changed to
'Skazhi' ('Tell me!').

The action of Mazeppa in its definitive form is as follows:

Act I. *Scene* 1. Garden of the rich Cossack Kochubey; girls are
fortune-telling by throwing wreaths into the river. Enter Kochubey's
daughter, Mariya (soprano), who after the departure of the girls confesses her love for their guest, the elderly hetman Mazeppa (whose
little adventure on the horse had happened some forty years earlier).
Enter the young Cossack Andrey (tenor), who tells her of his hopeless
love for her. Exeunt both. Enter Mazeppa (baritone), Kochubey (bass),
the latter's wife Lyubov (mezzo-soprano), Mariya, guests, musicians,
servants, etc. Entertainment with songs and dances. Left alone after
the entertainment, Mazeppa asks Kochubey for his daughter's hand;
Kochubey refuses on account of the hetman's age and the fact that he is
Mariya's godfather. They quarrel violently and the noise brings back
the others. Mazeppa fires his pistol, summoning his men, calls on
Mariya to choose between him and her parents—and carries her off.

Scene 2.[1] Room in Kochubey's house. With him are his wife and

---

[1] The division of the First Act was an afterthought. Apparently the action was originally
conceived as continuous, without change of scene.

friends, including Andrey and Iskra, governor of Poltava (tenor). Women lamenting for Mariya. Urged to revenge by his wife, Kochubey resolves to reveal to the Tsar Mazeppa's secret intrigues with the Swedes. Andrey volunteers to go to the Tsar.

Act II. *Scene* 1. Dungeon in Mazeppa's castle at Belotserkov; Kochubey chained to a pillar. The Tsar, trusting Mazeppa implicitly, has given his accusers into his power. Enter Orlik (bass), who demands to know where Kochubey's treasure is concealed; at the end he summons a torturer.

Scene 2. Room in the castle; Mazeppa is looking out into the starlit garden. Orlik comes to tell him that the torture has failed to make Kochubey reveal his secret. Enter Mariya, who knows nothing of her father's fate; she reproaches Mazeppa with his recent coldness and he reveals to her his plan to set up an independent Ukrainian state with himself as its head. Exit Mazeppa. Enter Lyubov, who tells Mariya the whole story and persuades her to plead with Mazeppa for her father's life.

Scene 3. A field by the scaffold. A crowd of people, including a drunken Cossack (tenor). Enter executioners, Mazeppa on horseback, Orlik, and Cossacks; later Kochubey and Iskra guarded. Kochubey prays. At the moment the axes fall, Mariya and her mother rush in. Curtain.

Act III. Symphonic picture: 'The Battle of Poltava.' The curtain goes up, revealing the same scene as Act I, scene 1, but everything is now neglected and half-ruined. Fugitive Swedish soldiers cross the stage, pursued by Russians, including Andrey. He sings a long aria, then hides as he hears horsemen approaching. Mazeppa and Orlik pause in their flight. Andrey emerges from concealment and attacks Mazeppa, who shoots him. Enter Mariya, out of her mind. Orlik drags Mazeppa away. Mariya takes Andrey's head in her lap and, thinking herself back in the days of their childhood, sings a lullaby as he dies.

That, as I have said, is the definitive form of the action; as the opera was originally produced, the end was more protracted, the chorus entered after Andrey's death and Mariya, remembering the floating wreaths in the first scene, threw herself into the river. But within a month after the first production Tchaïkovsky made up his mind to end with the lullaby, which he extended considerably. At the same time he cut some of the music at the end of the first scene, which tended to hold up the action, and made a number of drastic changes (mostly cuts but also some additions) in the big scene between Mariya and Mazeppa. At some later date he wrote an additional arioso in G flat for Mazeppa, to words by V. A. Kandaurov, to be inserted *ad lib.* just before this scene.

We have seen that Tchaïkovsky began *Mazeppa*, as he had begun *Onegin* and *The Maid of Orleans*, with a scene in the middle of the opera, a scene that specially appealed to him. The scene between Mariya and Mazeppa has not left its musical mark on the rest of the opera as the horn-theme in Ex. 16 did on so much of *Onegin*—though, oddly enough, Mariya's first words in the scene are sung to a motive very nearly identical with the opening of the horn-theme in the earlier opera, and the motive recurs elsewhere: in Act I when Mariya is left alone by the other girls, in the first scene between Mazeppa and Kochubey, in Kochubey's mono-logue in the dungeon scene, and in the accompaniment to Andrey's aria in Act III. But dramatically the scene is as important as Tatyana's letter scene or Joan of Arc's narrative, for it reveals at full length the character of the central figure—or in this case of the two principal characters. (The others are negligible; Kochubey comes to life only when he is half-dead from the torture, in the dungeon scene, a powerful, gloomy piece of work though over-praised by some Russian critics; and Andrey is simply a tenor with some attractive but not quite first-rate lyrical music to sing.) Both Mazeppa and Mariya are favourite types of Russian opera—and Russian fiction—but they are not quite stock figures from the Western point of view. Mariya is the less interesting, being one of those negative, all-suffering heroines in whom the Russian soul delights—or used to delight—and who inhabit the pages of every classical Russian novel and every classical Russian opera; like so many of her sisters, she lacks the positive traits which distinguish Sonya in *War and Peace* or Tatyana Larina in *Onegin*, both of whom really belong to this class. But Mazeppa is by no means the mere villain my bald summary of the action makes him appear to be; he is a romanticised, Byronised figure,[1] a 'divided' character like a Dostoevsky hero, or Pushkin's and Mussorgsky's Boris Godunov, or Ivan the Terrible in *The Maid of Pskov*. He is potentially first-rate material, and Tchaïkovsky's limitations as a musical dramatist are precisely defined by the nature of his failure with him. For Tchaïkovsky to paint a character successfully in music, it was necessary for him to feel strong sympathy, to experience at least partial self-identification, with it; and as we have seen he 'did not feel particularly attracted' by any of the char-acters in *Mazeppa*. Though himself a divided character, he was incapable either of entering into Mazeppa's or of drawing it objectively as a real, living whole. So, instead of a character living in terms of music like Mussorgsky's Boris or even Rimsky-Korsakov's Ivan the Terrible, we get only a character who behaves like an unmitigated villain and who has throughout the opera a sort of *Leitmotiv* suggesting his cruelty (Ex. 20)

---

[1] Pushkin's Mazeppa 'is treated romantically and, though he is painted as a villain, his dark cunning character is calculated to exercise a powerful charm over the reader', says D. S. Mirksy, in his *Pushkin*, London, 1926.

(I quote the form in which it is first heard, at the opening of the orchestral introduction to the opera), but who also breaks into beautiful and expressive music (e.g. the arioso in which he tells Kochubey of his love for

Ex. 20

Mariya) or poetises about the beauty of night in the Ukraine (beginning of Act II, scene 2) or sentimentalises over Mariya and her youthful love for him (the inserted arioso in G flat). But the only place in the whole score where his character even begins to become integrated is the big scene with Mariya, and even here his portrait is musically inadequate.

When Mazeppa is telling Mariya of his ideal of a free and independent Ukraine, neither 'under the protection of Warsaw' nor 'under the despotism of Moscow', Tchaïkovsky introduces a modified quotation, or rather allusion, of a kind common enough in literature but exceedingly rare in music: the orchestra underlines Mazeppa's words with a passage (see Ex. 21a) marked in the score by square brackets and the letters 'Zh.z.Ts.G.' (i.e. *Zhizn' za Tsarya Glinki*)—compounded of the mazurka from *Life for the Tsar* (Ex. 21b) and the 'Slavsya' from the same opera (Ex. 21c), symbols of Warsaw and Moscow respectively:

Ex. 21

The point is, of course, far too subtle for an opera audience, perhaps too subtle for any audience. More obvious and more effective, if much less interesting, are the musical symbols of Russian victory in the 'Battle of Poltava' intermezzo: the famous song of glorification 'Slava' (introduced by Beethoven in the second Razumovsky quartet, by Mussorgsky in the Coronation scene of *Boris*, and by Rimsky-Korsakov in *The Tsar's Bride* and his *Overture on Russian Themes*), the liturgical chant which Tchaïkovsky himself had used for the opening and climax of his *1812 Overture* only a year or two before, and a military march of the Petrine period.[1]

To what extent actual Russian, or rather Ukrainian, folk-tunes are introduced in the rest of the score I cannot say. But the folkish element plays an important part in the First Act. The beautiful opening chorus of girls in 5/4 time, for instance, might well have been written by Glinka.

[1] In a letter to A. F. Fedotov, Tchaïkovsky some years later expressed his distaste for the depicting in sounds of 'every sort of fight, assault, attack, etc.'

And the whole of the following scene—the entrance of Mazeppa, Kochubey and the rest, the choral song, and the ensuing hopak (generally known as 'the Cossack Dance')—is attractively dyed in national colours, though even in the hopak Tchaïkovsky rather unhappily uses a secondary cantabile melody of his own as a foil to the folk or folkish main theme (cf. the finale of the Second Symphony and the finale of the Serenade for strings). Otherwise the national element in the music is more or less limited to the 'folk scene', actually so called by the composer, with the song of the drunken Cossack which Tchaïkovsky hotly defended to Jurgenson, which precedes the grim and theatrical scene of the execution. (Incidentally, in Pushkin Mariya arrives not in time to see the execution but to see the scaffold being taken to pieces and 'two Cossacks lifting a coffin on to a cart'.) But here again Tchaïkovsky, challenging comparison with Mussorgsky in the field of choral realism, only demonstrates his inferiority, precisely as in the similar scene in *The Oprichnik*. Only in the irony of the contrast between the song of the drunken Cossack and the scene of death is there a dramatic value comparable with similar things in Mussorgsky, e.g. the lovely snatch of folk-song sung by Shaklovity over the body of the murdered prince in *Khovanshchina*. There are several touches of such irony in *Mazeppa*: for instance, the quotation of the melody to which Mariya has hailed Mazeppa as future Tsar of the Ukraine again when, mad, she faces him in the last scene (cf. the two appearances of the Archbishop's music in *The Maid of Orleans*), and—still more effective, indeed a real master-stroke—the lullaby which she sings over the body of Andrey.

This simple and beautiful song might well be given occasional hearings in our concert-halls, but there are few musically outstanding numbers in *Mazeppa*. The melodic inspiration neither rises to the level of Tchaïkovsky at his best nor falls to that of Tchaïkovsky at his worst. It keeps—particularly in such numbers as Mariya's arioso and duet with Andrey, Mazeppa's arioso in the First Act, the lament of Lyubov and the women, with its characteristic woodwind embroideries, and Andrey's aria in the last scene—to a respectable level of warm and always unmistakably Tchaïkovskian lyricism, but never leaves one with anything to remember. One favourite device of Tchaïkovsky's—the orchestral echoing of the voice part, usually by a solo woodwind instrument, to bridge the cæsuras (cf. the middle section of Lensky's aria in *Onegin* or the end of Ex. 17)—is used in *Mazeppa* more perhaps than in any other opera of Tchaïkovsky's; it becomes particularly wearisome when the voice part consists merely of short-winded arioso phrases.

Tchaïkovsky's choice of subject for his next opera[1] was once again decided by a single scene. His brother Modest tells the story:

[1] Among the other opera subjects that temporarily attracted Tchaïkovsky's attention in the early 1880s was the legend of Sadko, afterwards used by Rimsky-Korsakov.

Peter Ilyich was at that time [i.e. January 1885] in search of an opera subject. I happened to be in Moscow and one day mentioned quite in passing that the scene of the meeting between 'Kuma' and the young Prince in Shpazhinsky's drama *The Sorceress* would be very effective in an opera, though without recommending the drama itself for a libretto. Peter Ilyich immediately bought a lithographed copy of this play and went into raptures over the scene in question. That was decisive. The next day a letter was written to the author of *The Sorceress* with a request for the drama to be turned into an opera libretto.

Shpazhinsky agreed (21 January/2 February, 1885) and set to work forthwith, while Tchaïkovsky passed the time with the transformation of *Vakula the Smith* into *Cherevichki*.

The action of *The Sorceress* in its operatic form is as follows:

Act I. A low inn on the banks of the Oka, near Nizhny-Novgorod. Foka (bass) and Paisy (tenor), a vagabond monk, mingle with the drinkers who are gaming and quarrelling. Enter Foka's niece, the inn-keeper Nastasya (nicknamed 'Kuma' = 'gossip') (soprano) with her friend Polya (mezzo-soprano). Boats pass on the river; the young Prince Yury (tenor), his huntsman Zhuran (bass) and their men are returning from a bear-hunt; when Yury has passed, 'Kuma''s quietness suggests that she has fallen in love with him. Lukash (tenor), one of the drinkers, brings the alarming intelligence that Yury's father, Prince Nikita Kurlyatev (baritone), the Grand Ducal vicegerent of Nizhny-Novgorod, is approaching with the puritanical old clerk Mamïrov (bass), who has brought his master to see for himself the scandals of this inn of ill-repute. The drinkers are all frightened, but 'Kuma' keeps her presence of mind and at once bewitches the Prince by her beauty and simplicity. She brings him wine and calls the inevitable *skomorokhi* (tumblers) to amuse him. Mamïrov is furious and 'Kuma' mischievously induces the Prince to order him to dance too. General mockery of the old puritan.

Act II. The garden of the Prince's house. His wife, Princess Evprak-siya (mezzo-soprano), is pale and ill with jealousy, for he visits 'Kuma' every day. Her waiting-woman Nenila (contralto), who is Mamïrov's sister, vainly tries to console her, and Mamïrov himself inflames her jealousy still further. Enter Yury, who tries in vain to worm from his mother the secret of her trouble. Scene between Mamïrov and Paisy, who is ordered to act as a spy on 'Kuma'. Angry scene between the Princess and her husband, who makes no secret of his passion for 'Kuma'. Scene in which an angry crowd of townspeople break into the garden in pursuit of one of the Prince's men who—taking advantage of their master's preoccupation—have been committing all sorts of crimes; Yury pacifies them. Re-enter the Princess with Nenila; Paisy reports that the Prince has gone to 'Kuma' as usual and Yury thus learns the reason for his mother's grief. He swears that he will kill 'Kuma', the 'sorceress' who has bewitched his father.

Act III. 'Kuma' 's hut. The Prince is making love to her; she is cool, and when he becomes over-pressing she threatens to commit suicide rather than yield. Exit the Prince; enter Polya and Foka, who warn her of Yury's determination to kill her. 'Kuma' insists on being left alone, and presently Yury and Zhuran enter the moonlit hut. 'Kuma' reveals herself, and Yury is at once captivated by her beauty. She has little difficulty in convincing him of her innocence; Zhuran is sent away; love scene.

Act IV. A gloomy forest near the bank of the Oka. Hunting horns are heard, and the wizard Kudma (bass) emerges from his cave, only to retire on the approach of the hunters. They pass on but Zhuran waits to meet Yury. From their conversation it appears that he has arranged to meet 'Kuma' here and fly with her; exeunt both to join the bear-hunt. Enter Paisy with the Princess, who persuades the wizard to give her a poison for 'Kuma'; they go into the cave. On the Oka a boat appears with 'Kuma', who is set ashore with her belongings. The Princess, who is unknown to 'Kuma', comes out of the cave, gains her confidence and, pretending to give her a drink from the spring, administers the poison to the accompaniment of the wizard's mocking laughter. Hunting horns; the Princess bids 'Kuma' farewell; Yury rushes in joyously—but the poison is already beginning to work and 'Kuma' dies in his arms while his mother returns to rejoice in her revenge. 'Kuma' 's body is borne away by the hunters; exit the Princess, cursed by her son. Yury is left alone lamenting, when a number of boats appear on the river. It is the Prince with his men, in pursuit of 'Kuma' and Yury. The Prince thinks Yury is concealing her, will not believe the truth and—just as the Princess reappears—kills his son in an outburst of jealous fury. The young Prince's body is borne away and his father, left alone in the dark forest, goes mad to the accompaniment of thunder, lightning and the wizard's laughter.

It is difficult to understand why Tchaïkovsky was ever attracted by this extraordinary melodrama. Apart from its absurdities and unrealities, it contains far too much action, too many secondary characters and too many superfluous episodes. As the composer told his librettist's wife, 'He [Shpazhinsky] knows the stage admirably but he can't adapt himself to the demands of opera. He uses too many words; dialogue predominates too much over lyricism' (letter of 27 October/8 November, 1887). Tchaïkovsky himself had to make drastic cuts in the libretto—even, when the composition was finished, in his music—and the letter to Shpazhinsky in which he points out that after 'Kuma' has bewitched the son as well as the father 'it's impossible to drag out two more whole vast acts', has already been quoted.[1] But the attempt to cram the content of those two long acts into a single one only resulted in Act IV of the opera becoming ridiculously crowded.

Even more than in *Mazeppa* one feels the lack of sympathetic or even interesting characters. All these persons except 'Kuma' are lay figures, and she is not quite credible. Her beauty, her charm—which have the effect of witchcraft on every man who sees her—constitute the mainspring of the action; yet in musical fact she has not even the charm of Oksana in *Vakula*. But Tchaïkovsky *conceived* her as a more remarkable character, and it is worth quoting at length from a letter to Emilya Pavlovskaya, his favourite Tatyana and Oksana, for whom the rôle of 'Kuma' was conceived and who actually 'created' it (at the Maryinsky Theatre, St Petersburg (20 October/1 November, 1887). When Pavlovskaya first heard of his intention to compose *The Sorceress*, she had taken an opportunity of seeing Shpazhinsky's play and conceived a violent dislike to it, particularly to the leading rôle, which seems to have been originally conceived on coarser, more realistic lines—as Mérimée's Carmen is more realistic than Bizet's. 'My conception of Nastasya's type is quite different from yours,' the composer wrote to his prima donna (April 12/24, 1885).

Of course she is a *loose woman*, but her charm does not lie merely in her ability to talk well. That would be enough to attract the people to her inn. But it wouldn't be enough to turn the young Prince from a bitter enemy, who has come to kill her, into a lover. In the depths of this loose woman's soul lie a certain *moral power and beauty* which up to now have had no opportunity to unfold themselves. *This power is love.* She is a strong womanly nature who can love only once and can sacrifice *everything* for her love. While her love is still unborn Nastasya squanders her power so to speak in small change, i.e. she makes a joke of compelling everyone who comes in her way to fall in love with her. She remains a sympathetic, charming, though spoiled woman; she knows she is charming, is content to be, and—since she is neither guided by religious faith nor, being an orphan, has received a proper upbringing—pursues the single aim of having a good time. Then appears the man who has power to touch the slumbering better chords of her inward being and—she is transformed. Life loses for her its value so long as her goal is not reached; her charms, which hitherto have possessed an elementary, instinctive power of attraction, now

[1] See p. 120.

163

become a powerful weapon which in a moment overcomes the hostile power, i.e. the hatred of the young Prince. Then both surrender themselves to the mad torrent of love which leads to the inevitable catastrophe—her death—and this death leaves the spectator with a sense of peace and reconciliation. At any rate it will be so in my libretto, though it's different in the drama. Shpazhinsky understands perfectly well what I want and will work out the characterisation in accordance with my intentions. He will soften some of the rough edges of Nastasya's *manières d'être* and bring the hidden power of her *moral* beauty more into the foreground. *He and I*, later *you* too (if you will come to terms with this rôle), will so arrange it that in the last act everyone will have to weep. As regards costume and make-up, there's no need for headaches about that. We'll arrange it so that there's nothing repellent. If Savina [the actress whom Pavlovskaya had seen play the part in its original, non-prettified form] was badly dressed there's no need for you to be. . . . My enthusiasm for *The Sorceress* has not made me untrue to the fundamental requirement of my soul: to illustrate in music Goethe's words, *Das Ewig-Weibliche zieht uns hinan*. The circumstance that the power and beauty of Nastasya's womanliness long remain covered under a cloak of sin only heightens the theatrical interest. Why do you love the rôle of la Traviata? Why are you so fond of Carmen? Because power and beauty peep out from these characters, though in coarse form. I assure you that you will also grow fond of the *Sorceress*. I won't say much about the other characters. I will only tell you that in my version the Princess will also be a strong personality. If this character has struck you only as the type of a *jealous and amorous old woman*, it is probably because you have seen it badly played. She is not jealous of the elder Prince's person but on account of her noble rank; she is a rabid aristocrat to whom the preservation of the honour of her sex is everything and who is capable of giving her life or committing a crime for honour's sake.

There is no need to look any further for the reasons why *The Sorceress* is a failure. A dramatic composer may sometimes 'soften some of the rough edges' of a character with impunity—Verdi and Bizet and their librettists did so in the cases Tchaïkovsky mentions—but anxiety to conciliate a prima donna who disliked realistic rôles could only be unfortunate. *The Sorceress* is, or ought to be, a dramatic, realistic opera; as it is, it is only a convincing demonstration that Tchaïkovsky was not a truly dramatic composer. He was not objective enough; his power of dramatic expression was paralysed directly it was dissociated from more or less Tchaïkovskian types of character. Brutal Princes and haughty Princesses and enchanting hussies were quite outside his range, and the attempt to convert the enchanting hussy into something like a rustic Tatyana completely failed.

The Sorceress is particularly disappointing in that it begins so well. The First Act, where there is practically no drama but only lively tableaux, is delightfully colourful. These drunken roistering scenes may not be very realistic judged by Mussorgskian standards (as we can, unfortunately, hardly help judging them now), but by the conventional operatic standards still generally valid in the 1880s—Tchaïkovsky's own standards —they are first-rate. The instrumental introduction, mainly based on Nastasya's song later in the Act, sets the note: a folkish melody with Glinka-like treatment. And the opening chorus, the approaching chorus of girls, the 5/4 opening of the scene of the arrival in boats of more convivial citizens from Nizhny-Novgorod, the little scene between Nastasya and Lukash (the bell passage just before would pass unnoticed if transferred to Borodin's *Igor*), the sonorous E flat theme which permeates the scene of the passing of Yury and his men, Lukash's 'Come along you pretty girls' and the girls' reply, the thoroughly Russian character of the recitative in which the old Prince first addresses 'Kuma' and in which she replies, the song in which she defends herself and at the same time attacks Mamïrov, the recommencement of the jollification (with the Prince joining in)—all these are beautiful or racily characteristic music. Only the tumblers' dance at the end of the Act is a little less colourful than might have been expected, and the unaccompanied decimet with chorus, which opens the finale, though notable as a technical feat, is disappointingly operatic.

But when the drama begins, the music (one might almost say) finishes. There are a few good moments here and there in the three remaining acts, generally when the music recaptures the Russian flavour of Act I: the chorus of girls at the beginning of Act II, the music that accompanies Yury's first entry, the really lovely eight bars in which in Act III Nastasya addresses Yury as her 'falcon', the male chorus dying away in the distance as the old Prince is left alone on the stage towards the end of the last Act. But for the rest this Russianness is either strongly diluted—as in the prelude to Act IV, where a melody with a folk-song cadence, taken from the passage where the boat bearing Nastasya and her belongings comes into sight, is incongruously mixed with the conventional blood-and-thunder music of the theatrical hack. Nor is this weakening of the national flavour compensated for, as in *Onegin*, by the power of Tchaïkovsky's own peculiar lyricism. The duet for the Princess and her son in Act II, though pretty, is weak and utterly inexpressive of either the singers' characters or the words they sing. The elder Prince's love-song in Act III is again pretty in the Gounod vein. 'Kuma' 's arioso in the last act is pitifully weak by comparison with Natalya's arioso in *The Oprichnik* of twenty years earlier, while the 'poison' duet that has come just before is to English ears absurdly suggestive of Gilbert and Sullivan. Indeed, the high-water mark, such as it is, of Tchaïkovsky's more personally lyrical invention in *The Sorceress* is the phrase that crowns the love-duet at the end of Act III ('And began to forget everything: why I had come to thee'):

Ex. 22

That was the best he could do for the emotional culmination of the whole drama.

Nor does he rise to the wonderful opportunities offered by some of the dramatic moments. Consider the scene in which Nastasya, alone in the moonlit hut, awaits the coming of the man she loves—coming to kill her. (Incidently this scene is an excellent example of Tchaïkovsky's favourite device of using some attractive, unpretentious little orchestral theme, not a *Leitmotiv* or anything like one, to punctuate a scene and give it unity.) However adequate the declamation, the orchestral figuration—and they are no more than adequate—the stale diminished-seventh harmony deprives them of all force. Yury's actual entry and his immediate enslavement by Nastasya's beauty are even more completely thrown away. And the final scene of the elder Prince going mad in the forest is inferior to the scene of the Miller's madness in Dargomïzhsky's *Rusalka*, to say nothing of the hallucination scene in *Boris Godunov*.

Tchaïkovsky was, in his own words, eager 'to get his revenge after the unlucky *Sorceress*' and during this period, when he was 'ready to rush at any subject you like', he expressed regret that his brother Modest was preparing a libretto on Pushkin's story *The Queen of Spades* for another composer, N. S. Klenovsky. Vsevolozhsky, the Director of the Imperial Theatres, had first suggested the subject to Klenovsky in 1885; he thought at the very beginning that it would be 'necessary to idealise Hermann a little and to make the Countess a live human being, not a puppet as in Pushkin', and suggested that 'as regards costume' it would be a good idea to 'transfer the action to the eighteenth century'. A scenario was roughed out by Shpazhinsky, but nothing came of this and fully two years passed before Klenovsky invited Modest Tchaïkovsky to prepare a libretto. By March 1889 Modest had written and Klenovsky had composed four scenes—presumably the rough equivalents of Acts I and II as we have them, though the libretto was very different from the libretto we know—but then the project inexplicably collapsed. Tchaïkovsky had already at one point shown signs of hankering after his brother's subject, only to turn away to compose the Fifth Symphony: 'I shall write an opera only if I come across a subject capable of warming me through and through. A subject like *The Queen of Spades* doesn't move me and I should only be able to write perfunctorily.' Yet now, in December 1889,[1] when Klenovsky abandoned his claim on Modest's unfinished libretto and Vsevolozhsky wanted him to save his long cherished project, he hardly even hesitated. The libretto was approved by the Theatre Directorate, though with various changes including the addition of the scene by the canal, and Tchaïkovsky rushed off to Florence for peace and quiet, and set to work on 19/31 January, 1890, finishing the sketches on 3/15 March, the vocal score on 26 March/7 April and the full score on 8/20 June. Vsevolozhsky got his opera in time for 'the next season', and it was duly produced at the Maryinsky Theatre on 7/19 December of the same year.

Pushkin's Hoffmannesque short story, told with purely Pushkinian irony, may be summarised as follows:[2] A young Engineer officer named Hermann is fascinated by gambling, but being of German origin (hence, in Russian eyes, ridiculously prudent and methodical), never gambles himself. In his presence one of the gamblers, Tomsky, tells the story of how his aged grandmother acquired in her youth the secret of an infallible winning sequence of three cards. Hermann is fascinated by the idea of wheedling the secret out of the old Countess, begins hanging about outside her house, and is soon struck by the beauty of her orphan *protégée* and companion Lizaveta. The wretched, repressed Liza is captivated by this unknown admirer, and when he sends her a love-letter she gives him a rendezvous in her room. But Hermann takes the opportunity to conceal himself first in the Countess's room and, when the old lady is left alone, frightens her literally to death in trying to make her reveal her secret. He then visits Liza and cruelly tells her the whole story. Three days later he attends the Countess's funeral and approaches her coffin with the other mourners to give her a last kiss—and he has an illusion that she winks at him sarcastically. That night he is visited by her ghost, who reveals that the secret sequence is three, seven, ace. Hermann goes to a gambling club, where the wealthy Chekalinsky is banker, backs the three and wins an enormous sum; backs the seven and wins again[3]—and then by some blunder, instead of the ace, plays the Queen of Spades and loses everything. At that moment he has the illusion that the Queen is winking at

[1] A month or two earlier there had been some question of a libretto by no less a writer than Chekhov on Lermontov's *Bela*, which Tchaïkovsky wished to compose.

[2] There is a good translation in the Everyman's Library volume, *The Captain's Daughter, and Other Tales* by Pushkin, translated by Natalie Duddington.

[3] It appears that this mysterious game was faro: see Arthur Jacobs's introduction to his translation of the libretto, London, 1961.

him: 'he was struck by an extraordinary likeness'. . . . And in a brief epilogue Pushkin tells us that Hermann is now in an asylum where he keeps muttering with incredible rapidity, 'Three, seven, ace! Three, seven, Queen,' and that Lizaveta married 'a very nice young man in the Civil Service, son of the old Countess's former steward'.

Modest Tchaïkovsky took this dry and fantastically humorous tale and saturated it with the sham romanticism of the novelette, providing Liza with a wealthy fiancé, tagging on a gloomily tragic ending and making every opportunity for interpolating songs and even a whole 'pastoral interlude' that have nothing to do with the action. Among other changes, the Countess becomes Liza's grandmother instead of Tomsky's. The general result is as follows:

Act I. *Scene* 1. A public garden in St Petersburg; children, nurses, etc. Meeting between Chekalinsky (tenor), Surin (bass), Hermann (tenor) and Tomsky (baritone). Hermann confides to Tomsky that he is madly in love with an unknown beauty. Enter Prince Eletsky (baritone), whom they congratulate on his engagement. Enter the Countess (mezzo-soprano) with Liza (soprano), who turns out to be Eletsky's betrothed and Hermann's unknown. While the Countess is talking, Tomsky tells the other men the 'three-card' story. A thunderstorm disperses the promenaders; Hermann is left brooding over the story.

Scene 2. Liza's room. She, her friend Polina (contralto) and other girls are singing and dancing till the French governess (mezzo-soprano) comes in and stops them. Liza, left alone, reveals that instead of her betrothed she is fascinated by the unknown officer who looks like 'a fallen angel'. At that moment he enters from the balcony. Liza is with difficulty persuaded not to alarm the household, but she is about to dismiss him when the Countess enters, while Hermann hides—and the 'three-card' story comes back to his mind. When the Countess leaves the room, Hermann again protests his love and this time Liza yields.

Act II. *Scene* 3. A masked ball. Eletsky is disturbed by Liza's troubled mood. Surin and Chekalinsky, who have discovered the secret of Hermann's preoccupation with the 'three-card' story, play tricks on him; he takes their whisperings for spirit-voices. A 'pastoral interlude', Karabanov's *Faithful Shepherdess*, is performed for the amusement of the guests, the principals being Prilepa (soprano),[1] Milovzor (played by Polina) and Prilepa's wealthy admirer, Zlatogor (played by Tomsky). Liza gives Hermann the key to the garden so that he may get to her at night more easily. It is announced that the Empress is coming

[1] There was originally some idea, rejected by the composer, that Prilepa might be played by Liza. In Rosa Newmarch's English version Prilepa becomes Chloë and Milovzor, Daphnis.

—the period is that of Catherine the Great—and great excitement is built up. As Her Majesty is about to enter, the curtain falls.

Scene 4. The Countess's bedroom. Hermann conceals himself. The Countess is put to bed by Liza and her attendants. Hermann emerges and frightens the old lady to death. Liza appears and finds that Hermann's card mania is stronger than his love.

Act III. *Scene 5.* Hermann's quarters in the barracks. Hermann alone. Liza has not lost all faith in him and has written asking him to meet her by the canal opposite the Winter Palace. He fancies he still hears the singing at the Countess's funeral. The ghost enters and tells him the secret.

Scene 6.[1] Liza alone at the rendezvous by the canal. Hermann comes but can talk of nothing but the secret of the cards. He finally repulses Liza brutally and she throws herself into the canal.

Scene 7. The gambling club. Enter Hermann, who wins twice, then plays against Eletsky, stakes everything, and loses on the Queen of Spades. The Countess's ghost appears to him; in a frenzy he stabs himself and dies. The assembled gamblers sing a brief prayer for his 'suffering spirit'.

Although Modest Tchaïkovsky was mainly responsible for the libretto of *The Queen of Spades*, the composer took an active part in shaping it. Indeed, the manuscript reveals that Modest wrote only on the right-hand half of each sheet of paper, while the left half is often covered by his brother's comments, substituted verses of his own and musical sketches. The text of Eletsky's aria in scene 3, for instance, is wholly the composer's. As with Shpazhinsky, Tchaïkovsky had to press for cuts. 'You've done the libretto very well', he wrote on 23 January/4 February, 1890, 'but there's one thing wrong—*too many words*. Please be as short and laconic as possible. I shall leave out a few things.' These 'few things left out' include three couplets of Hermann's arioso in the first scene, much of his original monologue at the end of that scene, a second interlude—Derzhavin's 'Ode in Honour of Prince Vyazemsky'—in scene 3, and much of the original scene between Liza and the Prince. On the other hand he actually added a few words to the Prince's part 'so as to bring it forward'; he always liked to strengthen subordinate rôles.

Tchaïkovsky liked the text for recitatives to be in rhythmic prose. 'I'm awfully pleased with the way you've re-done Hermann's words in the chief scene—the scene of the old lady's death: Pushkin's text has remained almost unchanged, but there's rhythm,' he wrote (25 February/9 March).

---

[1] This scene was inserted by the composer (who wrote most of the text for it), against the advice of Modest and Laroche, partly because otherwise the last Act would have been practically womanless, partly because 'the spectator must know what becomes of Liza. Her rôle can't end with scene 4' (as it practically did in Pushkin's story).

And in song passages he disliked short lines, which would hamstring long-breathed melodic phrases: 'I've decided to leave out everything that Hermann says in short lines.'

But as Tchaïkovsky himself remarked, he stands 'not by the word but by the scene', and Yarustovsky makes some interesting comments on his skill in building, and inducing his librettist to build, effective scenes:

> The soundest dynamic development of a dramatic line in opera is usually constructed according to the so-called law of 'repeated complexes', one of the principal laws of dramaturgy which opera has acquired from drama. Let us examine, for instance, the composition of the second scene of *The Queen of Spades*. We clearly observe the threefold repetition of a scenic-emotional situation, each time interrupted by a counter-action: after a 'neutral' episode (romance, duet, dances) Liza is left alone; her emotional state gradually changes and develops; appearance of Hermann. Again a gradual development in the emotional condition of both, a culmination—and again an interruption—the appearance of the Countess; finally—the third 'wave', forming the climax of the whole scene. . . . We may observe a similar development in the letter scene in *Onegin*, in the scene of 'Kuma' and the young Prince in *The Sorceress*, and in a whole series of other scenes.

It may be added that the emotional parallel between the second and third 'waves' in scene 2 is reflected in the musical substance of each wave and thus helps to condition the musical form on an almost symphonic scale.

The Queen of Spades seems to offer little that could arouse a composer's sympathy as Tchaïkovsky needed to have his sympathies aroused if he was to do good work. Hermann is a contemptible figure (in Pushkin actually ridiculous), the old Countess a repellent one, and even the unfortunate Liza is not particularly attractive. But a letter which Tchaïkovsky wrote to his brother a few hours after the completion of the composition-sketch throws a valuable light on his emotional state and also perhaps explains why *The Queen of Spades*, by no means Tchaïkovsky's second best opera, is his second most popular:

> I composed the very end of the opera yesterday before lunch and when I got to Hermann's death and the final chorus I felt so *sorry* for Hermann that I suddenly began to weep violently. This weeping went on awfully long and turned into a very pleasant state of mild hysteria, i.e. it was awfully sweet to weep. Then I considered why (for I'd never before had this experience of crying about my hero's fate and I wanted to understand why I wanted to cry so much). I found that *Hermann* had been for me not a mere pretext for writing this or that music, but all the time a real, living man, and what is more a very sympathetic one.

Because *Figner* [the greatest Russian tenor of the day] is sympathetic to me and because the whole time I imagined Hermann in *Figner's* form—I shared most keenly in his sad fate. Now I think that, probably, this warm, living feeling for the hero of the opera is favourably reflected in the music.

The score of *The Queen of Spades* is saturated with hysterical emotion and, lying chronologically between the Fifth and Sixth Symphonies, belongs almost entirely to their emotional world.

The orchestral introduction, an odd piece of patchwork, might easily belong to either of the last two symphonies, particularly in its harmonic intensification and the almost *Tristan*-esque working up of the not very distinguished love-theme from scene 2 (which returns in the closing scene of the opera). So might the passage where Hermann realises that the Countess is dead, practically the whole of the scene by the canal, the mournful descending melody that accompanies Hermann's first entrance and his arioso in the first scene—indeed, most of the music associated with the 'hero' himself. That 'mournful descending melody' (cf. also the melody accompanying the appearance of Liza and the Prince in scene 3) has a close family likeness to the phrase which recurs throughout the opera when the 'three cards' are mentioned, itself an echo of Lensky's aria in *Onegin* and a foreboding of the opening of the finale of the Sixth Symphony[1]—as well as to Ex. 22 in *The Sorceress*. In each case this phrase is associated with the idea of death.

A particularly interesting point is Tchaïkovsky's transformation of the end of Hermann's phrase into a 'fatal' motto-theme, first heard in the introduction, which recurs dozens of times throughout the score as no other single theme recurs in any other of Tchaïkovsky's operas:

Ex. 23

The other main element in the music of *The Queen of Spades* is that of eighteenth-century pastiche. As we have seen, Tchaïkovsky always delighted in opportunities for this—the minuet in *Vakula*, Triquet's couplets in *Onegin* and many examples outside the operas—but he had never allowed himself so many as in *The Queen of Spades*: the duet for Liza and Polina (to a poem by Zhukovsky), the whole long interlude of *The Faithful Shepherdess* (a miniature dramatic cantata taking up twenty-eight pages of the vocal score), and Tomsky's song in the last scene (a setting of a poem by the eighteenth-century writer Derzhavin). And the Countess, recalling the days of her youth, actually sings the air 'Je crains

[1] See the musical example on p. 114.

171

de lui parler la nuit', from Grétry's *Richard Cœur de Lion*—anachronistic-ally, for the Countess's youth must have begun to fade half a century before the composition of Grétry's opera.

The borrowing from Grétry is frankly acknowledged in the score but there are other borrowings or near-borrowings which are not so acknow-ledged. (The Grétry itself is prefaced by an adapted snatch of 'Vive Henri IV' on the cor anglais.) Tchaikovsky took with him to Florence seven eighteenth-century opera scores: *Richard* and another opera by Grétry (*Les deux avares*), Salieri's *Fiera di Venezia*, Piccinni's *Didon*, Monsigny's *Déserteur*, Martin y Soler's *Burbero*, and Astaritta's *Rinaldo*. What use he made of them, other than *Richard*, I do not know; perhaps he only soaked in their style. But the love-duet in the interlude is derived from Mozart (the piano concerto, K.503, and the string quintet, K.406, in each case the second subject of the first movement, that of K.503 in the major)[1] and the minuet-theme of the finale is adapted from a chorus in an eighteenth-century Russian opera, Bortnyansky's *Le fils rival*:

Ex. 24

As for the polonaise for the arrival of the Empress when the interlude is over, Tchaikovsky took the words and imitated the music from the most famous of all late-eighteenth-century polonaises, Kozłowski's 'Thunder of Victory', which was used for a time as a sort of Imperial hymn.

But these rococo insets are not the only parenthetic episodes, padding out the length but holding up the action. There are, for instance, Polina's romance in the second scene (the best example of truly Tchaïkovskian melody in the whole score) and the girls' chorus which follows it (which, with the nursemaids' song in the opening scene, provides the sole whiff of folk-music). The polonaise heralding the spoof entry of the Tsaritsa was an effect devised by the composer himself, *vide* his letter to Modest of 20 February/4 March, 1890, in order to get an effective ending to the scene. Hermann's song 'What is our life? A game!' in the last scene,

---

[1] See N. Rukavishnikov, 'Kak sozdavalas "Pastoral" iz *Pikovoy dami*', *Sovetskaya muzïka* (1940), no. 3, p. 45.

though it has more point, more dramatic justification than these, is also a parenthesis; it must be reckoned among the 'French' elements in the score, with the episode of the boys playing at soldiers in the opening scene (standing midway between the scene that obviously suggested it in *Carmen* and the toy soldiers of *Nutcracker*), the governess's arioso (where the Frenchness is of course deliberate), and the opening of scene 4 (which stands in a direct line between the first movement of the Fourth Symphony and the Flower Valse in *Nutcracker*).

One other page of *The Queen of Spades* is worth looking at and performing: Liza's 'Ah, I am worn with my sorrow', sung as she waits for her lover by the canal. It is not first-rate Tchaïkovsky but it stands out in a score which, despite its popularity in Russia, Tsarist and Soviet alike, is decidedly weak from the lyrical point of view. Such things as the square-cut and painfully conventional 'Chorus of promenaders' in scene 1, Liza's monologue in scene 2 almost till the moment of Hermann's appearance, Hermann's 'Forgive me, bright celestial vision', Eletsky's aria in the fête scene, Hermann's pleading with the old Countess and the duet in scene 6 compare rather dismally with the lyrical beauties of Tchaïkovsky's early operas. They lack even the stamp of his personality.

Tchaïkovsky's last two stage works are of slight importance. They are the incidental music to *Hamlet*, written hurriedly and very much against the grain in January 1891, for Lucien Guitry's benefit on 9/21 February, and the one-act opera *Iolanta*, a setting of a libretto by his brother Modest based on Zvantsev's translation of Henrik Hertz's *Kong Renés Datter*, which in turn originated in a story by Hans Andersen. The *Hamlet* music cannot compare in interest or importance with the *Snow Maiden* music. The overture is a shortened version of the big overture-fantasia *Hamlet*, rescored for the small orchestra of the Mikhaylovsky Theatre, which also provides the material for two of the melodramas and the brief final march (presumably for the entry of Fortinbras). The entr'acte before Act II is a cut-down version of the 'alla tedesca' movement from the Third Symphony, the trio being omitted; that before Act III is note for note the same as the melodrama that accompanies Kupava's complaint in Act II of *Snow Maiden*; that before Act IV is a piece composed seven years earlier for the jubilee of the actor I. V. Samarin and later published as an Elegy for him. Only the entr'acte before Act V, used again later as a funeral march, was specially written.

Iolanta was a commissioned work, a one-act opera intended to be produced (as it actually was on 6/18 December, 1892) with the two-act ballet *Nutcracker*. The subject was chosen by Tchaïkovsky himself, though having chosen it he temporarily took a violent dislike to it, and the composition, begun in July 1891, at first gave him considerable trouble. The action is as follows:

Iolanta (soprano), the blind daughter of a fifteenth-century king of Provence, is picking fruit in her garden. She has never been allowed to know she is different from other people, and no stranger is allowed, on pain of death, to approach her. Her friends Brigitte (soprano) and Laura (mezzo-soprano) and her maids, help her to find the fruit; her old nurse, Martha (contralto), holds the basket. Iolanta is tired and sad, and after trying to divert her with music and flowers her companions sing her to sleep and carry her into the castle. Horn calls are heard. Martha's husband, the gate-keeper Bertrand (baritone), opens the gates to Almerik, the King's armour-bearer (tenor), who announces the arrival of King René (bass) with the Moorish doctor Ebn-Hakia (bass) who is to attempt to restore Iolanta's sight. After looking at her, Ebn-Hakia says a cure is possible but on one condition: Iolanta must *know* she is blind and *will* to see. The King refuses this condition. Exeunt both.

Enter Robert, Duke of Burgundy (baritone), with Count Vaudemont (tenor). Robert has been betrothed to Iolanta from childhood, but has never seen her, is (like everyone else outside the castle) ignorant of her blindness, and, being in love with another woman, is now making his way to King René's court unwillingly and in the hope that René will release him from his pledge. He and Vaudemont have come upon Iolanta's hiding-place quite by accident. The two young men see the still sleeping Iolanta, and Vaudemont is completely enchanted by her; the Duke thinks they have wandered into a sorcerer's domain and tries, in vain, to drag his friend away. Their voices awaken Iolanta. Robert rushes off to fetch their followers and rescue Vaudemont from the enchantment. Vaudemont soon discovers from his conversation with Iolanta that she is blind, and inadvertently reveals the fact to her too. Enter the King, Ebn-Hakia, and the rest; the King is overwhelmed by the apparent misfortune of the revelation, but Ebn-Hakia points out that his condition is now fulfilled. Yet Iolanta does not really long for sight, for she does not know what sight means. To give her a motive the King says that Vaudemont must die for disregarding the notice forbidding entrance to the castle-grounds—unless Iolanta's sight is restored. She says whe will bear anything to save this young man with whose voice she has fallen in love. She is led away by Ebn-Hakia and the women. The King tells Vaudemont that the threat was only a device to work on Iolanta.

The Duke returns with his followers. General explanation: that Robert does not love Iolanta but that Vaudemont does. Bertrand runs in to announce that the treatment is completed. Ebn-Hakia leads in Iolanta blindfold and removes the cloth from her eyes. She sees. General rejoicing.

One wonders what attracted Tchaïkovsky to this subject, even temporarily; perhaps the psychological point that the heroine's physical abnormality can be removed only when she recognises it and wills its removal strongly enough. But it is hardly surprising that he felt considerable distaste for it and that his already quoted confession to Fedotov that 'medieval dukes and knights and ladies captivate my imagination but not my *heart*' was written only a month or two after he had finished scoring *Iolanta*. As in so many earlier cases, he began with a crucial scene: in this case, the one between Iolanta and Vaudemont. 'You've done this scene splendidly', he wrote to Modest, 'and the music might have been very beautiful, but I feel I haven't succeeded particularly well. I keep falling into self-repetition, so that a good deal in this scene is like *The Sorceress*.' In the same letter he complains that, after this 'light' duet, there is 'too little music and nothing but explanation of the action'. A fortnight later (7/19 August, 1891) he reports that he is pleased with the Brigitte-Laura flower song and the lullaby. The whole work was completed in full score by mid-December.

Like *The Queen of Spades*, *Iolanta* reveals here and there affinities with *Nutcracker* on the one hand and the Sixth Symphony on the other. The dark colouring of the short orchestral introduction, which seems intended to suggest Iolanta's blindness and her sense of something lacking, is a weak anticipation—also mostly in B minor—of the Cimmerian darkness in which the last Symphony opens. A great many passages in the opera belong to the harmonic world of the Symphony, a world of increased harmonic tension. And when Vaudemont tells Iolanta 'Your wish is law to me' and when later she uses the same words to him, each sings the words to bars 3–4 of Ex. 1c on page 114. But the relationship to *Nutcracker* is still closer. One notices it in the pseudo-orientalism, otherwise so rare in Tchaïkovsky, of Ebn-Hakia's 'Two worlds: fleshly and spiritual', in Robert's 'Who can compare with my Mathilde?' (which might have come straight from the Confituremburg), in the charming orchestration of Iolanta's first conversation with Vaudemont (particularly when he empties the beaker of wine), and above all perhaps at the end when Ebn-Hakia takes the kerchief from Iolanta's eyes and a sweet but undistinguished tune first insinuates itself in the orchestra as she asks 'Where am I?', is later sung by her as she sinks to her knees in grateful prayer (Ex. 25 on p. 176) and is used to clinch the final 'Hosannas' as the curtain falls. But one feels that this if pretty and quite in place in a fairy ballet, is rather inadequate as the expression of the feelings of a lady who has just been almost miraculously given her sight. (Even the harmony, as static as that in Ex. 22, gives no help here.) So with other passages. The women's flower song and the lullaby will pass muster, but the melody to which Vaudemont sings of light as 'the wondrous prime creation, first gift to the

world by its Creator' is less pretty and even more inadequate than Ex. 25. Yet this, too, is used again considerably in the last scene. That is the criticism one must level against the music of *Iolanta* as a whole: it is often pretty but dramatically inadequate and rather characterless. Not that the score is entirely lacking in unmistakably Tchaïkovskian melodies. Vaudemont's *romance*, written at Figner's request after the first run-through is developed from an impudent plagiarism of the horn theme in Ex. 16. And nothing could be more typical than the cantabile melody:

that accompanies the knights' discovery of the sleeping Iolanta, or the pretty canon on an oramented version of it a few pages later. (Here and elsewhere in *Iolanta*, as on some of the most impassioned pages of *The Queen of Spades*, the musical centre of gravity lies in the orchestra, while the voice part is merely declamatory; by the end of his life Tchaïkovsky was quite at home with the procedure which fourteen years earlier had scandalised him more than anything else in Wagner.) Naturally there is nothing Russian in the score—except the regal phrase heralding the reappearance of Robert with his armed followers, just as in *The Maid of Orleans* the King thanks his 'good people' in decidedly Russian accents. But no one but Tchaïkovsky could have written, for instance, the passage where Vaudemont dries Iolanta's tears and that where she sings, a few pages later, 'Thou speak'st so sweetly! I have never known such happiness,' with its characteristic echoing of the voice by the orchestra. Both of these occur in the first scene to be composed, and one can only regret that, having written it, the composer's inspiration should have ebbed so completely. The ensemble following the discovery that Iolanta knows she is blind is an instance of that vulgarisation of his own melodic and harmonic idiom in which Tchaïkovsky sometimes forestalled the Arenskys and Rakhmaninovs who tried to imitate him.

In January 1891, a few months before Tchaïkovsky began the composition of *Iolanta*, Taneyev had written to him: 'Apropos of opera in general. The question of how to write operas interests me in the highest degree and I've long wanted to exchange thoughts with you on this topic. Your views, so far as they are given concrete expression in your operas, do not completely satisfy me.' To this Tchaïkovsky replied with what in effect is a just summing-up of his aims as a stage-composer:

The question how one should write operas I've always decided, do decide and shall decide extraordinarily simply. One should write them (just like everything else, for that matter) as God has put it in your soul to write them. I've always tried to express in music as truthfully and sincerely as possible what was in the text. Truth and sincerity aren't just the result of brain-work but the immediate product of inner feeling. So that the feeling should be warm and vital, I've always tried to choose subjects in which the characters are real living people, feeling as I do. That's why I find Wagnerian subjects, in which there's nothing human, intolerable; nor would I have chosen a subject like yours [Taneyev's *Orestes*] with monstrous crimes, with the Eumenides and fates as actual characters. So, having chosen a subject and set about the composition of an opera, I've given free rein to my feelings, neither resorting to Wagnerian methods nor striving to be original. In doing so I by no means prevented the spirit of the age from influencing me. I confess that if there'd been no Wagner I should have written differently; I admit there is even *Kuchkism*[1] in my operatic writings; probably also Italian music, which I passionately loved in childhood, and Glinka whom I adored in my youth, have strongly influenced me—to say nothing of Mozart. But I have never invoked either of these idols but allowed them to direct my musical inner being as they liked. It may be that as a result of this attitude there is no direct evidence in my operas that they belong to this school or that; it may be that one or another of these forces has predominated over the rest and I have fallen into imitations— but however that may be, it has all come about of its own accord, and if I am confident of anything it is that in my writings I have shown myself as God created me and as I have been formed by education, circumstances and the nature of the age and land in which I live and work. I have never been untrue to myself. But how I am—whether good or bad—let others judge.   1945

[1] The spirit of the *Kuchka* or 'handful'.

Much has been written about the relationship between what we might well call 'Rimsky-Korsakov's *Boris Godunov*' and Mussorgsky's, little or nothing about that of Mussorgsky's work to the Pushkin drama which after all is the 'original' *Boris*. Yet the one relationship is quite as interesting as the other. Mussorgsky's treatment of Pushkin's text was no less drastic, and often no less puzzling, than Rimsky-Korsakov's treatment of his own music. Mussorgsky, of course, had the excuse that a librettist adapting a blank-verse play for musical setting *must* take liberties, that he necessarily has a licence one denies to a composer 'revising' a dead friend's score. It is a good excuse, but, as we shall see, it is to some extent vitiated by the nature of Mussorgsky's liberties. Nevertheless I must emphasise from the start that my purpose is not to excuse Rimsky-Korsakov by showing that Mussorgsky himself, *mutatis mutandis*, was just as bad. (Though it is evident that the whole of their circle held very free-and-easy views about textual accuracy.) Mussorgsky's treatment of his poet, 'the greater part' of whose verses he claimed to have 'preserved',[1] is interesting for its own sake, for the light it throws on his mind.

The most obvious need in the adaptation of any play for musical setting is, of course, for shortening, for compression. Music holds back pace. Mussorgsky would not have agreed with Wagner's view that opera cannot successfully cope with non-emotional action that is perfectly in place in ordinary drama—the basis of Mussorgskian aesthetics is that music can cope with the prose of life as well as with its poetry—but his attempt to set Gogol's comedy *The Marriage* word for word, just as it stood, must have taught him among other things that the sung word, even the recitatived word, is far slower than the spoken word. When in 1868 he turned from the uncompleted *Marriage* to Pushkin's *Boris Godunov* with its twenty-four scenes—five in prose, the rest in blank verse —he saw at once that he must select and compress. The first (1868–9) version of his opera actually consisted of seven scenes only, the second —made in 1871–2, and produced and published in somewhat cut form in 1874—of nine. Obviously much has gone by the board, and western critics have sometimes complained that the opera, like other Russian operas (e.g. *Prince Igor*), is not an organic whole but a series of disconnected scenes. I do not propose to discuss this charge here,[2] but I must

---

[1] See the title-page of the Oxford University Press vocal score; all page and other references are to this edition.

[2] I have already done so in the first chapter of my *Studies in Russian Music*.

make it clear that this disconnectedness is equally a feature of Pushkin's 'dramatic chronicle'. Pushkin gives us twenty-four scenes selected from the sequence of historical events that began in 1598, when Boris Godunov was implored to accept the Muscovite crown, and ended in 1605 with his death and the murder of his widow and son. Mussorgsky has time to give us only seven (or nine) scenes, not all of which correspond to Pushkin. But the principle is the same in both cases: Pushkin and Mussorgsky have both painted series of stage illustrations to a story they could assume to be well known to their audience.[1] Mussorgsky could further assume that a Russian opera audience had read its Pushkin, and there is no need here to underline the difference between that audience, for which the opera was written, and a western audience ignorant equally of Pushkin and of pre-Petrine Russian history.

Pushkin begins with a scene in the Kremlin between two boyars, Shuysky and Vorotïnsky, which sets the stage by reminding the audience of the political situation when Boris was still pretending to refuse the crown, and also begins to build up the character of Shuysky. This was omitted by Mussorgsky, who begins with a crowd scene in the courtyard of the Novodevichy Monastery roughly corresponding to scenes 2 and 3 in Pushkin: crowd scenes in the Red Square and in the Maidens' Field outside the Novodevichy Monastery. I say 'roughly corresponding', for there is no detailed correspondence at all: Shchelkalov, the Secretary to the Duma, addresses the assembled people—and the people reveal their blind obedience to authority, their political ignorance and indifference—but in completely different terms and on completely different lines. The only verbal connection between Mussorgsky and Pushkin consists of three words, 'The Secretary speaks' (or as Calvocoressi translates in the O.U.P. score, 'Hark to the Provost's words'), which Pushkin gives to 'the people' and Mussorgsky to a police officer. There are, incidentally, no police officers in either of the two Pushkin scenes.

Pushkin's fourth scene is laid in the palace of the Kremlin where Boris addresses the Patriarch and the boyars after his acceptance of the crown and where, after his exit, Shuysky and Vorotïnsky resume (as it were) their conversation in the opening scene. From Boris's address Mussorgsky borrowed eight or nine lines for the soliloquy in his coronation scene in the Kremlin square, which was otherwise entirely of his own devising, and the manner of his borrowing is worth examining in some detail, since it is typical of his procedure throughout the opera. He selects, he sometimes condenses by omitting anything from a single word to a number of lines, he interpolates extra words, he transposes words or phrases, and

---

[1] In point of fact Pushkin's play was never staged in his lifetime and has never been very successful in the theatre since. Though based, in intention, on Shakespeare's chronicle plays, it is essentially a 'closet play' like the poetic dramas of Tennyson and Browning.

he quite often alters a word or a phrase for no apparent reason. The passage in question illustrates all these points. In Pushkin Boris begins by reminding the Patriarch and the boyars of his unwillingness to ascend the throne, and goes on to reflect, for their benefit, that he is the successor of 'Ivan the Terrible' and the 'angel tsar' Fyodor. Instead of this, Mussorgsky makes him sing (p. 43) 'My soul is sad! A secret terror haunts me. With evil foreboding ev'ry hour is haunted.'[1] He then goes on in Pushkin's words:

> O father mine, lend me thy strength and wisdom,
> From Heaven you see our anguish, our distress,

a passage which is quite incomprehensible when thus removed to a different context, for who could guess in the opera that the 'father' thus invoked is the 'angel tsar' Fyodor, Boris's pious brother-in-law and predecessor? Pushkin's next three lines:

> O let your blessing fall on [him
> Who loved thee, whom thou exaltedst here]
> And bring me strength, refit and guide me,

are compressed by the substitution of 'me' for the words enclosed in square brackets. That is legitimate and comprehensible. But what can have been Mussorgsky's reason for transposing Pushkin's next two lines and garbling one of them? Pushkin wrote:

> May I rule in glory my people,
> (*Da pravlyu ya vo slave svoy narod*)
> May I, like thee, be just and happy.

Mussorgsky made this:

> May I, like thee, be just and happy
> In glory rule my people . . .
> (*Da v slave pravlyu svoy narod*).

There was no question of moulding the words for the sake of a musical conception; a glance at the score will show that the words are set as simple recitative.

The remainder of Boris's solo is entirely based on Pushkin (after a five-line cut), with two or three minor alterations. Pushkin says 'Now let us [go and] bow before [the tombs of] Russia's sleeping rulers'; Mussorgsky takes out the words in square brackets and substitutes 'Rus', the old name for Russia, for the modern word 'Rossiya' used by Pushkin. The poet says 'Call all our people to the feast'; the composer takes out

---

[1] My translated quotations from Mussorgsky's text are often either borrowed from Calvocoressi's version (O.U.P. edition) or adapted from it for greater verbal precision.

'all our', obviously in this case so as not to clutter the melodic phrase with superfluous syllables. But why did he in the next line substitute 'ot boyar' for Pushkin's 'ot vel'mozh'? The words are practically synonymous—'vel'mozha' means 'grandee'—and both have the stress on the second syllable. There is no perceptible reason for the change, and I suggest that the explanation is simple carelessness, a carelessness equally apparent in much else that Mussorgsky transcribed—from the words of a number of his songs to the stage directions of Ozerov's *Oedipus in Athens*.[1]

The next scene, that in Pimen's cell—the fifth in the play, the third in the opera—is the first of which it can be said that Mussorgsky's action and text are really based on Pushkin's. He actually preserved rather more than half the poet's verses—at any rate in the original version; the slashing cut made in 1874 (Pimen's description of the murder) removed nearly six pages of vocal score and nearly thirty lines of almost pure Pushkin. There are more wilful changes of words: e.g. at the very beginning Pimen says 'finished the work' ('okonchen trud') instead of 'fulfilled the task' ('ispolnen dolg') (p. 50)[2] and at the very end Grigory speaks of 'the judgment of mankind' ('lyudskovo') instead of 'the judgment of the world' ('mirskovo') (p. 79). But there is no need to give a full list of these or of the transposed words or lines. The important point is that practically all the text is Pushkin, if not quite pure Pushkin. Some of the cuts are slashing, though skilfully done: who would guess that on page 67 of the O.U.P. score, where Pimen, speaking of Ivan the Terrible, says 'And quietly speech poured from his lips', the words 'quietly' and 'speech' were originally ten lines apart? The only things inserted by Mussorgsky are the phrases on the page before this about 'the royal sceptre and the purple' and seeking 'within a cloister cell the peace that lasteth', and the short choruses of monks behind the scenes. Of these only the last was included in the 1869 version, the others being afterthoughts. Pushkin follows this scene with one[3] between the Patriarch and the Abbot of the Chudov Monastery, in which the latter brings news of Grigory's flight and his boast that he 'will be tsar in Moscow'. This short prose scene was justifiably left out of the opera, but scene 7, consisting almost entirely of a soliloquy by Boris, though not used by Mussorgsky in its existing form, gave him the text for Boris's famous monologue 'I stand supreme in power' in the terem scene, which will be discussed later.

Scene 8, by far the longest of the five prose scenes, is the one in that unforgettable 'inn on the Lithuanian border'. (The English reader may

---

[1] See p. 194.

[2] It will be noticed that Calvocoressi's translation restores Pushkin's wording.

[3] There is also a scene between the fugitive Grigory and a 'wicked monk' outside the Monastery, but Pushkin omitted this from the definitive version of his play.

need to be reminded that in the early seventeenth century Lithuania was not a tiny Baltic state but a great dukedom united to Poland by a common crown and stretching from the Baltic nearly to Smolensk and Kiev.) In the second version of his opera Mussorgsky inserted the hostess's song about the duck and the business of the approaching guests, but the original version began exactly as in Pushkin with the entrance of Grigory and the monks, and the hostess's words 'What refreshment will you take, reverend fathers?' (p. 87). And, as in the cell scene, Mussorgsky has kept pretty faithfully to his author. There are inevitable cuts, Varlaam's first remark in the play is divided between him and Misail in the opera, there are all sorts of apparently unmotivated verbal changes, but on the whole, one can say that the inn scene, like the one in Pimen's cell, is mainly Pushkin and preserves the greater part of Pushkin. Even Varlaam's song about the taking of Kazan is prescribed in the poet's stage-directions.

The scene of Boris and his children in the terem, which follows a banqueting scene in Shuysky's home (wisely passed over by Mussorgsky despite the light it throws on the character of the crafty Shuysky), is not so easily measured against the Pushkin text. To begin with, there are two widely different versions to compare with Pushkin: the shorter original of 1869 and the version drastically rewritten in 1871, which in turn was altered and cut before publication of the vocal score in 1874. On the whole the 1869 version keeps a good deal closer to Pushkin than that of 1871, though in one or two details the later version is actually more faithful. For instance Xenia, in her first speech, speaks of her dead bridegroom lying 'in a dark grave, in a strange land'. In his original version Mussorgsky set the greater part of this little speech just as Pushkin wrote it, altering only the two adjectives 'dark' to 'damp' and 'strange' to 'far-off'. In the later version Mussorgsky discards all but four of Pushkin's words, yet one of these four is the restored epithet 'strange'. Another tiny phrase from this first speech of Xenia's was transferred, in a slightly altered form, to another passage two pages farther on in the 1871 version. Indeed even in the 1869 version Pushkin's text is treated with the utmost freedom and the action, too, is somewhat altered; in the 1871 version the action is still further altered by the insertion of the nurse's 'gnat' song, the clapping game, the parrot incidents and so on. The differences are most clearly shown in tabular form:

Pushkin	*Mussorgsky (1869)*	*Mussorgsky (1871)*
Xenia's lament.	Xenia's lament, with the Tsarevich's map-reading.	Xenia's lament, with the episodes of the chiming clock, the 'gnat' song and the clapping game.
Enter Boris, who addresses Xenia.	Enter Boris, who addresses Xenia and dismisses her and the nurse.	Enter Boris, who addresses Xenia and dismisses her and the nurse.

The geography lesson.	The geography lesson. Boris's monologue, 'I stand supreme in power' (based almost entirely on the text of his monologue in Pushkin's seventh scene).	The geography lesson. Boris's monologue (incorporating only about eight lines of the Pushkin text); noise behind the scenes.
Scene with Semyon Godunov; Boris dismisses Xenia and the nurse.	Scene with a boyar.	Scene with a boyar. The Tsarevich's account of the parrot.
Scene with Shuysky. Boris alone.	Scene with Shuysky. Boris alone.	Scene with Shuysky. Boris alone. Hallucination scene, with the clock.

In both versions Mussorgsky makes Shuysky enter softly and overhear Boris's remarks about him (which follow Pushkin exactly in the 1869 version, but differ entirely in that of 1871); in Pushkin the prince enters directly *after* these remarks, at fig. 35 on page 139 of the O.U.P. score. Boris's second monologue, after Shuysky's exit, begins in both versions with the first four lines of the equivalent passage in Pushkin, and then harks back to garbled versions of the end of the speech in Pushkin's scene 7, which has already furnished the text of the solo, 'I stand supreme in power'. The lines which conclude both Mussorgsky versions—'O God on high! Thou who willest not the sinner's death. . . . Have pity on me and grant my guilty soul forgiveness!'—owe nothing to either of the passages in Pushkin; they are entirely the composer's invention, as of course was the hallucination caused by the chiming and the moving figures of the clock.

Pushkin now turns from Boris to his rival, and in a series of five scenes shows the Pretender among his Polish supporters, enslaved by the beauty of Marina, daughter of Mniszek, the Wojewoda of Sandomierz, and later crossing the Russian frontier at the head of his troops. In the original version of his opera Mussorgsky passed over the whole of this sequence; indeed in the original version Grigory—'Dimitry'—disappears completely after the inn scene; the dramatic limelight is concentrated on Boris. But in the second version of his opera Mussorgsky inserted two scenes (constituting the Third Act) which correspond to the Polish sequence in Pushkin. Which correspond, that is to say, superficially and in general function, but not at all in detail. Pushkin's scene 11—Dimitry holding a reception in Prince Constantin Wisnioviecki's house at Cracow —has no parallel in the opera and yielded Mussorgsky only two proper names for the entirely unconnected final scene of his second version, the so-called 'revolution scene' near Kromy: that of one of the priests, Czernikowski, and that of the bated nobleman, Khrushchov. Except that the one is a Catholic priest and the other a Russian nobleman, these episodic figures have nothing in common with the characters who make fleeting appearances in Pushkin's scene 11. Textually Mussorgsky borrowed three words from it, an invocation of St Ignatius for *his* Jesuit, Rangoni, in his second Polish scene (O.U.P. score, pp. 265–6).

Mussorgsky's first Polish scene corresponds to Pushkin's twelfth scene. In both Marina is seen being adorned by her maidens, though Mussorgsky has transferred her father's castle from Sambor to Sandomierz. But textually the two scenes have only one phrase in common: Marina's demand for 'My diamond crown! (or as Calvocoressi renders it, 'My coronet and pearls!', p. 231). But the whole dramatic context is different. In Pushkin it is the maid Ruzia who does most of the talking; she praises Dimitry, and her mistress merely pooh-poohs her in brief interjections. Mussorgsky inserted these Polish scenes so as to have a prima donna part in the opera; so he had to write for Marina on prima donna lines. The whole of her part here had to be invented, and her vanity and cold egotism are baldly set forth in her musically weak mazurka instead of being gradually revealed in the later course of the action. The latter part of the scene, with Rangoni—indeed the character of Rangoni —is entirely Mussorgsky's.

Pushkin's thirteenth and fourteenth scenes are headed respectively 'A Suite of Lighted Rooms in Mniszek's Castle' (where a conversation between Mniszek and Wisnioviecki is interrupted by a polonaise in which the dancers, two and two, are heard discussing Dimitry and Marina) and 'Night. A Garden. A Fountain'. This fountain scene is long and dramatic. After a monologue by the waiting Dimitry, Marina comes to him and there follows a powerfully conceived scene in which both their characters are fully revealed. Marina shows that she is in love, not with the man but with the possibility of a crown, while Dimitry is so far lost in love that he cares no more about the great adventure he has embarked on. Anxious to be loved for himself, not for what he pretends to be, he even confesses his imposture. Marina is shaken, but her ambition steels her— and finally her stinging words steel Dimitry too. As she leaves him, he reflects:

> Ah no—'tis easier to fight with Godunov
> Or fence with courtly Jesuits
> Than with women. The Devil take them. . . .
> Serpent! Serpent! . . .

Now let us see how Mussorgsky has reshaped all this in the second scene of Act III. He begins with Pushkin's stage-direction, adapting it not only for his own stage-direction ('A garden. A fountain. A moonlight night'), but also for the opening of Dimitry's monologue, 'At midnight . . . in the garden . . . by the fountain'. But his monologue is otherwise indebted to Pushkin only for the reference to Marina's enchanting 'voice' (which actually occurs in the play *after* her appearance). The scene with Rangoni is, of course, entirely Mussorgsky's, but for the passing reference to St Ignatius, already mentioned. Then Mussorgsky shows us the 'lighted rooms' from outside, and the guests come out into the garden to the sound of the polonaise. But the dialogue which contains the substance of the Pushkin scene is replaced by a festive, patriotic and anti-Russian chorus. The duet for Dimitry and Marina, when the guests have gone indoors again, preserves the characters of the infatuated Pretender and the cold ambitious woman spurring him to action, but on much broader and simpler lines; Dimitry does not confess his fraud, and the scene ends with Marina asking, and being granted, forgiveness in a commonplace love duet—while the melodramatic Rangoni chuckles in the background. Textually Mussorgsky's libretto is indebted to Pushkin for nothing but single words here and there; the nearest it approaches even to paraphrase is at the bottom of page 288 ('Pray spare me all this bombast' in Calvocoressi's version):

> *Pushkin:* I made this rendezvous with thee, not so as to hear the tender speeches of a lover. . . .
> *Mussorgsky:* Not for loving conversation, not for empty and stupid speeches, did I come to thee. . . .

and at the top of page 294:

> *Pushkin:* Don't torture me, exquisite Marina . . .
> *Mussorgsky:* Thou woundest my heart, cruel Marina . . .

Pushkin's scene 15, the crossing of the frontier, has no equivalent in Mussorgsky. His sixteenth scene, Boris in council discussing the measures to be taken against the Pretender, also has no real equivalent in the opera, but it suggested the setting for the later death scene (which Pushkin laid in the Tsar's apartments) and also contains the text of what is generally known as 'Pimen's tale' in that scene (pp. 349–52). Only in Pushkin this account of the healing of the blind shepherd at the tomb of the real Dimitry is given not by Pimen but by the Patriarch; in the play, Pimen appears no more after the cell scene. Textually Mussorgsky follows the poet fairly faithfully, making only short cuts (with one of more than a dozen lines near the end) and a few verbal changes and inversions of the kind noted in earlier passages.

Mussorgsky left aside Pushkin's seventeenth, nineteenth and twentieth scenes—Boris's foreign mercenaries fleeing at the Battle of Novgorod-Seversk, the Pretender interrogating a prisoner and the Pretender seen in the forest after his reverse at the Battle of Dobrinichy—but the eighteenth gave him the memorable scene before St Basil's Cathedral, with the episode of the simpleton, which was the penultimate tableau of the opera as he first conceived it and the most serious of the losses in the definitive version, despite the wholesale transference of much of the simpleton music to the new final scene 'in the forest near Kromy' (pp. 314–17 to 381–4, and pp. 325–6 to 417–18). Mussorgsky's text for the crowd music, up to the entry of the simpleton and his tormentors, is a very free paraphrase of the poet's text, embodying only a few of his actual words and phrases. Mityukha is an invention of the composer's; Pushkin specifies only 'a member of the crowd', 'another', 'a third' and 'a fourth'. On the other hand Mussorgsky makes the simpleton say '*Simpleton*, arise, pray to God Almighty' (p. 315) instead of naming himself as in Pushkin '*Nikolka*, arise', etc. He also omits the incident of the old woman giving the simpleton the kopek which is stolen from him. But on the whole the simpleton episode, including his conversation with the Tsar, is quite close to Pushkin, though there are the usual unmotivated verbal changes: e.g. the Tsar says, 'Don't touch him' (p. 323) instead of 'Leave him alone'. The chorus of people begging for bread was Mussorgsky's idea; in Pushkin the crowd only cry, 'The Tsar, the Tsar's coming!' And so was that stroke of genius, the simpleton left alone on the empty stage; in Pushkin the scene ends with the words, 'It is not so ordered by God's Mother' (bottom of p. 324).

The last parallel between the poet's version and the composer's is in the death scene, the twenty-first in Pushkin's play, the seventh and last in Mussorgsky's first version, and the penultimate in his second version. Mussorgsky's really has very little in common with Pushkin's. As I have already mentioned, the very settings differ; indeed the whole action differs in the opera. In the play we see Boris in his palace conversing with his trusted general Basmanov—who will be the first to desert the Godunov family after Boris's death; Basmanov, left alone, reveals his ambitions in a short monologue; there is an alarm outside; the Tsar has been taken suddenly ill; he is carried in dying, surrounded by his family and the boyars. Compare this with the opera. The Council of Boyars is discussing a suitable punishment for the Pretender; Shuysky gives his account of the Tsar's odd behaviour, in the middle of which the Tsar himself enters in a half-lunatic frenzy; finally Shuysky introduces Pimen whose account of the blind shepherd, taken, as I have already explained, from the Patriarch's speech in an entirely different council scene in Pushkin, completes the Tsar's collapse; the Tsarevich is sent for. From that point there is a real parallel between play and opera: the Tsar takes leave of his son, giving him much good counsel, and dies—though in the play we do not actually see his death. But the Tsar's farewell in the opera owes surprisingly little to that in the play. He begins, 'Leave us! let all go away!' (in Pushkin 'Let all go away—leave the Tsarevich alone with me'), and the opening of his actual farewell is practically the same as in Pushkin: 'Farewell, my son. And now your time has come to reign . . .' (p. 355). Only the words 'I am dying' were interpolated by Mussorgsky. And when we get to page 358, with the injunction to take care of Xenia, we find Mussorgsky again incorporating a line and a half of Pushkin. But between those points paraphrase and condensation have been carried so far—sixty-three lines of blank verse providing no more than forty-seven bars of music—that Mussorgsky's intervening text embodies only thirteen of Pushkin's actual words. The death-knell and the chorus behind the scenes were Mussorgsky's idea. At the reference to the 'skhima' (the taking of monastic vows when on the point of death) at fig. 63 he again borrows one or two words and phrases from Pushkin, but the bulk of the text is his own.

Pushkin's play has three more scenes—Basmanov being persuaded to change sides, the proclamation of Dimitry in Moscow and the murder of Boris's widow and son—but they failed to inspire Mussorgsky. In 1869 he ended his opera with the death of Boris; and when in 1872 he added the so-called 'revolution scene' near Kromy he took for it from Pushkin nothing but a couple of proper names and the simpleton episode from the scene before St Basil's.

Those are the essential facts of the relationship between Mussorgsky's libretto and Pushkin's play. They need little comment; most of them speak for themselves. Some of Mussorgsky's changes are easily understandable and quite justifiable; others—particularly the minor verbal alterations—seem pointless. Some of the major changes—such as the introduction of Rangoni, the melodramatic treatment of Boris's hallucinations in the terem scene (particularly its second version) and in the council of boyars, the banalization of the scene between Marina and Dimitry by the fountain—are altogether regrettable. But one point does emerge very markedly; the seven scenes which constitute the 1869 version are not only the best musically and make a more satisfactory dramatic whole[1] than either the 1872 version or the cut version of the latter which Mussorgsky published in 1874 (the original Bessel vocal score); they are also much more faithful to Pushkin.

[1] A note on the autograph piano score of the St Basil's scene, describing it as 'Fifth Act. First Tableau', suggests that these seven scenes were, after all, only a selection from Mussorgsky's original design.

1945

XI—THE MEDITERRANEAN ELEMENT IN
BORIS GODUNOV

One of the most curious characteristics of the major Russian composers was their parsimony, their unwillingness to waste anything. Tchaïkovsky, for instance, scraps an opera but uses bits of
it in his Second Symphony and his incidental music to Ostrovsky's *Snow
Maiden*; Borodin puts the 'leftovers' from *Prince Igor* into his Second and
Third Symphonies; four of the Mighty Handful collaborate in an opera-
ballet, *Mlada* (the subject which Rimsky-Korsakov afterwards tackled
single-handed), and dump into it whatever spare music they can find in their
portfolios; *Mlada* is abandoned—and they at once pull it to pieces and
use the pieces elsewhere. Practically everything is salvaged. Mussorgsky
was even more ingenious, and more economical, than his fellows. He had
a piece of 'witches' music' on his hands for many years; it did service as an
independent orchestral piece and in various other works—and then, after
all, it was left for Rimsky-Korsakov to re-compose it into what we know
as 'Mussorgsky's *Night on the Bare Mountain*'. And then there was the
choral piece which came into existence as an alleged 'scene in Sophocles's
Œdipus' (priests and people in the Temple of the Eumenides), turned up
in the projected opera on Flaubert's *Salammbô* (the priestesses and people
rush into the Temple of Tanit, when Salammbô gives the alarm after the
theft of the zaïmph), and was later degraded to a fight episode between the
Polabians and the merchants of Novgorod in the market scene before the
Temple of Radegast in *Mlada*; not long before his death, Mussorgsky was
toying with the idea of putting it into *Sorochintsy Fair*. Greeks and
Carthaginians, Baltic Slavs of the ninth century and Ukrainians of the
nineteenth—Mussorgsky saw no incongruity in using the same music for
all of them.

Now this would not surprise us at all in an eighteenth-century composer. Everyone will recollect at once a dozen examples of that sort of
thing in Bach or Handel. But although the practice was by no means
peculiar to the Russians in the nineteenth century, it was not continued
by other composers on their wholesale scale. By the middle of the last
century (we are accustomed to think) music had acquired a certain precision of emotional expression, a sense of ambient non-musical atmosphere;
individual works had acquired a unity of style, so that, for instance, the
Tristan quotation in *Die Meistersinger* stands out as an incongruity. It is,
on the whole, less shocking to our sense of fitness to find Bach turning
the sleep-song of Voluptuousness in *Die Wahl des Herkules* into a lullaby

for the Christ-child (*Christmas Oratorio*) than to find Mussorgsky introducing in *Boris Godunov* music written for *Salammbô*.

But this last-mentioned case offers an incomparable opportunity to test the validity of this prejudice. Are we wrong in ascribing to nineteenth-century music, to Mussorgsky's music in particular, that definiteness of expression we think (and he thought) it possesses? How was Mussorgsky, with his insistence on dramatic truth in music, able to turn music originally conceived as a Cathaginian princess's prayer to Tanit, the Moon Goddess, into the dying Tsar's farewell to his son—one of the most moving passages in the whole work? The publication of the complete *Salammbô* music in 1939 at last enabled one to answer such questions. Until then we had had to rely mainly on the information of Stasov and others, who had told us of all these transferences, had even told us which passages in *Boris* came from which scenes in *Salammbô*, but left us to wonder how the thing was possible.

We shall find a clue in the adventures of that so-called 'chorus from Sophocles's *Œedipus*'. (My reasons for casting on it the aspersion of 'quotes' will be explained in the coda of this article.) In its original form this chorus expressed the agitated fears of a crowd of priests and people in face of a national calamity ('What will happen to us? With what will all this tribulation end?' etc.); in *Salammbô* the priestesses and people find that a national calamity has happened; on the stolen zaïmph depend the safety and prosperity of Carthage ('What is it? What mean these cries?'). The Greeks demand a victim; the Carthaginians demand the death of the thief. In the hushed *adagio* conclusion the Greeks pray, 'Accept our victim, O ye gods! Have pity on us!' and the Carthaginians pray, 'Protect us, O Tanit! Save us from woe!' The *Mlada* scene is not nearly such a close parallel, but here again there is a temple in the background and an agitated crowd scene—and the essence of the music lies in the rush of staccato quavers in the orchestra rather than in the superimposed choral cries. The projected further removal into the score of *Sorochintsy Fair* was doubtless made possible by the association with the market-music of *Mlada* which actually became the fair-music in the Ukrainian opera. Fight in a market—scuffle at a fair, or after a fair; again there is a parallel. But in music things that are parallel to the same thing are not necessarily parallel to one another; Gogol and Sophocles are not parallel at all. However, the transferences from *Salammbô* to *Boris* are removals by only one stage, not three.

Take the case already mentioned: the transformation of Salammbô's prayer to Tanit into the Tsar's prayer for his children. To begin with, the two musical ideas that are the basis of each were not simply copied from *Salammbô* into *Boris*. The voice-parts—in each case superimposed on an orchestral stream of thought containing the essence of the music—are completely different. And this orchestral part is also condensed and purified: four bars of banality cut out, the harmony made simpler and less luscious. It is instructive to compare part of the *Salammbô* passage:

Ex. 1

Pri - mi me - nya, pri - mi! K te - - be i - du

with the corresponding part of the *Boris* music:

Ex. 2

Krï-la - mi svet - lï - mi vï o - khrà - ni - te mo - e dï - tya rod-no - e ot bed i zol

The music is *essentially* identical. And there is good reason in the texts why it should be. Boris is praying as he dies; Salammbô is not dying, but she is going to sleep—at the end she goes to sleep—and she is praying. And though the substance of her prayer is very different from Boris's, there are key-words in both which establish a certain connection. She prays that the 'bright form' of the Moon Goddess may 'keep' her dreams and 'lead them from suffering and evil to love and happiness', and she ends: 'Hear me, O Tanit! Take me! I go to thee!' Boris prays to God: 'pour Thy beneficent light on my innocent children. . . . With Thy bright wings keep them from woe and evil.' (I am translating as literally as possible, so as to preserve the verbal identities of the Russian.)

A similar verbal link seems to have suggested to Mussorgsky the use of a choral cry, from the scene of the sacrifice to Moloch, in Boris's famous monologue in Act III. 'Woe to us, woe', cries Salammbô. 'In our hearts is sorrow!' And the voices of the people in the Grove of Eschmoûn are heard singing, 'Protect us, give us the victory':

Ex. 3

When Mussorgsky came to set Boris's monologue first in 1869, the words, 'No happiness for me,' must have touched some mysterious spring in his mind, for immediately the phrase:

Ex. 4

not Salammbô's own but the choral answer, is heard in the orchestra; indeed the motive is the thematic basis of practically the whole monologue in this original version. (It is also prominent elsewhere in the *Salammbô* scene.) But that the verbal connection is the real point of contact with *Salammbô* is, I think, proved by the fact that when Mussorgsky almost entirely rewrote the monologue two years later, with an altered text, he still set the words, 'And my *heart* is full of *sorrow*,' to the phrase in its original form (see p. 186 of the O.U.P. vocal score).

In the rewritten (1871) version of the monologue this passage is preceded by a setting of a passage which Calvocoressi has translated: 'How heavy is the hand of God in His wrath, how merciless a doom awaits the sinner! In gloom I tread; grim darkness surrounds me; no single ray of light brings solace.' The music of this, too, is modified from a passage in the same Moloch scene: the priests' 'Our sacred city is beset'. The parallel here lies not in the text but in the mood which lies at the heart of each situation: in each case, a sense of prostration before an angry and merciless deity.

When the sacrifice has been completed, the priests of Moloch form a procession, singing, 'Hail, O Moloch! Hail, O Avenger!' This music turns up in the last scene of *Boris*, the so-called 'revolution scene', for the appearance of the troops of the Pretender, the false Dimitry (p. 409 of O.U.P. score). Again there is a verbal connection, for the troops sing, 'Hail, O Tsarevich' (though the chorus parts are entirely different) and it might be argued that the Pretender is also an 'avenger' (he is so called elsewhere in the opera), the avenger of the true Dimitry, murdered by Boris. But the essence of the music lies, in both cases, in its triumphant, processional character.

The passage immediately before this in *Boris*, the attempted lynching of the two Jesuits (O.U.P. score, pp. 404–8), is also taken—and taken with far fewer changes than in most of these borrowings—from *Salammbô*: the point where Salammbô suddenly notices that Mâtho has taken the zaïmph and calls down curses on his head; instead of fleeing, Mâtho stays and, if he could get in a word, would plead his love once more, but his companion Spendius drags him away by force. The music might serve for almost any type of agitated scene, but there is the real pretext of a parallel between Salammbô's cursing of Mâtho and Varlaam's (and the crowd's) abuse of the Jesuits, between Spendius dragging off Mâtho and the crowd dragging off their victims. The score of *Salammbô* makes it clear that the orchestral figure heard two or three times:

Ex. 5

originated as a 'dragging' motive; it appears each time Spendius tries to get his companion away.

Two passages from an earlier part of this scene of the theft of the zaïmph were turned to account in the fountain scene of *Boris*, where the Pretender is making love in the moonlight. One ("'Tis you alone, Marina': O.U.P. score of *Boris*, p. 292) was originally the last portion of a choral hymn to Tanit sung while Salammbô sleeps and the thieves creep into the sanctuary—a passage for which Mussorgsky had planned extraordinary, Berliozian orchestration with glockenspiel, two harps and piano duet. The other ('You break my loving heart': O.U.P. score, p. 294) originated as a recitative in which the concealed Mâtho expresses his wonder at the 'divine, marvellous singing'. It is difficult to see any real parallel between these situations; one might, of course, plead that there is some connection between adoration of a goddess and adoration of a young woman, and that Mâtho and the Pretender are both amorous young men. But the truth is that the music is not very expressive and of little value.

Much more interesting is the transference of a whole group of themes from Act IV, scene 1, of *Salammbô* (Mâtho in the dungeon) to Act IV, scene 1, of *Boris* (the Duma of the boyars). The captured leader of the mutinous mercenaries foresees that his enemies will doom him 'to death and shame and torture'. And later the pentarchs come and read his sentence; among other unpleasant details, 'his tongue is to be given to the crows to feed on . . . his body itself is to be given to the flames . . . and his accursed ashes thrown to the four winds'. Both these passages are set to music which was used again in *Boris* at the point where the boyars pass sentence on the Pretender: 'Let the scoundrel taste the rack and thumb-screw. And then the gallows . . . on his flesh let crows and ravens feed. Let his body be burnt to ashes . . . and let his accursed ashes be scattered to the wind' (O.U.P. score, pp. 332-3). Mussorgsky had every justification for introducing the *Salammbô* music here. (As this scene does not occur in Pushkin, it is not impossible that Mussorgsky introduced it as a pretext for using an effective piece of music.) And this passing sentence on Mâtho and the Pretender not unnaturally suggested that the solemn music accompanying the arrival of the priests of Moloch, with the pentarchs, to read the sentence on Mâtho, might be used to herald the gathering of the boyars to pass sentence on the Pretender at the opening of Act IV of *Boris* (O.U.P. score, p. 327). But one other passage common to these two scenes needs a little more explanation. In *Boris* it is the orchestral commentary on Shuysky's account of the Tsar's hallucinations; he has been spying on his master: 'Pallid, aghast, in cold sweat bathed and quaking, he staggered moaning, oft muttering strange words, wild, unconnected words of terror' (O.U.P. score, pp. 340-1). In *Salammbô* it is the orchestral commentary on Mâtho's thoughts of the Numidian king, Narr 'Havas:

'Foul traitor! I had you like a worm under my heel and I pardoned you. Pretending to forget the insults at the drunken feast, you long harboured your grudge against me. And secretly sought the alliance of the enemy. And bartered the blood of a thousand brave comrades for the gold of the Carthaginian merchants.' There is obviously no connection between the two texts; the explanation, I suggest, lies in the character of Shuysky. Shuysky, too, is a crafty man who has plotted against Boris under a mask of fidelity. And so the *Salammbô* score throws light on this curious music, with which Mussorgsky must have intended afterwards to suggest not Boris's terror but Shuysky's treachery.

In practically every case, then, the transference of music from *Salammbô* to *Boris* was justified by identity or near-identity of emotional or dramatic context, an identity made more vivid in several cases by textual parallels. The transferences are never note-for-note and they concern the orchestral parts only; they vary considerably as regards the amount of alteration Mussorgsky found necessary, but it is clear that he preferred wherever possible to keep the passages in their original keys. Study of his emendations of harmony and part-writing is instructive; but these points lie outside the real subject of the present chapter.

But I cannot resist the temptation to clear up one matter which is not strictly germane to the subject: the 'quotes' with which I have had to qualify that chorus 'from Sophocles's *Œdipus*'. Everyone who knows anything at all about Russian music knows that during 1858–61 Mussorgsky was working at 'music to Sophocles's *Œdipus*'. This one chorus was publicly performed in 1861; it was published in vocal score by Bessel in 1883, and republished with French and German words in 1909. Yet for eighty years apparently no one troubled to find out just what part of Sophocles Mussorgsky set, or even from which of the two Œdipus tragedies. No one paid any attention to Mussorgsky's inscription on the earliest autograph, 'Temple scene from the tragedy *Œdipus in Athens*', for such a tragedy exists, though it is not by Sophocles. First performed in 1804, it is the work of a well-known Russian dramatist, V. A. Ozerov (1769 or 1770–1816). It covers the same ground as *Œdipus Coloneus* though it deviates rather widely from the Sophoclean and traditional account of things. Instead of giving Œdipus and his daughter sanctuary, the Athenians demand his death—at least the death of a victim—to avert misfortune from their country; Œdipus, Antigone and Polynices contend for this fate, but finally it is Creon who is, most properly, sacrificed.

Mussorgsky's temple-scene does not correspond precisely to any situation in Ozerov; but it is fully explained by Ozerov, whereas it makes no sense at all from the point of view of Sophocles and tradition. It stands in at least as close a relation to Ozerov as do most operas to the plays or novels they are based on, and one of Mussorgsky's stage directions is directly based on Ozerov's:

> *Mussorgsky:* 'Interior of the temple of the Eumenides. The temple is divided into two parts; in the farther one are seen an altar and three statues of gods (*sic*). . . .'
>
> *Ozerov:* 'The theatre represents the interior of the temple of the Eumenides, which is divided into two parts. In the farther one are seen an altar and three statues, representing the goddesses of this temple. . . .'

Mussorgsky was evidently writing, not music to Sophocles, but an opera on Ozerov. That he himself spoke of Sophocles may be explained in two ways: he may have believed Ozerov's play to be a translation of the *Coloneus*, or he may simply have been careless—as he was when he turned the Furies into male deities.

That this explanation has not been noticed by Russian critics is the more curious since Ozerov is by no means an unknown writer. Kropotkin (*Russian Literature: Ideals and Realities*) says his tragedies 'enjoyed a lasting success, and powerfully contributed to the development of both the stage and a public of serious playgoers', and according to Lavrin (*Russian Literature*) 'his *Polixene* is considered the best pseudo-classic tragedy in Russian.'

1942

Postscript: By 1946, when it fell to me to complete Calvocoressi's book on Mussorgsky in the 'Master Musicians' series, it had occurred to me that some of the *Œdipus* music may actually be preserved at third-hand in *Boris*. Mussorgsky told Balakirev on 26 September, 1861, that he had recently written two other choruses for 'the introduction to *Œdipus*': an *andante* in B flat minor ('my last mystical outpouring', as he calls it) and an *allegro* in E flat major. The first part of the Third Act of *Salammbô* answers exactly to this description and the dramatic situations are almost identical: terror-stricken people before a temple, priests preparing a sacrifice, the acclamation of a god or ruler. But, as I have shown above, the B flat minor chorus in *Salammbô* provided material for Boris's monologue and the one in E flat ('Hail, O Moloch!') was used for the acclamation of the Pretender.

It would perhaps be going too far to suggest that a certain parallelism between the tragedies of Œdipus and Boris may have played some part in attracting Mussorgsky to Pushkin's play.

XII—RIMSKY-KORSAKOV AS SELF-CRITIC

One of the most interesting traits of Rimsky-Korsakov's personality was his power of objective self-criticism, a product of that coldly logical, sometimes pedantic element in his nature which appears to be so strongly opposed to the fantastic character of so much of his music. (But only appears to be: the fantastic effects are often produced by coldly calculated means.) The extraordinary feature of this self-criticism is its detachment; it did not, apparently, function as a normal part of the creative process as with most composers—at least, not to any unusual degree—nor did it hamper Rimsky-Korsakov's productivity, except at times of physical or psychological depression, as excessive self-criticism has done with some composers (for instance, Duparc). It is as if he composed with one lobe of his brain and dispassionately contemplated the result with another.

These self-judgments are sometimes general and sweeping, sometimes passed on individual works or quite small details. The general tone is always the same: judicious, calm, unemotional. There is no suggestion of vanity in his self-approval or of false modesty in his self-depreciation. When he told his young admirer Yastrebtsev, who recorded his conversation over a period of eighteen years:[1] 'Do you not overvalue me? Study Liszt and Balakirev more closely and you will see that *much in me is not mine* ... I repeat (by no means from modesty), you overvalue me!' (8 April, 1893), it is true that he was speaking at a time of depression, but the whole context is calm and objective. On the same occasion he remarked that his opera *The Maid of Pskov* showed 'less individuality' than such other early works as the orchestral fantasia *Sadko* and *Antar*: 'in it one is conscious of the influence of Mussorgsky's ideas'—a criticism as accurate as the remark on the influence of Liszt and Balakirev. And similar protests against 'overvaluation' were sometimes made in even stronger terms: for instance, in a letter of 24 August, 1894;

> My dear Vasily Vasilevich, in the course of your letter you spoke of me as a genius. I remember that you have done this more than once already. I must tell you that your opinion of me is exaggerated, in the first place because of your affection for me but also (so to speak) because we happen to exist in the world at the same time. Don't speak of me

[1] Part of Yastrebtsev's reminiscences (only as far as 27 March, 1895) first appeared as *Moi vospominaniya o Nikolae Andreyeviche Rimskom-Korsakove*, Petrograd, 1917; they were published complete, but without the letters included in the original edition, in two volumes as *Rimsky-Korsakov: Vospominaniya V. V. Yastrebtseva*, Leningrad, 1959 and 1960.

in such terms, I beg you, either to my face or behind my back. . . .
Foreigners use this expression very often, but with them it means much
the same as 'talented'; we Russians will reserve it for more important
cases. Of Russian composers, only Glinka is a genius. I by no means
deny that I have some ability for composition; but I know my place.
Throw away that expression once and for all. And, I beg you, say no
more to me about this or you will annoy me.[1]

Again on 12 September, 1902, Yastrebtsev records that 'speaking about
the fate of his operas, Nikolay Andreyevich said: "All my operas (after
Sadko) have, I think, only temporary interest; then they will completely
and finally disappear from the stage and only *Snow Maiden* will remain
associated with my name." ' This again was a sound judgment, for he had
not yet composed *Kitezh* and *The Golden Cockerel*, and of his other operas
'after *Sadko*' only *Tsar Saltan* had much success.

The previously quoted remark, 'Study Liszt and Balakirev more closely
and you will see that *much in me is not mine*', is very characteristic; Rimsky-
Korsakov was always acutely conscious of the various influences that had
contributed to the formation of his style. Writing of his early 'musical
picture' *Sadko* in his autobiography,[2] he says:

What musical influences guided my imagination during the composition of this symphonic picture? The introduction—depicting the quiet
undulation of the sea—shares the harmonic and modulatory basis of
the beginning of Liszt's *Ce qu'on entend sur la montagne* (modulation to
a minor third lower). The beginning of the *allegro* 3/4, describing
Sadko's fall into the sea and his being carried off to the depths of the
Sea King's realm recalls the abduction of Lyudmila by Chernomor in
the First Act of *Ruslan*. . . . The D major part, *allegro* 4/4, depicting the
Sea King's feast, is harmonically and to some extent melodically reminiscent of Balakirev's 'Song of the Golden Fish', a favourite of mine
at that period, and the introduction to the Rusalka's recitative in Act IV
of Dargomïzhsky's opera, and partly to his chorus of magic maidens
[from the unfinished opera *Rogdana*] and certain harmonic details and
figurations from Liszt's *Mephisto-Walzer*. Completely original inven-
tions are the dance-theme of the third part (D flat major, 2/4) and the
ensuing cantabile theme. . . .

(An amusing point here is that, while noticing the indebtedness of his
opening passage to the Liszt symphonic poem, Rimsky-Korsakov overlooked the much greater debt to the opening scene of Serov's *Rogneda*:

[1] *Moi vospominaniya*, pp. 117–18.
[2] *Letopis moei muzikalnoy zhizni*, (fifth edition) Moscow, 1935, p. 77.

Ex. 1
(a) Serov (1865)
Andante lento

(b) Rimsky-Korsakov (1867)
Moderato assai

The Serov passage is immediately repeated a major third lower.) Again, describing the inception of his Berliozian programme-symphony *Antar*, he tells us among other things that 'the chief theme of Antar himself was composed under the undeniable influence of several of William Ratcliff's phrases' (from Cui's opera) and that 'the chief theme of the fourth movement was given me by Dargomïzhsky with his harmonisation, taken by him from Christianowitsch's volume of Arab melodies. For the beginning of the *adagio* of this movement I preserved Dargomïzhsky's original harmonisation (cor. ingl. and 2 fag.).'. But here his modesty went too far; the melody from Christianowitsch's *Esquisse historique de la musique arabe* (Cologne, 1863) with Dargomïzhsky's harmonisation is now preserved in the Houghton Library of Harvard University[1] and it is clear that Rimsky-Korsakov not only improved the borrowed melody but by no means 'preserved' Dargomïzhsky's harmonisation even in the original version of *Antar*:

Ex. 2
(a) Christianowitsch-Dargomïzhsky

(b) Rimsky-Korsakov (1868)

A still more ill-founded self-accusation is the pencilled note, 'David, Le Désert', in the margin of his own analysis of the Spring Fairy's aria from *Snow Maiden*.[2]

The chief monument to Rimsky-Korsakov's self-dissatisfaction, however, is the pile of his 'revised' scores. All his orchestral works up to and including the Third Symphony were afterwards revised and reorchestrated at least once, some of them more than once. The opera *The Maid of Pskov*, composed in 1868–72, was completely rewritten in 1877 and yet again in 1892.[3] These revisions are of every kind, from minute changes of

[1] See Miloš Velimirović, 'Russian Autographs at Harvard', in: *Notes*, second series, XVII (1960), pp. 542–3.

[2] N. Rimsky-Korsakov, *Literaturnïe proïzvedeniya i perepiska* IV, Moscow 1960, p. 417.

[3] The full score of the original version was published in the complete edition of Rimsky-Korsakov's works (*Polnoe sobranie sochineniy*) in 1966, too late for discussion in this study; the 1877 score remains unpublished.

tempo indication, phrasing, or orchestral detail to wholesale transposition or complete re-composition. The youthful First Symphony (1861–5)[1] in E flat minor was in 1884 transposed to E minor, the position of slow movement and scherzo reversed, valve-horns in F substituted for natural horns in various crooks, and a host of other changes made. Another composition later transposed from E flat minor to E minor is the song 'El i palma' (a setting of a translation of Heine's 'Ein Fichtenbaum steht einsam');[2] here the note values of the 1866 version were halved in 1888 and one or two touches added to the piano part, but the only essential change was the repetition of the last two lines with a musical setting of intensified emotion (bars 33–8 in the definitive form).

The *Overture on Russian Themes*, also composed in 1866, was more drastically altered in 1880.[3] Even the folk-tune, 'U vorot, vorot', which provides the first *allegro* subject, was modified—in fact, restored to the form in which it appears in Balakirev's *Sbornik russkikh narodnikh pesen* (St Petersburg, 1866) and in Tchaïkovsky's *1812 Overture*. In addition to the rewriting and rescoring common to all these revised scores—often in the direction of strengthening (e.g. a passage originally given to woodwind and harp only is now strengthened by the addition of a horn and pizzicato strings)—the end was completely changed: a thick and ineffective orchestration of the well-known 'Slava' melody—the worst orchestral tutti Rimsky-Korsakov ever put on paper—was replaced by a brilliant snatch of 'Slava' which then passes into a *vivace* coda in 2/4 time, combining two of the themes. Yet perhaps more interesting are the touches the composer adds in minutiae—for instance, details in a passage unchanged in scoring, such as the first appearance of the 'Slava' melody in its complete form:

Ex. 3
(a) 1866
Moderato ♩=76
Strs. *pp*

(b) 1880
Andante ♩=69
Strs. *pp*

Of the other orchestral pieces rewritten to a greater or lesser extent—

---

[1] *Polnoe sobranie sochineniy*, 16, p. 3; 1884 revision, ibid., p. 117.
[2] Ibid., 45, pp. 19 and 23.
[3] Both versions ibid., 20, pp. 7 and 55.

Antar, the Third Symphony, *Sadko* and the *Fantasia on Serbian Themes*[1]
—by far the most important case is *Antar*, the so-called 'Second Symphony'. The history of this work and its various versions is somewhat confused, and confusion has been made worse by mis-statements on two of the published scores. We are confronted by four versions in all:

A: The original version of 1868. Never printed in the composer's lifetime; first published in 1949.[2]

Ba: A revised and reorchestrated version made in 1875, still described as 'symphony', published by Bessel in 1880.

C: A much more drastically revised version made in 1897 ('symphonic suite'), published by Bessel only in 1913 (edited by Maximilian Steinberg) but marked 'Passed by censor. Spb.4 November 1903', the date which really belongs to B*b*.[3]

B*b*: A revision of the engraved plates of Ba, as 'symphonic suite (Second Symphony)', made in 1903 and published by Bessel the same year. This is quite falsely described on the familiar Eulenburg and Breitkopf miniature scores as 'Nouvelle rédaction (1897)'.

The muddle arose from Bessel's refusal during the composer's lifetime to scrap the old plates and engrave the entirely new ones necessitated by the real 'new version of 1897'.

There are thus three main versions of *Antar*, of which the second also exists in two slightly different forms: for instance, in the fourth movement the 'mélodie arabe' is marked *adagio, amoroso* in Ba, *andante amoroso* in B*b*. (In A it is *ochen medlenno* [i.e. 'very slowly'] and is not preceded by the 12 bars of *allegretto vivace*; in C it is simply *adagio*—and the passage is transposed from D flat to G flat, and the cor anglais with two bassoons is replaced by oboe with two clarinets.) But the three main versions differ in respects much more important than tempo markings, dynamic nuances or even modifications of scoring. The major changes include cuts and insertions, wholesale transposition and complete recomposition of passages, as well as reorchestration and modification of harmony or melody. The most important changes of actual substance occur in the first movement. A passage beginning in A at p. 22, bar 2, and in B*b* at p. 19, bar 4, was recomposed in C (p. 237, bar 1)[4] with a fresh counterpoint and the excision of 16 bars (Ex. 4, p. 200).

[1] Ibid., 17*a*–19.

[2] Ibid., 17*a*, p. 3; this volume also contains the earliest version—quite different in material, and in the key of B minor—of the second movement, p. 183.

[3] Republished ibid., 18*a*, p. 209. B*b* is 17*b* of the *Polnoe sobranie*.

[4] Page references for A and C are to *Polnoe sobranie sochineniy*, 17*a*, those for B*b* to the Eulenburg/Breitkopf miniature score which is more easily accessible. The practically identical harp parts—arpeggios on F sharp–C sharp (only the original version requires two harps)—are omitted in all three of my quotations.

Ex. 4

(a) 1868 Lively

(b) 1875 (1903) Allegretto vivace

(c) 1897 Allegretto

A little later $10\frac{1}{2}$ bars (C: p. 247, bar 2–p. 250, bar 3) with touches of imitation suggesting quasi-development replace $2\frac{1}{2}$ weak bars in the earlier versions (cf. B*b*, p. 31, bars 2–4), and the thematic semiquaver figure is continued as a viola counterpoint in the ensuing passage—already much strengthened in B*a* as compared with A. Characteristically, the version in B*b* (p. 32) merely adopts 'suggestions' from C for the improvement of B*a*.

The transpositions in C are particularly interesting. A passage in the composer's autobiography,[1] written presumably in the early 1890s, reveals a certain disquiet about the key-scheme of *Antar*:

The tonalities of the four movements of *Antar* present an unusual sequence: F sharp minor–F sharp major: C sharp minor: B minor–D major: and finally D flat major (as dominant of F sharp).

As already mentioned[2], the original second movement—discarded before performance—was in B minor like the third movement. The substituted movement in version A, substantially the same in B*a* and B*b*, is in C sharp minor—but in version C (with a modified modulating passage at the opening) it is changed to D minor. The above-mentioned transposition of the 'mélodie arabe' in version C, from D flat to G flat, has the appearance of being an attempt to reinstate F sharp (=G flat) as the tonal centre of gravity of the whole work; yet this attempt is abandoned almost immediately and the finale proceeds and concludes in D flat as in the earlier versions. The transposition in version C of the last 12 bars of the slow introduction to the first movement, as compared with A and B, was obviously intended only to avoid key-monotony.

Space does not allow discussion of the innumerable smaller changes of melodic line, harmony, part-writing and orchestration, but it may be observed as a general principle that Rimsky-Korsakov tended at first to increase the weight of his scoring, then to refine it;[3] a typical case is the end (last 5 bars) of the first movement where in A the *Antar* theme is played only by the violas, over brass chords, whereas in B it is given to flutes, cor anglais, violins and violas in octaves, while in C the thick, heavy texture of B is poetically lightened and transformed. Just before embarking on the C version, Rimsky-Korsakov remarked to Yastrebtsev that it would be necessary 'above all to heighten the significance of the strings'.[4]

Not all the changes in C are for the better. Even the faithful Yastrebtsev found some of the passages in the first two movements 'rather heavy-handed'[5] and one can only endorse his disapproval of the piccolo (C: p. 265, bar 5) replacing the flute (A: p. 48, bar 6; B*b*, p. 44, bar 13). Nevertheless, while C may not be in every respect the best version it is certainly that which Rimsky-Korsakov himself regarded as the definitive one and it is very regrettable that *Antar* should still be best known in a form (B*b*) which, though the 'latest' in date, represents only an unhappy *pis aller* forced on the composer by a niggardly publisher.   1963

---

[1] *Letopis*, p. 89.

[2] See footnote 2, p. 199.

[3] One detail may be mentioned: the tendency to replace harp arpeggios in A and B*a* with glissandi in B*b* and C.

[4] *Rimsky-Korsakov: Vospominaniya* I, p. 455.

[5] Ibid., I, p. 480.

XIII—RIMSKY-KORSAKOV'S SONGS

If Rimsky-Korsakov was not one of the world's great song-writers he was one of Russia's great song-writers, and though his eighty songs are by no means all masterpieces they do include perhaps as many as a dozen that only a very cautious critic would refuse admission to that select company. These eighty songs are not, as one might expect, spread fairly evenly over his long creative career. They fall into three widely separated groups: about two dozen early songs, a little group of nine dating from about 1882, and a tremendous outpouring in 1897 (overflowing to some extent into 1898). Obviously the most convenient way of examining them is to take each group separately.

The earliest of all Rimsky-Korsakov's songs was 'a sort of barcarolle, fairly melodious and in pseudo-Italian style' as he says, written in 1861 while he was still a seventeen-year-old naval cadet.[1] But when the composer came across the manuscript in 1906 he was sufficiently interested in it—obviously for autobiographical, sentimental rather than musical reasons—to copy out 'this nonsense' and send it to his friend and Boswell, Y. Y. Yastrebtsev. Then in March 1865 came a setting of Pushkin's 'V krovi gorit', which has disappeared, and in November of the same year the earliest surviving song: a setting of Mikhaylov's translation of Heine's 'Lehn deine Wang' an meine Wang' ' (Op. 2, No. 1). 'Whence came the wish to compose it, I don't remember', the composer wrote in after years. 'Most probably from a desire to imitate Balakirev, whose songs aroused my enthusiasm. Balakirev approved of it moderately but, finding the accompaniment insufficiently pianistic, wrote a completely new one. And with this accompaniment my song was printed.' Balakirev's arpeggio accompaniment, though pianistic enough, is no more distinguished than Rimsky-Korsakov's melody.

But one has no right to expect distinction in an Op. 2, and it is the more remarkable that of the other three songs that make up this opus, written early in 1866, two are among Rimsky-Korsakov's best songs: the setting of Koltsov's 'Enslaved by the rose, the nightingale' (Op. 2, No. 2), which is probably the most popular of all Rimsky-Korsakov's non-operatic songs, and the cradle song in the First Act of Mey's drama *The Maid of Pskov* (Op. 2, No. 3), one of his most haunting melodies (Ex. 1 on facing page). When later he made an opera of *The Maid of Pskov* he omitted the First Act from his scheme, but it was inserted in the second version of the opera as a prologue (1877) and in it he naturally included his

[1] It is printed in the preface to Vol. 45 of his collected works, Moscow and Leningrad, 1946.

Ex. 1

(*Lulla, lullaby, my little Olga*)

early setting of the lullaby. Finally (1898), the prologue was largely re-written as an independent one-act opera: *Boyarinya Vera Sheloga*. In *Vera Sheloga* the lullaby is transposed up a tone to E flat, the accompaniment is altered, the original harmonies are modified here and there; but the melody remains the same as in 1866—and it is still the loveliest thing in the whole score.

There was something warm and vital in the early, naïve Rimsky-Korsakov that tended to disappear, except for sporadic glimpses, from his later, technically accomplished music; something one finds in *Antar* and misses in *Sheherazade*, finds in *May Night* and misses in *Christmas Eve*. And 'Enslaved by the rose, the nightingale', slight as it is, also has that something. It is interesting as the earliest of the composer's essays in the pseudo-oriental, essays that bulk a good deal larger in the average concert-goer's estimate of his output than in the output itself; still more interesting for the amount of colour he manages to squeeze out of very limited harmonic means: double-pedals, diminished sevenths and very little else. The 'oriental' melodic stock-in-trade is even slighter: nothing more than flattened seconds and a little arabesque ornament that also crops up in other songs of this period, e.g. in 'Lehn deine Wang' ' and 'In the dark grove the nightingale is silent' (Op. 4, No. 3). Characteristic of Rimsky-Korsakov's essentially 'instrumental' approach to song-writing is the fact that 28 of its 48 bars are for piano only; and when the voice enters, in bar 13, it is unaccompanied:

Ex. 2

Ple - niv - shis ro - zoy, so - lo - vey I den i noch po - et nad ney;
(*Enslaved by the rose, the nightingale sings to her day and night*)

During the next few years (1866–70) Rimsky-Korsakov produced the eighteen songs that constitute his Op. 3, 4, 7 and 8—plus (if we may trust his often inaccurate autobiography) another Heine song, 'Mir träumte einst von wilden Liebesglühn', written in 1870 but not published till some twelve years later as Op. 25, No. 1. Heine—or rather, Heine-Mikhaylov—also attracted him twice more in 1866 and he set Russian versions of 'Ein Fichtenbaum steht einsam' (Op. 3, No. 1), orchestrated in 1888, and

'Mein Knecht! steh auf und sattle schnell' (Op. 4, No. 2). I deliberately say 'attracted' rather than 'inspired', for Heine's lyricism oddly failed to evoke a response from a composer who, whatever his shortcomings, did possess a true lyrical vein; Rimsky-Korsakov's early songs tend to be declamatory, but even so one might have expected Heine to release again the stream of melody evoked by Mey's little lullaby. As it is, the dramatic 'Mein Knecht!' is more successful than 'Ein Fichtenbaum'.

The oriental vein is continued too, notably in the setting of Nikitin's 'In the dark grove the nightingale is silent', a more beautiful companion-piece to the better known 'nightingale' song of Op. 2 and, like it, very nearly a piano-piece with vocal obbligato—the voice is silent in 24 bars out of 43. The piano part sounds like a preliminary study for *Antar*.

Ex. 3

(Similarly, the setting of Pushkin's 'My voice for thee is sweet and languid', Op. 7, No. 1, betrays in both melody and accompaniment that it was written in the same year as the orchestral picture *Sadko*, Op. 5.) Mey's 'Hebrew Song' (Op. 7, No. 2) naturally called for 'oriental' treatment and is based on the scale F sharp–G–A sharp–B–C sharp–D–E–F sharp, while the settings of Pushkin's 'On the hills of Georgia' (Op. 3, No. 4) and Lermontov's 'Thy glance is radiant as the heavens' (Op. 7, No. 4) belong to that semi-oriental genre, beloved of all the classical Russians and now cultivated more authentically by natives like Khachaturyan—the Caucasian. Actually there is very little that can be called even semi-oriental in 'The Hills of Georgia': only the single *poco meno mosso* phrase, 'Nothing torments, disturbs my melancholy':

Ex. 4

That phrase is also the only genuinely melodic phrase in the song. The rest of the voice part is expressive arioso; the piano part consists only of the manipulation of a few slender harmonic ideas. Yet 'On the Hills of Georgia' is a very beautiful miniature, and it is run very close by several other of these early songs; particularly by 'The golden cloud had slept' (Op. 3, No. 3), inspired by one of Lermontov's loveliest lyrics, and the setting of Pleshcheyev's 'Night' (Op. 8, No. 2):

Ex. 5

(Night has flown over the world, scattering dreams; on the dark blue vestment are strewn the twinkling stars)

The Fet serenade in the same mood, 'Quietly evening falls', Op. 4, No. 4, also has a charming and characteristic accompaniment but here the voice part is once more insignificant:

Ex. 6

(The sultry air grows cool; sleep, my child!)

In these songs Rimsky-Korsakov has discovered an essentially Russian type of arioso; the piano figures are strikingly evocative of mood;[1] the harmonic idiom is limited but unconventional. Altogether one feels that

[1] When Rimsky-Korsakov tries to write an 'ordinary' piano accompaniment he collapses into dull conventional figuration, usually simple arpeggios, as in 'Southern Night' (Op. 3, No. 2), 'I believe I love' (Op. 8, No. 6) and 'Switezianka' (Op. 7, No. 3). Incidentally, the last-named song has an interesting history; it is a setting of the water-spirit's words from Mickiewicz's ballad of that name, a poem that is said to have inspired Chopin's Ballade in F, in a Russian version by Mey. When in 1897 Rimsky-Korsakov set the whole poem for soprano and tenor soli, chorus and orchestra, he incorporated his much earlier setting of part of the words but with some interesting modifications.

Rimsky-Korsakov seldom stood closer to Mussorgsky than in 'Night', 'The golden cloud had slept' or the Pushkin setting 'What is my name to thee?' (Op. 4, No. 1), while his own artistic individuality is clearly manifested both in these and a number of other early songs.

The dozen years that lie between the latest songs of this group and those of 1882 (Op. 25, No. 2, Op. 26 and Op. 27) were remarkably eventful. In that interval Rimsky-Korsakov had discovered that he was a musical illiterate, subjected himself to drastic self-education, turned himself into a professor and pedant, and then recovered his true musical personality in two delightful lyrical operas, *May Night* and *Snow Maiden*. As one would expect, the songs of 1882 are much more conventional than the early ones; the voice parts are more melodious, the accompaniments less evocative and almost entirely dependent on the commonplace devices of ordinary piano figuration. Least conventional are 'Zuleika's Song' (Op. 26, No. 4), based on a free paraphrase of 'This rose to calm my brother's cares' from *The Bride of Abydos*, and the powerful and gloomy setting of Pushkin's 'Evocation' (Op. 26, No. 2) which reverts to the earlier declamatory style and picturesque type of accompaniment ('drum' triplets in the bass):

Ex. 7
Andante lugubre

O, es - li prav-da, chto v no-chi, Kog-da po - ko - yat-sya zhi - vï - e,

(Oh, if it's true that in the night, when the living are at rest....)

Of the others, the best are another Byron song, 'In moments to delight devoted' (Op. 26, No. 1), to which it is unfortunately impossible to fit the original English text, and the settings of Alexey Tolstoy's 'Softly the spirit flew up to heaven' (Op. 27, No. 1) and Pushkin's 'Thou and you' (Op. 27, No. 3) (Ex.8). All three possess genuine lyrical *élan*. The last of the Heine songs, 'Wenn ich in deine Augen seh'' (Op. 25, No. 2), and the setting of Pushkin's 'For the shores of thy far native land' (Op. 26, No. 3), which Borodin too had composed only the year before, are both disappointing.

Then comes another, even longer, hiatus in Rimsky-Korsakov's songwriting: the fifteen years in which he evolved into the supreme orchestral virtuoso of *Sheherazade* and the *Spanish Capriccio* and produced his great trio of fantastic operas: *Mlada, Christmas Eve* and *Sadko*. He had not long finished *Sadko* when his fancy took another of those curiously sudden turns that mark the whole of his creative career. In the field of opera it resulted in *Mozart and Salieri* and *The Tsar's Bride*, but only after it had

Ex. 8

Allegro

Pu - sto - e vï ser - dech - nïm tï O -

- na, ob - mol - vyas, za - me - ni - la

(By a slip of the tongue she changed the empty 'you' to a fond 'thou'....)

produced a huge crop of songs. He has told the story himself in the *Chronicle of my Musical Life*:

'It was long since I had written any songs. Turning to Alexey Tolstoy's poems, I set four of them [Op. 39] and felt that I was now composing in a different way. The melodies turned out purely vocally, i.e. were vocal in their very inception, with no more than hints of harmony and modulation. I worked out the accompaniments after the melodies were finished, whereas before, with few exceptions, the melodies had been conceived instrumentally so to speak, i.e. not in close connexion with the text but only harmonising with its general content, or evoked by the harmonic basis which sometimes preceded the melody. Feeling that the new method of composition had produced genuine vocal music and being satisfied with my first attempts in this direction, I composed one song after another on words by A. Tolstoy, Maykov, Pushkin and others.'

These forty-six songs of 1897–8 (Op. 39, 40, 41, 42, 43, 45, 46, 49, 50, 51, 55 and 56) cannot be discussed here as fully as the earlier songs. But they do not deserve to be discussed as fully; although 'genuine vocal music' and technically blameless, the majority are as uninspired as the bulk of the work of an over-productive composer is almost bound to be; few indeed bear the marks of Rimsky-Korsakov's musical personality. Still, there are some plums worth picking out. The most convenient way of dealing with them is according to the poets who inspired them, the great majority being based on Pushkin, Alexey Tolstoy and Maykov in practically equal proportions, while a mere half-dozen or so owe their origin to Lermontov, Fet and others By far the most successful—at any rate, in my opinion—are the Maykov songs. Even these vary enormously. The pale orientalism of 'I love thee, moon' (Op. 41, No. 3) compares sadly with such juvenile productions as 'Enslaved by the rose, the night-ingale', and 'Look in thy garden' (Op. 41, No. 4) suggests not Rimsky-Korsakov but Bantock imitating Rimsky-Korsakov. But the arioso, 'I waited for thee at the appointed hour' (Op. 40, No. 4) is more character-istic—and more 'instrumental' in character, like the earlier songs. In some details it foreshadows *Tsar Saltan*, begun two years later, and one of its themes refers, perhaps unintentionally, to the beautiful Lermontov song, 'When the golden cornfield waves', which opens the same set:

Another more characteristic and unconventional song—it is practically a scena—is 'Doubt' (No. 4 of the cycle *To the Poet*, Op. 45)[1] and the whole set, Op. 50, inspired by Maykov's translations of modern Greek lyrics is worth looking at. 'The Girl and the Sun' appeals immediately:

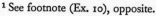

and both 'The Singer' and 'Quiet is the blue sea' grow on one, though No. 4 collapses into a mere 'well-made song'. Rimsky-Korsakov's last

[1] See footnote (Ex. 10), opposite.

two songs, 'The Nymph' and 'Summer Night's Dream' (Op. 56, Nos. 1 and 2), are both Maykov settings—and both charming, particularly in

(*Long last night I could not sleep: I got up, opened the window....*)

---

[1] The canon between voice and piano near the end of this song:

(*And thou involuntarily dost bestow on these appearances the loveliness of life*)

is an instance of the only really distinctive device Rimsky-Korsakov uses at all frequently in these later songs: see, for example, Op. 45, No. 5, Op. 49, No. 1, Op. 51, Nos. 2 and 4, Op. 55, No. 3.

the orchestral versions. (Rimsky-Korsakov orchestrated them in 1905 and 1906 respectively.) I quote the opening of the second one (Ex. 12 on p. 209). Incidentally, we also owe the best of Rimsky-Korsakov's few vocal duets, 'Pan' (for mezzo and baritone, Op. 47, No. 1) to Maykov.

The best of the Tolstoy songs is 'The west dies out in pallid rose' (Op. 39, No. 2), but this poet never tapped Rimsky-Korsakov's best lyrical vein as he so often did Tchaïkovsky's. Take, for instance, the first song of the Op. 39 set which opened this great outburst of song-writing, 'Oh, if thou couldst for one moment', and compare it with Tchaïkovsky's setting of the same words (No. 4 of his Op. 38):

Ex. 13

(Oh, if thou couldst for one moment forget thy grief, forget thy misfortunes!)

The Tchaïkovsky may not be one of the world's masterpieces of song, but the poet's outpouring of passionate grief has at least produced a corresponding outpouring of lyrical music; Rimsky-Korsakov was, of course, entitled to translate the poem more soberly but his setting, if 'vocal', lacks any true lyrical impulse. Again, Tchaïkovsky's 'Silence descends on the golden cornfields' (Op. 57, No. 2) does at any rate convey an emotional experience, as Rimsky-Korsakov's version (Op. 39, No. 3) does not. Only in the fourth song of this set, 'Sleep, my poor friend', albeit a rather feeble echo of the lullaby from *The Maid of Pskov*, does the Rimsky-Korsakov bear comparison with the Tchaïkovsky version (the latter's Op. 47, No. 4).

It is difficult to believe that the composer who has given us the most enchanting of spring operas, *Snow Maiden*, could have written the *Spring* cycle, Op. 43: three poems by Alexey Tolstoy and one by Fet, all turned into utterly conventional, perfectly German *Lieder*. No. 4 ('Early Spring') again unsuccessfully challenges Tchaïkovsky (his Op. 38, No. 2). And in the five songs that make up the cycle *By the Sea*, Op. 46, the only mark of the composer's individuality is the appearance in the last song of the curious conventional 'wave' motive to be found in *Sheherazade* and *Tsar Saltan*. The fourth song of *By the Sea*, 'Do not believe me, friend', can also be compared with Tchaïkovsky (Op. 6, No. 1); neither setting rises higher than uninspired competence and neither bears the personal stamp of its composer.

Of Rimsky-Korsakov's later Pushkin songs the only ones that call for special comment are the two striking bass ariosos, 'The Upas Tree' and 'The Prophet' (Op. 49, Nos. 1 and 2), written for the famous operatic bass, F. I. Stravinsky (to whom 'The Upas Tree' is dedicated), father of Igor Stravinsky. Rimsky-Korsakov afterwards orchestrated them, 'The Prophet' in 1899, 'The Upas Tree' in 1906, in which form they are most effective; 'The Prophet', in particular, was a favourite warhorse of Shalyapin's. But it attempts the impossible. 'The Prophet' is not only one of Pushkin's greatest poems but one of the greatest poems ever written in any language; it is one of the few writings other than the Apocalypse that one can without hyperbole speak of as 'apocalyptic',[1] to set it adequately would tax the powers of one of the greatest masters, and Rimsky-Korsakov was far from being that. But if his setting is no match for the poem, it is at any rate a fine challenge to an intelligent bass singer.

To sum up: even among the mass of colourless and rather conventional music that Rimsky-Korsakov gave birth to in 1897–8 there are at least eight or nine songs thoroughly worth singing. And in the earliest group the proportion is very much higher. It is time English singers realised that Rimsky-Korsakov wrote something more than 'Enslaved by the rose' and a few hackneyed opera numbers.   1944

---

[1] Readers who know no Russian can judge its quality by Maurice Baring's prose version, printed in his *Outline of Russian Literature* (Home University Library) and also in the introduction to *The Oxford Book of Russian Verse*. Personally I prefer this to Baring's later verse rendering.

XIV—RANDOM NOTES ON LYADOV

Lyadov is not a composer who ever impinges very forcibly on one's consciousness. We all know a few things by him: the enchanting orchestral arrangements of *Eight Russian Folk-Songs*, two or three brief orchestral impressions of the more fantastic side of Russian folk-lore (*Baba-Yaga*, *Kikimora*, *The Enchanted Lake*), a handful of polished, Chopinesque piano-pieces. We may know something about the man himself: the friend and disciple of Rimsky-Korsakov, the great talent who achieved so little because he was so indolent, the man whose failure to write *The Fire Bird*—from sheer laziness—gave Igor Stravinsky his first big opportunity. And perhaps there is not so very much more by him or about him that is worth knowing. One would certainly never dream of 'studying' him. Yet if chance happens to throw one or two of Lyadov's better works in your way—he wrote no large-scale ones—they are apt to hold your interest. They have no depth, yet they have something more than superficial charm and technical polish. They glint with suggestions of the brilliant might-have-been, suggestions which one can sometimes extend and deepen and link together with the help of such writings as Yastrebtsev's *Reminiscences of Rimsky-Korsakov*[1] and 'V. Karenin's' article in the *Muzïkalny Sovremennik* for March 1916.

Chief among these might-have-beens is the unwritten opera, *Zoryushka* which began to occupy Lyadov's mind at least as early as 1879 and of which all he had put on paper in a definite form at the time of his death in 1914 is contained in the two little orchestral pieces *Kikimora* and *The Enchanted Lake*. *Zoryushka* was to have been based on a play by Dahl, *The Night at the Crossroads*, and in the spring or summer of 1879, the year after Lyadov had left the Petersburg Conservatoire, Mussorgsky's friend and collaborator, Golenishchev-Kutuzov began to prepare the libretto. But Kutuzov was temperamentally too nearly akin to Lyadov; he worked slowly and fitfully, and finally his interest in the subject petered out altogether. All that remains of his libretto is a charming *rusalka* scene. Some ten years later V. V. Stasov induced the well-known poet Polonsky to take up the libretto, which was now called *Princess Zorka*; he too contributed a few scenes. Finally Stasov's daughter, 'Vladimir Karenin', prepared a fresh scenario in collaboration with Lyadov himself. This scenario underwent various changes, some of them fairly drastic, but the general course of the action was more or less as follows:

Act I.—Prince Vïsheslav—like Svetozar in *Ruslan and Lyudmila*—is giving a feast to his daughter Zoryushka's suitors, who include the

[1] *Moi vospominaniya o N. A. Rimskom-Korsakove* (cf. note on p. 195).

Carpathian prince Udacha. Among the revellers is the half-witted
Tumak, a protégé of Visheslav's, whom in jest they call 'Zoryushka's
betrothed'. Tumak takes the jest seriously, demands his bride, and
frenziedly attacks the real suitors. Visheslav orders him to be torn to
pieces by dogs, but the suitors beg for him to be pardoned.

Act II, *Scene* 1. In her chamber Zoryushka, surrounded by waiting-
women, is mournful at the prospect of leaving her father's house.
Visheslav comes to enquire which of the suitors she prefers. She replies
that she will obey his wishes, but it is evident that she really prefers
Udacha.

Scene 2. A crowd of people at an inn are discussing the banishment
of Tumak who, it appears, is no ordinary half-wit. He is a degenerate,
'son of a woman possessed with a devil'; even Satan serves him and
he is in league with the Water-Spirit and the Wood-Spirit. Fortunately,
Udacha also has an ally in the friendly House-Spirit who is devoted to
Visheslav. The crowd sings and drinks and dances.

Act III, *Scene* 1. By the White Stone at the crossroads, the neutral
point where the domains of the three Spirits—the lake, the forest,
and the Prince's court—meet. Tumak invokes the Wood-Spirit, who
appears at first tall as the trees, though his stature diminishes as he
approaches. The theme of his approach has been recorded by Yastrebtsev:

Ex. 1

Tumak asks the Wood-Spirit's help in getting his revenge; the Spirit
agrees on condition that he may have Zoryushka 'over the border' (i.e.
in his realm and hence in his power).

Scene 2. By a lake near the Stone. The 'lake music' recorded by
Yastrebtsev

Ex. 2

was used in the *Enchanted Lake* of 1909. Rusalkas (water-nymphs)
appear and ask Tumak to give them Udacha 'over the border': he
willingly agrees. The rusalkas dance a khorovod. Visheslav, Udacha
and Zoryushka enter with courtiers and attendants. The princess is
soon enticed 'over the border' into the Wood-Spirit's power and
Udacha, going in pursuit, is captured by the rusalkas. The benevolent

House-Spirit appears and sends Vïsheslav and his company into an enchanted sleep by the White Stone. The Spirit's lullaby was years later used for the cor anglais solo (the tom-cat's lullaby) at the beginning of *Kikimora*:

Ex. 3
Adagio

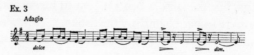

and I suspect that the 'marvellous mystical progression' which Yastrebtsev recorded[1]

Ex. 4

and which was afterwards introduced in a slightly altered form in *The Enchanted Lake* (cf. p. 13 of the score) was also connected with this magic sleep.

The rusalkas come out and resume their play. A shepherd's pipe is heard:

Ex. 5

and presently the rusalkas dance to the piping. But the 'shepherd' is really the House-Spirit who presently seizes one of the rusalkas and will only give her up in exchange for Udacha.

Act IV. Zoryushka mourns in the forest, probably to this theme recorded by Yastrebtsev:

Ex. 6
Lento

But the rescued Udacha, directed by the House-Spirit, is cutting his way through the seemingly impenetrable thickets. His sword sets fire to the dry wood; the whole forest is soon ablaze; the Wood-Spirit flees discomfited; and Udacha carries off his bride through the flames.

In Dahl's play Zoryushka's rescue was effected by an inundation which the Water-Spirit is forced to produce; but when Lyadov saw the first Petersburg performances of the *Ring* in 1889, he was seized with a desire

[1] I have corrected a number of obviously wrong accidentals in the published version of Yastrebtsev's *Reminiscences*.

to write some fire-music of his own. At the same time the clumsy staging of certain Wagnerian effects seems to have exercised a discouraging influence. Lyadov was constantly damped by the thought of his fantastic characters being embodied in the stout singers of the Maryinsky Theatre. He toyed with the idea of using Maskelyne-and-Devant methods, plus characteristic orchestral music, instead of flesh-and-blood actors, to represent the supernatural beings. He would have liked Zoryushka and Tumak to be the only 'real' beings in the action. And the half-bestial, half-comic Tumak himself underwent various modifications; sometimes he was to be the son of the Wood-Spirit, 'a sort of Russian Caliban' with 'a touch of Smerdyakov' (from *The Brothers Karamazov*); after the *Ring* performances of 1889 he acquired some of the characteristics of Mime. And in the end, of course, he failed to materialise at all. Mingled with all the pretexts which ingenious indolence finds for not doing something was also a vein of paralysing humour. 'I'm afraid', Lyadov wrote to his scenarist, 'that *Zoryushka* will soon become *Ipecacuanushka* for you.' But it was he, rather than the scenarist, who became sick of her. Yastrebtsev records a remark of his in 1894 that 'it was not worth writing music for purely fairy-tale subjects like *Zoryushka*,[1] and that a really good dramatic subject [for an opera] was nowhere to be found'. 'Vladimir Karenin' has suggested that her own literary shortcomings were partly responsible for Lyadov's abandonment of his opera and that, had he found the right poet, he would have written the music. I doubt it. The composition of an opera demands a sustained energy quite foreign to Lyadov. We need not doubt that the best of the *Zoryushka* material was put into *The Enchanted Lake* and *Kikimora*, and probably *Baba-Yaga* too; not only the themes identified by Yastrebtsev and 'Vladimir Karenin' but others as well. Even some of the orchestrations of *Eight Russian Folk-Songs* may well have been originally intended for Act II, scene 2 of *Zoryushka*.

Nothing could be in stronger contrast with the fantasy, raciness and harmonic piquancy of these Rimsky-Korsakovian orchestral fragments from *Zoryushka* than the drawing-room polish of the host of little piano-pieces, mainly Chopinesque preludes and mazurkas, that constitute the main bulk of Lyadov's music. The only common features are miniature scale, fine workmanship and a curiously static quality, a lack of vital rhythm. Here and there one comes across a page of real if not very original poetry, such as the elegiac Prelude in B flat minor, Op. 31, No. 2; but far too often Lyadov is content to set a pattern in quintuplets spinning in one hand against a pattern of triplets in the other, or two-against-three or some other cross-rhythm (though one pattern is usually in quintuplets) and to call the result a prelude or étude or variation (cf. the first and third

[1] Though as late as 1902 we find him writing to Stasov that he 'badly needs Dahl's *Night at the Crossroads*' in a great hurry.

Preludes of Op. 40, Nos. 9, 10 and 11 of the *Variations on a Theme by Glinka*, Op. 35, or Nos. 1 and 5 of the *Variations on a Polish Theme*, Op. 51). It is a Chopinesque device, of course, but Lyadov added something of his own—while subtracting some of Chopin's poetry—and when one comes across the same sort of thing in early Skryabin (e.g. the early Étude in B major, Op. 8, No. 4) one feels he has picked it up through Lyadov rather than direct from Chopin. We know that Skryabin admired Lyadov; and Lyadov returned the compliment, even revealing some influence from the younger man in the harmony as well as the titles—*Grimace, Ténèbres, Tentation, Réminiscence*—of his last four piano-pieces, Op. 64. The *Four Pieces* are not altogether successful, but they have a certain piquancy and atmosphere lacking in so much of Lyadov's piano-music.

The hollow elegance is much more tolerable in the variations than in the preludes, for the patterns acquire sense through being referable to a theme. The elegance is in fact no longer hollow, the void being filled by the implied theme. Lyadov was not one of the world's great variation writers; he did not possess anything even comparable with Beethoven's power of producing a series first of rabbits, then of larger fauna from a miserable little Diabelli trilby; his variations even have a curious tendency to model themselves on his own early works (e.g. the eighth *Glinka* variation on the Prelude, Op. 13, No. 1 or the seventh *Polish* variation on No. 4 of the *Biryulki*, Op. 2) or on other people's (e.g. Var. 6 of the *Glinka* set on Chopin's Étude in E flat, Op. 10, No. 11). All the same, both works—particularly the *Glinka Variations*—are well worth playing; either would make a pleasant alternative to the Glazunov *Theme and Variations*.

Both sets of variations are, to my mind, thrown into the shade by the magnificent *Ballade* (*In the Old Days*), Op. 21, which has a strong claim to be considered Lyadov's best work. Beginning with a slow introduction in which an old *guslar* seems to be summoning up the memory of some heroic tale of Russia's epic past, the *Ballade* passes, with a quickening of the tempo, into the tale itself:

Ex. 7

It is difficult to believe that this broad and dynamic work, comparable in more than one respect with the ballades of Brahms, could have been written by the composer of all the graceful Chopinesque trifles. Some sixteen years later, in 1906, Lyadov orchestrated this *Ballade* as Op. 21*b*, not only scoring it in those bright, transparent colours he was accustomed to borrow from Rimsky-Korsakov's palette[1] but altering the tempo-markings, bar-lengths, even melodic outlines, patching in a brilliant new 16-bar peak to the final climax, and adding an inscription from the twelfth-century *Epic of Igor's Army*:

> 'Let us tell, my brothers, a tale
> From the ancient times of Vladimir. . . .'

In its orchestral form the *Ballade* seems to me a decidedly finer work than the 'symphonic picture' *From the Apocalypse*, Op. 66, which attempts to illustrate *Revelation* x. 1–3, with the methods of Rimsky-Korsakov's *Easter Overture*, and is sometimes put forward as evidence that Lyadov could have succeeded in the grand manner if he had tried. *From the Apocalypse* is a brilliant orchestral piece, as colourful as an ikon—and as static; but it is not Apocalyptic.[2] The *Ballade* is dynamic, epic, full of genuine life and power.

If I were writing anything more than random notes on a few aspects of a minor composer which struck me as worth drawing attention to, I should have to speak of Lyadov's *Children's Songs*, his fugues and canons, his folk-song arrangements (particularly the choral settings, Op. 59) and his poignant little *Nenia*, Op. 67, for small orchestra, which was probably the last thing he wrote. But after all they add only a few not very important strokes to their composer's portrait.

1945

[1] The convention of representing the *gusli* by a combination of harp and piano, as in the introduction to the *Ballade*, was invented by Glinka in *Ruslan* and adopted also by Tchaïkovsky and Rimsky-Korsakov.

[2] 'Vladimir Karenin' tells us that Lyadov contemplated a companion-piece on *Revelation* iv. 4–11.

XV—GLAZUNOV AND THE STRING QUARTET

The Russian string quartet has a considerably longer history than the Russian symphony;[1] Alyabiev wrote his first string quartet in 1815, to say nothing of the three quartets by a certain Taneyev—possibly an ancestor of one or both of the two late-nineteenth-century Taneyevs—published by Breitkopf at the end of the eighteenth century, of which the last traceable copies seem to have been destroyed in the Dresden holocaust of 1945. Yet the quartet has never achieved the importance in Russian music that it enjoys in other countries; numerically there are plenty of quartets but they are the stepchildren of Russian music. The Balakirev circle was in its early days actively hostile to chamber music, though Borodin eventually conquered his friends by his two fine compositions. Tchaïkovsky's three are not as bad as seems to be commonly supposed but they can hardly be reckoned among his masterpieces and the world would be little poorer if it were for ever deprived of the quartets of Glinka and Rimsky-Korsakov. The only nineteenth-century Russians who took the quartet seriously enough to write a whole series of them were Glazunov and S. I. Taneyev (whose unrelated or only distantly related namesake, A. S. Taneyev, also produced three respectably written but very lightweight quartets), and their only twentieth-century successors have been Myaskovsky and Shostakovich.

Glazunov produced altogether seven full-length quartets, as well as a Suite, Op. 35, a set of *Novellettes*, and various short pieces, some of them still unpublished. Indeed, with a String Quintet in A (with two cellos), a brass quartet and a quartet for saxophones, they represent the whole of his output of chamber music. It will be useful to list them here, with dates of completion:

Five pieces[2] (1879–1881)
Fugue in D (unpublished) (1881)
Quartet No. 1 in D, Op. 1 (1882)
Quartet No. 2 in F, Op. 10 (1884)
Five Novellettes, Op. 15 (1886)
'El paño', Spanish melody arranged for quartet (1886)
Finale of Quartet on the name 'B-la-F' (1886)
Fugato on the name 'B-la-F' (1887)
First movement of 'Name-Day' Quartet (1887)

---

[1] Bortnyansky's so-called Sinfonie concertante of 1790 is a piano septet.
[2] Edited by A. M. Rivkin (Leningrad, 1951).

Quartet No. 3 (*Slavonic*) in G, Op. 26 (1888)
Suite in C, Op. 35 (1891)
Quartet No. 4 in A minor, Op. 64 (1894)
Theme and variations (converted for string orchestra, but unpublished) (1895)
Prelude and Fugue, and Courante ('Fridays') (1895)
Variation III from 'Variations on a Russian Theme' (1898)
Quartet No. 5 in D minor, Op. 70 (1899)
Quartet No. 6 in B flat, Op. 106 (1921)
Elegy (in memory of M. P. Belyaev) Op. 105 (1928)
Quartet No. 7 in C, Op. 107 (1930)

It will be noticed that Glazunov's earliest music for string quartet was written at the age of 14, the last, six years before his death. One could say that it covers his entire life-span but for the fact of that curious twenty-two-year gap between the Fifth and Sixth Quartets.

I propose to consider first and mainly the seven full-length quartets, though, as will be seen, it is not possible to put them firmly in one category and the usually lighter separate movements (so far removed from the austerity commonly held to be proper to chamber music) in another. It is impossible to get Glazunov's quartet music in right perspective without some reference to the circumstances out of which it arose. He began to write chamber music as a boy because it was played in his mother's home, and he soon participated in it as either violist or cellist—though by no means as a master of either instrument. It was natural, therefore, that he should feel the need of a not too demanding repertory of quartet 'miniatures' and that, directly he began to study composition with Rimsky-Korsakov, some of his earliest essays should take the form of quartet pieces. Earliest of all seem to be a Lento and Intermezzo, dating from the end of 1879; they were originally connected, though when Rïvkin published them in 1951 he saw fit to separate them by a Scherzo in E, written in August (not March, as he says) 1880. A second Scherzo, in C, followed in October, and a third, in A, 'Scherzo alla ongaressa' (sic) in 1881. In August 1881 Glazunov wrote a Fugue in D 'a due soggetti', still (I believe) unpublished,[1] which he then decided to use as the finale of a full-length quartet in D.

In the spring of 1882 Glazunov duly completed this Quartet in D, his Op. 1, although he now threw out the fugue and wrote a different finale. It is a remarkable work for a 17-year-old, well-made, with a strong

---

[1] I am indebted for a good deal of information concerning unpublished works, sketches, etc. to Viktor Belyaev, *Glazunov*, I: *Zhizn* (Moscow, 1922), and L. N. Raaben's chapter on the instrumental chamber music in *Glazunov: Issledovaniya, materiali, publikatsii, pisma*, I (Leningrad, 1959). Belyaev lists *two* scherzos in C, op. cit., p. 39, but I suspect this is an error.

Russian flavour, reflecting Rimsky-Korsakov in the outside movements, a rather characterless scherzo, and a short *andante* (in C sharp minor). The transformation of the opening theme of the introduction into that of the main *allegro* is striking.

One can endorse Tchaïkovsky's judgement after buying the score: 'I was pleasantly surprised. Notwithstanding the imitation of Korsakov, the innumerable repetitions of ideas in a thousand keys instead of development of them (which is intolerable), notwithstanding the disdain for melody and the pursuit of harmonic curiosities, a significant talent is revealed. The form is so smooth that I am surprised, and suspect that the teacher helped' (letter to his brother, 12 September, 1883).

The Second Quartet, F major, Op. 10, written during 1883–4, shows a considerable advance in both individuality (despite the obvious influence of Borodin) and technique. The opening subject of the first movement is decidedly folkish, as are the 4/4, D flat, trio of the scherzo (which again comes second), and the chief theme of the finale; but the second subject is one of those soft, plastic singing tunes with which the mature Glazunov sometimes wearies us but which are one of the hall-marks of his personal style. The scherzo proper, in 3/8 time, is rhythmically curious: written in three-bar phrases of which the first two bars are nearly always fused to suggest one 3/4 bar, so that the effect to the ear is of a perpetual 3/4 + 3/8. Cui paid tribute to the 'inspired depth' of the *adagio molto* and its 'strong impression of genuine grief' in his notice of the performance (*Nedelya*, 1884, No. 52): it is unquestionably the finest movement of the Quartet and the opening may be quoted as an illustration of Glazunov's long-breathed polyphonic thought.

The festive finale is the weakest movement. The sketches, in D flat and with an indication of 'timpani' at bar 13, show that it was conceived for a different—orchestral—work; the reduction for quartet was an unhappy afterthought. In his Third Quartet Glazunov reversed the process, re-scoring the finale as a separate orchestral piece, *Slavonic Festival*.

This Third Quartet (G major, Op. 26) came into existence in a peculiar way. Both its predecessors had been tried out first at the Friday chamber-music evenings in M. P. Belyaev's house. In these surroundings Glazunov —like others—was tempted to experiment with lighter forms of chamber-music, really salon music for string quartet. In particular he was attracted by the idea of quartet 'suites'. The *Five Novellettes* were originally styled 'Suite' and only re-named, on Hans von Bülow's suggestion, after the first performance. And the *Slavonic Quartet*—at first not numbered, and designated '3' only by implication when its successor was numbered '4'—was also conceived as a suite. Indeed the first movement, then in F and entitled 'Chetverka' ('Thursday', i.e. intended for the Glazunovs' own chamber-music evenings), was composed separately in April 1886. On 10 July, 1886, Glazunov wrote a 'Prelude' (now the 'Interludium' of the Quartet) followed by an arrangement of a Spanish melody, 'El paño'; on 7 November, 1887, he finished the 'Alla mazurka' and on 5 July, 1888, the Ukrainian dance finale. Finally the Spanish piece was rejected, and never published, and the transposed and revised 'Thursday' was prefixed to the three other movements in November 1888. Thus it is hardly sur-prising that the Quartet makes a suite-like impression. All the same, the easy polyphonic flow, the charm of the folk-like melodies, and the gaiety of the last two movements have made it the most popular of all Glazunov's quartets, and some of Shostakovich's quartets must be numbered among its descendants.

In his Fourth and Fifth Quartets Glazunov sharply changed course: instead of a 'national' idiom, a 'universal' one, instead of rather loose, suite-like works, firmly integrated ones. The change (due to the influences first of Tchaikovsky, then of Taneyev) is, of course, obvious in all fields of composition; the first manifestation of it in his chamber music is the A major String Quintet, Op. 39. The very opening of the Fourth Quartet (A minor, Op. 64) leads us into this more austere world:

Ex. 3

To mid-twentieth-century ears the austerity may not sound very remark-able; paradoxically, Glazunov's sound-ideal of polished euphony—long-breathed, essentially pentatonic or hexachordal melody rising and falling without real climax, equally smooth harmony and polyphony without clash or even sharp contrast of lines—is so remote from our norm of consonance-dissonance as to present as great an obstacle to our appreciation of his music as the harmonic asperities of Schoenberg, Stravinsky and Bartók did to the average concert-goer half a century ago. But Glazunov's contemporaries felt the impact they were intended to feel. When he played this first movement to Stasov, 'after the first bars, beginning with the canon in thirds, Stasov exclaimed: "This is a cry of despair! What's happened with you?" I then told him that I had composed the quartet under the impression of gloomy memories.'

The way this introduction is worked round to the first *allegro* subject still with the violins in thirds, still beginning with the motive '*x*' (which also opens the slow movement and the finale):

Ex. 4

is typical of Glazunov's subtly monothematic thinking; in the symphonies it is usually more obvious. Similarly, the way the second subject:

Ex. 5

flows out of the first is characteristic of both Glazunov's strength (spontaneity) and his weakness (a tendency to sameness). As both Raaben and E. Bogatïreva[1] have remarked, Glazunov's first and second subjects are usually complementary rather than antithetic. Similarly the long-breathed chief melody of the *andante* is a meditation taking off from the beginning of Ex. 5, while tucked away in the middle of the movement is a complete transformation of Ex. 4:

Ex. 6

The whole quartet is welded together by many tiny links subtler than these, as well as by frank quotations (of the first movement in the finale, and so on). The scherzo is, incidentally, one of the most brilliant pieces of quartet-scoring ever written.

[1] 'Zametki o muzïkalnom stile A. K. Glazunova', in the annual *Voprosi muzïkoznaniya*, I (1954).

The first movement of the Fifth Quartet was conceived in 1897 at the time of the production of the ballet *Raymonda* and, as the composer confessed, in reaction from the composition of dance music. It belongs to the same world as the Fourth. Again an *andante* grows imperceptibly into an *allegro*—both fugal; indeed the earliest autograph shows both as *moderato*, with the present *allegro* written in half note-values and with two bars as one. Again the lyrical second subject has what one might call a homosexual relationship with the first, which becomes fully apparent when the first appears in the development section with doubled (later quadrupled) note-values. But this time the scherzo is demure and humorous, showing a doubtless deliberate affinity with that of the first of Beethoven's 'Razumovsky' quartets, and brilliance is reserved for the rather empty finale.

Belyaev died in 1903 and the break-up of his circle deprived Glazunov of the direct incentive to write quartets. But there was also a general slowing-down of his productivity. The composition of the Seventh Symphony, conceived during the winter of 1902–3, dragged on until the autumn of 1906. When in later years the stream began to flow again, it brought little that was really fresh. The Sixth Quartet (1921) is technically masterly: the *andante piangevole* a typical Glazunov slow movement, the final variations a set of delightfully fashioned miniatures comparable with the well-known Piano Variations, Op. 72. But the only genuinely new music comes in the second movement, 'Intermezzo rusticano' in 8/8 time (3 + 2 + 3), which begins with second violin solo and soon develops a curious texture in which Bogatïreva[1] sees a resemblance to Russian folk-polyphony:

Ex. 7

In the Seventh Quartet (written in exile in Paris, in 1930) Glazunov frankly goes back to his beginnings, to the suite-like structure and the idiom of the 'Mighty Handful': the first movement is headed 'Reminiscence of the past' and the allusion to Balakirev at fig. 15 was obviously not accidental. (Once again a fugato *adagio* generates a theme which is to become the first subject of the very attractive *allegro*.) The other movements have titles too: 'Breath of Spring' (*andante affectuoso*), 'In the mysterious forest' (a deliciously scored *allegretto scherzando*), and the finale is a 'Russian festival', though unlike the festive finale of No. 3 in everything except its need of orchestral weight and colour. It is perhaps

[1] Op. cit., p. 296.

an 'Easter festival', a 'slava' (glorification) rather than a merry-making
—despite the 'quasi balalaika' episode in four-note chords for all the
instruments.

The other quartet works hardly deserve more than passing mention;
practically all date from the period 1886–95. The *Five Novellettes* were
begun as salon-essays in pseudo-national styles: Spanish, oriental,
Hungarian-gypsy. Then the Schubertian waltz was inserted and finally
the grave, very Russian 'Interludium in modo antico'. This last is perhaps
the best, but there is a lot of delightful light scoring in the other pieces.
As has already been mentioned, the 'Novellettes' were originally entitled
'Suite', and the Suite actually so-called, Op. 35, is similar in style. It, too,
includes an 'Orientale' (suggested by Tatar songs heard in the Crimea)
and a 'Valse' as well as an 'Introduction and Fugue' (a very square-cut
fugue, naturally on the same theme as the Introduction), a scherzo,
and a set of 'character'-variations which might well be played on their
own. The much more Bach-like 'Preludio e fuga' in D minor, and the
'Courante' (originally entitled 'Sarabanda') in G major, published in
Les Vendredis, represent the beginnings of another suite that was never
finished; they date from late April–early May, 1895.

Glazunov's contributions to the collective tributes for Belyaev's name-
day in 1886 and 1887 are cheerful, effective, extrovert pieces. Between
them chronologically came a 'Fugato on the theme B-la-F' (Andante
sostenuto) written in Weimar on 25 May, 1887. But the best of all the
'B-la-F' pieces came forty years later: the touching Elegy which Glazunov
dedicated to Belyaev's memory in 1928. An evening gathering took place
in Leningrad that year to mark the 25th anniversary of the publisher's
death, and M. M. Kurbanov—a friend of both—asked Glazunov to write
a funeral march: 'No one in the world has yet written a funeral march
for quartet! It will be magnificent!' Glazunov accepted the challenge and
produced this moving short piece, very personal, very expressive, on the
B-la-F motive which does in the end settle into the ostinato of a funeral
march.

Ex. 8

1965

XVI—THE BEST OF SPONTINI

Spontini [wrote Wagner] was the last link in a chain of composers whose first link was Gluck; what Gluck aimed at, and first seriously attempted, the most complete possible dramatisation of the opera-cantata, was achieved by Spontini—in so far as it is possible to achieve it in the form of opera. . . . Spontini is dead and with him a great, noble and much to be respected artistic period has manifestly gone to its grave: it and he no longer belong to life, but—solely to the history of art. Let us bow low and reverently before the tomb of the creator of the *Vestale*, of *Cortez* and of *Olympie*.[1]

Last of the Gluckists, a composer whose work lives only in the pages of the history books—and who keeps his place in these only on the strength of three of his two dozen or more operas: that places him very fairly. If he had not had such a good opinion of himself, one would wonder whether a prophetic gleam did not flash across his mind when he made that angry death-bed retort to Berlioz's 'Comment pouvez-vous penser mourir, vous, mon maître, qui êtes immortel!' (The old master did not want to die, whatever he thought of his works, and he snapped 'Ne faites pas d'esprit!')

To many of us, perhaps, Spontini means *La Vestale* only, though we may remember *Olympie* because of the eclipse of its second (Berlin) version in 1821 by *Der Freischütz*, produced in the same city five weeks later. But if *Olympie* was conquered at the time by the more racy native product, it was not killed. If Spontini failed to capture the Berlin stage with the later operas he wrote specially for it—*Nurmahal* (1822), *Alcidor* (1825) and *Agnes von Hohenstaufen* (1829)—his three masterpieces of the Paris period, *La Vestale* (1807), *Fernand Cortez* (1809: second version 1817) and *Olympie* (1819: second version 1821), were among the ordinary repertory pieces of the German opera-houses throughout the period of 1820–50, and when Julius Cornet published his survey of opera in Germany[2] in 1849 he observed of these works that 'the novelty of this stately-pathetic style, the grandiose original rhythms, the sonority of the instrumentation, these fully accompanied, singable recitatives full of fire in their expression—all this surprised and rejoiced the musician's heart and occupied his mind; they marked a new form and phase in operatic style'. And, as we have just seen, Wagner was prepared to bow low before the tomb

[1] Richard Wagner, 'Erinnerungen an Spontini', *Gesammelte Schriften*, Vol. V.
[2] *Die Oper in Deutschland und das Theater der Neuzeit aus dem Standpunkte praktischer Erfahrung*, Hamburg, 1849.

of their creator. As for Berlioz, he bracketed Spontini with Beethoven and Weber as the masters from whom he had learned expressive instrumentation and admitted that every page of *Les Francs-Juges* 'bears traces of Spontini's powerful influence'.[1] But Berlioz's admiration of Spontini is more understandable than Wagner's. Wagner was indebted to Spontini for little more than a few hints in *Rienzi*; Berlioz might have disputed with him the claim to be the last of the Gluckists.

Gluck's head must intrude in any study of Spontini almost as pertinaciously as King Charles's in Mr Dick's memorial, for it was the impact of Gluck that struck Spontini's three masterpieces out of him. We are assured by those who know them that Spontini's fifteen Italian operas written between 1796 and 1801, and the three French works produced at the Paris Opéra-Comique in 1804–5 are for the most part simple essays in the familiar style of the late eighteenth-century Neapolitans, the style of Piccinni, Cimarosa and Paisiello. By far the best of them is said to be the one-act *Milton* of 1804, in one scene of which the poet dictates part of the Fourth Book of *Paradise Lost* to his daughter Emma, who sings it to harp accompaniment, and to Arthur, son of 'the late Lord Avenan', who acts as amanuensis. In *Milton* Spitta[2] detected the influence of Mozart and in the hero's 'Hymne au Soleil' 'something of the mild solemnity which Mozart contrived to import to the *Zauberflöte* and also to his compositions for the Freemasons'; Charles Bouvet, Spontini's most recent biographer,[3] agrees that the hymn is 'une fort belle chose qui fait pressentir la prière de la *Vestale*'. But it was not Mozart—though Mozart remained one of his lifelong idols—it was not Mozart but Gluck, the Gluck of *Alceste* and the two *Iphigenias*, who enabled Spontini to find himself. 'Like his hero Ferdinand Cortez', says Bouvet, 'he saw a new world open before him.' And the first result of his advance into this new world was *La Vestale*. As for *Cortez* and *Olympie*, they represent not further exploration, but rather consolidation of the territory first trodden in their predecessor.

For Spontini was one of those artists who find a successful formula and go on succeeding by sticking to it or, at most, varying and elaborating it. In *La Vestale* he found his formula: a simple conflict of strong human passions set against a spectacular background. Here it is the sinful love of the Roman general, Licinius, for the Vestal virgin, Julia, against a background of military triumphs and religious ceremonies (Vestal). In *Cortez* it is the unpatriotic love of the Mexican princess, Amazily,[4] for the Spanish leader, set against a background of military alarms and excur-

[1] *Memoirs.*

[2] Article in the second edition of *Grove*. The passage has since been cut.

[3] *Spontini*, Paris, 1930.

[4] Apparently a favourite name for exotic young women in early nineteenth-century opera. It is also borne by the sister of the heroine of Spohr's *Jessonda*, a Hindu maiden.

sions and mutinies—and of religious ceremonies (Mexican). In *Olympie* it is the love of the heroine, daughter of Alexander the Great, for her father's supposed murderer, Cassander, shown against a background of military rivalry and (for the third time) religious ceremonies (Ephesian). And in each case this unhappy love must be happily consummated, though in *La Vestale* and *Olympie* the happy endings are as forced and unnatural as that of Gluck's *Orpheus*. Jouy, the librettist of *La Vestale*, felt it necessary to apologize for Julia's reprieve, admitting in his preface that 'historic truth demanded that the guilty Vestal should suffer the death to which her sin had exposed her; but was this fearful catastrophe—which might have been introduced by means of a narrative in regular tragedy —of such a nature that it could be consummated before the eyes of the spectator? I do not think so.'

And the happy ending had to be hammered home. Wagner in the same essay decribes Spontini's annoyance when he came to Dresden in 1844 and found that, as in all German theatres of the period, the production was to end with Julia's rescue; the composer insisted on the change of scene to the Temple of Venus with its ballet and chorus of rejoicing. *Olympie* was *imitée de Voltaire* and the original version did follow Voltaire's tragedy fairly closely; the librettists, Dieulafoy and Brifaut, had even preserved some of his verses. They introduced a certain amount of spectacle, it is true: a sacrifice to Diana and the coronation of Alexander's widow, Statira. But the heroine did die; Statira did commit suicide. The craving for a happy ending was only half-satisfied by a final scene in which their spirits were greeted in the Temple of Immortality by the spirit of Alexander. The opera failed; Spontini blamed the libretto; and in the Berlin version of two years later everything was altered. So in the opera as we have it—for Spontini seems to have tried to destroy every trace of the first version—the villainous Antigonus is exposed and killed, Statira lives and reigns, and Olympia marries Cassander.

These three works are written not only to the same dramatic formula, but to the same musical formula. And this musical, or rather operatic, formula is of great historic interest. Nor is it without interest for its own sake. For these three great operas of Spontini's are 'composed through' with a real continuity of musical texture and even musical thought such as Gluck never attained and which pointed the way for the German romantics: Weber (in *Euryanthe*), Spohr (in *Jessonda* and *Der Berggeist*), Schumann (in *Genoveva*) and of course Wagner. Not that Spontini outgrew the number-opera; no one did before Wagner. But he took considerable pains to strengthen, if not to conceal, the joins, and of the two main tendencies that ultimately led to the overthrow of the number-opera—Gluck's magnification of the rôle of recitative and Mozart's magnification of the proportions of the *durchkomponirt* finale in *Die Zauberflöte*—one, the former, was considerably accelerated by Spontini. (His finales—particularly those of the Second Act of *La Vestale* and the Second Act of *Olympie*—are dramatically fine, though as regards length they are not out of the common. But whole acts in Spontini are as closely knit as the *Zauberflöte* finales.) Spontini's recitatives are not only sensitive and expressive and fairly free from routine formulas; they have richly—contemporaries said 'heavily'—scored accompaniments, accompaniments that often consist, moreover, of something more substantial than the conventional interjections of the period. After the morning hymn of the Vestal Virgins in the First Act, part of the hymn is played by the woodwind in the middle of the Grande Vestale's recitative, as her subordinates withdraw. In the First Act of *Olympie*, a *marche religieuse* serves as the background to Antigonus's recitatives.

The *Vestale* passage also draws attention to another aspect of Spontini's work: his tendency to repeat a theme or a passage, less for dramatic effect than to satisfy his sense of musical architecture. Thus at the happy dénouement in the Third Act the orchestra returns to the calm evening music heard at the beginning of Act II, and the duet of the happy lovers in the epilogue is simply a reprise, in the same key, of the end of their duet in the Second Act. Similarly in the First Act of *Olympie* the music that accompanies the first appearance of the Hierophant recurs later in the same Act at his recitative, 'Diane a désigné'; and into the Third Act, into the triumphal march for Statira's coronation—said to be the only piece of music in this Act that survived from the original version of the opera—is woven a passage from the already mentioned *marche religieuse* in the First. The chorus of Spanish soldiers at the beginning of the Third Act of *Cortez* introduces a reference to Cortez's 'Suivez-moi, Castillans' from the finale of the Second Act. It is noteworthy that when Spontini returns in this way to music previously heard, he does so in almost every case in the original key.

These triumphal and religious marches, with their sometimes noisy scoring—that in *Olympie* demands four trumpets, as well as bass trumpet, horns, ophicleide, bass drum and cymbals—and the stage spectacles that accompanied them,[1] are the features of Spontini's operas that seem to have most deeply impressed the minds of musical historians. He has been blamed in consequence for setting the fashion that was followed by Meyerbeer and the Wagner of *Rienzi*, and blamed quite justly. But it is only fair to him to recognise to what extent his art was influenced, if not formed, by his surroundings—both his artistic and his political surround-

[1] The librettist of *Cortez* tried to justify the introduction of horses on the stage at the beginning of the work (the beginning of the Second Act as we now have it): 'they are by no means intended as a mere spectacular effect; their object is to recall the surprise and terror felt by the Mexicans on first seeing them, and the part they played in this memorable enterprise'.

ings, for the two were closely connected. The French Revolution, as everyone knows, generated a curious pseudo-classical style in all the arts; the French Republic was felt to be, in some respects, a resuscitation of the Roman Republic. Opera did not escape the general infection, and the operas of such men as Grétry, Lesueur, Méhul, Catel and Berton—all of them Gluckists, like Spontini—show a predilection for what one can only call 'the heroic style'.[1] Under the Empire the pseudo-classicism of the Republic took the same turn as the Republic itself: it developed pomp and rather tawdry display—and Spontini was the composer *par excellence* of the First Empire. He was recognised as such by Napoleon himself. The emperor did not care for the heroic style in music, and his personal attitude to Spontini is wrapped in a certain amount of mystery, but after the success of *La Vestale*, says Charles Bouvet, 'he considered him the composer best qualified to serve his projects and add lustre to his reign'.

The subject of *Cortez* was actually dictated by Napoleon in 1808 when he had just embarked on the Peninsular adventure. The official poet Esménard accordingly produced a libretto with a Spanish hero (to flatter Spanish vanity) but with a parable—the Spaniards breaking the power of the fanatical and superstitious priesthood of Mexico—of France's mission of enlightenment in the Peninsula. Unfortunately the opera inadvertently became such a glorification of Spanish bravery that the Police Minister had to order the withdrawal of the work in full career of success. But in intention, at any rate, *Cortez* is the most 'Napoleonic', though musically the least fine, of Spontini's three masterpieces. And it is in *Cortez*, above all, that Bücken sees the closest connection with the operas of the Revolution period, e.g. in the first scene with its 'powerful unison passages, effects of sharp contrast, the violent emphasis on weak beats, the frequent employment of the favourite chromatic motive of the Revolution epoch'. According to Bücken, Spontini's long-built-up climaxes are also *ein echter Revolutionseffekt*. Certainly Spontini loved the long-drawn crescendo of dynamics and scoring: e.g. the chorus 'Aveugle ambition' in the finale of Act II of *Olympie*, the coronation march in the same opera, the chorus of Spaniards at the beginning of the last Act of *Cortez*. The two latter may even have given Beethoven hints for the treatment of the 'joy' tune in the Ninth Symphony. All the same, before putting these effects down to the account of the Revolution, we should bear in mind that Spontini had crescendo in his blood, as it were: the Neapolitan crescendo, commonly but erroneously attributed to Rossini. We shall be on surer ground if we attribute Spontini's 'heroic' common-chord melodies (e.g. the duet 'Vous amis de la gloire' in Act I of *Olympie* or Cassander's 'Mais

---

[1] See Ernst Bücken's *Der heroische Stil in der Oper*, Leipzig, 1924.

déjà retentit' in Act III) to the example of his predecessors of the Revolution. Here, too, we may note a point of contact with Beethoven.

But Spontini would hardly have commanded the admiration of men so different as Weber,[1] Berlioz and Wagner, had he not possessed something more than these 'Napoleonic' qualities. He certainly did. The formula that he exploited so successfully consisted not only of spectacular background but of strong, conflicting human passions in the foreground, and it is in his expression of these passions that he appears at his best—and his most Gluckish. Spontini's melody had most of the qualities that we call classical, yet one detects in it a note of something else: Berlioz was not exaggerating so very much when he spoke of Spontini's 'passionate sensibility'; as Julia's prayer in the *Vestale* (Act II, finale) particularly reminds us, Spontini was one of the spiritual parents of Bellini (*Norma*) as well as of Meyerbeer. Sometimes even, as in the Grande Vestale's 'O ma fille, ton cœur s'égare', the sensibility becomes dangerously like sentimentality. But there is also here and there a surprising affinity with Schubert, as in Licinius's 'Les dieux prendront pitié' in Act II of *La Vestale*. As a specimen of Spontini's vein of romantic tenderness I quote the opening of Amazily's 'Hélas! elle n'est plus' in Act II of *Cortez*:

Ex. 1
Andantino passionato

Hé - las! — el - le n'est plus, el - le n'est

plus — toi seul as su char - mer, —

But to illustrate Spontini's real dramatic power by quotation is almost impossible, since it needed space to develop itself. The scene of Licinius's appearance in the temple, for instance, which—technically at any rate—nearly bridges the whole gap between Gluck and Wagner, would have to be quoted at length. But one short example, from Cinna's aria in Act I of *La Vestale*, an example of Spontini's melody at its more purely Empire-classical, will illustrate several characteristic mannerisms: the predominance of falling melodic lines, the seventh drop, the descent to a 6/5

---

[1] Weber is said to have considered the duet for Licinius and the High Priest in Act III of *La Vestale* 'one of the most astounding known to him' and to have thought very highly of the overture to *Olympie*.

chord, the cadence-formula of the voice and the cut of the orchestral
theme in the last bar:

Ex. 2

All these recur frequently throughout Spontini's work, though seldom
all packed together in such a small space as here. Another favourite, and
irritating, cadence-formula:

was destined to leave its mark on both Meyerbeer and Wagner. And the
predominance of symmetrical phrases is undeniable. Yet Spontini's
melody can be very bold at times (cf. the ninth drops in the Grande
Vestale's 'L'amour est un monstre', at the words 'sur des tombeaux, sur
des abysmes') and it very frequently shows the same sort of fusion with
recitative elements that one finds on so many pages of *Fidelio*. It gets little
help from the harmony which, despite the opinion of Spontini's contemporaries, is generally limited in range and, to modern ears, rather inexpressive (though one notes some striking changes of key). On the other
hand, Spontini was a masterly orchestrator. He was a rather poor instrumental composer—the overture to *Olympie* and the rather feebly exotic
ballet music of *Cortez* are probably the high-water marks of his achievement in this field—but he could score superbly. Students of Berlioz's
Traité will remember the passages in praise of the death march in *La
Vestale* and of the solo horn which 'murmurs in duet with Julia's "Toi
que j'implore"'. But Berlioz has not acknowledged his debt to Spontini
for one of his own most curious effects, the 'muted' clarinet, wrapped in a
leather bag, in *Lélio*; in the chorus 'O doux moment' in Act III of *Cortez*,
Spontini directs that both oboes and clarinets are to be muted 'en renfer-
mant le bas de l'instrument dans une bourse de peau'. His scores are,

indeed, full of striking effects. Not only freakish ones like this, and theatrical ones like the terrific unison B of the trombones which announces Cinna's arrival to warn the lovers in the Second Act of *La Vestale*, but such subtler things as the sobbing figure, given first to oboe then to clarinet, when Julia takes farewell of the other Vestals and the deep and threatening horns in the chorus of Spanish soldiers, 'Nous redoutons le plus funeste sort', in *Cortez*. In one passage that I have already mentioned —the quotation of the morning hymn in the middle of the Grande Vestale's recitative—the dovetailing of the woodwind anticipates a characteristic feature of Wagner's scoring. It was not for nothing that he bowed low and reverently before the tomb of the creator of the *Vestale*, of *Cortez* and of *Olympie*.

1942

XVII—HOFFMANN AS COMPOSER

Lovers of *Les contes d'Hoffmann* tend to forget that E. T. A. Hoffmann was as real a person as the Cologne Jew who composed him into his own stories, that Hoffmann was not only a writer of fantastic tales, a music-critic and a character in an opera, but himself a composer—and an opera-composer at that—of considerable merit. Not quite such a good composer as Offenbach, but all the same a musician whose compositions deserve to be considered seriously, not patronisingly dismissed as the diversions of a man of letters. He was no mere Nietzsche of a composer; he has a by no means unimportant place in the history of German romantic opera; and in one respect—his use of *Leitmotiv*, or rather of the sort of thematic reminiscence that was the forerunner of the *Leitmotiv* proper—he was, if anything, in advance of his time.

The couple of pages devoted to Hoffmann's compositions in the sixth volume of the *Oxford History of Music* do him rather less than justice. Dannreuther concerns himself only with the opera *Undine*,[1] Hoffmann's best work, and although he admits a number of good points—'characters and situations well depicted . . . declamation remarkably direct and spirited . . . an acute sense of instrumental colouring and considerable knowledge of [orchestral] effect'—he sums up that Hoffmann 'never rose above the level of a highly-gifted dilettante. His opera did not and could not gain a firm footing on the stage; it was far too tentative.' But Dannreuther did recognise Hoffmann's role as one of the forerunners of Weber and Marschner: 'The overture and the short instrumental pieces which serve as introductions to the Second and Third Acts—rather poor and somewhat incoherent—are made up of scraps and hints of things to come.' Writing in 1904, he says 'the music has not been published' and speaks of 'manuscript copies of the score, preserved at Berlin'. One wonders whether he really knew *Undine* at first-hand at all thoroughly. But two years later Pfitzner prepared an edition from these 'manuscript copies' (there are two: the original draft and the composer's own fair copy); his excellent vocal score was published by Peters; and the work has since been given a number of times on the German stage (e.g. at Aix-la-Chapelle in 1922 and at Leipzig in 1933–4).

[1] Based, like Lortzing's *Undine* of twenty years later, on La Motte Fouqué's story of the water-spirit who marries a mortal and gains a soul, but who loses her husband (Huldbrand) to a mortal (Berthalda). Fouqué himself prepared the libretto, a circumstance less advantageous than one might suppose, for as Weber drily commented: 'Herr von Fouqué knows the tale much too well and is therefore liable to the delusion that others do too.' The later popularity of Fouqué's story deprives the jibe of its sting, but Weber was writing in 1817 barely six years after its publication.

However, before looking more closely at *Undine*, composed in 1813 and produced in Berlin in 1816, it will be worth while to glance for a moment at Hoffmann's previous career as a composer, which began in 1804 with a group of piano sonatas.[1] These are obviously 'prentice-works, written partly under the influence of C. P. E. Bach and showing polyphonic leanings that are justified neither by the thematic material nor by the composer's ability in this direction. The piano-writing is of this type:

Ex. 1

Earlier in the movement—the finale of the Second Sonata—the same theme is treated fugally. About the same time Hoffmann wrote a Mozartean, or would-be Mozartean, Symphony in E flat, presumably for the symphony concerts he was conducting in Warsaw, where he held not a musical post but one in the service of the Prussian Government. A little later came another Piano Sonata, in C sharp minor, a Harp Quintet, and a Piano Trio in E (1809), the scherzo of which is said by Bücken (*Musik des 19. Jahrhunderts*) to be 'a really imposing structure, concise in form and keeping a firm grip on the basic idea'. These later compositions begin to show the influence of Beethoven, as does the 'Miserere' in B flat minor written at Bamberg (where Hoffmann settled in 1808, his official career having been abruptly terminated by the war, and where he conducted the opera for four or five years). He had already at Warsaw written a Mass in D minor, influenced by Mozart's Requiem, but the 'Miserere' is considered his best choral work. Despite the influences of Beethoven and Cherubini, it is, says Istel (*Die Blütezeit der musikalischen Romantik in Deutschland*) 'absolutely original. Particularly fine is the way in which, at the beginning of the five-part final chorus, Hoffmann looks back to the first movement, takes up its themes and works them out on fresh lines'. On the other hand, most of Hoffmann's choral works (e.g. the *a cappella Hymns to Mary* of 1808) reveal his admiration for the Italian masters of vocal composition —particularly those of the baroque period, the Lottis and Durantes. It must be admitted, however, that these works are overshadowed in importance by the great essay 'On Old and New Church Music', of 1814, which exercised a very real influence on the development of German church music in the early nineteenth century. In the same way the other vocal compositions of the Bamberg years, the canzonettas of 1808, the

---

[1] There are two modern editions: that by Gustav Becking in his *Gesamtausgabe* of Hoffmann's compositions. and that by G. von Westermann in the series of attractive little *Musikalische Stundenbücher* published in the early 1920s by the Drei Masken Verlag, Munich.

duettini of 1812–13, and so on, matter a great deal less than the 'Kapell-meister Kreisler' sketches which began to appear in 1810.

Hoffmann seems to have put the best of himself as a composer, not into these odds and ends, but into his dramatic works: his *Singspiele* and operas, his incidental music, and the ballet, *Harlekins Reise auf den Blocksberg*. There is no need to catalogue them here—are not their names written in the dictionaries of music?—but it is worth pointing out that his *Aurora*, an opera on the Cephalus-and-Procris theme produced at Bamberg in 1811 and revived in 1934, anticipates *Undine* in its nature-painting and its use of *Leitmotiv*. *Undine* is his masterpiece; it is on that score alone that he must base his claim today to be considered seriously as a musician. It is emphatically worth looking at; for, although it contains nothing that one can hail as great music, it is in many respects—quite apart from the fact that it was composed by a distinguished man of letters—a remarkable work.

One expects to find technical awkwardness and one is not altogether disappointed. But very nearly. Hoffmann was, on the evidence of *Undine*, by no means the mere gifted dilettante Dannreuther makes him out to be. Because he wrote at the time of, and therefore in many respects in the styles of, Beethoven and Schubert, one inevitably tends to measure his technical accomplishment against theirs: a too severe test. Measure it against that of a musician of his own class and you realize he was not such a bungler after all; put *Undine* beside Spohr's *Faust*, written in the same year and produced in the same year, and you find Hoffmann quite well able to hold his own beside a composer who, whatever his weaknesses, can hardly be accused of technical incompetence. There are flaws, of course; Weber drew attention to them in his otherwise enthusiastic article on the *Undine* production:

(1) The predilection for little, short figures which tend to lack variety and to obscure the *cantilena*, the bringing out of which consequently demands great care on the part of the conductor.

(2) The predilection for cellos and violas; for diminished-seventh chords; for too abrupt cadences, which—at any rate at first hearing—are somewhat disturbing and, if not exactly incorrect, are often unsatisfactory; of certain motives in the inside parts which, thanks to their frequent use by Cherubini, tend to set people looking for plagiarism.

Yet even these 'short figures' to which Weber objects are a symptom of the future, of that more symphonic handling of the opera orchestra which infected Weber's own later works. (*Der Freischütz* was begun the year this article was written, 1817.) However, the diminished sevenths are undeniable, though Weber was hardly the man to point them out; and in commenting on Hoffmann's penchant for the lower strings he might have added, 'for the lower male voices'—for the hero is a baritone and of the remaining male parts only one, the Duke, a minor role, is a tenor, while the other three are basses. This must have led to a certain monotony in performance; but one of these bass roles, that of the dæmonic Kühleborn, Undine's uncle, who first opposes her marriage to Huldbrand, and then avenges her betrayal, is worked out with remarkable power and imagination. Kühleborn is really characterised musically, above all in his vocal line with its bold, wide leaps (one is reminded of Pizarro in *Fidelio*) but also orchestrally in threatening rhythms and brassy colours; as Weber put it 'the instrumentation remains always true to him'. Indeed the whole score is strewn with picturesque or romantic orchestral effects, such as the suggestion of Undine's silvery laughter by rapidly repeated staccato woodwind chords, the painting of the waterfall:

or the theme:

first heard, *fortissimo*, in the introduction to Act II but repeated in the form quoted when the mist first rises from the water to envelop Undine at the end of the Act, again when she disappears, and which pervades the whole scene in the Third Act, when she returns and is reunited with the faithless Huldbrand in a *Liebestod*. (It is worth noting that this word is actually used in the libretto.)

The almost all-pervading sense of a watery background is conveyed by—admittedly rather conventional—murmuring figures that often remind one of *Die schöne Müllerin*, composed ten years later. Indeed it is not only the accompaniments that recall Schubert's cycle; Hoffmann's melodies often suggest rather poor Schubert, occasionally not so poor Schubert, just as his more symphonic passages (e.g. the *allegro con spirito* of the overture) suggest Cherubini or second-rate Beethoven. These likenesses are, of course, mainly period likenesses; Hoffmann cannot have known anything of Schubert, or Schubert anything of Hoffmann, though the direct influence of Beethoven is undeniable. Again, one sometimes notices affinities with some of the older North German composers of the

Zopf period, the Zumsteegs and Reichardts, or with contemporary Italians: a certain melodic stiffness here and there, very occasional coloratura.

To tell the truth, melodic fertility was not Hoffmann's strongest point; the duet at the beginning of the Second Act:

Ex. 4

a characteristically German tune lapsing diconcertingly into an Italianism at bar 7, is typical of his lyrical vein at an average moment. But he can rise well above this level, and when Undine sings her farewell at the end of this Act he sounds real depths of warm emotion. Yet even here the expression is not essentially melodic, but rather contrived by the interplay of harmony and orchestral colour and texture. The novel elements in Hoffmann's music are harmonic or orchestral: e.g., the ending of a number on a dominant seventh, repeated—after a couple of dozen lines of spoken dialogue—at the beginning of the next number, and only then resolved. But the real novelty of Hoffmann's opera consists not in any details but in its quality as a whole, its sense of ambient nature impinging on human happenings, its full-blooded—there is no escaping the word—romanticism, a romanticism which made the strongest impression on Weber.

The future composer of *Der Freischütz* heard *Undine* several times in Berlin in November 1816, and wrote of it to his fiancée that 'the music is uncommonly characteristic, clever, indeed often striking and thoroughly effective, so that it gave me great joy and gratification. It was given very well, and the beauty of the décor is really extraordinary. I was so filled with it that directly after the performance I hurried to Hoffmann to express my thanks and interest.' And shortly afterwards he publicly proclaimed *Undine* in the *Allgemeine Musikalische Zeitung* in the article I have already quoted from, to be 'one of the most gifted works we have been given in recent times . . . marked by beautiful, warmly felt melodies' and went on to speak of its 'great effectiveness of scoring, knowledge of harmony and often new progressions, correct declamation'. The last is certainly generally better than in Ex. 4.

'But if all this is true,' the reader may object, 'why did not *Undine* keep the stage? Was not Dannreuther right after all?' *Undine did* keep the stage of the Berlin Schauspielhaus with great success for nearly a year. Then the theatre was burned down, destroying the scenery and costumes, and Hoffmann himself refused to allow his opera to be produced in the Opernhaus on the ground that the latter was too large. It was commonly believed that even the score had been destroyed in the fire, and so the opera was gradually forgotten[1] and then superseded by those maturer operatic fruits of German romanticism, the first of which, *Freischütz*, Hoffmann lived just long enough to hear and to greet, first with a laurel wreath and then with a spiteful article in the *Vossiche Zeitung*.

1942

[1] According to Hans Ehinger, *E. T. A. Hoffmann als Musiker und Musikschriftsteller*, Olten, 1954, p. 215, it was produced at Prague a few years later.

XVIII—WEBER AS NOVELIST AND CRITIC

The list of distinguished musicians who have tried their hands at literature or journalism is not a long one. Nor, with the exception of Schumann and Berlioz, does it record any conspicuous successes. We read Wagner's prose works, it is true, but he had no real literary flair and such essays in fiction as the 'Pilgerfahrt zu Beethoven', whatever their autobiographical interest, have no literary distinction. Debussy had a witty touch, but was only a clever amateur at the game of criticism. Tchaïkovsky must be relegated to a still lower class, though his newspaper articles make interesting, and sometimes unintentionally amusing, reading—simply because they were written by the composer of the *Pathétique*. Probably not many people would think of including Weber's name in the list at all, for his writings seem to be almost unknown to the general musical public. Benedict says little about them in his well-known *Life of Weber*, only making a passing reference to an article on Morlacchi's *Isacco* and quoting from a notice of Meyerbeer's long-forgotten *Alimelek*. But some readers may remember that Grove, in *Beethoven and his Nine Symphonies*, speaking of the Fourth Symphony, says: 'Carl Maria von Weber, then in his hot youth, was one of its sharpest opponents, and in a *jeu d'esprit* in one of the journals of the period—if that can be so called which exhibits neither *jeu* nor *esprit*—has expressed himself very bitterly. It is supposed to be a dream, in which the instruments of the orchestra are heard uttering their complaints after the rehearsal of the new work.' And Grove goes on to quote Weber's skit at considerable length.

As a matter of fact, Weber's writings, spread over the period 1809–1821, cover a fairly wide field—concert notices, analyses, fiction and even poetry.[1] But by far the most interesting of all these productions is the unfinished novel, *Künstlerleben*, a work which gives him a unique place among composer-authors. And, as it happens, the lampoon on the Fourth Symphony was actually intended to form part of this novel.

Künstlerleben—or, as Weber first thought of calling it, *Tonkünstlers Leben, eine Arabeske*—must have been begun when the composer was still in his early twenties, at the time when he was private secretary to Prince Ludwig of Württemberg, for one episode appeared in the Stuttgart

---

[1] Including an 'Ode on Vogler's Birthday', 1810, which was set to music by Weber's fellow-pupils, Meyerbeer and Gänsbacher. It begins:

> Willkommen, teurer Vater, hier
> In deiner Kinder Reihen,
> Wo alle eng vereinigt dir
> Die wärmste Liebe weihen.

Morgenblatt in 1809. Other fragments were afterwards published in the *Muse* and in the *Taschenbuch zum geselligen Vergnügen* edited by Friedrich Kind, the librettist of *Der Freischütz*, but the novel as a whole was never finished. It remained somewhere at the back of Weber's mind for a number of years and at long intervals he worked at it afresh. But all that we have is the first, third, and seventh chapters fairly worked out, fragments of the second, eighth, ninth, and twenty-second chapters, one or two other passages expressing views on æsthetics and life in general, which might have been inserted almost anywhere, and a synopsis of the contents of the chapters according to a second revised draft of the whole. From this last it appears that there were to have been twenty-three chapters in all, though curiously enough the fourth, fifth, and sixth are omitted from the synopsis. *The Artist's Last Will and Testament* was to form an epilogue. Another curious feature is the C below the bass clef, which heads the first chapter. Weber intended that each chapter should have a similar note-heading; and at the end, when the hero looked back over his life, the headings were to join in a chorale. The notes were also to form a *Cirkelkanon*, which would moreover sound the same backwards and forwards, and at the same time be 'to some extent a picture of human life'.

It would be idle to pretend that *Künstlerleben* has great merit as a novel. Yet it is far more than an interesting curiosity, a mere freak of a man of genius. It has real value in that it gives us not only Weber's opinions on many points connected with music, but many unique glimpses of the workings of a composer's mind. *Künstlerleben* is not an autobiographical novel in the usual sense, though some circumstances in the life of the composer-hero, variously referred to as 'Felix' and 'A', are identical with those of Weber's own (for instance, the early loss of his mother, his father's laxness, and his life at a court). But the book is almost certainly a spiritual autobiography. If Felix is not Weber, his thoughts and feelings are clearly Weber's. The opening chapter, for example, gives us a graphic description of a state of mind which Weber himself must have often experienced: the torment of the creative artist who for the time being *cannot* create.

> Vague longing, stretching out into a dim distance where one hopes to find alleviation, without being able to say exactly *how*; painful excitement of inward power on which consciousness of a high ideal lays heavy fetters, fetters from which one sometimes gives up all hope of release; irresistibly violent impulses to work, calling up giant pictures of would-be accomplishment which immediately dissolve into a pure void of thought. . . .

These phenomena could be described only by one who had experienced them.

The very position I had taken up to work *at the piano* was, as my last resource, a bad sign. The composer who gets his material from *there* is almost always born poor or well on the way to handing over his mind to the banal and commonplace. For these hands, these damned 'piano-fingers' which from constant practice acquire a sort of independence and self-willed intelligence, are quite unconscious tyrants of the creative power. *They* invent nothing new, in fact everything new is uncomfortable to them. Quietly and cunningly, like true mechanics, they botch old, familiar limbs of sound into whole bodies, which look almost like new figures, and which, because they sound clear and euphonious, are accepted at a first hearing by the corrupted ear. How differently does the man create whose *inner* ear is the judge of things simultaneously invented and criticised. This spiritual ear . . . is a divine secret, peculiar to music and incomprehensible to the non-musician. For it hears whole passages, even whole pieces at a time, and takes no notice of little gaps and unevennesses, leaving the filling in and smoothing out of these to later consideration. . . .

Again, further on in the same chapter:

With me everything must conform to musical shapes. The sight of a stretch of country is to me the performance of a piece of music. I sense the whole, without dwelling on the details of which it is composed; in short, the scene, curiously enough, moves in time. It is a *successive* pleasure.

The plot and characterisation of *Künstlerleben* are very weak. It is easy to see from the completed fragments that there would have been only one real character, the hero himself. The others are lay-figures seen through the medium of Felix's own personality. And even Felix is not very interesting apart from the fact that he is a composer; in other respects he differs in no way from the numerous sentimental-romantic heroes of early nineteenth-century German fiction. He has any amount of temperament— but no character. Weber obviously lacked the novelist's most essential quality—the power to create and definitely visualise scenes and characters, still more, the ability to make the reader share his vision. He could only set down his own experiences naïvely and directly; and, as most of his experiences were inward rather than active the novel would probably have become a rather self-conscious soliloquy, interrupted by melodramatic incidents and outbursts of bitter, somewhat heavy sarcasm directed at the musical fashions of the day.

The most amusing of these episodes, unessential to the action and interpolated in the manner of the 'Confessions of a Beautiful Soul' in *Wilhelm Meister*, are the dream of the orchestral instruments and the parodies of French, Italian and German opera which occur in Chapter Seven. Felix, who has fallen in love with a girl named Emilie (of whom he knows nothing but her Christian name), goes to a masked ball, where his disguise is quickly penetrated by various other masks. The scene is merely sketched, and the curiously haphazard punctuation shows that it was to have been re-written later:

A girl touched me and offered me an orange. For your beautiful playing a few days ago. A devil pushed against me and said, 'compose this for me'; I read 'to Emilie', snatched it and said: 'even from the devil I adore whatever bears her name, you shall have it at the next ball.' A nun took my arm; the bad music must annoy the ear of a connoisseur.—No, my dear, but what does annoy my ears is that the whole world can find nothing to talk to an artist about but what he never likes to discuss, only to feel—his art.

Then comes the masque-like interlude of the opera-parodies. A clown appears and announces a 'grand declamatory, dramatic, melopoetic, allegorical representation in verse'. First comes a figure symbolising Italian opera, heralded by 'a noise made in the orchestra to make the audience quiet, which in Italy is called an Overture':

SCENA

Recit. O Dio . . . addio. . . .
Arioso. Oh non pianger mio bene
   Ti lascio—Idol mio—
   . . . oimè. . . .
Allegro. Già la Tromba suona. . . .

  .   .   .   .

Colla parte. Per te morir io voglio. . . .

  .   .   .   .

più stretto—O Felicità. . . . .
(A ten-bar trill on 'ta', the public applaud frantically.)

DUETTO

—Caro . . .!
—Cara . . .!
a Due. Sorte amara. . . . .
(The sweetest passage in thirds on 'amara', because of the 'a'.)

Allegro.—oh, barbaro tormento—

(No one has been listening, but a connoisseur shouts *Bravo, Brava,* and the whole audience joins in *fortissimo.*)

The parody of French grand opera is taken from a skit published in Paris in 1670, but is worth quoting for its own sake:

ACT I

La Princesse: Cher Prince, on nous unit.
Le Prince: J'en suis ravi, Princesse.
Peuple, chantez, dansez, montrez votre allégresse.

CHORUS

Chantons, dansons, montrons notre allégresse.
END OF ACT I

ACT II

La Princesse: Amour!

(Warlike sounds; she falls unconscious. The Prince appears fighting his enemies, and is struck down.)

La Princ: Cher prince.
Le Pr: Hélas!
La Princ: Quoi?
Le Pr: J'expire!
La Princ: O Malheur!
Peuple, chantez, dansez, montrez votre douleur.

CHORUS

Chantons, dansons, montrons notre douleur.
(A march closes Act II)

ACT III

(Pallas appears in the clouds)
Pallas: Pallas te rend le jour.
La Princ: Ah, quel moment!
Le Pr: Où suis-je?
Peuple, chantez, dansez, célébrez ce prodige!

CHORUS

Dansons, chantons, célébrons ce prodige!

There is a long pause before the appearance of the German opera which as the clown has to explain to the impatient audience, is in a bad way. But *Agnes Bernauerin*, described as a *romantisch-vaterländisches Tonspiel*, appears eventually and proves at least that Weber did not mind laughing at himself, as well as at other people. A quotation from the First Act must suffice:

FIRST SCENE

(*The scene changes*)

SECOND SCENE

Duke (with retinue): Knight, follow me to the hall of state. She shall give thee her hand today, or snakes and vipers in the castle-dungeon, according to their wont. . . . Thou understandest. . . . (Exit.)

(*Scene changes*) *Albrecht (appears):* Kaspar, thou followest me.

(*Scene changes*) (*A ghost appears warningly*).

Albrecht: Who art thou, incomprehensible being?

Ghost: I have power to do everything—but hasten, noble youth, I will rescue thee later.

Albrecht: Rescue or die.

(*Two Minnesingers appear):* Wait, noble sir; we will sing you the whole story.

(*Scene changes.*)

FINALE

(*Wooded rocky scene. Left, in the background, a castle; a vineyard on the other side; nearer, a hermit's hut. Left foreground, a cave; nearer, a bower; in the middle, two hollow trees; nearer the front, a subterranean passage.*)

(*Hermit enters singing prayers. Agnes sings an aria in the castle, accompanied by chorus of grape-pickers from the other side. Albrecht is sleeping in the bower and sings disconnectedly in his dreams. The terrified Kaspar sings a polonaise in the hollow trees. Robbers in the cave sing a wild chorus. Protecting spirits hover over Albrecht. Sounds of battle behind the scenes. A march is heard from the other side. Naturally all at the same time. Two lightning flashes come from different directions and shatter something.*)

All: Hah!

The Curtain Falls.

In the Second Act Agnes is thrown over a bridge and left hanging by a nail, while Albrecht and the chorus sing at great length that no time is to be lost, etc. It will be seen that there was nothing very subtle about Weber's humour.

This interlude is no sooner over than the plot at last begins to develop. The mysterious Emilie, unknown to Felix, is at the ball too, and Felix in his disguise is mistaken for a dissolute prince (suggested perhaps by Prince Ludwig of Württemberg) who has planned to abduct her. Instead of rescuing Emilie himself, Felix, haunted by Poe's 'Imp of the Perverse', entrusts this gratifying task to Dihl, his friend. Dihl accordingly substitutes a little acquaintance of his own for the real Emilie, whom he escorts safely home, leaving the pseudo-Emilie to the hoodwinked Prince. Unfortunately, in the excitement of the moment Dihl has forgotten to make a note of the real Emilie's address, and Felix, thus having lost yet another chance of making her acquaintance, spends a sleepless night. Here again the personal note creeps in. After speaking of those unfortunates, like himself, who live in extremes of emotion, Felix goes on:

> I flew to music and hoped, driven by these passions—inflamed to fever heat, indeed—to be able to express my feeling in tones; but in vain. My ideas were in a state of chaos. The abundance of my emotion consumed itself. So that I proved the falsehood of the usual remark that the merry compose well merrily and the sad sadly. Whoever repeats that remark does not know mankind. Profound emotion is *felt*, but not expressed (*Alles Tiefempfundene* fühlt *sich, aber* sagt *sich nicht*). The creative impulse must be a fundamental element of that tranquil mood which is capable, so to speak, of leaving the individual Ego entirely and passing over to the other, the creative.

That is a clumsy way of defining poetry as 'emotion recollected in tranquillity', but it is valuable to have Weber's endorsement—or rather, since he could hardly have known Wordsworth's dictum, his independent testimony. Again, in Chapter Ten, when Felix's creative ability is reawakened by the finding of the poem given him by the Devil at the ball, there is an illuminating snatch of dialogue when Dihl appears and interrupts him. Dihl asks Felix if he is disturbing him, but Felix tells him to go on talking:

> *Dihl:* Now I can't understand that, and I have long wanted to ask you how you can carry on a conversation and work at the same time.
> *Felix:* Yes, I could almost believe with Plato that men—or at least I—have two souls; at any rate, I evidently have two things in me, of which one is trained to deal with sounds and the other with conversation. For I find it quite easy to talk connectedly of entirely different matters and yet with my whole soul, quite occupied with my subject, to form musical ideas and compose. Yet I must admit that it overfatigues me and that at such times I am like one hypnotised, since my tongue speaks of things concerning which I really know and think nothing.
> *Dihl:* And do you find that to be the same with all kinds of composition?
> *Felix:* No, not quite. In the so-called really strict forms, such as fugues, I find it more difficult to do anything else at the same time.

Dihl: That is curious, for I should have thought that that kind of thing called for less exercise of the imaginative faculty than any other type of composition, and that you only needed to have your Kirnberger, Fux, Wolf, or whatever the animals are called, thoroughly ground into you.

Felix: As a matter of fact, it is supremely necessary to have feeling as a guiding-star in these abstract forms, so as not to allow oneself to be led away by academic learning into the dry sand of boredom.

Dihl: Since you are now talking so sensibly I take it that you are not writing *fugues*.

Felix: If only you laymen would leave the poor fugues alone. No! I've just been composing a song.

There, but for a few fragments, the novel ends, though the working out of the plot is fully sketched in the synopsis, which probably served Weber as a working plan. While acting as accompanist to a travelling reciter, 'a genuine wayfaring vagabond', Felix is invited by an amiable old gentleman to give his daughter music-lessons. The hero goes to the house, finds the room empty and sitting down at the piano begins to improvise; the daughter enters, unnoticed, and listens. Felix turns round and sees, needless to say, Emilie. In the course of 'a delightful musical evening' (Papa and Mamma having appeared in the meantime) Emilie shows him the compositions of her favourite composer. It is again needless to say that they are his own, which he has published under a pseudonym. He plays them 'like one inspired', Emilie is enraptured, and he can hardly refrain from proclaiming his identity. He goes every day to the house and introduces in his improvisations favourite mannerisms from which the intelligent Emilie recognises him as *her* composer. ('Renewed joy and admiration of his modesty', notes the sketch. And then were to follow some 'remarks on certain shapes peculiar to every composer' which one is sorry to have lost.)

Obviously the work interested Weber only so far as it gave him opportunities of writing about music and the artistic temperament. That the provision of the love interest merely bored him is amusingly betrayed by the note for the contents of Chapter Sixteen, in which Emilie was at last to discover that she owed to Felix her rescue on the night of the ball: 'She is overpowered with love. Declaration, etc. Wearisome love scene.' The course of Felix's true love now for a while runs a little more smoothly, for the attitude of Emilie's parents is not unfavourable, though they express a strong wish that he should abandon the Bohemian life of an artist for the safety of an official career. But at this point a complication of a more original nature arises. Felix has, in the meantime, made the acquaintance of the Prince, who has involuntarily attracted him, overcoming

Felix's distrust by his cordiality and his intelligent interest in art and artists. Finally he offers Felix a post as his companion. Since Emilie presses her lover to accept the offer, he tells her the full story of the attempted abduction. But even this does not shock the lady's parents and, after some meditations on 'the vanity of women, even the best'— which suggest that Weber was smarting from the caprices of Margarethe Lang or, if the draft is of a later date, of Caroline Brandt—Felix accepts the position. The consequences are roughly indicated in the synopsis:

New conditions. Court life. Relationship between Felix and the artists reversed. The latter's curious judgment on him *qua* dilettante. The greater his attachment to Emilie, who seems to have one soul, one thought with him artistically, the further their views of life diverge. She, who is full of equivocations and half-truths, is weakly deceitful. He, full of purity and uncompromising honesty. Strange uneasy feeling which arises between them.

In the twenty-first chapter another character is more fully sketched, the Prince's favourite, Dario, who has already made a short appearance in the scene of the attempted abduction.

Dario is cold and dry; of Italian parentage. Mathematician, despiser of music, atheist, under a mask of the grimmest seriousness with which diabolical smoothness and suppleness are sometimes mingled. Like the rattlesnake he attracts even Felix, who defends him against Dihl— who cannot bear him at all.

Felix, unhappy both in his love and in his position at court, oscillates between wild excesses and moods of blackest melancholy; and the dream interlude was to have been inserted at this point. Finally a *liaison* springs up between Emilie and the Prince. Her weak and worldly parents wink at it, and the disgusted Felix decides to turn his back on them all and devote himself once more to his art.

Of the remaining fragments of *Künstlerleben*, the most valuable is a conversation between Felix and Dihl, in which the former puts forward a surprising defence of the practice of cutting dramatic works. The poet, he says, often puts too much into his work. Wishing to make it as complete as possible, he includes much that is secondary and unessential (though it all seems essential to *him*), with the consequence that the spectator, apart from the fatigue of listening to an overlong work, cannot see the wood for the trees. A competent theatre director is more likely to be able to select the essential points so that the spectator shall get a clear idea of the main outline at once. Later, when, as with Shakespeare and Schiller, the public demands complete performances, it is better able to appreciate the working out of the details.

Then the conversation turns to the topic of opera and Felix emphasises the peculiar difficulty which besets the opera-composer—that of building up a number of complete musical wholes into one greater whole, so that only the latter, and not the individual parts, shall impress itself upon the spectator's mind, 'a difficulty which only the heroes of art have been able to overcome'. Later Dihl, attacking 'the excessive demands made on the resources of art, which must soon lead to total bankruptcy', says further:

> The musical wealth brought to light by the latest developments of instrumental music has been misused in the most criminal way. Luxuriance of harmony and overloading of instrumentation in the most trifling and unpretentious things have been carried to extremes. Trombones are quite the usual seasoning, and already no one can do anything without four horns.

Clearly it is the early critic of Beethoven who speaks here, not the composer of *Der Freischütz*.

When we turn from *Künstlerleben* to Weber's purely critical writings we find the same clear grasp of sound theoretical principles and the same conservatism in actual judgment. Since we know that his opinion of Beethoven underwent a fundamental change in later life, it would be of the highest interest to know his considered judgments of individual works of the older composer. Unfortunately all we have are criticisms (written at Prague about 1816–17), of three of Beethoven's poorest compositions, *The Mount of Olives*, the Choral Fantasia, and *The Battle of Vittoria*. Naturally the tone is not enthusiastic. The notice of *The Mount of Olives* is politely hostile:

> The effective choruses often remind one of the theatre and awaken a desire to hear them there, though that, of course, speaks more for their liveliness than for their suitability to this type of music [i.e. to oratorio].

Weber also notes the absence of 'the crown of the more serious style, the fugue', although a fugal subject is put forward and then quickly abandoned:

> When the great masters of the art take such liberties and treat significant things so carelessly, their example has an unfortunate effect on the serious study of the art, which is, in any case, continually becoming more and more superficial.

In the Choral Fantasia he can find nothing more to praise than the fact that the title has not been used as an excuse for formlessness. He refuses to pass any opinion on the *Battle of Vittoria* at a first hearing, 'as the fearful uproar of cannon, etc., made the real music practically inaudible'.

Yet 'the "Victory Symphony" shows obvious traits of genius, such as are never absent from the works of this powerful (*mächtig*) composer'. The notice of the second performance is still more carefully worded. Evidently Weber thought little of the 'real music' when he did hear it—a fact which in no way reflects on his critical ability.

One of Weber's most interesting essays is that in which he replies to the criticisms of the poet Müllner, who had complained of three bars:

Ex. 1

will ich sein   im – mer bei ihm,   e – wig treu ihm

in his setting of Brunhilde's song in the drama, *Yngurd*. Müllner had pointed out that the note-values did not agree with the prosodic quantities of the syllables:

The prosody gives: will ich sein—immer bei ihm, ewig treu ihm.

The notes, however, give: will ich sein—immer bei ihm, ewig treu ihm, In this way *ich* and *ihm* are emphasised as the main ideas, and the lines are given the sense: *Ich* will sein Leichenstein sein, immer bei *ihm*, ewig *ihm treu*, instead of the more correct: Sein *Leichenstein* will ich sein, immer *bei* ihm, ewig *treu* ihm. Besides, directly the singer gives 'bei' and 'treu' as short syllables, the spondaic feminine rhyme '*bei* ihm' and '*treu* ihm', becomes the incorrect '*ihm*' with '*ihm*'.

Weber, in his reply, acknowledges that the poet must be allowed to know best about the prosody and meaning of his own verses, but goes on to show that his declamation, if wrong, was not careless. He had taken the view, he says, that Brunhilde's love for her son was the underlying idea of the song:

She and *he* and again *her* love for *him*. Hence my underlining, by tone and accent, of all the words relating to it; the main point seemed to me to be that *she* will be his tombstone, that *she* will ever be near *him* and *true* to him: *hence:*

Ex. 2

Sein   Lei – chen–stein will   ich   sein

After pointing out that a slight natural accent in speaking may be distressingly exaggerated if music attempts to follow it too exactly, he gives examples of correct declamation of the words and asks whether they are not worse than his original setting (Ex. 3 on p. 250).

Ex. 3

Regarding the whole question of setting words to music, Weber states his view that correct declamation is less important than the bringing out of the 'inner life' expressed by the words:

> The great danger of too anxiously sought correctness is that the inner truth of the melody may lose its bloom and freshness. The decision as to whether music or poetry is to have the upper hand in a particular case is the rock on which so many have come to grief.

Weber's merits as a writer, apart from his ability as a critic, may be summed up under three headings: humour, imagination, and a sense of style. As we have seen, his humour was by turns naïve, coarse, exaggerated, and bitter, and his imagination strictly limited in certain directions. But his style is often attractive, though sometimes slipshod, and he had something of the power shared by the Goethe and the Schiller of the *Xenien* of crystallising his thought into striking aphorisms. In literature, as definitely as in music, he was a typical German romantic—the exact counterpart of E. T. A. Hoffmann, with the literary and musical roles reversed. *Undine* proves that Hoffmann could have been a notable composer, as *Künstlerleben* demonstrates that Weber had at least the germs of authorship in him. The essential stuff of their minds must have been strikingly similar.   1934

XIX—MARSCHNER AND WAGNER

To most English musicians, I imagine, the name of Heinrich Marschner is little more than a name. One murmurs to oneself: 'Oh, yes—disciple of Weber—*Hans Heiling* (one has heard the overture)—*Templer und Jüdin*—didn't Schumann quote 'Du stolzes England, freue dich' from it in the finale of the *Études symphoniques* as a compliment to Sterndale Bennett?—and *Der Vampyr*, of course.' If one is the sort of person who uses the word *Zeitgeist*, one adds a lightly learned comment on *Schauerromantik* and E. T. A. Hoffmann and the early nineteenth-century German *Schaueroper*. But was Marschner really nothing more than this, a composer of operatic thrillers, a weak link in the chain that connects Weber with Wagner? He certainly had two characteristics in common with the fat boy in *Pickwick*: he liked to make your flesh creep and he—or, at least, his creative ability—was always liable to drop off to sleep. But has posterity been quite fair in dismissing him as the fat boy of German romantic opera?

Admittedly Marschner put his best work into two thrillers, *Der Vampyr* (1828) and *Hans Heiling* (1833), and in his other operas comes nearest to success when he depicts evil or demonic characters: Bois-Guilbert in the *Ivanhoe* opera, *Der Templer und die Jüdin* (1829), the Marchese del Orco in the otherwise complete failure, *Das Schloss am Aetna* (1836). But he not only portrays these demonic figures with considerable musical power; he gives them a subtlety lacking in their Weberian prototypes. To the accusation that he had merely followed in Weber's footsteps he could reply with some justice that he had 'gone a bit further than Weber and touched on points that he had left alone' (letter to his publisher, Hofmeister, 29 October, 1850). He was decidedly Weber's inferior as a musician, equally in technique and inspiration; but he did surpass his master—of whom he was a disciple, but never a pupil in the strictest sense—in this one point, the demonic Weber's Kaspar and Samiel are all black; Marschner's demons and demon-possessed characters are skilfully shaded. It might appear an impossible task to make Byron's (or, rather, his physician-secretary Polidori's) Ruthven, the vampire who has undertaken to sacrifice three brides to the Prince of Evil, into an almost sympathetic figure. Yet Marschner has done so. Not so much by the suggestions he undoubtedly made to the librettist, his brother-in-law Wilhelm August Wohlbrück (also the librettist of *Der Templer* and several of his other operas), who adapted Polidori's story very freely, as by the nature of his music, above all in Ruthven's confession to his friend Aubry in Act II, the big scena 'Strauchle auf der

Bahn des Rechten'. Ruthven has committed a sin and his fearful punishment is that he has become a vampire and must do evil though he loathes it. There is a parallel scene in the Second Act of *Der Templer*, where Bois-Guilbert reveals that he too is not wholly bad—a scene which Wagner himself praised as 'a creation of the greatest originality of feeling, and of striking (even, in parts, inspired) melodic invention'. Again, in *Hans Heiling* the unhappy Hans—a goblin prince who longs for warm, human love—expresses his dual nature in the aria 'An jenem Tag': he loves Anna with true devotion and overwhelming passion, but if she is faithless—and she is, in fact, a Senta who prefers Erik to the Dutchman—he already 'feels the dark powers that will drive him to a terrible vengeance'.

Now these three big arias, or rather scenas, which epitomize the central ideas of Marschner's three greatest operas very much as Senta's ballad epitomizes *The Flying Dutchman*, also illustrate Marschner's general attitude to the problems of operatic style. Ruthven's scena is a continual alternation of recitative and arioso; the orchestra is completely subordinate to the voice and has a great deal of tremolo and sustained chords, with conventional 'dramatic' figuration, though there is a slight thematic thread holding the whole together. Only two things about the scena are noteworthy: the declamatory power and (what is really significant) the fact that Marschner chose this loose, purely declamatory form for such an emotional climax. Bois-Guilbert's scena in *Der Templer* is more striking, for in the first part the orchestra definitely has the upper hand and the voice merely comments:

Ex. 1

The text is prose and Marschner sets it with complete disregard of conventional recitative formulas on the one hand and balanced phrasing on the other. In the *allegretto* section that follows, 'War ein Ritter je im Leben' (the beginning of the aria proper, quoted by Dannreuther in the *Oxford History of Music* as the part specially admired by Wagner), the text changes to verse and the voice part becomes more lyrical as well as symmetrical in build—though even here it is the agitated accompaniment that bears the main burden of emotional expression. The latter part of the aria is still more conventional; but it is significant that, according to his biographer Georg Münzer, Marschner himself 'regarded the concluding aria as a "tail-piece" that could even be omitted if the singer had fully expressed what had gone before'. Heiling's 'An jenem Tag' has a little more in common with the older type of aria, though the orchestra, if subordinate to the voice, is handled almost symphonically and there is a startling innovation at the end—spoken dialogue breaking in most effectively against the background of the orchestral coda. But the most interesting part of *Hans Heiling* is the so-called *Vorspiel* which precedes the overture, just as 'As God the Lord of Israel liveth' precedes the overture to *Elijah* (possibly Mendelssohn took the hint from Marschner). But here it is a case, not of a dozen bars of recitative, but of a whole scene in the subterranean realm of Heiling's mother, the Queen of the Earth-Spirits: twenty-seven pages of vocal score *durchkomponiert* without a break, and, with all its changes of key, as clearly related to a central tonic as any symphonic movement.

All these characteristics—symphonic handling of the orchestra, blending and interweaving of recitative and arioso, the long *durchkomponiert* scene—point unmistakably in one direction: Wagner. It is well-nigh impossible to see minor masters like Marschner as their contemporaries saw them—without regard to, or knowledge of, the greater masters who came along a little later and used the same technique to very much better purpose. But if at this point the intelligent reader fears he is in for a dissertation on 'Wagner's debt to Marschner', I shall to some extent agreeably disappoint him. Whether or not Marschner did exercise a strong direct influence on Wagner I propose to leave an open question. Like every other German musician of the day the young Wagner knew his Marschner very thoroughly. He added an *allegro* to Aubry's aria 'Wie ein schöner Frühlingsmorgen' in *Der Vampyr* for his brother Albert. He occasionally expressed a certain amount of admiration for Marschner; on the other hand readers of *Mein Leben* will remember a very sarcastic account of the first performance at Dresden in 1845 of *Adolph von Nassau*, one of Marschner's failures. But to those who know Wagner as a man his verbal praise or disparagement of a contemporary composer means very little; it was by no means proportionate to the amount of his indebtedness. I do not propose here to try and calculate the amount in this case, but only to show to what extent Marschner and the pre-*Ring* Wagner, eighteen years his junior, belonged to the same artistic world and breathed the same musical atmosphere.

The similarities are quite as striking in the dramatic material as in the musical. The Dutchman, for instance, is a direct descendant of Ruthven and Hans Heiling; Lohengrin, too, is a sort of spiritualised Heiling. The parallel between Rebecca, waiting for the unknown champion whom she is confident Heaven will send to save her from the stake, and Elsa in the First Act of *Lohengrin* is very striking. Even more so is that between the appearance of Ruthven in *Der Vampyr* to Emmy, who has just been singing about the vampire (the ballad, 'Sieh, Mutter, dort den bleichen Mann'), and that of the Dutchman to Senta. Yet even here Wagner can hardly be accused of plagiarism, for in Heine's *Schnabelewopski* (1831) his main source for the *Dutchman* legend, the Scottish heroine has been familiar from girlhood with the gloomy old portrait of the Dutchman. Perhaps the idea of Senta's ballad owes something to *Der Vampyr*, but, the music does not, nor does the appearance of the demon lover long familiar by repute. At the most one can only surmise that the situations in the *Templer* and *Vampyr* may have done something to make those in *Lohengrin* and the *Dutchman* more attractive in Wagner's eyes. The same may be said of the already mentioned prologue to *Hans Heiling* and *Das Rheingold*—the parallels between Heiling and Alberich, with their longing for love, and between the toiling subterranean earth-spirits and the slaves of Nibelheim.

And what about the musical parallels? In addition to those already mentioned, Marschner's harmony, with its chromaticism and free use of appoggiaturas, sometimes sounds what we are accustomed to call 'Wagnerian'. Like Wagner, he was accused of ruining voices, and Eduard Devrient (as Bois-Guilbert) and the original Rebecca were said to be hoarse after every performance. Marschner, like Weber and Spohr and various other composers, is also said to have anticipated Wagner in the use of the *Leitmotiv*. But this, it seems to me, is hardly correct. Marschner would quote an earlier theme for dramatic effect; for instance, the Queen's 'Sonst bist du verfallen dem rächenden Grimme' in Act II of *Hans Heiling* is appropriately recalled by a solo trumpet when she appears as *dea ex machina* in the finale of the last Act, and the semiquaver figure of the *Tannhäuser* overture appears several times in *Heiling*, apparently as a symbol of evil. But there is a world of difference between this sort of musico-dramatic point-making and the systematic, symphonic use of characteristic themes as the basis of a whole score. No doubt the 'clue theme' (*Leitmotiv*) sprang from the 'thematic reminiscence' (*Erinnerungsmotiv*) but it is by no means the same thing. Nor will the melodic reminiscence-hunter find much sport in comparisons of Marschner and Wagner; though bearing in mind the other Marschnerian connection of Senta's ballad he will note with interest a feeble anticipation of its refrain in an early work of Marschner's—the overture to *Schön Ella* (1822), a play by Kind, the librettist of *Der Freischütz*. The third and fourth bars of Rebecca's prayer in *Der Templer*:

Ex. 2

Herr, aus tie - fen Jam-mers Nö-then hör'__ der See - le brünstig Fleh'n

may not have inspired certain phrases in Elisabeth's prayer in *Tann-*

häuser and Elsa's 'Einsam in trüben Tagen', but they certainly belong to the same family. Their echoes may be heard in German music as late as 1897, in the second of the *Michelangelo-Lieder* of Hugo Wolf, who had a great admiration for Marschner.

More important than particular traits are general ones. Consider, for instance, this from *Adolph von Nassau*:

Ex. 3

Hab' ich die Dankbar-keit ver - ges - sen,   zollt' ich Dir nicht den reich - sten Lohn

Has it not the very ring of a good deal of the vocal writing in early Wagner? The likeness is much intensified by the context—the melodic interplay of voice and orchestra, and, still more, the symphonic handling of a terse little orchestral motive, partly in sequence, partly in passage-work. Indeed this despised *Adolph*, a work of which Wagner declared that 'the principal effect lay in a drinking song for a male quartet', is at least as rich in premonitions of Wagner as any other of Marschner's works. Siegfried Goslich, in his *Beiträge zur Geschichte der deutschen romantischen Oper*, has drawn attention among other things to the relationship between Adolph's address to the knights in the opening scene of the opera and the King's address in the opening scene of *Lohengrin*. Nevertheless, Wagner's sneer at the drinking song touches one of Marschner's weakest points. Weber's *Vaterlandslieder* and the huntsmen's choruses in *Silvana* and *Der Freischütz* had innumerable progeny; Marschner in particular delighted in them—and added profusely to the progeny. In addition to his independent male-voice compositions his operas are full of drinking songs, choruses of peasants and the like. No doubt they contributed enormously to the contemporary popularity of his operas; indeed he had a certain gift for this vein. But today all but the very best of these songs strike one as extremely banal. In view of this leaning towards simple *Volkslieder* and humorous scenes from peasant life it is a little surprising that Marschner was not more successful with comic opera. But his best-known work of this type, *Des Falkners Braut* (1832), despite some good pages, is inferior to the operas of Lortzing and Nicolai, and even the far superior *Der Bäbu* (1837), an oriental comic opera not altogether unworthy of comparison with Cornelius's *Barber of Bagdad*, completely failed to keep the stage.   1940

XX—THE SCORES OF MENDELSSOHN'S
HEBRIDES

The publication by Amerbach-Verlag, Basel, of a facsimile of the autograph full score of the version of *The Hebrides*, which Mendelssohn completed at Rome in December 1830, throws new and important light on the somewhat complicated history of this orchestral masterpiece. It has always been known that the overture was originally entitled *Die einsame Insel* and a score so inscribed was found among family archives by the composer's grandson, Paul Benecke, and is now in the possession of Miss Margaret Deneke, Honorary Fellow and Choirmaster of Lady Margaret Hall, Oxford; it was described and compared with the final version of the overture by Dr Ernest Walker in *Music and Letters* (Vol. XXVI, No. 3). Both Dr Walker and Grove (article, *Hebrides* in the *Dictionary*) supposed this to be the Rome version; the Amerbach facsimile shows that it is not. It is not in Mendelssohn's own hand, but contains corrections that appear to be in his hand.

It will facilitate explanation if we call the three known scores A, B and C.

> A—*Ouvertüre zur einsamen Insel* (undated), of which I have been able to study a photostat, thanks to the courtesy of Miss Deneke and the B.B.C.
>
> B—*Die Hebriden* (dated 'Rom. d. 16 Dec. 1830'); now published in facsimile.
>
> C—*The Hebrides* (dated 'London, 20 June, 1832').

That A is earlier than B is demonstrated not only by the title but by the very first page of the score. In A the second bassoon enters with the very first bar; B shows its first five bars written down and then scribbled through. In A the first bassoon in bar seven plays

Ex. 1

which in B has been changed to the final form. In the first six bars of A the double-bass part is notated in crotchets; the facsimile of B shows the actual alteration of these crotchets to minims as in the final version. There are similar slight differences in later passages. For instance, in the equivalent to bar 77 et seq. of the published score the first violin part of A has

Ex. 2

while that of B has

Ex. 3

(with parallel changes in the second violin and viola parts). After bar five of the coda occurs a bar which has been vigorously scratched through in B and has disappeared from C (between bars 221 and 222) but which stands in A. Two pages later B has four bars crossed through; again these stand in A. On the other hand, Mendelssohn sometimes rejected his second thoughts; in the passage in B equivalent to that beginning at bar 112 of the printed score he began to deviate from A but scratched through four bars so that B remains at this point the equivalent of A. And indeed, despite these differences and various other tiny ones, A and B are broadly and essentially the same; it is in C that we find the big and important changes: the new transition from first to second subject, the new end of the exposition, all the new matter in the development and so on, to say nothing of innumerable smaller changes of varying degrees of importance.

How do these different scores fit into the history of the overture, as we can trace it from letters and other documents? The trouble is that we know so little about the early part, the most interesting part, of its history. One fact is very well known: that Mendelssohn sent home to his family a very full sketch of the opening, practically in its final form, headed: 'On a Hebridean island, 7 August, 1829. Just to show you how odd a state of mind I have got into on the Hebrides, the following has come into my head!' This opening is given in facsimile in all editions of Hensel's *Die Familie Mendelssohn* and is reproduced in the preface to the Amerbach facsimile of B. What is not generally realised, however, is that this was written before Mendelssohn had seen Staffa and Fingal's Cave;[1] on 7 August he and Klingemann were at Tobermory on the island of Mull, and it was not till the next day that they made the expedition to Fingal's Cave. Moreover, it appears from Klingemann's very amusing letter of 10 August printed in *Die Familie Mendelssohn*, that on the 8th the sea was very rough and Mendelssohn was seasick ('he gets on with the sea better as an artist than as man or stomach') and therefore in no condition to conceive or note down orchestral compositions. There are two references to what he playfully calls 'die Hebridengeschichte' in letters written from Wales on 2 September and from London on 10 September: 'The Hebrides business can also go crazy' (he is referring allusively to various compositions he has on hand) and 'the Scottish

[1] Tovey, in one of his wilder flights of fancy, speaks of 'the moment when Mendelssohn, while actually standing in Fingal's Cave, jotted down, in crotchets and quavers, the first bar' (*Essays in Musical Analysis*, Vol. IV, page 91).

Symphony, as well as the Hebrides business, builds itself up bit by bit'. But after that I have been able to discover no reference to it for more than a year when he writes to his sister Fanny from Rome (16 November, 1830), 'Now I want to get the *Hebrides* overture finished.' On the anniversary of their Hebridean expedition he had written to Klingemann recalling the fact and quoting a scrap of tune that they must have heard during the trip (Munich, 6 August, 1830): 'A year ago today we came to Fort William and hurried along the sea shore,

Ex. 4

in Ba - la - hu -- lish in Ba - la - hu -- - lish

found the steam-boat next morning, and so set off to the Hebrides' (i.e. to Mull). But there is no reference to the following day's trip to Fingal's Cave—or to the overture, although later in the letter he goes on to say, 'I have since written my great *Reformation* Symphony.' The snatch of tune happens to be in the same key as the overture—a not uninteresting detail—but has no thematic connection with it. (I do not think we can reasonably connect it with a violin figure in the coda of A and B.)

But after the reference of 16 November, soon come others. On 23 November to his sisters: 'I just wanted to work at the *Hebrides* when in came Herr Bank.' On 30 November: 'I'm now writing daily at the *Hebrides*.' Then in December he tells his father in a peculiarly interesting sentence: 'As [birthday] present I think of finishing writing my old overture to the *Lonely Island* tomorrow, and if I put "11 December" under it and take it in my hands it seems to me as if I were actually giving it to you.' This reference to 'meine alte Ouvertüre' and to the original title is indeed the only one to version A in the whole of his published letters, so far as I have been able to discover; it suggests that A had been in existence since, perhaps, the end of 1829. The passages in the letters of 16, 23 and 30 November refer to B, which is actually dated '16 December'; taken alone, they suggest a work of actual composition—but the relatively slight differences between A and B show that 'finishing', 'working' and 'writing' amounted only to copying and revision of detail.

Then for a year Mendelssohn let the work lie, without bringing it to performance. He was dissatisfied with it. On 21 January, 1832, he wrote to his family from Paris: 'However I can't give the *Hebrides* here because, as I told you at the time, I consider it not yet finished; the middle section, *forte*, D major, is very stupid, and the entire so-called development smacks much more of counterpoint than of oil and sea-gulls and salt-cod, and it ought to be the reverse. I'm too fond of the piece to perform it in an imperfect form, but I hope to set to work on it soon and have it ready for England and for Michaelmas.' The score that resulted from *this* revision, which was used for the first performance (at a Philharmonic Society Concert) on 14 May and the second (at Moscheles' concert) on 1 June, seems to have vanished completely. Score B had been given to Moscheles on 1 May, and on 6 June Mendelssohn wrote—in English—to Sir George Smart offering the Philharmonic Society 'the score of my Overture to the *Isles of Fingal*, as a sign of my deep and heartfelt gratitude for the indulgence and kindness they have shown to me during my second visit in this country'. Nevertheless, the score is not in the possession of the Society; perhaps it was the pre-revised form of C.

Score C, it will be remembered, is dated a fortnight later. Mendelssohn afterwards gave it to Sterndale Bennett, from whom it passed into the possession of his son-in-law Professor Thomas Case; it now belongs to Professor Case's grandson, Mr T. G. Odling, thanks to whose kindness I have been able to examine it. This score in turn shows a considerable number of changes and I shall call its original form C*a*, its finally revised form—which agrees in all essentials with the published version—C*b*. The most important differences are the excision in C*b* of six bars that originally stood between bars 84 and 85 (the rising wood-wind scale in dotted rhythm that survives in bar 86 of C*b* is a continuation of a pattern that originally started in the lower strings) and of two repeating bars that in C*a* came between bars 174 and 175 of C*b*. Of the other changes, the most interesting is the transference of the theme in bars 264–5 from first flute to first clarinet. On the face of it, it seems probable that C*a* was the version used for the first performances and that this was the score Mendelssohn offered to the Philharmonic Society; that he then held it back, or asked for its return, to make further corrections in the light of the performances. On the other hand the date 20 June seems to refer to C*a*—the point might be decided by closer examination of the ink than I was able to make—and C*b* may easily have been arrived at later still; moreover there is the evidence of the letter to Smart and the Philharmonic programme that the completely lost score bore the title *Isles of Fingal* (though Mendelssohn calls it *Die Hebriden* in his letter of 18 May to his father).

One other curious point in this strange history: the fourth title, *Fingals Höhle*, does not appear until April 1835, when the first edition of the full score was issued by Breitkopf & Härtel. (The parts, published in May 1834—which disagree with the score in bars 7 and 87—had still been entitled *Hebrides*.) As we have seen, the most striking and evocative part of the overture—the opening—was written down the day *before* Mendelssohn saw Fingal's Cave on the island of Staffa. The first title, *Die einsame Insel*, seems just as likely to refer to another Hebridean island, Iona, which the friends saw on the same day as Staffa and which struck Klingemann at any rate by its 'most desolate loneliness'; Mendelssohn apparently did not recover from his seasickness till later in the day. *Isles of Fingal* is only a poetic synonym for *The Hebrides*, though the reference to the Ossianic hero is a useful reminder that the overture is not merely a seascape: it contains epic and heroic elements as well. But the connection with the specific place, Fingal's Cave, was first suggested more than five years after the original conception of the piece.

1948

XXI—SCHUMANN'S OP. II AND III

It is 'common knowledge' that 'Schumann wrote nothing except for the piano until 1840'. Like so much else that is 'common knowledge', it is not true. Apart from the early G minor Symphony, three songs by Schumann composed in 1827–8 have been in print since 1893. They are settings of Justinus Kerner's 'An Anna', the same poet's 'Im Herbste' and a certain Ekert's 'Hirtenknabe', and Brahms published them in the supplementary volume of the Breitkopf *Gesamtausgabe* with an explanatory note in the preface:

> The songs are taken from a manuscript collection of eleven un-printed songs marked Op. II and bearing a dedication to Schumann's sisters-in-law, Therese, Rosalie and Emilie.[1]

The most interesting point about this is that Brahms, who had peculiar views (exemplified also in Schubert's case) on what should and what should not be included in a 'complete edition', does not mention why he chose to rescue just these three songs, except that the various items selected for this supplementary volume are 'either of intrinsic value or else of special interest'. As we shall see in a moment, he had a good reason; but it is characteristic that he did not tell us it. In 1933, six other songs from Op. II[2] were published in the Universal Edition by Karl Geiringer who must have been perfectly familiar with the three others but does not refer to them in his preface or give a hint that his six are not the complete Op. II. The sixth of these *Sechs frühe Lieder* is a setting of another poem of Kerner's entitled 'An Anna'; but none is of 'special' interest.

Earlier in 1933 Geiringer also edited for Universal Edition Schumann's Op. III: *VIII Polonaises/pour le Pianoforte à quatre mains/composées et dediées/à/ses frères/Eduard, Charles, Jules/par/Robert Schumann /Op. III/ /(faites en Août et Septembre de l'an 28)*. As the editor pointed out in an article in *Die Musik* ('Ein unbekanntes Klavierwerk von Robert Schumann', June 1933) the Polonaises were clearly written under the immediate influence of Schubert's four-hand Polonaises, particularly the four of Op. 75, for which the young Schumann is known to have had an enormous admiration. That is interesting but much more interesting —very much more interesting—is the connection between the Polonaises and *Papillons* (which Schumann began to compose in 1829). Geiringer

---

[1] To whom eventually the definitive Op. 2, *Papillons*, was dedicated.

[2] I keep Schumann's own Roman numerals for Opp. II and III to distinguish them from the definitive Opp. 2 and 3: *Papillons* and the six *Paganini Studies*.

drew attention to this in his editorial preface and went into the matter in some detail in his *Die Musik* article, but on the whole confined himself to pointing out borrowings without analysing the rather extraordinary *manner* of the borrowings. Two of the *Papillons*, Nos. 5 and 11, are almost entirely based on material from the four-hand Polonaises: No. 5 on the trio of the seventh Polonaise, and No. 11 mainly on the fourth Polonaise but with a passage added from No. 3. This is the more interesting of the two but even No. 5, which is little more than an improved transcription of the Polonaise trio,[1] offers a fascinating study of Schumann's methods of working on his earlier, rather jejune ideas. Compare the opening of the trio:

Ex. 1

with the opening of the *Papillon*: in the later form the fussy turns are taken out and the conventional polonaise rhythm of the *secondo* part has become even quavers. Most important of all, Schumann has found the *basso cantando* motive hidden and unsuspected in the block chords of Ex. 1,[2] and he has added a lovely touch in bar 4. Bars 6 and 7 of the Polonaise, an outburst of brilliant *fioritura*, were entirely scrapped, even harmonically; there is no hint of the minor subdominant touch in the earlier version. And bar 8 of the *Papillon*, identical harmonically with bar 8 of the original, acquired its triplet figure in the left-hand from the equivalent bar of the trio of the *eighth* Polonaise.

The patchwork of *Papillon* No. 11 is still more curious. The three opening bars are simply the three opening bars of the third Polonaise, transposed a minor third down, except that the tonic chord of the original third bar was F *minor*. But the first bar of the main theme is a transposed and improved version of the first bar of the fourth Polonaise, which opens as follows:

Ex. 2

As the quotation shows, the original Polonaise then took quite a different

---

[1] An intermediate version, for piano solo, appears in one of the Zwickau sketch-books.

[2] But a similar bass motive does figure in the fourth Polonaise (see Ex. 2) and the trio of the fifth.

course—a very feeble one—and the rest of its first eight-bar period contributed nothing to the *Papillon*. Yet, as we shall see in a moment, this part of the *Papillon* is otherwise indebted to the Polonaise. The debt in the next part is obvious enough; the eight bars following the double-bar-and-repeat are simply a revised version of the corresponding portion of the fourth Polonaise. I quote the last four bars from the latter:

Again, comparison with the later version provides an object-lesson in the craft of musical composition of the kind one gets from study of Beethoven's sketches. From the heavy crudity of Ex. 3—*ff*, be it noted —to the *pp* lightness and sparkle, and the contrast of registers, of the corresponding passage in the eleventh *Papillon* is a very big step, taken by the young Schumann in a very short time.

One other point: the revised form of bars 3 and 4 of Ex. 3 was also in the *first* portion of the same *Papillon*, only in D major instead of G minor. Consequently the opening of the *Papillon* is seen to be a most odd piece of patchwork:

3 bars from Polonaise No. 3.
1 bar from first section of Polonaise No. 4.
1 fresh bar.
2 bars from second section of Polonaise No. 4.

So much for the Polonaises and *Papillons*. But Schumann's later use of his own juvenilia did not end there. Niecks—and, so far as I have been able to discover (admittedly without exhaustive study of the Schumann literature), Niecks alone—noticed why Brahms elected to print two of the Op. II songs in the supplementary volume of the *Gesamtausgabe*, and even Niecks says nothing of his discovery in the body of his book (which he did not live to finish), only at the end of his list of works: 'three early songs, two of which were afterwards developed into the slow movements of the Sonatas Opp. 11 and 22'. As for the third song, 'Hirtenknabe', even Niecks seems to have failed to detect its later embodiment.

A note at the end of the autograph of the G minor Sonata, Op. 22, tells us that, whereas the first and third movements date from June, 1833, and the finale (the original *presto* finale afterwards published among the posthumous works) from October, 1835, the *andantino* was written as early as June, 1830. In other words, the *andantino* was written first as an independent piece; it is, moreover, hardly more than an elaborated transcription of the little song, 'Im Herbste', written in 1828, with its two exactly similar strophes (each only five bars long) and four-bar piano epilogue. Comparison of the opening:

Ex. 4

with the beginning of the Sonata movement shows the nature of Schumann's changes: transposition from E flat to C, the rewriting of each 2/4 bar as two of 6/8. It will be noticed that the composer now varies the accompaniment of the second strophe and elaborates its conclusion. Otherwise the first twenty-one bars of the *andantino* are simply a transcription of the song. The middle section and coda, though developed from the first idea, were of course new.

Schumann must have been quite satisfied with his experiment in turning juvenile songs into sonata movements for he repeated the feat in the F sharp minor Sonata, Op. 11 (written during 1833-5, i.e. at the same time as the other three movements of the G minor). Here the 'Aria' is a transcription—and in this case even more simply a transcription—of 'An Anna' (dated July 31, 1828). The music is again transposed (from F to A major) but the accompaniment of the first and third parts of the song is not re-arranged, only redistributed, the repeated right-hand chords now being given to the left hand which also has to sketch in the bass. The harmonies are slightly altered, the melody changed in unimportant details but the only real difference is the substitution of the dropping-fifth figure for the crossed right hand in bars 6-9 in place of the vocal echoes of the piano part in the original song:

Ex. 5

The middle section of the sonata movement, in F, is a rather freer transcription of the middle part of the song, in D flat, and is reached by a much simpler, less forced modulation. The semiquaver right-hand figure is quite new; in the song the accompaniment continues its repeated quaver chords. The third part of the sonata movement—again reached by a less inept transition—corresponds, except for the five-bar coda, almost exactly with the third part of the song, which repeats the first part note for note and word for word. The words, incidentally, tell how the poet thinks of 'thee, dear life, not in the valley of the sweet homeland but borne, pale, from the field of battle'. In the middle section he reflects that all his friends are fallen and mournfully welcomes the pale Messenger who will guide him to the 'sweet homeland'.

The substitution of the dropping-fifth figure for 'bleich getragen . . . aus dem Schlachtfeld' in Ex. 5 is, of course, a reminder of the introduction to the first movement of the Sonata, where the slow-movement—'An Anna'—melody already makes fragmentary appearances. And this slow introduction was in 1834–5 added to an *allegro vivace* completed in 1832 as a *Fandango: Rhapsodie pour le Pianoforte. Oeuv. 4*. By such patchings and furbishings-up of earlier works, with inserted cross-references, did Schumann hope to construct sonatas! Is it surprising that we find the sonatas rather unsatisfactory?

The third song printed by Brahms in the supplementary volume of the *Gesamtausgabe*, 'Hirtenknabe' (dated August, 1828) shows that Schumann did not confine to the piano sonatas his borrowings from his vocal juvenilia. The naïve, folk-songish melody:

Ex. 6

Kindlich und innig   poco rit.

Bin nur ein ar - mer Hir - ten - knab, das Hift - horn ist mein gan - zes Hab,

repeated unchanged for each of three stanzas, seems much more suitable in its original form, with the simplest chordal accompaniment, than in the form we generally know it: as the Intermezzo, Op. 4, No. 4.[1] Perhaps we have hitherto missed the full significance of the superscription, 'Meine Ruh' ist hin' over the middle section of the second Intermezzo. For one thing, the *Gesamtausgabe* prints it close above the notes, not vaguely skied as in some editions: drawing attention to the fact that the music was not only inspired in a general way by Goethe's words but to a certain extent actually fits them. Can there be much doubt that it was originally conceived as a vocal setting of Gretchen's song?

And can we doubt that Schumann continued this practice of drawing immediate inspiration for his instrumental melodies from the words of poets (perhaps omitting the intermediate stage of a vocal setting)? There are many rather square-cut stanzaic melodies among his lyrical piano pieces which sound a good deal more like song-transcriptions than the

[1] The introductory bar and the coda of this Intermezzo are based respectively on the first four bars and last eight bars of a projected *Papillon* in 3/4 time, sketched in a Zwickau note-book.

andantino of the G minor Sonata. To take only five of the more obvious examples, look at the Intermezzo from the *Faschingsschwank*, the trio of the first *Novellette*, the first two of the *Drei Romanzen*, Op. 28, and the 'Abschied' of the *Waldszenen*. In the last case, I would even hazard a guess—though it is a pure guess—at an actual poem: Wolfgang Müller's 'O danke nicht für diese Lieder'. We know that Brahms often sought inspiration in this way from his earliest to his latest years; was not the idea in all probability suggested to him by Schumann?

It would be almost equally interesting to trace through Schumann's music the influence of polonaise rhythms in works not actually so called, such as the Intermezzo in the third movement of the F sharp minor Sonata (1834–5) and the fifth *Novellette* (1838). In them we seem to catch the gradually dying echoes of Schubert's duet polonaises, still faintly perceptible at the very end of Schumann's creative life in the finale of the Violin Concerto.   1946

XXII—SCHUMANN'S *JUGENDSINFONIE*
IN G MINOR

When the nineteen-year-old Schumann wrote to Friedrich Wieck on 6 November, 1829, that he had 'begun many a *symphony* and finished nothing' it is clear from the context that the remark is to be understood in a Pickwickian, or rather Jean-Pauline, sense: 'You know I have little use for absolute *theory* and so I have silently lived my life away for myself alone, improvised a great deal and played little from the printed page, begun many a *symphony* . . .' The surviving compositions of that period—songs, four-hand polonaises, and other fragments—though individual enough for parts of them to be used again in later, published works, show that at this period Schumann was ill-equipped to embark on the construction of a large-scale instrumental work such as a symphony. The 'symphonies' he speaks of probably ended as they had begun, in improvisation: symphonic day-dreams not even written down in sketch-form Schumann's first serious attempt at symphonic composition dates from nearly three years later, though as we shall see in a moment he did note down a theme for a 'third symphony' in 1831 or thereabouts.

Between July 1831 and April 1832 Schumann had worked at thorough-bass and counterpoint—rather spasmodically, it seems—with Heinrich Dorn, and by this time he was able to construct more extended works: a Piano Sonata in B minor, of which the first movement was afterwards published as Op. 8, and the Fandango which was later expanded into the first movement of the Sonata in F sharp minor, Op 11. In April 1832 Dorn declined to continue the lessons and Schumann then worked on his own with Marpurg's *Abhandlung von der Fuge* as his guide and the *Wohltemperiertes Klavier* as his collection of models. In a letter of 27 July to his old teacher Kuntzsch at Zwickau, Schumann after paying tribute to Marpurg as 'a theoretician worthy of great respect' says he has been analysing the Bach fugues *seriatim* 'down to the finest details', and then goes on: 'Now I must set about score-reading and instrumentation. Do you happen to possess older scores, perhaps of old Italian church music? Concerning my plan, I will write later . . .' Whether that 'plan' was the composition of a symphony, it is impossible to say, but in just over three months the first movement of a symphony had been completed —as we learn from two letters published in the *Jugendbriefe*. The first is dated 2 November, 1832, and is addressed to 'Musikdirektor G. W. Müller' (whom Niecks no doubt rightly indentifies with Gottlieb

Christian Müller, at that time one of the Gewandhaus violinists and conductor of the Leipzig Euterpe concerts):

> The undersigned begs to enquire whether you would be inclined to
> give him instruction in instrumentation, and to express the humble wish
> that, to this end, you would go through with him a symphonic move-
> ment of his composition which is shortly to be played at Altenburg.
> I cannot say how greatly obliged I should be for this, for I have
> worked almost entirely according to my own ideas and without guid-
> ance and am moreover somewhat distrustful of my symphonic talent . . .

The second was written four days later to his mother in Zwickau:

> . . . we shall certainly see each other within a fortnight . . . Wieck and
> Clara are giving a concert in our town . . . and a symphony movement
> of mine is to be played at it[1] . . . For the last fortnight I have been
> working uninterruptedly, and I am almost anxious and doubtful whether
> I shall be ready by then. I have put my apartment up to let for two
> months . . . and hired my piano to Lühe—in short everything except
> the symphony is ready to set off.

Some confirmation that the Symphony had been begun only in October
is given by one of Schumann's lists of works in his diary:

> Sinfonie p. gr. Orchestre. Oeuv. 7.
> Im October [1832] bis Mai 1833.[2]

Whether the movement had the benefit of Müller's touching-up or advice
it would be impossible to say without examination of the autograph manuscript, of which I have seen only a copy. But it was completed in time for
the concert on 18 November and duly performed in the Zwickau Gewand-
haussaal, the composer (according to Wasielewski) listening unseen from
a hiding-place. An (unpublished) entry in Clara's diary (made by her
father) records that: 'The first movement of Schumann's symphony was
given—but not understood. It was also not effective enough—at least
for such a public—but is well devised and worked out—but too thinly
scored.'

But Schumann was not discouraged. Settling down for the winter at
Zwickau—his two months' absence from Leipzig ultimately became four,
for a reason that will appear in a moment—he quietly continued work on
the remaining movements of the symphony. On 7 December he writes to
Rellstab, not yet known to be hostile, that he hopes to see him soon in

---

[1] The Wiecks had planned a little tour in the neighbouring Saxon towns of Zwickau,
Schneeberg, and Altenburg; in the interval between 2 and 6 November, it was evidently
decided to have the symphony-movement played at Zwickau instead of Altenburg.

[2] *Robert Schumanns Briefe: Neue Folge.* (2nd ed.), Leipzig, 1904, p. 537.

Berlin: 'I shall come with a symphony under my arm.' On the 17th he tells Hofmeister how he is 'working industriously at the symphony in my little familiar nursery':

> To be sure I often take yellow for blue in the instrumentation of the first movement, but I consider this art so difficult that only a [many-year?] study can bring sureness of mastery. If only you could help to bring about a performance this winter in L[eipzig] that would probably be the finest encouragement for me. I hope that doesn't sound immodest! . . .

And Clara in Leipzig teases him with news that 'Herr Wagner' has 'outsoared' him with a symphony that is said to be as like as two peas to Beethoven's A major. (Wagner's C major Symphony was tried out at the Euterpe in December, a fortnight before the first performance at the Leipzig Gewandhaus on 10 January, 1833.)

At the New Year Schumann received an offer from Carl Thierfelder, *Stadtmusikus* of the nearby town of Schneeberg, to perform the first movement there. He replied on 3 January, 1833:

> I am delighted by your invitation but regret that at the moment I can send neither score nor parts as I have completely revised the first movement and have not yet written out the separate parts. One thing will strike you as an improvement in this revision. When I first composed this movement I actually had the rhythm ♩ ♩.. ♪ throughout: only towards the end I let it resolve into the friendlier and easier ♩.. ♪ ♩; for the hurried Zwickau concert, however, I kept the latter form throughout but in the new score have changed it back to the original, since it is more fiery and unusual, though there is also something very perverse about it. Well, you will hear and judge for yourself!
>
> When I know the exact day of your concert, I will come myself a few days before, so as to go through everything with you in detail. You can reckon confidently that the parts will be in your hands by tomorrow week (Wednesday). If you consider the time from then to the concert too short for proper rehearsal, please let me know by return so that I shall not have to write out the parts in less haste. I should prefer it if you would let me know the precise date of the concert, so that I can do everything with suitable artistic calm.

On 9 January Schumann wrote to his sister-in-law Rosalie, who lived at Schneeberg, in leisurely tone without mentioning Symphony or concert—at any rate in that part of the letter published in the *Jugendbriefe*; but a letter of the following day to Wieck in Leipzig is breathless:

> Great concert at Schneeberg—Thierfelder wrote for the symphony—complete upheaval of the first movement—rewriting of parts and score

—addition of the other movements—up to the ears in work. . . . At the beginning of February I shall certainly come with the complete symphony under my arm. If you could help to bring about a performance, that would be the finest encouragement . . . (the concert is on the 17th) . . .

But was the Symphony publicly performed in Schneeberg on 17 January? Wasielewski has caused some confusion on this point; in earlier editions of his biography[1] he says, perhaps correctly, that the concert 'was postponed till 12 February', when the first movement was repeated. But in his 'fourth, revised and considerably enlarged edition'[2] he asserts that

at the beginning of January 1833 Schumann found an opportunity to hear the first movement of his symphony again on the orchestra, namely at Schneeberg, where there was a repetition on 12 February. On the first of these performances he reported to Wieck (10 January) [followed by the passage quoted above].

Wasielewski clearly blundered in taking this letter of 10 January to refer to a *previous* performance in Schneeberg 'at the beginning of January', but Schumann certainly heard the Symphony, or the first part of it, at Schneeberg in January—though apparently only in rehearsal. On 29 January he writes to the publisher Hofmeister, still from Schneeberg:

The symphony goes forward. It (with Beethoven's A major Symphony) is being rehearsed here with great diligence and is scarcely to be recognised by comparison with the Zwickau performance. As the concert is not till 18 February, Leipzig won't see me before March.[3]

In the same letter he thanks Hofmeister for the 'very fine' scoring paper and asks him 'to send the parts of Onslow's First Symphony and Kalliwoda's last (D minor)[4] here'.

In March Schumann returned to Leipzig with his score. On 5 April he claimed, in a letter to his old friend Töpken, to have finished the work:

During the whole of the past winter a big symphony, which is now finished, took up my time; from it I expect, without vanity, the most for the future.

This was not quite true. But the revised first movement was to have one

[1] e.g. 2nd ed., Dresden, 1869, p. 94, third footnote.
[2] Leipzig, 1906, p. 103.
[3] *Briefe: Neue Folge.* 2nd ed., p. 414. I am unable to resolve the discrepancy between this date and the one given in all editions by Wasielewski.
[4] Actually Kalliwoda's Third Symphony, Op. 32. I have not been able to see the Kalliwoda work but a violin figure from the first movement of Onslow's Symphony No. 1, in A, Op. 40, was worked into the revised version of Schumann's symphony. Perhaps the Onslow also suggested the addition of trombones.

more performance—its last. On 29 April Clara Wieck gave a 'grand concert' at the Gewandhaus[1] and once again the first movement was brought out under her auspices. It is doubtful whether it was carefully rehearsed, for only three days before the concert Schumann sent it to Matthäi, the Gewandhaus leader, with a request that he should look through it.[2] Schumann reported to his mother that his Symphony had 'won him many friends among the greatest art-connoisseurs, such as Stegmayer, Pohlenz, and Hauser' but since he waited exactly two months before telling her about the performance we may safely conjecture that the success was not brilliant. More eloquent still is the fact that in May (according to the entry in the list of works referred to above) he stopped work on the Symphony, which was—as the autograph manuscripts show—still unfinished.

The foregoing information has long been known to Schumann-students though the full story of the Symphony has never been told, so far as I am aware, in a connected form. But the Symphony was long supposed to be lost. However Wolfgang Boetticher in his monumental *Robert Schumann: Einführung in Persönlichkeit und Werk*[3] drew attention to the fact of its continued existence. In his list of 'Unpublished Works' (p. 638) he gives:

Symphony in G minor (*Jugendsinfonie*)	Sketches, on two staves, with indications of separate instrumental effects. 25 bars E flat, 32 bars C major, 17 bars B flat major. 40 bars beginning of a final fugue in G minor.
	Second copy. All three movements preserved complete . . . The first movement (*allegro*), is scored, was performed at Zwickau and Schneeberg in 1832, in revised form at the Leipzig Gewandhaus in 1833.

Apart from the inaccuracies the reader will notice in that last piece of information, Boetticher is wrong in other respects. 'All three movements' are not preserved complete. What actually survives is the first movement in both the first, Zwickau form (hereafter called Z; 478 bars long) and the second (Schneeberg, hereafter called S, 490 bars), both complete and fully scored;[4] the second movement complete and fully scored; the greater part of another version of the second movement, scored but unfinished; sketches, partly in score, for a scherzo and trio; sketches for a finale, some

[1] Dörffel, *Geschichte der Gewandhauskonzerte*, Leipzig, 1884, p. 209.
[2] See Gustav Jansen's notes to the *Briefe: Neue Folge*. 2nd ed., p. 493, note 30.
[3] Berlin, 1941.
[4] There is indeed a third score, a variant of S, two bars longer, which I have been unable to consult.

of them fugal. Thanks to the great kindness and courtesy of Dr Georg Eismann, curator of the Robert Schumann Museum at Zwickau, I have been able to study not, unfortunately, photostats but manuscript copies of practically all the surviving material.

The greatest interest naturally attaches to the first movement, the only one (apparently) that was ever performed. It will be most convenient to discuss it mainly in terms of Z, with cross-references to S. Both versions are scored for pairs of timpani, trumpets, horns, flutes, oboes, clarinets, and bassoons, with strings (in that order in the scores); S has staves for three trombones—alto, tenor, and bass—at the bottom of the score but they are used for only two short passages in neither of which do they add anything but weight. Z is 478 bars long, excluding repeat of exposition; S, 490. Z begins with an 8-bar introduction, *moderato*: three statements of the leaping motive *a* in Ex. 1, in bare octaves, separated by whole-bar rests, the third statement releasing a brief oboe cantilena. The movement proper then begins, *allegro molto*:

Ex. 1

S rejects the jejune introduction and with two brusque, Beethovenian tutti chords, dominant and tonic, plunges straight into Ex. 1, which is now marked *allegro*. Small differences are at once noticeable in scoring and other details: double-stops for second violins and violas, the pairs of quavers in the clarinet part (Ex. 1, bars. 7 and 8) become dotted quavers with semiquavers in S. Very soon in Z Schumann begins to use the empty staves at the bottom of the page for revision of instrumental details (e.g. trumpets and woodwind repeating a chord rhythmically instead of sustaining it) and for verbal comments:[1] 'The quavers shorter and the first of the bar well marked', 'The figure in the inside parts as strong as possible', 'Wind instruments not too strong', 'Bassoon strong', and so on. (It is interesting to note how he has, for instance, 'strengthened the bassoon' in S.)

---

[1] Only examination of the originals or photostats would determine whether these comments are all Schumann's or whether they were made by Müller, but they *seem* to have been made by Schumann after the Zwickau performance.

A certain amount of tossing to and fro of motive *a* culminates in a cadential passage considerably altered in S:

The introduction here of the 'perverse' rhythm mentioned in the letter to Thierfelder, indicated below the score of Z on an empty staff, foreshadows the transition theme which actually embodies that rhythm. In Z this transition theme takes the form:

S has the change of rhythm described to Thierfelder, the grace-notes in bar 3 have disappeared, bar 4 is altered—and incidentally the accompanying texture is made less pianistic.

The general affinity of Ex. 4 with *Papillons* will not have escaped the reader. Indeed Schumann himself quoted in his diary, with approval, a friend's comment on the parallel passage in the recapitulation, where this

theme returns in the major to herald the second subject in the tonic major:
'Becker's thought on the transition to G—"Hurrah! There the butterfly
flies away! High, high in the air"—is very poetic.'[1] The second subject
itself:

belongs equally to the world of *Papillons* and is also closely related to the
alternativo of the Intermezzo, Op. 4, No. 5, which like the symphony
makes much play with the figure x and might well pass for a page from
its development section.

    This—the development—is, as one might expect, the weakest part of
the movement. Sometimes in Z Schumann's efforts to weave a texture out
of various permutations and combinations of thematic fragments, further
weakened by his inexperience as an orchestrator, are pitiful:

Ex. 7 shows the equivalent passage in S: less desperately thematic in every
part but with a better sense of orchestral sonority:

   [1] Quoted by Boetticher, op. cit., p. 319, where the entry is misdated 'June 1832' instead
of 1833.

Schumann's experience at Zwickau had at least taught him something of the ineffectiveness of double-basses on their own; one of the most curious features of Z is this independent treatment of the double-basses and their frequent notation (as in Exs. 2 and 6) an octave lower than the composer presumably intended them to sound.

A number of passages in the development were altered quite as drastically in S; two bars were cut from Z and another passage considerably expanded. Yet the result is still unsatisfactory; there are some pleasant, unmistakably Schumannesque paragraphs, but even Schumann's published symphonies tend to offer thematic mosaic instead of symphonic development—and this, his first attempt, is naturally his poorest mosaic. In both Z and S the recapitulation—purely conventional, and not too happy in the change of modulatory course after the 'transition' theme (Ex. 4) especially in Z—is heralded by the unison passage that opens Z but is here heard for the first time in S; it is marked *adagio* in both scores, and in S Schumann brings in the trombones for the first time. At the point that suggested to Becker the flying away of the butterfly—the double bar and change to the major—the pace changes to *più moto* in both scores (preceded by four bars *un poco andante* in S), and in S the beginning of the coda is marked by another double-bar and a further acceleration (*più mosso*). S brings in the trombones again for the final 13 bars; whereas Z ends abruptly with the leaping-sixth motive:

Ex. 8

S prolongs the final chord from one bar to three, swelling on it to a final crash.

Of the two versions of the second movement, the complete one is shown to be the later of the two by the inclusion of trombones in the score, though again they have only one five-bar passage in the whole piece. As we shall see in a moment, there is yet other evidence that this is the second version—though we can no longer speak of Zwickau and Schneeberg scores, for there is no evidence that the second movement was ready for the Schneeberg concert or, if ready, was performed at it. Nor was it played at Leipzig, apparently. Description of the complete version of the movement will be better left until after a survey of the incomplete form and the other fragments, however.

The first version of the second movement is marked *andantino con moto*; it is one of those slow-marchlike movements fashionable at the period—cf. Schubert's great C major Symphony, Mendelssohn's *Italian Symphony*, and Berlioz's *Harold en Italie*, none of which Schumann could then have known—which are probably to be reckoned as the progeny of the *allegretto* of Beethoven's Seventh. The choice of key, B minor (minor parallel of the dominant), is strange but explicable by the fact that the third movement, scherzo, was planned in D major. The influence of the Beethoven *allegretto* is evident alike in the main idea:[1]

Ex. 9

in the contrasting flute solo (A major and F sharp minor, even crotchets), and in a triplet counter-subject:

Ex. 10

which Schumann was later to transfer to the 'Marche des Davidsbündler' of *Carnaval*. The movement proceeds steadily for 92 bars, then begins a gradual acceleration *poco a poco al doppio movimento* spread over 35 more. The texture thins out to nothing, and the repeat begins, *tempo primo*, only to break off after 28 bars. But the scoring is complete up to the 28th bar (middle of a phrase), suggesting that the movement was actually completed in some sketch that has now disappeared.

Scherzo and trio are again in 2/4 time, the trio even returning to B minor. There are two substantial fragments, neither with any indications of tempo:

28 bars of scherzo (plus repeats) sketched on four or two staves; 50 bars of trio (plus repeats) sketched on two staves and gradually petering out. 31 bars of scherzo, of which the first 20 are fully scored; 12 bars of trio in rather sketchy scoring.

[1] Boetticher (op. cit., p. 570) quotes this theme in the same key and with only slight differences as that of an *Andantino quasi Allegretto* for a 'Sinfonie III' in a sketch-book dating from about 1831. Boetticher adds that it 'does not belong to the pre-studies for the so-called *Jugendsinfonie*': a statement that shows again how casually he must have looked at those 'pre-studies'.

It will be sufficient to quote the opening of the scored form of the scherzo:

and the beginning of the sketch of the trio:

These two attempts at a scherzo are separated and also immediately followed in Schumann's sketches by a number of brief essays in fugal treatment of the theme consisting of two falling fifths, which is the real theme of the *Impromptus über ein Thema von Clara Wieck*, Op. 5; almost at once Schumann hits on something practically identical with the first 12 bars after the double-bar and three-flat key-signature in the last Impromptu. The 'C F G C thought' had occurred to him a year before: to be precise on 29 May, 1832.[1] The Impromptus on Clara's *Romance*, for which he himself had supplied the bass, were composed 'from 26–30 May, 1833',[2] that is to say, at just about the time when he had abandoned work on the G minor Symphony. At first sight one might conclude merely that sketches for Op. 5 had got mixed up with those for the symphony—the sort of thing one finds so often in Beethoven's sketchbooks. But the matter is not quite so simple. No other sketches for Op. 5 appear here, and as we shall see in a moment Schumann did actually try to work a fugue on this 'falling fifths' theme into the finale of the Symphony. On the other hand, the passages that approximate to the last movement of Op. 5 all have a three-flat signature and are written in 6/8 while most, not all, of the sketches actually marked as belonging to the finale of the Symphony are in 6/16

---

[1] Litzmann, op. cit., Vol. I, p. 50. A sketch-book from the same period contains a 'Fuge No. 3' which is the earliest form of that in the symphony and in Op. 5.

[2] *Robert Schumanns Briefe: Neue Folge*, p. 537.

(in the thirties a favourite finale pattern with Schumann: cf. the original finale of Op. 22 and the finale of Op. 14 in the original edition). But the weight of evidence appears to me to support the view that the C minor portion of the last Impromptu was originally devised as part of the finale of the Symphony.

There is one five-part fugal working for 32 bars of open score; then a short passage is C minor, 6/8, all in the incessant ♩ ♪♩ ♪ rhythm characteristic of the finale of the Symphony; then a fresh idea which must be quoted:

Ex. 13

We shall meet this again later in another connection. At last, after another snatch of the C minor, 6/8, not used in the last Impromptu though belonging to it, comes an extended sketch on two staves for 'Finale. Presto'. It is headed 'Corni in Es. Tromba C. Clarinette in B' and begins with a borrowing from the trio (cf. Ex. 12, bars 4–6), though whether this implies that Schumann intended to quote the trio here or that (as I am inclined to believe) he had already made up his mind to scrap the trio, it is impossible to say:

Ex. 14
Presto

The 'right-hand' rhythm continues remorselessly almost without interruption for 79 bars,[1] of which the first 61 are marked to be repeated, after which we get a more sustained theme not unlike that which was to appear in the course of the finale of the C major Symphony:

Ex. 15

Very soon the dropping-fifths theme appears (C F G C) only to be scratched through; at bar 137 it reappears in a 'heralding' form (B flat, E flat, F, B flat); then after bars left blank for later filling-in, in Schumann's customary manner in first sketches, we get:

[1] The spirit, if not the precise letter, of this music is preserved in Impromptu No. 9 (1850 edition) of Op. 5.

Ex. 16

etc. for seven more bars

There the sketch peters out and is followed by a number of disconnected fragments: an attempt to work the flute theme from the second movement in four parts canonically, a scrap of entirely new music in E flat, 2/2, in half-finished orchestral score, chromatic chord-progressions, an attempt to combine the fugue-theme with itself in diminution:

Ex. 17

and a fresh opening of the fugue

Ex. 18

sketched on two staves, which also comes to nothing after 40 bars when the trombones have just entered with the theme. At no point are more than two simultaneous parts noted.

Finally, with a return to three flats and 6/8, we get a two-stave sketch, fully worked out, equivalent to (indeed partly identical with) a substantial section of the last Impromptu of Op. 5. But the 57 bars of sketch were reduced to 33 in the piano version. The culmination of the sketch[1]

Ex. 19

with its sudden (unmarked) return to 6/16 may be compared with the last four bars of the fugal middle section of the final Impromptu (before the double bar and cancellation of the flat key-signature). There the sketches for the finale end.

It remains to say something about the completed version of the second movement. The tempo-marking is *andantino quasi allegretto*—a return to

---

[1] The flat key-signature is cancelled in the sketch 28 bars earlier.

the original marking of the theme when it was intended for 'Sinfonie III'—but internal evidence, as well as the addition of trombones, suggests not only that this is the last version of the movement but that it was put together rather hastily with the help of discarded materials. In this form the movement opens with the 'Davidsbündler' fanfare of clarinets and bassoons (Ex. 10), now in B minor, played against F sharps sustained by the rest of the orchestra, which immediately follows with x from Ex. 12, the original opening of the now-discarded trio. We can say with confidence that the trio was 'now discarded', for the Symphony's scherzo is now incorporated in the second movement. The main part of the second movement, apart from minor details and one or two interpolations of Ex. 12, is unchanged; but the long-drawn accellerando now leads not to a repeat but to an 'Intermezzo quasi Scherzo', *allegro assai*, in 6/8, opening with the theme quoted above as Ex. 13. The dropping-fifths figure appears here and there as a bass, and the influence of the first movement of Beethoven's Seventh Symphony is obvious; but the whole of this 'Intermezzo' is very weak. At the end the pace is slowed down and the *andantino* repeated in slightly altered form. After the final double-bar there are two more attempts to work the flute theme in canon.

It must be admitted that the rediscovery of the G minor Symphony has not given us back a lost Schumann masterpiece. But it does enable us to fill out our picture of Schumann's creative personality in these early days and we can perhaps date his thick, cautious orchestral doubling from the evening when he must have blushed at the sound of the *zu mager instrumentirt* first movement at Zwickau.

1951

XXIII—THE THREE SCORES OF
SCHUMANN'S D MINOR SYMPHONY

The bare facts of the history of Schumann's D minor Symphony are well known: composed in 1841 as a 'second' symphony, it was revised and reorchestrated in 1851 as 'No. 4'. In 1891, at the instigation of Brahms and rather against the will of Clara Schumann, the original version of 1841 was published by Breitkopf and Härtel—thereby dispelling some curious legends concerning its nature and the nature of the changes. 'The alterations in the score were confined for the most part to a redisposition of the wind band', Fuller Maitland had said in his book on Schumann in the once popular 'Great Musicians' series, 'and to the omission of a guitar, which was at first included in the accompaniment of the Romanza, its place in the new recension being taken by the *pizzicato* strings'. The Breitkopf score showed that the alterations had been far more drastic than a mere 'redisposition of the wind band' and that the guitar was purely mythical; it also showed that the original form of the work, though inferior to the more familiar one in some respects, was actually superior in others. The orchestration, in particular, of the 1841 version was found to be much lighter and more transparent than that of 1851, the latter being typically Schumannesque in that thick unnecessary doubling produced by the composer's constant playing for safety in a medium where he never felt particularly happy.

Nevertheless the original version of the Symphony has been strangely neglected by conductors and critics alike. Tovey, who combined both roles, not only performed it but discussed it at some length in the second volume of his *Essays in Musical Analysis*. But so far as I am aware no critic has yet subjected the two versions to close and detailed comparison. Even less known than the 1841 versions is the existence of yet a third score of the Symphony: that made by Mahler. It is not uncommon for distinguished conductors to modify the scoring of Schumann's orchestral works, but only Mahler—who also laid sacrilegious hands on Beethoven's Ninth—published his versions of the four symphonies. Whatever one's views as a purist, one must admit the interest and value of his re-scorings to the student of orchestration. In discussing Schumann's own changes of orchestration, therefore, I have noted Mahler's views when they differ materially from Schumann's final version.

Mahler naturally altered only the orchestration of Schumann's 1851 version. But the 1851 version differed in much more than orchestration from that of 1841; Schumann made changes in melody, harmony, bass, inner texture, connecting links, and even metre. Except in the transition

281

from scherzo to finale there is no hint in the original score that the movements are to succeed each other without a break. The notation of both first movement and finale were changed, two bars being turned into one in each case. Neither movement originally had its double-bar and repeat. Even the tempo indications were altered from Italian to German:

1841	1851
Andante con moto—Allegro di molto	*Ziemlich langsam—Lebhaft*
Andante	*Ziemlich langsam*
Presto	*Lebhaft*
Largo—Allegro vivace	*Langsam—Lebhaft*

The very opening of the 1841 score differs strikingly from the familiar version. Instead of the sustained A, beginning on an up-beat, of flutes, oboes, horns, first violins, celli, basses and rolling kettledrums, it begins on a down-beat with a full A major triad, and neither flutes, oboes nor timpani participate in the sustained A. The rest of the introduction is practically as in the final version up to the point of transition to the *allegro*, where instead of the seven bars in which the first violins now introduce the motto-theme of the whole Symphony—a fine touch—there was originally a commonplace ten-bar *stringendo* of staccato chords with a chromatic scale in the bass. Schumann substituted a subtle and organic transition for a naïve and clumsy one. And it must be admitted that in the original the opening of the *allegro* proper is at once less brilliant and less anticipatory of Brahms than in the familiar form

Ex. 1
(a) 1841   Allegro di molto   (b) 1851   Lebhaft

(Mahler here contented himself with transferring the violas from their inside harmony part to the principal melody, making them play in unison with the first violins.)

Not all Schumann's changes tended to strengthen the organic and thematic unity of the work. The important new violin theme that enters later in this structurally very unorthodox first movement was on its first appearance (and most of its subsequent appearances) originally accompanied by the motto-theme on the violas *poco marcato* and bore a fresh tempo marking: *animato*. This interesting feature disappeared from the 1851 version (with the *animato* indication), being replaced by a commonplace pianistic figure on the second violins. Again, as in Ex. 1, flute and oboe were enlisted to reinforce the first violin melody. (Here Mahler altered nothing but the dynamic markings, modifying the *p* of all except the violins to *pp*, and shading off the first violin part in the fourth bar with a ══════.)

As opposed to this change, the introduction of the motto-theme on the lower strings at the opening of the finale was an afterthought converting it from an allusion into an actual quotation from the first movement:

Ex. 2

(Mahler here only took out the trumpet parts in bars 2 and 4.)

In the bars that follow Ex. 2, a passage too long for quotation, Schumann's changes are more radical than in either of the preceding examples. Indeed, the finale, with the latter part of the transition leading to it, was revised more drastically than any other movement. The two middle movements underwent only a few minor changes even in scoring, nor did Mahler consider it necessary to do any but slight and comparatively unimportant retouching. In the first movement Schumann's alterations were mainly in the scoring. In the finale even the relative tempi were modified. Whereas in the final version the marking *lebhaft* remains constant throughout the greater part of the movement, the *allegro vivace* of the original applies only to the first sixteen bars (equivalent to eight of the 1851 score); then comes a double-bar and the marking *più vivace*, which remains the principal tempo of the movement. Clearly these first few bars were originally conceived by Schumann as purely introductory; they are omitted from the recapitulation even in the final version, and in the first version, owing to the absence of the double-bar-and-repeat, they are not heard a second time. In the final version, with its conventional repeat of the exposition section, the introductory nature of this passage is obliterated.

Again: near the end of the finale as we know it occurs a double-bar, a change of time-signature from 4/4 to 2/2, and the direction *schneller*, followed twenty-three bars later by another double-bar and the marking *presto*. In the original score both these quickenings take place earlier. The fresh melody on violas, clarinets and bassoons which appears sixteen bars before the indication *schneller* is already marked *stringendo sin al Presto*. (The melody was originally given to a solo clarinet only, an octave higher than in the definitive version.) And the *presto* marking and double-bar duly occur forty-eight bars later (i.e., at the equivalent of eight bars after the *schneller* indication in the 1851 score). The four bars of string scales that follow each statement of this *stringendo* theme were also considerably recast in the equivalent two bars in 1851.

The finale is marked by a number of very drastic changes of scoring. For instance:

'Nothing is more characteristic in the difference between the two scores than the natural dialogue of single wood-wind instruments [*sic*] which Schumann wrote here, and which he afterwards turned into a thick plaster for full wind-band,' comments Tovey—not quite accurately. (Mahler, whose emendations to Beethoven and Schumann so often take the form of strengthening the melody, made no attempt to restore the original dialogue form of the passage. Indeed, all his alterations here tend to lighten the accompaniment: taking out the second oboe that doubles the second flute, altering the second violin and viola double-stopping to *divisi*, and marking the cello and bass parts *pizzicato*. In addition Mahler marked everything down to *pp*—cellos and basses even to *ppp*.) A still more essential change was made in the working-out section of the finale, the square four-bar periods being extended in four places by the interpolation of two extra bars (written as two half-bars owing to the changed time-signature):

Ex. 4

Furthermore, the beginning of the recapitulation had an imitative effect which Schumann did not retain in the revision. (Ex. 5, p. 286).

Parallel with this alteration was one made in the first movement, where the motto-theme is, in the familiar version, played by all the strings and woodwind in octaves. Originally this was a piece of imitation, such as

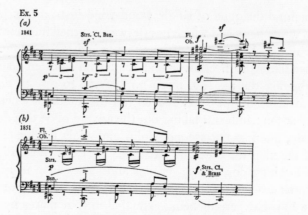

occurs about a dozen bars later in the definitive form, first and second violins being echoed by the lower strings. Schumann evidently wished to tie his little canonic knot by way of climax and punctuation; to anticipate the effect was to rob it of half its value.

This little point in the first movement, too (three bars after letter B), is obviously an improvement melodically and harmonically:

But no less obviously the addition of an opaque daub of woodwind was by no means an improvement. Ex. 6, in fact, puts the cases for the two versions in a nutshell. As regards the essential musical substance the 1851 score is preferable in most respects—though not in all. But, despite the increased sonority of the tuttis, obtained by much freer use of string double-stopping and by a more skilful disposition of wind and brass in full chords, the scoring of the definitive version is on almost every page more clumsy than that of the original. Tovey asserts that 'the ideal version of the symphony would undoubtedly be arrived at by taking the latter version as the text and striking out all superfluous doublings until we reach the clarity of the original'. He is probably right. But however that may be, it seems a pity that conductors do not give us opportunities of hearing Schumann's finest symphony both in its original form and (since we tolerate Mozartean Handel and Rimsky-Korsakovian Mussorgsky) in the clearer sonority given it by Gustav Mahler.

1940

XXIV—ON A DULL OVERTURE BY SCHUMANN

I doubt whether Schumann ever wrote a duller work, a work less characteristic of his real genius, than his overture to *Hermann und Dorothea*. I have never heard it in the concert-room and probably the majority even of assiduous concert-goers, unless very elderly indeed, could say the same. I never want to hear it. It is completely neglected and deservedly neglected. Yet that very dull score, considered thoughtfully, may throw some light into a dark and tortuous place: Schumann's mind. Not that the music is subjective in expression; it is the facts of the music, and behind the music, that are enlightening.

Now the chief fact of the music is that it is very largely based on the Marseillaise, which is one of the principal elements of the 'first subject' and dies away in the 'wrong' key at the end, a puzzle apparently solved in a note to the score:

> By way of explanation of the introduction of the Marseillaise into the overture, it may be remarked that the latter was intended for the opening of a *Singspiel* based on Goethe's poem, the first scene of which represented the retreat of soldiers of the French Republic.

And it is certainly true that round about this time (December 1851) Schumann did discuss with Moritz Horn, the poet of *Der Rose Pilgerfahrt*, the possibility of turning Goethe's idyll into a *Singspiel*; they even toyed with the idea of making it a 'concert-oratorio' before they dropped it altogether. So the presence of the Marseillaise is 'explained'. But is it satisfactorily explained? Somehow the explanation does not quite carry conviction. It seems an odd notion to base the greater part of a full-length overture—as distinct from a short orchestral introduction to an opening scene—on anything so inessential as a 'retreat of French soldiers' must have been in a dramatic version of *Hermann und Dorothea*. Dorothea is a war-refugee; Hermann a young man who takes pity on her and falls in love with her; we hear of Dorothea's heroism in dealing with French looters when the Revolutionary troops came to her village; but the story is pure idyll and the only element of dramatic conflict in it is the opposition between Hermann and his father, not the opposition of French Republicans and patriotic Germans. The more one thinks of it the odder it seems, the more difficult not only to justify the extensive use of the Marseillaise on so slight a pretext but to connect this bustling, strenuous overture at all with Goethe's rustic comedy. Even the *dolce* second subject lacks lyrical warmth; it is more like the trio of a march. And when one turns up Schumann's correspondence with Horn the mystery only grows more mysterious. On 21 November, 1851, he tells the poet:

Hermann und Dorothea is an old and favourite thought of mine. Get a firm hold of it! When you want to set to work on it seriously, please let me know directly so that I can tell you my thoughts on it in more detail.

On 8 December, however, he writes again:

I have not yet been able to collect my thoughts on *Hermann und Dorothea*. Still you might consider whether the material can be so treated as to fill out a whole evening, which I almost doubt. In any case there must be no *speech* in the *Singspiel*, a point on which we are certainly in agreement. The whole must be kept—both musically and poetically—in simple German folk-style.

The idea was at this stage—Schumann's own conception still inchoate, nothing yet discussed in detail with the librettist—when, between 19 and 23 December, he completed a full-length overture having little or no connexion with the work as a whole but very largely concerned with the not at all essential opening scene. And when he next mentions *Hermann und Dorothea* to Horn, on 6 February:

Hermann and Dorothea still lies deep in my mind. Before you set about working it out, it would of course be a good thing to settle the sketch first. . . .

he says not a word about the overture or the already determined opening scene; if the 'sketch' (i.e. presumably, of the general outline of the action) was not yet 'settled' in February, was it not risky in December to link the overture with the opening scene? After that the letters reveal no other thought of the subject for exactly a year, when Schumann writes to Horn 20 December, 1852:[1]

I wouldn't mind making a concert-oratorio out of *Hermann und Dorothea*. Let me know what you think! An overture is already done, as I probably wrote you.

'An' overture, observe; not 'the' overture. Does not this in itself suggest 'an overture that could be used for *Hermann und Dorothea*,' an overture independently conceived? It is not impossible, of course, that the notion of opening with the scene of the 'retreat of Revolutionary soldiers' had

[1] Wasielewski printed this letter in the first edition of his biography, misdating it '1851'; a reference to the title-page of *Der Rose Pilgerfahrt*, published in November 1852, proves it to belong to 1852. The correct date is given by Jansen in his notes to *Robert Schumanns Briefe: Neue Folge*, second edition, 1904.

long played a part in that 'old and favourite thought'; if so it seems to have played a strangely important part. But is it not equally possible that the overture sprang from some other exciting cause and that the idea of the scene with the French soldiers arose out of the overture, as a pretext for using it, not vice versa? I suggest that the exciting cause may well have been the *coup d'état* of 2 December, 1851, by which Louis Napoleon overthrew the Second Republic, and the events that followed—when liberty was being crushed to the ground in France.

That is only a theory, of course; it could probably never be proved. But in weighing its probability we have to consider two questions: 'To what extent are we justified in disregarding Schumann's own account of the inspiration of his own music?' and 'Was Schumann interested enough in politics to be excited to composition by an event such as the *coup d'état*?'

The first is easily answered. Schumann was quite capable of deliberately giving a false account of the origin of his works. One case will suffice. In letter after letter he told various correspondents that the *Papillons* were inspired by the last scene of Jean Paul's *Flegeljahre*. Take, for instance, this perfectly clear and categoric statement to Castelli (April 28, 1832):

> I will add concerning the *Papillons* that the thread connecting them is difficult to grasp if the player does not know that the whole was composed after reading the final scene of Jean Paul's *Flegeljahre*.

Yet we now know that most of the *Papillons* were inspired not by Jean Paul but by Schubert, and to some extent by Weber's *Aufforderung zum Tanz*, that the majority of the twelve numbers were salvaged from a set of waltzes written in imitation of Schubert's waltzes and a set of four-hand polonaises written in imitation of Schubert's four-hand polonaises. Indeed Schumann himself once frankly admitted (to Henriette Voigt, 22 August, 1834) that 'only the last . . . was awakened through Jean Paul'. There was no 'thread connecting them'; the statement to Castelli is a mask covering what Schumann knew to be the weakness of the work: its heterogeneity.

Everyone knows Schumann's love of enigmas and mystifications and disguises in his music; perhaps we do not realize how often he wore a mask in his life as well. It becomes startlingly evident when we begin to study his interest in political events. To judge from his published letters no artist could have been more detached from and indifferent to public happenings. Commenting on this, Julien Tiersot once wrote (*S.I.M.*, 15 April, 1913):

> In general he avoids speaking to his correspondents of external

events and one is surprised to read the dates of certain of his letters, written amid the gravest disturbances, and to find that he speaks exclusively of Bach or Mendelssohn, of piano pieces and quartet music, above all of *Faust* and *Genoveva* which he was composing during this period of troubles. So did Archimedes refuse to allow the incursion of the enemy to distract him from the solution of his problem!

Or if he does mention the disturbances, it is only in conventional terms and in passing: e.g. to J. B. Laurens (3 November, 1848): 'What times we're living in, what a fearful rising of the masses, among us too! Well—enough of that; let's rather talk about our beloved art. . . .' Again, in the following May when the Dresden rising in which Wagner had been playing an active part had driven the Schumanns to take refuge outside the city at Bad Kreischa, Robert writes a longish letter to Liszt in which there are only two passing references to the insurrection: a regret that, owing to 'the revolution', he has only been able to see Reinecke once and so could not answer some inquiry about 'the scene from *Faust*', and a statement that they 'are living here very quietly—driven out by the revolution—and although the great events of the world occupy one's thoughts my delight in work grows rather than diminishes'. (But perhaps the laconic postscript is significant: 'Where is *Wagner*?' [1]) And a few days later Clara wrote to Wenzel:

> It's heavenly here and we've never enjoyed the spring more than in this very year of hubbub in the outer world. It is as if external horrors had excited exactly opposite emotions in my husband; for actually he has just been composing the most lovely, peaceful songs [the *Lieder-album für die Jugend*, Op. 79] when everyone expected him to let himself go in the most frightful battle-symphonies.

That was one side of Schumann's nature: the escapist, the man who sought in art and in the circle of his family the peace and balance lacking in the external world. The other side was very different. So different that we realize his escapism was an absolute necessity. His detachment was not due to indifference; it was a mask, worn probably not so much to deceive the world as to help him to assume the character he had to assume if he was to keep his mental equilibrium.

But there were occasions when the mask slipped. One, little known, was during April 1848, when Schumann so far forgot his customary caution as to set three stirring revolutionary poems for male chorus with *ad lib.* military band accompaniment. The very titles and poets' names speak for themselves: 'Zu den Waffen!' (To Arms!) by Titus Ulrich of whom Schumann said at this very time, 'He has been the true prophet of

---

[1] 31 May; by that time Wagner was safe in Switzerland.

Revolution'; 'Schwarz-Roth-Gold' (Black-Red-Gold, the old Imperial colours adopted by the democrats) by Ferdinand Freiligrath, democratic leader in the Rhineland, twice exiled for his political opinions; and 'Freiheitssang' (Song of Freedom) by J. Fürst. The three together were numbered Op. 65. But then Schumann readjusted the mask, suppressed the choruses (which later fell into the hands of Charles Malherbe and were bequeathed with the rest of his collection to the Library of the Paris Conservatoire) and transferred their opus-number to an innocuous set of male-voice *Ritornelle* with words by Rückert. They were first published in 1913 in *S.I.M.* by Tiersot, in connection with the article from which I have already quoted.

We get another glimpse behind the mask fifteen months later when 'on 12 June, on the way from Kreischa to Dresden', as he writes on the manuscript, he composed the first of the *Four Marches*, Op. 76. The other three, together with the 'Geschwindmarsch', Op. 99, No. 14, which originally followed No. 3, the 'camp scene', were composed during the next four days and the set was posted to the publisher Whistling on the 17th with a covering letter that speaks for itself:

> You receive herewith some marches—not the old Dessauer type—but, rather, republican. It was the best way I could find to express my excitement—they have been written with real fiery enthusiasm.
>
> Condition: they must be printed *at once*.
>
> They must be engraved with very large notes.
>
> And as I always wish the appearance of my compositions to correspond with the content, I want on the title-page nothing more than appears on the inside—this little however in the largest lettering—that is, with my name unobtrusive, as I don't know how otherwise to bring in the 1849, which it is important not to leave out.
>
> Similarly I should like a *cover-title* if possible with still larger lettering —as is now fashionable.
>
> . . . . . .
>
> If you can't take it on, send it me back straight away.

And when the Marches duly appeared, he at once sent them to Liszt—leaving all mention of them, however, to the postscript of a fairly long letter. Yet this guarded postscript is significant enough:

> I enclose a novelty—IV Marches—I shall be pleased if they are to your taste. The date they bear has a meaning this time, as you will easily see.
>
> O time—O princes—O people!—

According to C. G. Ritter, the Marches were known among the intimate circle of Schumann's Dresden friends as 'Die Barrikadenmärsche'. And

Wasielewski, commenting on Schumann's crypto-liberalism and its 'strange contrast' with his apparent indifference and neutrality, says that 'one must think of him not in public gatherings but at his desk, in his hand the pen from which came the Marches, Op. 76.' Let us spare our irony on the man who sat quietly at Kreischa writing his peaceful children's songs while it was dangerous to stay in Dresden, and composed heroic marches when the fighting was all over. Schumann reacted to events as an artist, perhaps, ought to react, although Wagner undoubtedly appears in the better light as a man and citizen. At any rate Schumann produced four or five marches, albeit mediocre ones, as a direct result of the Dresden rising while Wagner produced nothing.

My point is that Schumann is revealed as an inwardly agitated, if outwardly calm, spectator of political events: a composer liable to musical excitement from contemporary political happenings. We know that the Marseillaise had a special attraction for him. I say nothing of 'Die beiden Grenadiere'; everyone will remember how the tune dances in disguise for a moment through the *Faschingsschwank aus Wien*. Is it not highly probable that the man who responded to the triumph of reaction in Dresden in 1849 by writing the 'barricade marches' should have responded to the triumph of reaction in Paris in 1851 by writing an overture based partly on the Marseillaise, partly on themes that are closely related to the themes of those marches? It is at any rate much easier to relate the overture to the *coup d'état* of 1851 than to Goethe's *Hermann und Dorothea*.

1946

XXV—WAGNER'S SECOND THOUGHTS[1]

One of the cardinal errors of criticism is the judgment of a work of art by standards its creator would not have recognised as valid: standards of a different age, of personal taste, or some scale of mythical 'absolute values'. The critic's first effort should be to place himself beside the artist, if possible even inside the artist, to see with his eyes what he is trying to do and the world in which he is trying to do it. Unless his aim is simple exegesis he must presently withdraw some distance and try to assess how far the artist has achieved his purpose, yet even this detachment may not make him a sharper critic than the artist himself. However artists may vary in their powers of self-criticism, such self-criticism as they do apply must be directed by an insight superior to that of any outsider, the critic who wishes to judge an artist by his own standards therefore seizes eagerly on every piece of evident self-criticism.

In Wagner's case the evidence falls into two classes: his re-writings in maturity of the works of his immaturity, and his treatment of his first rough sketches. The latter provides a subject which must be left untouched in the present study. Fortunately he has given us a number of instances within the first category, the most important being those in the 1855 revision of the *Faust* overture and the post-*Tristan* revisions of *Der fliegende Holländer* and *Tannhäuser*. We even know that he would have approved our study of them, for he wrote to Liszt in the letter enclosed with the revised version of the *Faust* overture (16 February 1855):

> I am childish enough to ask you to compare it [the revised score] really closely with the original version, since it gives me pleasure to show you this manifestation of my experience and the finer sensibility I have acquired; it seems to me that it is from rewritings of this kind that one can see most clearly whose spiritual child one has become and what crudities one has sloughed off.

The original version of the overture, it will be remembered, was written in Paris in January 1840, in the middle of *Rienzi*; the revision dates from

[1] In 1938 I began a book on Wagner's musical style which I intended to dedicate to Ernest Newman, who (in the phrase I thought of using) 'should have written it himself'. Part of the book was written, nearly the whole of it exists in notes or in rough draft, but during the war my thoughts were diverted into other channels; fresh interests and more urgent work have kept me from Wagner ever since. Nevertheless I hope to finish the book some day, and in the meantime Mr Van Thal's *Fanfare for Ernest Newman* seemed an appropriate opportunity to offer Newman, not an excerpt from it, but a study written from the notes for two different chapters. In reprinting it here, I have extended it by inserting part of an article on the revision of the *Holländer*, published in *Music and Letters* in October, 1939.

fifteen years later, when Wagner was in the middle of *Die Walküre*. The most far-reaching changes were in the scoring, which was lightened throughout, the 'rather too abundant brass' being no longer to Wagner's taste as he had told Liszt as early as 1852 (letter of 29 May). Some of the tuttis certainly had a more brutal, *Rienzi*-like orchestration, with full trombone chords, but the demisemiquaver triplet figure of the strings in bars 11 and 14 of the slow introduction was not given to the brass as in the parallel passages of the *Enzio* and *Feen* overtures. The revision was by no means confined to the scoring and, although the 1840 score has never been published in full, Michael Balling's introduction to Vol. XVIII of the still incomplete *Gesamtausgabe* of Wagner's works and an article by Richard Sternfeld[1] who had been shown the score by Balling, tell us what the other alterations were:

(1) The first two bars were originally written as four, in double note-values.

(2) The cadence closing into the A major repeat of the second-subject melody was originally:

Ex. 1

(3) This A major passage ended as follows:

Ex. 2

leading directly into the F major working of the subject at letter L (page 23 of the Eulenburg miniature score); thus page 22 of the

---

[1] In *Die Musik*, June 1923. Since the original publication of this essay I have—thanks to the kindness of my friend Irving Kolodin—been able to study a photostat of the autograph score.

miniature score is entirely new music, the 'extension of the middle (2nd motive)' of which Wagner spoke in his letter to Liszt of 19 January, 1855.

(4) The climax after letter O (pages 31–2 of the miniature score) was altered rhythmically and harmonically.

(5) The whole of page 47 of the Eulenburg score was inserted in 1855. Originally the passage on page 46 was followed by a bar of half-close, tutti, like the corresponding passage in the exposition, and the first bar of page 48 followed.

(6) The last twenty bars of the overture were also added in 1855. In the original version the *pp* restatement of the principal theme on the first violins, soli, was followed by a bar of silence and a for-tissimo D minor chord, tutti.

Now the most important of these changes are not really the most infor-mative. The striking and beautiful conclusion added in 1855 merely tells us that Wagner had come to prefer quietly poetic to noisily sensational endings, a preference confirmed by the definitive ending of the *Holländer* overture and by his general practice in his mature compositions. And the inserted passages which constitute pages 22 and 47 of the Eulenburg score only show Wagner taking more pains with what Tchaikovsky called the 'seams' of musical form, substituting gradual transitions for abrupt ones and, in the first case, writing some very beautiful music into the bargain. But the changes which transformed Exs. 1 and 2 (miniature score, page 21) are much more enlightening.

To begin with, the square ♩ ♩. ♪ | ♩ pattern, the heavy down-beat even emphasised by the turn, is subtly disguised; taking a hint from the original form (the opening of Ex. 2). Wagner now eliminates all the turns and begins the motive each time on the up-beat half a bar earlier. The inept Bellinian cadence which vulgarises the motive in Ex. 1[1] is replaced by a purely harmonic cadence, the separate parts moving stepwise, even chromatically, with a much less decisive cadential effect rhythmically. The still more inept cadence at the end of Ex. 2, ending on a formula typical of the *Rienzi* period, is treated in exactly the same way, vulgar melody being dissolved and the underlying harmony lightly disguised under the rising chromatic scale in the top part. And how skilfully Wagner turns to account even the bits he appears to have discarded! Just as the first flute part in the second bar of Ex. 1 could be divided between first and second flute, with totally different effect, the last four notes of the banal cadence of Ex. 2 could be made to flower into the inspired oboe melody

---

[1] It survives in slightly less vulgar form in Wolfram's 'Gegrüsst sei uns, du kühner Sänger, *der ach! so lang' in unsrer Mitte fehlst*' (*Tannhäuser*, Act I, scene 4).

Ex. 3

sehr zart

p

of the 1855 version.

Orchestrally, too, these passages reveal a great deal of self-criticism. One notices at once the wealth of dynamic nuances marked in the 1855 score and almost completely lacking in the original version; in the original score the A major string passage connecting Exs. 1 and 2 is simply marked *p*, without the six-bar crescendo and two-bar diminuendo indications, though the actual notes are the same. The direction to begin a very gradual slowing of the tempo throughout Ex. 2 was also added by way of preparation for the entirely new passage inserted in 1855. The re-scoring of Ex. 1 was necessitated by the textual changes but is none the less symptomatic of the fifteen-year advance in Wagner's orchestral technique. First flute and first clarinet, doubling the violins and then completing the melodic phrase on their own, are replaced by first oboe and first bassoon an octave lower than the violins, each simply holding its D through the heart of the cadential complex. The entry of the flutes only at bar 2 and at the original pitch completes the breaking up of the melodic phrase as it stood in Ex. 1. Two other points: in Ex. 1 each wind instrument enters on a down-beat, whereas in the revised score half of them come in on off-beats or up-beats; and in the later version the final chord of the wind cadence overlaps the string entry by a semibreve instead of merely a crotchet. Entries and joins are wherever possible made less obtrusive; everything is made less block-like.

Similarly in Ex. 2 each entry of the motive—practically identical with the 'glance' theme in *Tristan*—half a bar earlier not only shades off the squareness of the motive itself but, having obliged the composer to give the second appearance of the theme to other instruments (first flute and first oboe) instead of repeating it on first violins and celli, automatically produces dovetailing. Equally characteristic of the more mature Wagner is the lightening of the diminished sevenths in bars 2 and 4 of Ex. 2; the bassoons, the four horns and the drum-roll are taken right out of bar 2, leaving a purely string chord, and in bar 4 reduced to one clarinet, one bassoon and one horn.

The revision of *Der fliegende Holländer* was a more complicated matter. Wagner returned to this score several times, the first as early as 1846, lightening the brassy orchestration as he had done with the *Faust* overture, but the most vital changes were not made until after *Tristan*. 'Now when I had written Isolde's final transfiguration', Wagner wrote to Mathilde Wesendonk (10 April, 1860), 'I was at last able to find the right end for the *Holländer* overture—as well as for the horror of the Venusberg.' Both here and in the earlier letter to Mathilde (3 March, 1860) in which he first mentions this 'new end to the *Holländer* overture, which pleases me very much and also made an impression on the audience' (at his three Paris concerts a month or so earlier), he mentions only the overture, not alterations to the opera itself; but certain passages in the opera were altered too. And apparently even this was not the definitive version. Guido Adler[1] speaks of changes made in 1864: perhaps further revision of the overture and certainly alterations to the end of Act III, obviously made for the Munich production of 4 December of that year. (This was not only the first Munich performance of the *Dutchman*, but the first performance in Munich of any opera of Wagner's since Ludwig II had taken him under his protection.)

I have not been able to study the original full score of the overture. Only twenty-five copies of the full score of the opera were lithographed for the composer by the Dresden publisher Meser in 1844, and even the British Museum does not possess a copy. But, extraordinarily enough, the vocal score of the original version is still published by Novello in their well-known Original Octavo Edition, and the nature of the changes in the orchestration can easily be seen by comparing certain passages in the overture with corresponding ones in the opera itself, where the scoring was unaltered.

Adler, who had seen the score, says that 'in the instrumentation Wagner tried to smooth down certain uneven—not to say rough— passages of the first version and perhaps injured the sonorous effect in some places by substituting strings for trumpets and trombones'. The 1846 toning down of the brass, for a projected performance at Leipzig which came to nothing, has already been mentioned. Again, in 1851 Wagner told Bülow, then at Weimar, that if Liszt wished to introduce the *Dutchman*, 'the brass might be moderated a little with discretion. The cadenzas in Daland's aria and Erik's cavatina (Acts II and III) must be omitted'. And then in 1852, in view of the Zürich performances in April of that year, he thought of the 1846 revision and tried to reconstruct it. 'I was too easy-going to enquire after the Leipzig score', he wrote to Uhlig (9 April, 1852). 'Rather, I set to work afresh to retouch the instrumentation, but at last lost patience, so that—as you will have perceived— I often, and mostly, contented myself with minor alterations.'

Wagner had explained his view of the necessary changes still more clearly in an earlier letter to Uhlig (25 March):

> At first I did not wish to systematically revise this score: for on closer examination I found that to rearrange the instrumentation in accordance with my present experience, I should have for the most part to do all the work over again; and naturally the desire for such a

[1] *Richard Wagner*, Leipzig, 1904.

task cooled down at once. In order to reduce the whole brass, for instance, to reasonable proportions, I should have had to alter everything consistently therewith; for the brass was not merely incidental here, but was determined by the whole manner not only of the scoring, but of the composition itself.

This discovery certainly vexed me, but—I would rather confess the fault than improve it in an unsatisfactory manner. Only, therefore, where it was purely superfluous have I struck out some of the brass, here and there given it a somewhat more human tone, and only thoroughly overhauled the coda of the overture. I remember that it was just this coda which always annoyed me at the performances; now I think it will answer to my original intention. The changes must be clearly indicated in the score, and often it would be best for them to be written out on fresh sheets of stout paper: better spend a little money on it than have anything unclear![1]

This shows, I think conclusively, that in 1852 the end of the overture was not changed very drastically, except as regards the scoring. (Wagner wrote to Liszt on 8 January, 1853: 'In particular I entirely altered the instrumentation of the last section of the overture.') Newman (in *The Life of Richard Wagner*, Vol. II) says: 'It was on this occasion that Wagner . . . changed the ending of the overture,' which seems to imply that he then made the definitive change in the actual substance of the music. This assumption appears to me unfounded. As we have seen from the letter to Mathilde Wesendonk, already quoted, the definitive change was not made till eight years later.

The same reduction of the brass was made in the re-scoring of sixty-one bars of the Dutchman's recitative in the finale of Act III.[2] For instance:

Ex. 4

in the 1842 version, at the words 'Wohl hast du Treue mir gelobt', became as shown in Ex. 5 in the final form:

---

[1] J. S. Shedlock's translation.
[2] The original version of the passage is printed as a supplement to the miniature full score in the Fürstner edition.

Ex. 5

surely an improvement rather than an 'injury to the sonorous effect', as Adler calls it.

The orchestral passage where the Dutchman's ship appears at the end of the Steerman's song in Act I corresponds exactly to the first dozen bars or so of the overture. In the latter, as we now have it, the second statement of the 'curse' theme is given only to trombones and tuba; in the parallel passage, which no doubt presents the original form of the overture, it is played by two trumpets and the string basses as well as the lower brass. Again, compare these two scorings of an identical passage (*a*) in Senta's ballad (1840s), (*b*) in the revised form of the overture (1860s):

Ex. 6
(a)

(*a*) is merely a broad effect, (*b*) is a broad effect refined and beautifully shaded; (*a*) is opaque, although Senta's sustained F has to sound through it, (*b*) is transparent.

The most striking change in both overture and opera is a parallel to the 1855 edition of *Faust*: the replacement of a boisterous tutti fortissimo by ten quiet bars, *un poco ritenuto*, on a new motive:

which had played an important part in *Tristan* as the theme of 'fate' (cf. the Prelude, bars 16–17, where it grows out of the 'desire' theme, the opening of the fifth scene of Act I, and dozens of other places).

Of the changes made in the coda of the overture but *not* in the end of the opera, the most important begins at bar 25 of the coda as we know it. Originally the music continued from this point as follows:

battering rowdily along more or less in the main key and culminating in
a six-bar fanfare on the tonic chord. For this passage Wagner substituted
one in pure *Tristan* style, dramatically changing the dynamics and
orchestral colouring:

Ex. 9

This excursion into extreme subdominant regions is balanced by another
in E major, and the music returns to its original course through a passionate and extended climax, of which the second violin part in itself,
mere 'inside' filling, yet as finely wrought as a part in a string quartet:

Ex. 10

is enough to show that the music belongs not to the world of the *Holländer* but to that of *Tristan*. A wealth of music-type would be needed to
illustrate how Wagner, sometimes without altering the original melodic
line, recasts the texture in terms of his technique of twenty years later.
Block changes of harmony at each half-bar are now avoided; a chromatically moving inner part played by second oboe and clarinet and first
bassoon not only makes the whole texture more plastic, more 'singing',
but points the harmonic brickwork. The new treatment of the melody is
still more instructive. Ex. 9 shows how Wagner cunningly began his
patching operation with the *second* bar of the melody, more than half
concealing the join by putting it a bar later than the point where it would
have shown most obviously; the change of scoring seems to dissociate
this entirely new variant of the 'redemption' theme from its conventional
♩ ♩. ♪|♩ opening. Eight bars later this impression is confirmed and the
heavy ♩ ♩. ♪|♩ pattern, an obsession of which Wagner was evidently pain-
fully conscious in later years, is disguised by the orchestral lay-out.
Originally the melodic line had been drawn right through on the same
instruments, and very firmly drawn by violins, woodwind (including
the piercing piccolo) and a horn (cf. page 673 of the Fürstner miniature
score of the complete opera); now it was distributed between different
ones and the phrase-join further concealed by the semiquaver up-beat of
first violins and viola (Ex. 11 on p. 303).

Whether Wagner was aesthetically right in thus tinkering with a completed work as definite in style as the original *Holländer* is debatable. How
ever much finer the new music may be than anything in the original score,

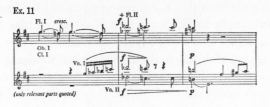

(only relevant parts quoted)

it is glaringly out of place. If we were all as sensitive to style as we like to think we are, we should be startled every time we hear Ex. 9 and shiver with horror when we are hurled back, twenty bars or so later, from the world of *Tristan* into something that is only just round the corner from *Rienzi*. But our sensitiveness is hopelessly blunted by familiarity.

The same clash of styles in the Paris version of *Tannhäuser* worried many musicians from the first. That stout Wagnerian, Wendelin Weissheimer, who had the score of the Paris revisions in his possession for a considerable time, says he returned it to Wagner at the latter's request in 1865

> with a heavy heart . . . for their music is as much like the *Tannhäuser* music as chalk is like cheese. But since he wanted them, I had to return them—convinced that he would thus deform and distort his noble work. Which indeed happened! At the large opera-houses the innovations were introduced and thus the work composed with such unity was broken across by two entirely different, even inimically opposed, styles with the result that one can no longer enjoy even the untouched parts.[1]

Yet however much he may agree with Weissheimer's aesthetic judgment, the student of Wagner's style must rejoice unreservedly in the richness of the opportunity to compare the Wagner of 1844 with the Wagner of 1860, to see how the composer of forty-seven criticises the composer of thirty-one. For the changes in *Tannhäuser* cover a very much wider field than those in the *Faust* overture or the *Holländer*.

There are two popular misconceptions about the Paris version of *Tannhäuser*: that the rewriting was confined to the Venusberg music, and that Wagner cut the end of the overture so as to lead without a break into the new Venusberg music. Actually, in addition to minor changes, such as the insertion of three bars in F sharp major for the cor anglais in the shepherd boy's song, practically the whole of the first two scenes of Act I was rewritten, as was the orchestral passage at Tannhäuser's melting in scene 4 (the passage leading up to his 'Zu ihr! Zu ihr!'). Drastic

---

[1] *Erlebnisse mit Richard Wagner*, Stuttgart, 1898.

alterations were made in the Tournament of Song; for instance, Tannhäuser's original reply to Wolfram and Walther von der Vogelweide's song were both cut. Tannhäuser's reply to Walther now being extended and made to apply, with much altered music, to Wolfram[1] and the end of the Act was rewritten. The end of the last Act, too, was rescored and this rescoring was further revised, presumably for the Munich production of the Paris score in 1867; moreover, as the Paris music was composed to French words, the vocal lines of the new passages were now readjusted in many places to fit a German text. As for the fusion of the overture with the Venusberg music, this seems to have been thought of only in 1872 for a concert performance in Vienna (on 12 May) and was first used in the theatre on the occasion of the Vienna production of the Paris version, under Richter, on 22 November, 1875.

These changes are of every degree and kind, ranging from tiny details to the insertion or substitution of entirely new material as in much of the Paris Venusberg music and in the latter part of Act I, scene 2 (from Venus's 'Suche dein Heil, und find es nie!' to the end). For the purpose of the present study the latter, the most obvious and important changes, are of no interest; the differences are too wide. But where the new has something in common with the old there still remains a rich field for investigation, a field rich enough almost to provide in itself a basis for an empirical study of Wagner's whole musical aesthetic.

One naturally looks at once to see how Wagner has dealt with the ponderous ♩ ♩. ♪|♩ rhythm. It is remoulded again and again in various ways. One very simple example occurs at the end of scene 2, in the treatment of Tannhäuser's decisive cry:

In two passages, the sirens' chorus 'Naht euch dem Strande!' and Venus's 'Geliebter, komm! Sieh' dort die Grotte', the remoulding is made easier by the replacement of common time—the predominance of which makes so much early Wagner sound so dreary—by triple time. In this passage from the sirens' chorus:

---

[1] This change was motivated by the inadequacy of the Paris Walther; see Ernest Newman, *The Life of Richard Wagner*, III, London, 1945, pp. 70 and 89–90.

Ex. 13

as Rietsch points out,[1] the original pattern ('Naht euch dem', 'wo in den' 'glühender', 'selig Er-') is replaced by three different ones. 'Geliebter, komm!' has a further point of interest:

Ex. 14

In the Paris version—set not to German words but to Charles Nuitter's translation—Wagner disguised the cliché in the third bar of the original version but actually inserted another, hardly concealed form of it to 'Viens, cher amant'. It was not until he came to prepare the German text of the Paris version that he not only changed this but, altering the verbal punctuation and inserting a phrase-mark, erased the last trace of the obnoxious pattern from 'sieh' dort'.

Recasting of 4/4 passages as 3/4 is one of the most characteristic of Wagner's revisions, a sign of painful consciousness of the squareness of his original conceptions. The last stanza of the *Meistersinger* prize-song, 'Huldreichster Tag', was conceived in common time as we have it in the overture and only later softened into triple time. (The ♩ ♩. ♪ |♩ opening could be left for the 'Mastersingers' theme where stiffness and pomposity were appropriate.) Again, when Wagner in 1869 borrowed from his string quartet of five years earlier[2] the passage beginning, 'O Siegfried,

---

[1] Heinrich Rietsch's *Die Tonkunst in der zweiten Hälfte des neunzehnten Jahrhunderts*, Leipzig, second edition 1906, contains an interesting study of the Paris Venusberg music.

[2] See the preface to my conjectural reconstruction of the Quartet Movement, London, 1947.

Herrlicher! Hort der Welt! (*Siegfried*, Act III, scene 3), he preserved the original 4/4 pattern; when, in the following year, he used it again in the *Siegfried Idyll*, he remoulded it in 3/4 time to its great advantage.

The little ornament on 'asile' is also characteristic of the revised *Tannhäuser*. Although Wagner insisted very firmly that there were no recitatives in the original *Tannhäuser*, he evidently came to recognise that his vocal line often looked on paper remarkably like recitative, that his declamation generally was too often stiff and could well afford more lyrical expansion. However much we allow for the circumstance that he was setting a new French text, the rewritten passages—particularly in the part of Venus—constantly reveal this desire for lyrical expansion both in the vocal line itself and in the orchestra. Venus's very first phrase in scene 2, 'Geliebter, sag', wo weilt dein Sinn?', was originally set as dry unaccompanied declamation. In the Paris version the C on 'sag'' was lengthened from dotted crotchet to semibreve-tied-to-crotchet and intensified by orchestral harmony, while 'wo weilt dein Sinn?' was expanded into a more melodic shape (which inadvertently drops, more noticeably in the later German version, into the ♩ ♩. ♪ pattern). Almost every phrase in the part of Venus is, if not completely recast, expanded and orchestrated in this way. There is a particularly striking example of this at 'Ha, was vernehm' ich? Welche tör'ge Klagen!' where not only is the voice-part made more lyrical but the perfunctory string chords and agitated scurries of conventional recitative accompaniment are replaced by a *dolce* wind-and-horn chord throbbing irregularly in the same manner, if not precisely in the same rhythm, as 'O sink hernieder,' in *Tristan*, similarly rhythmised string chords replace the 'scrub' tremolo that originally accompanied Venus's 'Hin zu den kalten Menschen flieh'; but almost every page of the new *Tannhäuser* music reminds one of *Tristan*.

One can sum up the broad guiding principles of Wagner's touching-up —as distinct from the complete rewriting—of his vocal line as lengthening of note-values, imparting a freer, bolder sweep to the line, avoidance of repeated 'reciting' notes and elimination of vocal cliché, with a (doubtless unconscious) moulding of outlines into more 'personal' melodic shapes. Not that he does all or any of these things constantly, but his tendencies are in those directions. He had left a familiar vocal-cadence formula in Walther's prize-song in *Die Meistersinger*, but in Venus's part he disguises the same formula by syncopation:

The other points, and the rejection in certain passages of details conditioned by the French text, may be illustrated by a few bars from the
Wartburg scene (Act II, scene 4):

in which perhaps the most notable feature is the substitution of a seventh
for a second on 'sangest', producing once again the *Tristan* 'glance'
motive (cf. Ex. 2). The line is kneaded, made more plastic. Similarly, the
bass also, though less often, is made more mobile; when Tannhäuser
bursts out in the Venusberg scene 'Dein übergrosser Reiz ist's, den ich
fliehe!', his part (in the definitive German version, though not in the
intermediate Paris text) and the diminished seventh harmony, are left
unchanged and the orchestration is but slightly touched up, but the bass
is given life:

Some of the harmonic changes—also in the direction of softened, more
plastic outline—are shown in Ex. 13; chromatic and diatonic passing-
notes, and in one case a double suspension, are used to break up some
of the earlier block-chords. But, while the new music is composed in the
harmonic idiom of *Tristan* and motives from the Venusberg music are
now worked up with heightened harmonic pungency, there is little that
can be described as harmonic touching-up, little that is of interest from
the point of view of the present study.

It is quite otherwise with the orchestration. Small details and large
patches of drastic rescoring alike show Wagner's finer mastery of the
orchestra in the 1860s. One typical change is the frequent substitution
of trills for 'scrub' tremolo as at bars 57 ff. of the original Venusberg
music. (The equivalent passage begins with the thirteenth bar after the
rise of the curtain in the new Venusberg music.) Not that Wagner abandons scrub tremolo altogether; he actually returns to it here; but his

general tendency is to replace it by trills. The same passage illustrates both his new rhythmic use of the triangle to give fiery intensity and his laying on of thicker colouring; the bacchanalian woodwind figure is now doubled by the violas and half the second violins. Wagner adds an oboe counter-subject here (Tannhäuser's 'Ach! schöne Göttin, wolle mir nicht zürnen!'), there makes the cello line more singing and continuous, instead of interjectional (Venus's 'Hin zu den kalten Menschen flieh'). Detached tutti chords are often laid out differently.

But the most characteristic changes are generally those which seek to conceal squareness and rigidity. It is amusing to find Wagner reverting to a favourite old device of his—a rhythmic figure on the trumpet—in an attempt to galvanise that originally rather sticky passage, Tannhäuser's 'nach Freiheit doch verlangt es mich'; but much more typical in this same passage are the efforts to breathe rhythmic life into the original dead down-beat chords for second violins and violas and to the cello part.[1] The upward-rushing scale up-beats to the tutti chords on the word 'Freiheit' are extended equivalents of the semiquaver up-beat of the first violins quoted in Ex. 11 from the revised version of the *Holländer* over-ture. In one case where such a scale up-beat existed already in the old music (Venus's 'der Freude Götter, wir, entflohn'). Wagner took some pains to elaborate it, carrying the pattern across the heavy down-beat on 'Freude'.

Yet another typical change in the 'nach Freiheit' passage is the greater plasticity given to the first-violin line:

Ex. 18
(a)
1844

(b)
1860

The violin parts are touched up in this way at many points in the revised *Tannhäuser*. Sometimes an entirely new *Tristan*esque line is drawn boldly across the original pattern to give it fresh life; there is a striking instance at the point in Act I, scene 4, where Tannhäuser, 'deeply moved', em-braces Wolfram and his companions and demands to be taken to Elisabeth (see pages 235 and 953 of the Eulenburg miniature score of the complete opera). Every change is thoroughly characteristic of the mature Wagner: the new violin part (adapted from a hint half a dozen bars later in the old

---

[1] Just before, at 'Doch hin muss ich zur Welt', Wagner syncopated similar inner parts for second violins and violas, making them enter a quaver before the beat, instead of on the beat as he had originally written them.

version), the rescoring of the original violin figure and the removal of its down-beats, the new rhythmic interest given to the solid wind and lower string chords, the lively viola part, and (not least) the upward rush of the lower strings in the first bar. It is worth noticing, too, how with typical care to distribute the interest more equally between the players, Wagner interchanges the violin roles when the passage is immediately repeated a tone higher, giving the new semiquaver part to the seconds, the original figure to the divided firsts. When a number of such alterations are made simultaneously, with almost completely rewritten voice-parts into the bargain, it is sometimes almost impossible to recognise the connection with the original music.

In a famous passage in a letter to Mathilde Wesendonk (29 October, 1859) Wagner declared that his 'subtlest, deepest art' was 'the art of transition' from one emotional extreme to another. The longdrawn and gradual transitions in his mature works are very familiar, and we have already noticed something of this in the 1855 *Faust*. But it is peculiarly instructive to study how in the revised *Tannhäuser* Wagner contrives to subtilise a strong and fairly sudden change of emotion, such as the descent from the climax at pages 146 and 856 of the miniature score to the soft voluptuousness of Venus's 'Geliebter, komm'. In the 1844 score the violins rush up to their high B, which is cut off abruptly; there is a long bar of complete silence; then three bars of soft woodwind harmony, a piccolo call, and a brief reference to one of the Venusberg themes introduce the most seductive of Venus's advances, 'Geliebter, komm!' (see Ex. 14). In the revised score the violins descend again from their high B; a solo clarinet, prolonging Venus's B, summons up the violas from the depths of the orchestra and then echoes the violin descent five bars later; only then do we reach the silent bar. It is followed by the woodwind harmonies, though differently scored and no longer soft, now repeated instead of being played once only; and there are six more *andante* bars of new music before we reach the Venusberg motive and Venus's song.

Such new or extended transitions are among the most striking features of the revised *Tannhäuser*. Rietsch draws attention to one instance at the beginning of the bacchanale: the insertion of twelve bars—he erroneously says ten—immediately after the rise of the curtain in the Paris version:

> The reason is an aesthetic one. The theme beginning with the arpeggioed diminished seventh [the so-called 'enticement' theme] is not to enter immediately in its complete form; instead the hearer's attention is to be aroused by fragmentary up-rushes and his interest in the theme heightened.

The excited orchestral passages leading to each strophe of Tannhäuser's song to Venus were all three rewritten; not only made more powerful and more plastic in texture but extended in the first case from three to eight bars, in the second from four to six, in the third from three to four. The object in each case is obviously to whip up a more frenzied climax from the peak of which Tannhäuser can launch his impassioned song. Similarly, in the original Tournament of Song a mere five bars of bacchanalian music sufficed to bridge from the choral acclamation of Wolfram's song to Tannhäuser's reply, merely four after Walther's song. Walther's song (it will be remembered) disappeared from the Paris version, but the transition from Wolfram to Tannhäuser's 'O Wolfram, der du also sangest' is now not only spread over fourteen bars but is far more finely shaded. Finally, at the very end of the Second Act, after the song of the younger pilgrims has died away in the distance, the original four-bar scurry of violin quavers leading to the general cry, 'Nach Rom!' was extended to eight, made more plastic, more *Tristan*-like in outline, and rescored more powerfully with violas 'pointing' the first three or two quavers of every four.

Not only are such transitions made less abrupt; the actual joins in the musical fabric are more skilfully welded. To take a single example: the entry of the siren chorus does not overlap the preceding orchestral motive in the original score. In the Paris version it does overlap this same motive—but very differently scored and, incidentally, reached through one of the most wonderful transitions in the whole of Wagner. In the original the supporting B of the third horn is, characteristically for the 1840s, cut off at the end of a bar; in the Paris version it is, characteristically for the 1860s, tied to a quaver in the next bar: a tiny detail but a significant one.

The only other completed work in which we can study Wagner's second thoughts is the set of *Fünf Gedichte* for soprano and piano, the so-called 'Wesendonk-Lieder', written in the period 30 November, 1857, to 1 May, 1858. The changes are of minor importance by comparison with those we have been discussing, but they have a special interest in that they were made in works of Wagner's maturity within the relatively short time before they were published (in 1862). Or even in a much shorter time: the second version of the piano postlude to 'Schmerzen' was sent to Frau Wesendonk on a separate piece of paper the day after she had been given the original, and the third version followed 'soon' after.[1] Most of the changes are trifling: e.g. the insertion of the turn five bars before the end of 'Der Engel' and the addition of two introductory

---

[1] The covering notes are garbled and reversed in order in the well-known volume, *Richard Wagner an Mathilde Wesendonk*, Berlin, ninth edition, 1904, p. 22. The particulars are given correctly by Balling in his preface to Vol. XV of the *Gesamtausgabe*, where the variants are printed.

bars for piano to 'Stehe still'. A few slight but telling touches were added to 'Im Treibhaus', notably the sharpening of the D in the piano-part at 'öder Leere' which thus produces the consecutive fifths with the voice which, as Balling remarks, so subtly suggest the 'barren waste'.

But the three versions of the postlude to 'Schmerzen' throw light on Wagner's quick changes of mind. The original three bars were brief and perfunctory, with consecutive fifths which—far from being expressive—are simply a grammatical ineptitude. Nor does the Neapolitan cadence make a convincing end to the song. The passage might have come from any incompetent amateur; it is almost as bare and crude as one of Wagner's composition sketches. Next day, however, 'after a lovely, refreshing night my first waking thought was this improved postlude':

Ex. 19

(The piano enters on the last note of the voice-part.) Here at any rate there is some lyrical expansion; the descending-line idea of the original form is now continued as in the introductory bars and at other points earlier in the song; the triumphant last two also refer to an earlier point ('wie ein stolzer Siegesheld'); the Neapolitan cadence has left only a shadow in bar 2, instead of ending the song. But still Wagner was not satisfied. Before long Frau Wesendonk received 'yet another ending! It has to be ever more beautiful!' and even this was touched up before publication. The descending line is now given an upbeat and, instead of being tamely repeated an octave lower or continued a sixth lower, is now treated sequentially—one of the rare cases of a descending sequence in Wagner—as it had been earlier in the song ('und gebieret Tod nur Leben'), only that the first two members now become the *Stollen* of a miniature *Bar* (as Hans Sachs called it to Walther von Stolzing) of which the *Abgesang* is provided by an echo of the last vocal phrase, 'O wie dank ich, dass gegeben solche Schmerzen mir Natur!', which in turn is mortised into the last three bars of the second version (Ex. 19). The greater harmonic subtlety of the definitive version will be self-evident to anyone who takes the trouble to compare it with Ex. 19. The finer workmanship of the left-hand part will be equally obvious. But, above all, the definitive version—unlike the earlier ones—is a satisfactory musical organism based entirely on elements used earlier in the song but nowhere brought together as they are here. Incidentally, it is the longest of the three versions. With Wagner improvement nearly always entailed expansion, seldom condensation.

1955

XXVI—NIETZSCHE'S ATTITUDE TO WAGNER: A FRESH VIEW

It is rather unfortunate that when we think of Nietzsche's connection with music, it is almost invariably the history of his personal relations with Wagner which springs to the mind—the close friendship, followed by the bitter hostility of *The Case of Wagner* and the other pamphlets of later days. Accident threw the shadow of Wagner's art over all Nietzsche's thoughts on musical matters, but, Wagner or no Wagner, Nietzsche would still have devoted a great part of his thought to music. Even in boyhood he loved music more passionately than literature. He began to compose—it was his life-long hobby—and years afterwards he imagined he heard in *Parsifal* echoes of things he himself had said in his youthful compositions. At first his favourite composer was Schumann, a curious fact when considered in the light of the reasons he gave for his admiration of Chopin, in a letter written while he was still a scholar at the Fürstenschule Pforta: 'I particularly admired in Chopin his freeing of music from German influences, from the tendency to the ugly, dull, pettily bourgeois, clumsy and self-important. Spiritual beauty and nobility, and, above all, aristocratic gaiety, freedom from restraint and splendour of soul, as well as southern warmth and intensity of feeling, were expressed by him for the first time in music.' The letter is of great importance, for in this explanation of his Chopin worship is revealed the secret, not only of the spell exercised on him by *Tristan*, but of the Bizet worship of nearly thirty years later. Here already is the feeling which later found expression in the cry, 'Il faut méditerraniser la musique!' It was the constant element in Nietzsche's musical life, underlying all the apparent changes of taste and opinion.

It is important to establish this point, for there is a widespread impression that Nietzsche, like many brilliant people, was fickle. The Wagner episode, tremendously important as it was, was essentially only an episode. And, as we shall see, even as regards Wagner, Nietzsche's emotional reaction to the master's music was always fundamentally the same; it was only that he interpreted the reaction in quite a different way. Indeed, a sound case might be made for the view that Nietzsche was not so much a Wagner-worshipper as a *Tristan* worshipper. If you probe deeply into one of his commentaries on the gospel of Wagnerism, in nine cases out of ten you will find *Tristan* at the bottom. His attitude towards the *Ring* was always more cautious. At the height of his enthusiasm, a few weeks before he first met the master in person, we find him writing to his friend, Baron von

Gersdorff, 'I have played but little as I have no piano here in Kosen, but I brought along the piano score of Wagner's *Walküre*, in regard to which my feelings are so confused that I dare not venture an opinion on the subject. The greatest beauties and virtues are offset by equally great short-comings and positive ugliness at times. And according to Riese and Buch-binder *plus a+minus a=*o.' (11 October, 1868.) Again; when the friend-ship was drawing near the snapping-point, Frau Förster-Nietzsche specifically says of some hostile criticisms consequent on her brother's disillusionment at the first Bayreuth Festival in 1876: 'It must not be for-gotten that all this criticism was directed against the Nibelung tetralogy and its author, not against *Tristan* and its creator. At that time, *Tristan* had practically been relegated to the background, or made the object of scathing criticism by some of the most fanatic Wagnerians. Even in Wahnfried, *Tristan* was seldom mentioned. . . . Had *Tristan* been the work chosen for performance at the first Festival, it is quite certain that my brother's criticisms would have been of quite a different character and his disappointment by no means so keen.'[1]

Nietzsche's first book, *The Birth of Tragedy from the Spirit of Music* (1871), maintains the thesis that the greatness of Greek art was a conse-quence of early Greek pessimism—the book was afterwards resubtitled *Hellenism and Pessimism*—and that its decline dated from the optimistic teaching of Socrates. The book, in spite of its confused and rhapsodic style, is an important contribution to the metaphysics of art. Unfortunately it is a mere torso of a much larger projected work on Hellenism in general, indeed a torso of only a part of it—and that recast and patched in order to please Wagner. Nietzsche had completed the first part of his study of Hellenism in April 1871, when he visited Tribschen and found the com-poser in very low spirits. Wishing to make a practical gesture of friend-ship, he returned to Basle, cut out those chapters of his book not concerned with Greek tragedy and inserted a great deal of fresh matter demonstrating that the spirit of Greek tragedy, dead for two thousand years, had been reincarnated in modern German music—but only fully, of course, in the Wagnerian music-drama. A book so constructed could hardly fail to be unclear. Nietzsche was trying to say and to prove far too much that was not perfectly clear even to himself, and the reader is only bewildered and irritated by Nietzsche's second-hand Schopenhauerism and his poetico-metaphysical jargon about the 'antagonism and reconciliation of the Dio-nysian and Apollonian principles'. Except the rhapsodic account of the author's reactions to *Tristan*, to which I shall return later, there is not much in *The Birth of Tragedy* to interest the musician of today.

But while writing and redrafting the book Nietzsche, in accordance with his usual habit, made innumerable notes and sketches, all carefully

[1] *The Nietzsche-Wagner Correspondence*, London, 1922.

preserved, and one of these, an essay 'On Words and Music', published posthumously in Vol. IX of the complete German edition of his works, contains some important observations on the nature of musical inspiration, particularly its inspiration by poetry. Nietzsche, following Schopenhauer, denies that such inspiration is ever given and contends that, while musical emotion may excite the activity of the visual or sentimental imagination, the converse is never the case—no musical idea is really born of a non-musical, a poetic or visual conception. Nietzsche is prepared to go even further than Schopenhauer, for while the latter held that music can express, not any particular joy or sorrow (or love or hate or ecstasy or serenity), or any subject of joy or sorrow, but ideal joy or sorrow, Nietzsche says that genuinely inspired music does not express even joy or sorrow, but only indeterminate emotion. In other words, there is such a thing as purely musical emotion. Definite feelings only 'serve as symbols to music'. The lyrical poet, who is half a musician, is conscious of this musical emotion, but he 'gives an allegorical translation of it in the form of feelings. So with all those listeners who experience a definite emotional reaction to music. The power of music reaching them only from a distance, appeals to an intervening world which gives them, as it were, a foretaste, a symbolic pre-notion of music properly so called, and this world is that of the feelings. . . . But all those who are affected by music only through the feelings must be told that they will always stay in the outer court and will never be admitted to music's Holy of Holies, for this cannot be manifested, but only symbolised, by feeling.'

Nietzsche's dictum is corroborated by modern scientific investigation. A Swiss, Dr Odier, as a result of careful research (discussed in W. J. Turner's *Music and Life*), came to the conclusion that the most musical class of listener, though numerically the smallest, consists of 'those who experienced an emotion *sui generis* and not to be compared with any other psychological phenomenon; in other words, a purely musical emotion inexpressible in other terms'. And Turner, who apparently knew nothing of Nietzsche's theory, wholeheartedly agrees that this is so.[1]

But, it may be objected, what happens when a composer sets words to music, then? Does it follow that his music is necessarily uninspired, merely 'made'? What about the world's undeniably great songs? 'When a musician composes a song,' Nietzsche replies, 'it is neither the imagery nor the feelings expressed in the text which inspire him as a musician; but a musical inspiration from quite another sphere chooses this text as suitable for its own symbolic expression.' In case this sounds rather too fanciful we may compare it with the explanation given by a modern composer of genius—

[1] Compare also the unanimous conclusions of Vernon Lee, Gurney, Ortman, Hanslick, Myers and Clive Bell, cited in Max Schoen's study of 'The Experience of Beauty in Music' in *The Musical Quarterly*, January, 1931.

Igor Stravinsky—of his own choice of literary subjects for works conceived as abstract music: 'Suppose I am a painter. I paint, say, a portrait of a lady in *toilette de bal*, with her jewels. My portrait resembles the person painted. None the less it is painted for the pleasure of painting, despite its subject. Or I paint a picture of a street fight. The fight is a pretext for the picture, but the painting of it may be pure painting.' To return to Nietzsche: if the poem is only the 'pretext' or opportunity for the crystallisation of a vague purely musical emotion, 'there can be no question of any essential connection between poem and music; the two worlds of sound and image here brought into contact are too far removed from each other to be linked by any but an external bond; the poem merely provides a symbol and is to music what the Egyptian hieroglyphic of bravery is to the brave warrior himself. The highest revelations of music make us feel, in spite of ourselves, the clumsiness of all the feelings and pictorial representations in which people pretend to find some analogy with them. Thus Beethoven's last quartets make all definite representations ridiculous. Symbols here lose their meaning and even offend by their materiality.'

Developing this idea, Nietzsche argues that a poem wedded to great music makes no impression at all *as a poem*, and that, if it did, it would only detract from the effect of the music; the text exists only for the singers; the composer uses the human voice simply because it is the finest of instruments. He goes on to illustrate his theory by reference to Beethoven's Choral Symphony, where he thinks 'Schiller's "Ode to Joy" is entirely disproportionate to the redeeming, dithyrambic intoxication of the music, and is even submerged like a pale moonbeam in a sea of flame. Further, who can deny that, if we are not keenly conscious of this when listening to the music, it is only because, the music having already annihilated our sensibility to words and imagery, *we hear nothing at all of Schiller's poem*? All this splendid transport, the very sublimity of Schiller's verses, has a disturbing effect beside the naïve truth of the melody of "joy", and even makes a coarse and unpleasant impression; fortunately, amid the ever more and more splendid development of the choral song and the orchestral masses, we do not hear it, and that alone prevents our being conscious of the clash.'

But is not all this, the logical consequence of Nietzsche's ideas at the very time when his friendship with Wagner was at its height, the most shocking heresy against all that Wagner taught? Unquestionably. Not quite such heresy as might appear, for Wagner himself was not always a Wagnerian in his practice. (We know, for instance, that the *Meistersinger* overture—that is, the *music* of a great deal of the Third Act—was finished before the *words* of the Third Act were written.) But it was heresy all the same. And, immediately after the passage last quoted, Nietzsche goes on to ask what one can think of the 'monstrous aesthetic superstition according to which this fourth movement of the Ninth was Beethoven's solemn profession of faith as to the limits of absolute music, and even opened, somehow or other, the gates to a new art in which music would now be able to make itself understood even by the "conscious mind" '. The 'superstition' was, of course, one of Wagner's pet theories.

What is the explanation, then, of Nietzsche's attitude? The fact that this essay was published only after the author's death gives us a clue to it. As far as one can see, Nietzsche was never a true Wagnerian at all. His enthusiasm for Wagner's music—above all for *Tristan*—may have led him to try to persuade himself that he was one; but even that is doubtful. Nietzsche's was an enigmatic personality. As he said himself, he was 'a labyrinth of a man'. We can only guess at what really went on in his tortuous mind and soul. His attitude in writing publicly in praise of a theorist in whom he had no whole-hearted belief, was disingenuous, but there can be no doubt that Nietzsche was personally devoted to Wagner at this period and was prepared to go to any length to please him. 'To Wagner or to his wife?' someone may ask—not without justice, for it is now definitely established, in spite of the ridicule Frau Förster-Nietzsche pours on the idea, that Nietzsche did love Cosima. But there is no reason why a man should not be a sincere and devoted friend of the husband of the woman with whom he has had the misfortune to fall in love, though no doubt the fact accounts for much of Nietzsche's extraordinary bitterness after the break. We may put it, then, that Nietzsche admired the man and the composer, but, in spite of praise of Wagner's theories patched into his published writings for friendship's sake, was at least undecided about the author of *Oper und Drama*. But the man began to weary him; Wagner's personality, his coarse humour and insatiable appetite for admiration, jarred his highly strung sensibility; no doubt secret jealousy played its part. And as early as 1874 he had lost most of his illusions about the composer.

In one of Nietzsche's note-books for that year occur these remarkable sentences: 'Wagner's youth was the aimless one of a universal dilettante. ... Not one of our great composers was still, at twenty-eight, as bad a musician as Wagner. This insane doubt has often crossed my mind: Is Wagner really musical?' Here again we find a discrepancy between Nietzsche's private thoughts and his published ones, for two years later he told the readers of his 'Richard Wagner in Bayreuth' that 'the enterprise of Bayreuth signifies in the realm of art the first circumnavigation of the globe', and that it was a voyage that had resulted in 'the discovery not merely of a new art, but of art itself'. As for Wagner, 'no artist of what past soever has yet received such a remarkable portion of genius'. And this of a man about whom he had come to the conclusion at least two years before, that he was 'an actor out of his proper sphere. He relies principally on music, but his attitude to music is that of an actor. . . . Wagner brings together all possible effective elements at a time when popular taste is dulled and demands extremely crass and vigorous methods. Everything is employed—the magnificent, the intoxicating, the bewildering, the grandiose, the frightful, the clamorous, the ecstatic, the neurotic. . . . Himself possessing the instincts of an actor, he wishes to imitate mankind only in the most effective manner. . . . Painting for effect is an extremely dangerous thing for artists. The intoxicating, the sensual, the unexpected, the ecstatic, the being-moved-at-any-price. Alarming tendencies.' As Pierre Lasserre says,[1] 'The whole substance of *Der Fall Wagner* is already embodied in these notes of 1874. The difference lies in the tone. Here Nietzsche coldly confesses to himself what he sees in the work of a master whose friend he still is and who reckons on his open attachment. When he wrote *The Case of Wagner* he had grown to hate the pleasures as well as the painful impressions given him by Wagner's music.'

Nietzsche's attitude, from first to last, was that of a defender of the 'purity' of music. Now on this ground, now on that, he is always, as in the early essay 'On Words and Music', asserting the superiority of music over the other arts and insisting that its temple must not be defiled. He had, of course, always been familiar with Wagner's doctrine that music in the drama is only a means, not an end in itself. But in his admiration for the music *as* music, feeling as almost everyone does the infinitely greater value of the music than of the other elements in the Wagnerian art-work, he had devised an ingenious explanation of the latter, given in *The Birth of Tragedy*. He addresses 'not those who make use of the scenic pictures, the words, and the emotions of the performers, in order to approximate thereby to musical perception; for none of these speaks music as their mother tongue and, in spite of the aids in question, do not get farther than the precincts of musical perception', but 'those to whom music is, as it were, a mother's breast and who are connected with things almost exclusively by musical relations'. And he asks 'these genuine musicians' 'whether they can imagine a man capable of hearing the Third Act of *Tristan and Isolde* without any aid of word and scenery, purely as a vast symphonic period, without expiring? Would not a man be *shattered* who, so to speak, had put his ear to the heart-chamber of the cosmic will, where he could feel the wild will-to-existence pouring out into all the arteries of the world? . . . Here interpose, between our highest musical excitement and the music itself, the tragic myth and the tragic hero—in reality only as symbols of the most universal facts, of which music alone can speak directly. . . . Suddenly we imagine we see only Tristan, as he lies there motionless, saying to himself, "The old tune. Why does it wake me?" And what before seemed to us a hollow sigh from the heart of all existence,

[1] *Les Idées de Nietzsche sur la musique*, Paris, 1907.

now only tells us "how waste and void is the sea". And whereas, breathless, we felt we should expire through a convulsive distention of all our feelings, and only a slender thread bound us to our present existence, we now hear and see only the hero wounded to death and still not dying, with his despairing cry, "Longing! Longing! In dying still longing! for longing not dying!" ' The stage-picture and the individual characters of the drama are a necessary veil to protect us from the too-overwhelming emotional effect of the music. Nietzsche is, in fact, only saying in his extravagant way what many of us express with less exaggeration, though with ridiculous coldness, when we say that the music of *Tristan* is 'more effective in the concert hall, without voices, than in the theatre'.[1] He was so convinced of the 'absolute' nature of the *Tristan* music that he went so far as to say that 'any number of actual scenes might be used as passing manifestations of the same music. They could never exhaust its essence, but would always remain mere externalised copies of it.'

Nietzsche's disillusionment with Wagner was the natural consequence of his discovery that the music was for the most part—above all in the *Ring*—exactly what Wagner had always said it was, a means to a dramatic end; that when Wagner was an 'absolute' musician it was only by accident and in spite of himself. He probably began to wonder, as others have wondered since, whether so many themes based on the arpeggio of the added-sixth chord were the natural fruits of a genuinely fertile musical intelligence. He saw that Wagner was 'obliged to make patchwork—"motives", attitudes, formulæ, reduplications, centuplications; as a musician he remained a rhetorician'.[2] Neither Wagner's enlargement of the resources of music nor his colossal skill in handling these resources, which Nietzsche never denied, compensated in the eyes of the disillusioned admirer for the absence of pure 'musical emotion'. Hence the 'insane doubts' and other questionings of 1874, which may be compared with this passage in *The Case of Wagner*, written fourteen years later:

Was Wagner a musician at all? At least he was something else in a *higher degree*, namely an incomparable *histrio*, the most astonishing

---

[1] Romain Rolland remarks in *Musiciens d'aujourd'hui*: 'I cannot help feeling that scenic reality takes away rather than adds to the effect of these philosophical fairylands. Malwida von Meysenbug told me that at the Bayreuth Festival of 1876, while she was following one of the *Ring* scenes very attentively with her opera-glasses, two hands were laid over her eyes, and she heard Wagner's voice say impatiently: "Don't look so much at what is going on. Listen!" It was good counsel. . . . One might say that the best way to follow a performance of a Wagner opera is with the eyes shut. So perfect is the music, so powerful its hold on the imagination, that it leaves nothing to be desired; what it suggests to the mind is infinitely finer than what the eyes may see. I have never shared the opinion that Wagner's works may be best appreciated in the theatre. His works are epic symphonies. As a frame for them I should like temples; as scenery, the illimitable land of thought; as actors, our dreams.'

[2] *The Case of Wagner.*

theatrical genius that the Germans have had, our *scenic artist par excellence*. His place is elsewhere than in the history of music, with the grand true geniuses of which he must not be confounded. Wagner *and* Beethoven—that is a blasphemy—and in the end an injustice even to Wagner. . . . He *became* a musician, he *became* a poet, because the tyrant in him, his stage-player genius, compelled him to it. . . . Wagner was *not* a musician by instinct. He proved this himself by abandoning all lawfulness and all style in music, in order to make out of it what he required, a theatrical rhetoric, a means of expression, for strengthening attitudes, for suggestion, for the psychologically picturesque. Wagner might here pass for an inventor and an innovator of the first rank—*he has immeasurably increased the speaking power of music*; he is the Victor Hugo of music as language. Provided always one grants that music *may*, under certain conditions, not be music, but speech, tool or *ancilla dramaturgica*. Wagner's music, *not* taken under protection by theatrical taste, a very tolerant taste, is simply bad music.

Nor is there any reason for supposing that Nietzsche's emotional (or, more accurately, *sensuous*), as distinguished from his æsthetic, reaction to Wagner's music underwent any change. Even in the *Case of Wagner* he could say of *Parsifal*, the very work which, through its Christianity, had snapped the last threads of the friendship, 'I admire that work. I should like to have composed it myself; not having done so, *I at least understand it*. . . . Wagner was never better inspired than at the end.'[1] Most people would probably consider that an error of judgment, for it is generally agreed that there is a falling off in the musical inspiration of *Parsifal*. But Nietzsche had not had so much time to weary of its magic as in the case of the *Ring*, and the clarity and serenity of the music harmonised better with his predominant mood at that period. 'Dionysiac frenzy' no longer seemed to him the highest spiritual condition of which man is capable; Socrates had been forgiven. In his comments on the passage in *The Birth of Tragedy* dealing with *Tristan*, Lasserre, who thinks the passage is to be regarded 'merely as a description of impressions', points out that 'a day was to come when, in order to criticise this same work adversely, it was hardly necessary for Nietzsche to ascribe to it any other qualities than those he finds in it here. It was only that the "convulsive distension of all our feelings" no longer struck him as admirable or divine. . . . The "metaphysical" now seemed the "pathological"; the heaven of ecstasy became the hell of neurosis; and that impression of "infinity" given by the music of *Tristan*

[1] Compare this with a passage in a letter to Peter Gast, written ten years earlier, speaking of the music, as apart from the subject of *Parsifal*: 'Recently I heard the Prelude to *Parsifal* for the first time (in Monte Carlo!). . . . Quite apart from all irrelevant questions (such as what purpose this music *can* serve and is *meant* to serve), but purely from an æsthetic standpoint, has Wagner ever written anything *better*?' (21 January, 1878.)

was attributed to the cunning of the composer in turning to account his very impotence to create beautiful, healthy and definite forms, in order to produce an effect of vague and intoxicating seductiveness.' Which is only another way of saying that although *Tristan* still affected Nietzsche as powerfully as ever, he now recognised that its effect was emotional rather than musical. But whereas most people, better balanced because less sensitive, would have concluded only that the æsthetic element was, after all, less important than the emotional—not, as they had thought, the reverse —Nietzsche could now see *nothing* but the merely emotional where before he had seen only the purely musical. We must remember that, on such points, Nietzsche was as sensitive as the scales used by scientists, turned by a speck of dust.

Only one thing remains to be added in explanation of Nietzsche's *volte-face* with regard to Wagner's music. Long after he had discovered its 'impurity', but years before he wrote *The Case of Wagner*, his musical *taste* underwent a change, he tells us, a change interestingly connected with the conception of *Also sprach Zarathustra*. Nietzsche's own account of this may be found in *Ecce Homo*. After telling how the idea of 'eternal recurrence', the underlying 'motive' of his own masterpiece, came to him in August 1881, he goes on; 'If I reckon back a few months from that day, I find, as a premonitory symptom, a sudden and profound change in my taste, above all in music.' The change, which took place in the spring of 1881, while staying with his musician friend, Peter Gast, at the little mountain spa of Recoaro, near Vicenza, was perhaps not so sudden and so profound as he imagined; it was probably only that he was suddenly and profoundly conscious of the change; but it explains a great deal— including the tone of *Der Fall Wagner*. (It is inconceivable that spite against Cosima did more than deepen the colours.) 'On the contrary', it may be objected, 'it seems to confuse the whole business. If Nietzsche was aware of Wagner's "non-musicalness" as early as 1874, what has a change of taste in 1881 to do with it? And does it not invalidate your theory that Nietzsche's emotional reaction to Wagner's music underwent no fundamental change?' I do not think so. One may *know* that something is bad art, yet still like it;[1] and one may intensely dislike a work of art and yet be profoundly excited by it. I think we need attach no particular importance to this 'conversion at Recoaro', except as indicating that the exciting in art, though it had not lost its power over Nietzsche's senses, now offended his taste instead of seducing it in spite of itself. It put the stamp of warm, definite feeling on what had previously been only dim *Ahnung* and cold, intellectual judgment.

[1] 'In my student days I said: "Wagner is a romanticist, not of the art in its zenith, but in its last quarter; soon it will be night!" Despite this insight I was a Wagnerian; I *knew* better, but I could not do otherwise.' (Note-book of 1874.)

To sum up: apart from Nietzsche's two *published* writings on Wagner—*The Birth of Tragedy* (which we know was patched and adapted to please his friend) and 'Richard Wagner in Bayreuth' (a more or less formal *Festschrift*, which may have been written from a sense of duty, almost as much as of true friendship)—there is no evidence that Nietzsche was ever a true Wagnerian at all. In 1868, at twenty-four, before he had met Wagner, he was criticising *Die Walküre* adversely; in 1871, when his admiration of the composer was at its height and he was on the most intimate terms with the Tribschen family circle, he was secretly laughing at one of Wagner's most cherished theories as a 'monstrous æsthetic superstition', while even *The Birth of Tragedy* contains a very unorthodox commentary on *Tristan*; and three years later he was conceiving 'insane doubts' as to whether Wagner was a true musician at all. The very interesting personal relations of the two men, to which so much attention has been given, have very little to do with the case; they only befog the plain facts that Nietzsche was powerfully excited by Wagner's music and that he was profoundly disappointed and disgusted when he found that the excitement was not musical but emotional.   1932

Mahler is still [in 1932], twenty years after his death, an unsolved enigma for the greater part of the musical world. His position is comparable with Berlioz's in that musicians who know his work thoroughly are divided into two camps, those who consider him a very great master and those who deny him any creative gift at all. The same sort of complete contradiction exists in Mahler's own personality. He was a Jew, with all the Jew's lack of restraint and his susceptibility to outside influences; yet he must be given a foremost place among Austrian nationalists, for no composer has been more deeply influenced by folk-music—the music of both the races that meet on the Bohemian-Moravian border where he was born and where he spent the first fifteen years of his life. His childlike, almost childish, *naïveté* of spirit was at war with a profoundly philosophical mind continually worrying at the eternal problems that trouble the soul of man. His musical style seems a thing of shreds and patches, made up of borrowings from Beethoven, Schubert, Brahms and Bruckner, and yet it is unmistakably his own. A master of the orchestra, he often seems to score with wilful perversity. One is never sure whether he is a pessimist pretending to be an optimist, a weary Faust trying to comfort himself with the illusion that, unlike Brahms, he has actually found 'den Weg zurück zum Kinderland', or whether he is merely another Schopenhauer, quietly enjoying the pleasant things of life, while preaching a purely theoretical pessimism and enjoying a purely poetic luxury of melancholy. He indulges in irony and parody as freely as any Satie or Berners, and yet he expressly directs that the soprano soloist is to take the child's heaven of the finale of the Fourth Symphony quite seriously, *ohne Parodie*. The whole man and his music are one great paradox. We must take into account, too, his peculiar theories—that the symphonic art of the future must be 'popular' in the broadest sense of the word,[1] that each symphony must be 'the building up of a world', must be long enough to occupy a whole programme, as an opera does, without the intrusion of other music, and must, like the real world, contain the everyday, the homely commonplace. Is it surprising that English musicians who know him only through one or two performances of five out of ten big works (the nine symphonies and *The Song of the Earth*) a year or two ago, plus a few of his songs, have failed to understand his music?

There is another hindrance to the understanding of Mahler. He needs

[1] Again one thinks of Berlioz and his *Symphonie funèbre et triomphale* of which Wagner said that, though it is 'big and noble,' 'any little street boy would understand it perfectly'. Hindemith and some of the other younger Germans seem to be following, in their own fashion, the trail blazed by Mahler.

to be known as a whole, not piecemeal. Just as each of his symphonies, except perhaps the First, is a 'world', so his work as a whole is a sort of planetary system of inter-related worlds. Each work matters for its own sake—and also because of its connection with another in mood or point of view, often even thematically. The First Symphony is connected with the *Lieder eines fahrenden Gesellen* (which we are beginning to know fairly well) of five years earlier; the second of the *Lieder*, 'Ging heut Morgens übers Feld', appears in three of the movements, and the trio of the funeral march is based on another quotation from the cycle. In the third movement of the Second Symphony there is a similar quotation of his setting of 'Die Fischpredigt des Heiligen Antonius' from *Des Knaben Wunderhorn*, and in the next movement an alto soloist is introduced to sing another of the lyrics from Arnim and Brentano's anthology. Another of the *Wunderhorn* songs (not in his set of twelve so-called *Wunderhorn-Lieder*, but No. 11 of the *Lieder aus der Jugendzeit*), 'Ablösung im Sommer', is the basis of the third movement of the Third Symphony. The chorus (fifth movement) of the Third Symphony and the soprano solo (last movement) of the Fourth are both settings of verses about heaven from the *Wunderhorn* and are thematically related. And so this knitting of work to work goes on. The Seventh is full of references to earlier works. The Ninth is not only connected with the *Song of the Earth*, composed at the same time, but looks back to the Fifth Symphony and the *Kindertotenlieder*, two other contemporaneous works written about seven years earlier. A composer who writes in this lordly way, taking it for granted that we know everything he has written previously, and at such unheavenly lengths, is asking for trouble. Many people will naturally feel that if they cannot understand a not very attractive composer without knowing the whole of him they would rather leave him alone altogether. It is for people who feel like this about Mahler that I want to offer a sort of bird's-eye view of his work as a whole, to map out the planetary system I have spoken of, so that when they come across a single 'world' they may have some understanding of its relation to the others. And I should like to do this as far as possible without obtruding my personal opinions.

In laying out this 'map' we have the authority of the composer as regards the main outlines, the 'periods' beloved of every musical biographer since Wilhelm von Lenz. Not long before his death Mahler told Alfredo Casella that he considered his first four symphonies to constitute his 'first period' and the next four his 'second', while he regarded the Ninth as the beginning of a third period. Mahler's friend, Guido Adler, in his monograph on the composer, accepts this classification broadly, but dates the first period of ripe creative activity from 1883, when Mahler was twenty-three, and is unable to see any fresh elements in the Ninth. Let us see how this works out.

We may neglect everything written before 1883; the young Mahler ranged over a wide field—chamber music, opera, orchestral pieces—before he found his true sphere. Of these early productions only five songs the first book of the *Lieder aus der Jugendzeit*, have survived. The present form of *Das klagende Lied* (based on the familiar folk-tale of the murdered man's bone made into a flute which, when played, betrays the murderer), written about 1878–80, dates from eighteen years later and is the result of drastic revision.

The first period proper begins, then, with the composition in 1884 of the four *Lieder eines fahrenden Gesellen*, for which Mahler wrote the words as well as the music, and the first sketches of the First Symphony. But these were not fruitful years. Mahler the composer was to the end hampered by Mahler the conductor. He had time to write only in the holidays. As his enemies sneered, he was a 'summer composer'. (And has not the same fate overtaken the later Strauss?) In the eighties he was still a nonentity trying to establish himself, forced to content himself with assistant-conductorships at Prague and Leipzig. From this period dates his completion of Weber's unfinished comic opera, *The Three Pintos*. Late in 1888, just after he took up his first important post, the directorship of the Royal Opera at Budapest, he finished his First Symphony in D major. Nothing could be more typical of Mahler's mentality, for it is linked with his own work, the *Lieder eines fahrenden Gesellen*, as we have already seen, and reflects his love of nature, his affection for folk-music and his literary leanings—in this case towards the favourites he shared with Schumann, Jean Paul Richter and E. T. A. Hoffmann, particularly the former. The symphony was originally entitled *Titan*, after the greatest of Jean Paul's novels; the second movement, a typical Austrian *Ländler*, is connected with another of Jean Paul's books, *Siebenkäs*; while the third, 'The Hunter's Funeral Procession' (with the animals marching behind and—apparently—singing the old student canon, 'Bruder Martin, schläfst du noch?'), was originally subtitled 'Funeral March in Callot's Style,' just as Hoffmann had called his first book (containing the 'Kreisleriana') *Phantasiestücke in Callots Manier*. The march, the first of Mahler's experiments in the musical expression of pessimistic irony, might well have been composed by Kapellmeister Kreisler; at any rate there is far more of Hoffmann's mad musician in it than in Schumann's pleasant day-dreams. But the symphony as a whole takes its tone from the first movement, 'Spring—and no end'. There is the earliest stirring of nature before the dawn; the cuckoo calls across the fields—first of the many nature sounds Mahler loved to introduce in his works, though they are usually less definite than this; and then his 'wayfaring man' comes along, an Austrian peasant enjoying the sparkle of the early morning and quite agreeing with the finch:

Guten Morgen! Ei du, gelt?
Wird's nicht eine schöne Welt?

In the same year, 1888, Mahler came across Arnim and Brentano's famous anthology of old German folk-song poetry, *Des Knaben Wunderhorn*.[1] It was strange that neither his literary interests nor his love of folk-songs had led him to it before. Now, the *Wunderhorn* poems, so belatedly discovered, went to his head and heart—and stayed there. During the next twelve years everything he wrote was closely connected with them. Indeed, someone has said that *Des Knaben Wunderhorn* might stand as the motto to Mahler's life-work. Perhaps that is why we English fail to understand him, for the *Wunderhorn* means nothing to us; at least, no more than *A Shropshire Lad* to a German. The earlier *Wunderhorn* songs (up to 1892) appeared with piano accompaniments as the second and third volumes of the *Lieder aus der Jugendzeit*; 'Scheiden und Meiden' is probably the best known in England. Twelve others (including the contralto solo, 'Urlicht,' from the Second Symphony, and a solo version of 'Es sungen drei Engel' from the Third) are grouped together as a cycle of *Wunderhorn-Lieder* with orchestral accompaniment. 'Trost im Unglück,' the delightful 'Wer hat dies Liedlein erdacht?' and the 'Rheinlegendchen' all belong to this group. In addition there are two later settings, 'Revelge' and 'Der Tambourgesell,' with which the *Wunderhorn* period closes at the turn of the century. And as we have already seen, the Second, Third and Fourth Symphonies (finished in 1894, 1896 and 1900 respectively) are all intimately connected with the *Wunderhorn* poems.

Already with the Second Symphony (in C minor), the so-called *Resurrection* Symphony, Mahler begins to enlarge the scope of the symphony, to 'build up worlds'; though in this case he goes no further than Beethoven had done in the Ninth, except in length. The 'world' is tragic, but the end of the symphony is optimistic. The character of the first movement gave rise to a report that it had been inspired by the death of Bülow, and the composer acknowledged that the idea of a choral finale on Klopstock's hymn, 'Aufersteh'n, ja aufersteh'n', came to him during the memorial service to Bülow in the Michaeliskirche in Hamburg. After the third movement, a *Ländler* which Mahler himself quaintly compared with the watching of distant dancers whose music one cannot hear, an alto soloist sings some consoling verses from the *Wunderhorn*, in which more than one of Mahler's German admirers sees 'something naïvely moving' in the false accent on 'abweisen' (properly: '*ab*weisen'):

[1] Arnim and Brentano brought out their collection in three volumes, Heidelberg, 1806–8. Bettina, Arnim's wife and Brentano's sister, was that celebrated minx who apparently p ti vated both Beethoven and Goethe and was responsible for bringing about the meeting the two giants in 1812.

Ex. 1

Passionately, but tenderly

Ach nein! Ich liess mich nicht ab - wei - sen, Ach nein! ich liess mich nicht ab - wei - sen

And then, after a long orchestral episode, a Doomsday march in which Mahler tried to show 'the great procession of the dead, rich and poor, kings and people, the *ecclesia militans* and the Popes' (to use his own words), the chorus sing Klopstock's hymn, 'Thou shalt arise, my dust, after short rest' to which Mahler added four stanzas of his own.

The Third Symphony in D minor is immensely long—it plays for two hours—and yet the Fourth (in G major) is so closely related to it as to seem almost a continuation. It must certainly be regarded as a sequel. In contrast with the Second, the Third was originally to have been called 'Meine fröhliche Wissenschaft'—apparently with reference to Nietzsche's book. After a huge first movement, 'Pan's awakening; the entry of Summer', come five shorter ones originally entitled: 'What the meadow flowers tell me', 'What the animals of the forest tell me', 'What Man tells me', 'What the Angels in Heaven tell me' and 'What Eternal Love tells me'. Man's message is Nietzsche's Midnight Song from *Zarathustra*, the message of Delius's *Mass of Life*; that of the angels is a choral setting of some naïve verses from the *Wunderhorn*. The finale of the Fourth Symphony really belongs to its predecessor; Mahler thought of this as 'What the Child tells me' and it is yet another vision from the *Wunderhorn* of a heaven which can best be described as a German version of the negro heaven of *Green Pastures*. The three earlier movements of the symphony are, even thematically, little more than a prelude to it. The Fourth Symphony closes the *Wunderhorn* period.

Mahler's second period, like his first, opens with a group of songs which unmistakably point the direction for his symphonic thought. These are all settings of Rückert, the cycle of five *Kindertotenlieder* and five other songs, 'Ich atmet' einen linden Luft', 'Liebst du um Schönheit', 'Blicke mir nicht in die Lieder', 'Ich bin der Welt abhanden gekommen' and 'Um Mitternacht'. All ten date from the period 1901–2, though they did not appear till three or four years later. The *Kindertotenlieder*, by the way, have no autobiographical significance for, although Mahler actually lost his elder daughter, she did not die till 1907—indeed had not been born when these songs were written. But the tragic nature of the songs impregnates the next three symphonies—No. 5 in C sharp minor (1902), No. 6 in A minor (1904) and No. 7 in E minor (1905)—particularly the Sixth, which Mahler himself called his 'Tragic'. And just as the Fourth Symphony appears to be a gigantic footnote to the Third, the Seventh seems to be an appendix to the Sixth. In the Seventh, too, there is a sentimental looking back, in the middle movements, to the *Wunderhorn* period when there were problems and contradictions just the same, it is true, but when the problems of life seemed to have a solution and when one could forget the contradictions by becoming as a child. Musically these three symphonies show a deepening, a growing complication of style. But no one, I think, finds any difficulty in understanding Mahler musically; he is far too obvious and diatonic. The difficulty lies in this very obviousness and in ignorance of the meaning of what we must call 'personal *Leitmotive*', such as the enigmatic alternation of major and minor triads which plays such an important part in the Sixth and Seventh Symphonies. The clue to that cryptogram is in the Third Symphony, where Mahler (like Strauss a year or two before) had used it to underline the message of the questioning Zarathustra:

Ex. 2

These symphonies in fact are further sermons on Rückert's text, 'Ich bin der Welt abhanden gekommen.'

In 1897 Mahler had confessed to Arthur Seidl that when he conceived a great musical painting, he always came to a point where he was compelled to 'use words as the vehicle of the musical idea', though Adler insists that the words are merely the accompaniment to, or commentary on, the music, not *vice versa*—a doubtful point. Now these three symphonies, the Fifth, Sixth and Seventh (like the Ninth), are purely orchestral, but in the Eighth (the so-called 'Symphony of the Thousand', finished in 1907) Mahler flies wholly to words. The Eighth is a 'symphony' only in Mahler's sense, 'a world built up by all available means', though it is true the first part, the setting of the 'Veni creator spiritus', is musically shaped to sonata-form, and the second, the *Faust* part, contains the elements of the conventional slow movement, scherzo and finale.

It is curious that Mahler's third period, if we accept his own classification, begins like his first and second, with a song-cycle—this time a setting of poems from Hans Bethge's *Die chinesische Flöte*. But in this case the song-cycle, *Das Lied von der Erde* (finished in 1908), was given an orchestral accompaniment and itself grew to symphonic proportions so that the composer himself styled it a 'symphony'. The weak Ninth Symphony was finished a year later than *The Song of the Earth* and stands in the same relation to it as the Fourth to the Third Symphony, and the Seventh to the Sixth. The work of a sick and exhausted man, it is a disappointing pendant to the work which is usually considered to be Mahler's masterpiece. One point in connection with Bethge's poems must be made clear, though of no great importance, for it led a well-known critic badly astray on the occasion of the first English performance of the *Lied* a couple of years ago. Bethge's lyrics are not *translations* from Li-Tai-Po and other Chinese poets of the eighth century, but *Nachdichtungen*, re-creations such as Rückert made from Hafiz and Firdusi and, to come nearer home, such as Fitzgerald made from Omar. *Das Lied von der Erde* covers many moods—hedonistic pessimism, reminding one of Omar, in the first song; naïve happiness, taking one back to the early days of the 'wayfaring man' and *Des Knaben Wunderhorn*, in the third and fourth movements; irony, tempered with good humour, in the fifth, 'The Drunkard in Spring'.

> What's the Spring to do with me
> So long as I can drunken be?

These all have their counterparts in the earlier Mahler. But it is the second and last movements, 'Autumn Loneliness' and 'Farewell' (the only ones, as it happens, of which the words are not after Li-Tai-Po) that strike the key-note of the whole, the melancholy longing for rest after futile striving that is echoed in the Ninth Symphony. One line near the end of 'Der Abschied' ('Mir war auf dieser Welt das Glück nicht hold!') sounds like a paraphrase of one of the Rückert songs. It is true the very end speaks of eternal Spring, but Mahler's last gesture was really a question mark, the line he himself inserted in three places in the opening poem—'Dunkel ist das Leben, ist der Tod.' The whole thing was never a darker mystery than at the very end. The only consolation was the beauty of the earth, of nature.

Finally, something must be said of Mahler's music *as* music. Obviously it is hardly ever 'absolute' music, even though it seldom verges on the definitely programmatic. Whatever Mahler's champions may say, these symphonies are intensely subjective. They convey a 'message', embody a philosophy of life (or the longing for one), and music which tries to do that is naturally repugnant to some people. It is arguable that music can do nothing of the kind, even when harnessed to words. But the conviction that it can is apparent in all Mahler's music, and no one who does not bear that in mind can hope to understand him. Still, purpose is not achievement. Art attaches no value to moral aims, and every artist will agree that a beautiful little tune about nothing at all may be worth more than a colossal symphony about the cosmos. Mahler's music, like everyone else's, must stand or fall on its purely musical merits. Not many people will grumble nowadays at the 'looseness' of Mahler's structures, however much they may object to their size. Mahler had acquired, at any rate from the time of the Fifth Symphony, a technique fit for any task. His idiom, diatonic through and through, offers no more difficulty to our ears than Mendelssohn's does. His wildest excesses are a few consecutive seconds or sevenths. (Yet his music is admired by such advanced composers as Schönberg and Casella.) The attacks of Mahler's adversaries are all centred on his thematic material, which is said to be almost entirely 'derivative,' 'platitudinous,' 'saccharine' and 'characterless'. And it does appear to be all this. Far from trying to be original, to hammer out a musical speech of his own, Mahler seems to have been quite content to express what he had to say in the language of his predecessors. Instead of avoiding melodic resemblances, he seems to have taken pleasure in drawing attention to family likenesses, for instance, by playing them on eight horns *unisono* as in the opening of the Third Symphony:

Ex. 3

Perhaps he felt that they proved his rightful descent. And, in fairness, we must remember that some of the likeness to Schubert and others is due to the common influence of German folk-song. Inspiration is only the drawing up of a bucket from the well of memory, particularly memories of childhood. Genius does something we don't understand to the water; but the water is the basis. If we want to make good composers of our children we should see that their minds are packed with the right sort of memories. The poor little Jewish boy who used to hang about the barracks at Iglau, sometimes marching beside the troops, who at four years old used to play the soldiers' songs and military marches on his mouth-organ, was storing up bad material for a symphonist worried about the universe. It is generally agreed that Mahler's love of march-rhythms and fanfare-like themes and his curiously individual use of the percussion are due to these early impressions. Their other consequences are perhaps less obvious but more serious. And unfortunately the genuine folk-music of the district, which left an equally deep mark on his musical character, is not much more valuable artistically.

On the other hand, it is only fair to remember that the banality of Mahler's material was not always unintentional, a matter of bad taste, but was sometimes intended ironically, sometimes as a sincere attempt to express the homely, bourgeois feelings which, in his view, had a place in art as in life. You may think his view wrong-headed, just as you may deny the possibility of expressing irony in music, but it is unjust to ascribe everything commonplace in his work to poverty of invention. And before we finally decide that Mahler's material is hopelessly bad, I should like to draw attention once more to the parallel with Berlioz. Beside a reflection by Berlioz on his own melodies I will put one by Weingartner on Mahler's.

Berlioz says—and those who appreciate his music will agree that he is stating no more than the simple truth:

> They are often on a large scale; and an immature or short-sighted musical vision may not clearly distinguish their form; or, again, they may be accompanied by secondary melodies which, to a limited vision, may veil the form of the principal ones.

Weingartner uses almost the same expressions:

> Characteristic of Mahler is the significant spread (*Breite*) of his themes. I believe, for example, that those who . . . considered the first movement of the Second Symphony to be meaningless nonsense, had altogether failed to grasp as a whole the massive dimensions of the principal theme; it must naturally have been difficult for them to follow its development!

Is that the explanation of Mahler's 'banality'? That the blocks are so huge that we cannot get far enough away from them to see anything but the coarseness of the texture, as Gulliver was revolted by the skins of the Brobdingnagians? Or is it that Mahler's melodic line has a subtle something which eludes all who are not his compatriots? Can it be that our lack of understanding of Mahler is the precise equivalent of the foreign musician's inability to hear anything but folk-song and platitudes in Vaughan Williams? All these possibilities must be carefully examined before we can attempt a final valuation of Mahler's music.

1932

XXVIII—DELIUS AND HIS LITERARY SOURCES

It is only during the last ninety years that the study of a composer's literary sources has been of any assistance to the understanding of his work. Till then, the period immediately following Beethoven's death, the points of contact between music and literature were few and usually accidental. Not only was music essentially self-contained (even the best dramatic music was only concerned with the poorer journalism of drama) but musicians were, as a professional body, only divinely gifted craftsmen. The few wealthy amateurs, men of all-round culture, who flit through the pages of musical history were insufficiently gifted as musicians or too much concerned with conformity to the professional conventions of their time to act as fertilising influences. When music concerned itself with any text not drawn from the Bible, its function was precisely that of the philosopher's stone.

The change came only with quite a new type of composer, the cultured man who yet had music in every fibre of his being and who had adopted it as a serious career. For instance, and no better could be found, Schumann. We find at once that we cannot fully understand Schumann unless we realise what he drew from Jean Paul, from E. T. A. Hoffmann, above all from Heine. On the other hand the study of Berlioz's literary enthusiasms leads us nowhere. His attitude was not that of the man of culture but of the craftsman-musician who often got ideas from good books: the same attitude as Beethoven's, who struck it less often and who in allying himself for a divine moment with Schiller only proved that he had nothing in common with him. It is scarcely credible that Beethoven loved and lived with the 'Ode to Joy' for more than thirty years and at the end was never truly fertilised by it; though perhaps we should look in the Seventh Symphony rather than the Ninth for the real fruit.

Obviously the effect a book exercises on a man's work is as illuminative as the initial attraction itself. We learn nothing at all from the fact that Gounod wrote a *Faust* (except the already apparent facts that he was commercially minded and had some ability for writing tunes), but we do learn from Liszt's *Faust* Symphony that he was capable of getting inside Goethe's mind and, still more important, we learn what aspects of Goethe's work attracted him most and what aspects he did not understand or from which he was unable to draw musical warmth. Then again we find Schubert, always able to touch doggerel into pure gold, taking at the crown of his career a tiny masterpiece of Heine like 'Still ist die

Nacht' and making of it a masterpiece of quite a different kind. It is only when we realise how beautifully another man might have set those words that we realise how colossal is Schubert's achievement. Schumann apparently could always find the precise musical equivalent of Heine (so inevitable do we feel his settings), but Schubert, whose gifts seem essentially as purely lyrical as either Heine's or Schumann's, transmutes this beautifully sentimental heart-break into something infinitely bigger and more tragic. All this preamble is, I think, necessary to a proper understanding of the work of Delius, or, more accurately, of the particular analytical process to which I propose to subject it.

Few other composers, probably none, have drawn so heavily on literature for their sources of inspiration. (I do not mean for the subjects of their compositions.) Certainly none have shown sympathies so cosmopolitan and apparently so eclectic. A glance at Heseltine's book shows that at various periods he has been under the spell of half a dozen Scandinavians (Ibsen, Bjørnson, Jacobsen and lesser men), of Tennyson, Shelley, Verlaine, Nietzsche, Gottfried Keller, Walt Whitman, Arthur Symons and Ernest Dowson. His two loveliest songs (to me) are settings of Ben Jonson and Fiona Macleod. He has drawn on the lyrics of Henley, Herrick and Shakespeare. Most of these names are, of course, to be neglected; they mark only single jewels and are quoted only to remind the reader of his catholic, yet predominantly Anglo-Saxon, taste. But the musician whose major works have been inspired by contact with such different minds as Jacobsen, Whitman, Nietzsche and Gottfried Keller would seem to be possessed of exceptional breadth of sympathy, sentimental and intellectual. As a matter of fact Delius's treatment entirely destroys the apparent evidence of his choice. Generally speaking the truth of the proposition as to his exceptionally wide angle of vision remains true, but leaving the cultured man for the musician we find that either every literary masterpiece touches the same musical nerve in him (which is highly improbable) or his selective instinct functions with great acuteness not only in picking out the most curiously diverse books for musical treatment but in finding there scope for the display of that very limited range of musical moods of which Delius's whole art consists.[1] They are few, they recur monotonously, their limitations almost deny Delius the right to be considered as great as he undoubtedly is, but they are of intense and unique beauty—for no one else has ever done anything quite like them.

Delius's 'Scandinavian' period began in 1885 with a Hans Andersen

[1] I discovered the explanation a few years later when I learned from Eric Fenby's *Delius as I knew him* that 'from 1895 onwards, with the exception of the text of the *Mass of Life* ... the composer's wife chose almost every word that he set. Whenever she came upon a poem that matched the mood of that sad longing which she had first sensed in his improvisation, she copied it out and left it on his desk.'

song, and culminated in 1908–11 with the two great Jacobsen works, *Fennimore and Gerda* and *Eine Arabeske*. The Scandinavian bias no doubt originated in one of those natural personal prejudices that everyone forms for a beautiful foreign land where one has made charming friends. It was strengthened by meetings with distinguished Scandinavian musicians and literary men in Paris and Leipzig, as well as in the north, so that throughout the greater part of his creative career, Delius has been in more or less personal contact with the finest minds of Scandinavia—Strindberg, Knut Hamsun, Bjørnson, Grieg and Ibsen, to mention only a few at random. The artistic fruits of this connection long consisted only of songs, minor works in every sense, the best of them settings of that morbidly voluptuous genius, Jens Peter Jacobsen, who was later to strike two masterpieces out of him.

The American impressions began to work on him too, and in 1898, the impact of Nietzsche produced as results the setting of 'O Mensch! Gib Acht!' (on which Mahler had just been trying his hand) from *Zarathustra* and a few songs. Already the *Mass of Life* must have been fermenting in his mind.

Then in 1901 the line of great masterpieces begins with *A Village Romeo and Juliet*, after Gottfried Keller's story. Delius's opera is another example of the sort of transmutation that we noticed in 'Der Doppelgänger'. Keller's simple, poignant *Dorfgeschichte* (from *Die Leute von Seldwyla*) has suffered a sea-change into something far more 'romantic' and elusive. Sali and Vrenchen are no longer simple peasants; Keller's restrained narration with its plain realism is warmed with sentiment and interpreted as symbolism; the Dark Fiddler, good-natured ne'er-do-well, is as mysterious as Dalua in *The Immortal Hour*. Heseltine admits this much; but he forgets to mention the losses as well as the gains, scarcely indeed makes clear at all the relation between Keller and Delius. Delius's distant boatmen with their lovely

Ex. 1

at the end are a distinct gain, but the interpolation of the dream-wedding in the fourth 'picture' could well be dispensed with. Musically it is below the general standard of the work, artistically it is Teutonically sentimental without Humperdinck's excuse of catering for the child mind. Keller's Vrenchen dreamt more naturally, of festival clothes and dancing, and that so common sensation of trying in vain to reach someone; his Sali of going on an endless road through a wood, with Vrenchen beckoning in the distance 'and then it was like being in Heaven. That's all!' But in the opera their dreams are of Seldwyla church—and they both dream the same thing.

But the central theme of *A Village Romeo and Juliet* recurs again and again in Delius. It is generated by his view of life as something inexorably cruel to the individual, meltingly beautiful in its cruelty and with infinite power of renewal. He accepts it passively and underlines the beauty. Not for him the protest and struggle of Beethoven, the joyous all-embracing acceptance of Wagner, the renunciation of Brahms (but do we not love Brahms best when he looks back over his shoulder?); he takes life as Thomas Hardy took it. This brooding over beautiful cruelty would be repulsively morbid were it not for the ever-present faith in rebirth, the Nietzschean 'ewige Wiederkunft'. Sali and Vrenchen, the lovers who find life together impossible, are mirrored in *Sea-Drift* and in Flecker's *Hassan*. The same situation recurs with variations in *Fennimore and Gerda*. In Jacobsen's book fate is too much even for Niels and Gerda (though poor Niels is essentially a lonely person and the author certainly loaded the dice against him). But in this case Delius could not resist the call of spring that ever rings in his ears. In the book Niels makes his memorable visit to Gerda's father 'on a hot summer's day'; Delius's stage direction asks for 'spring' (and the flute twitters like an April morning): a trifling point but significant. He has allowed *Fennimore and Gerda* to end on this note. The *Requiem*, too, turns finally to spring and the rather bleak *North Country Sketches* end with 'The March of Spring'. Even the heartbreaking intermezzo ('The walk to the Paradise Garden') in *A Village Romeo and Juliet* hints at *The First Cuckoo*:

Ex. 2
Moderato

Sounding a deeper note, the *Mass of Life* dwells finally on 'tiefe, tiefe Ewigkeit'—which is the same thing (or, rather, the thing itself instead of the visible sign of it). Very different is the conclusion of *Sea-Drift*, with its sad 'no more', yet something in the music contradicts it or at least neutralises it, even while it seems to underline it. Delius did not bring that sympathy to Whitman which both Holst and Vaughan Williams evidently feel, the kindred aspiration and the intellectual acquiescence. But he found a poem whose central mood was that of his favourite motive, clothed it with lovely sound (*smothered* it, in truth, judging from performance) and made a masterpiece. I feel that the unity of mood between poem and music is due to the common vein of nostalgia rather than to any force exercised by the poem on the composer's creative faculty. Rather, the music seems to have absorbed the words. *Sea-Drift* probably has a parentage no more literary than that of *Appalachia*, the work that immediately preceded it. Indeed the words, such as they are, that emerge at the end of *Appalachia* deal with the same motive of love and parting. Both works were probably generated by that vague revelling in misery that is apparently native to the air of southern North America. Unfortunately we are accustomed to associate this sentiment with particularly abominable music, but, on a higher level, Coleridge-Taylor's arrangement of 'Deep River' (in his *Twenty-four Negro Melodies*) might be instructively compared with *Sea-Drift*. Despite the complete disparity of works on such totally different planes the same basic sentiment is expressed in both in the same harmonic 'over-ripeness'. Coleridge-Taylor's chords exist in a different world from those of Delius, but they spring from the same voluptuous love of pathos.

Since the *Mass of Life* (1905) and the two big Jacobsen works (1908–1911) Delius has been less obviously inspired by literature. The choral *Song of the High Hills* is wordless; the 'book' of the *Requiem* seems to have been compiled by, or for, the composer; the *Hassan* music is not of first-rate importance.

The self-assertive Nietzsche and the retiring poet Jacobsen would seem to have little in common but the highly nervous tension betrays itself in both cases in occasional hysteria. It is curious to see how Delius has fastened on both and drawn to the fore other common factors by a process of sympathetic exaggeration. Any attempt to draw a parallel between works so different in type and scope would, of course, be ridiculous; in any case Delius is far too sensitive not to have been deeply influenced by the difference between Nietzsche's resonant, excited rhetoric and Jacobsen's nervous prose, 'each drop from the well of his speech . . . heavy, strong as a drop of elixir or poison, scented like a drop of costly essence,' as Georg Brandes put it. The trend of Delius's later harmonic development also emphasises the sensitiveness of *Fennimore and Gerda*. Yet each figure—Niels Lyhne, hopeless, passive, bitter and Zarathustra, heavy with knowledge, but supported by his unconquerable will and hope—goes his lonely way, bitter and misunderstood, along a path of exceptional natural beauty. In choosing from *Also sprach Zarathustra* his 'book' for the *Mass* Delius has, consciously or not, picked such passages as are remarkable for their poetry rather than their philosophy. His music drowns the surviving philosophy of the words here as effectually as it softens the harsh realism of the tragedy of Fennimore and Erik. In both works (as in almost everything else Delius has done) responsiveness to the moods of nature, expressed in music of extraordinary sensuous beauty, overwhelms human thoughts and feelings. The fjord at night, the beech forest in autumn, the murmur of the fountains of Rome ('Nacht ist es: nun reden lauter alle springenden Brunnen'), the mountains with the distant horn-calls—in such moments is gathered all that is worth remembering in both works. Zarathustra dreams while 'glowing mid-day sleeps on the fields'; Niels Lyhne takes his ease in the idyllic tenth 'picture' in the old farmyard at home at Lönborggard. The maidens in the green meadow in the evening dance as Zarathustra passes, much as Gerda's sisters frolic when Niels calls to see their father. These things are really trivial episodes but Delius expands them and dwells on them with such loving care, lavishes on them such loveliness of sound that they remain with us when the memory of more crucial points has faded.

So we are brought back to the position of *Sea-Drift*. Judging from the vocal score only (a treacherous guide in Delius's case) the setting of Jacobsen's *Arabeske* is similar. The poem is more or less contemporary with the *Gurrelieder* and therefore much earlier than *Niels Lyhne*; Jacobsen was a poet before he was a novelist.

In every case the human element is overwhelmed by the natural background. Given almost any poem or book that attracts him by the presence of one or other of his favourite themes, Delius is stirred to music—and the music, however varied in manner, is in essence the same. Often, too, amusingly the same (or nearly so) in very substance, for Delius has many favourites beside his cuckoo-calls. But, as they are so very lovely, who complains?

There is just one other point that may be mentioned in connection with Delius and his literary loves. It is a matter of prosody, important not only for its own sweet sake, but because it may be used as evidence on the oft-debated point of the composer's 'Englishness'. Delius is notoriously careless, if sometimes surprisingly happy, in the setting of his native language, and one sometimes hears the fact cited as one more proof that he is 'not in the least English'. I am not concerned to prove that he is. The matter seems of small importance. But it seems worth while to mention that, if his national sympathies are international (if one may venture on an Irishism), Delius is equally impartial in his ill-treatment of foreign tongues. He is not only careless in setting difficult German vowels to high notes but in simple points of verbal accentuation. He sets 'In dein Auge schaute ich jüngst, o Leben' with 'In' heavily stressed. Nor would a German composer, I think, have written:

Ex. 3
Andante molto tranquillo
pp Bassi I soli

Nacht —— ist es.

Surely one feels it much quicker, quickly and lightly, a dactyl ('Nacht ist es'), like a puff of the night breeze.

Obviously Delius cares nothing for such points. When words have struck music out of him he wants to have done with them. That they have to be woven into the music strikes him as a nuisance—and, judging from a great many passages, an unnecessary one. How gladly he uses the chorus for wordless passages (*Appalachia*, the *Mass of Life* and the *Song of the High Hills*). The most beautiful vocal line in the whole of *Fennimore and Gerda* is that of a distant tenor in the second 'picture', singing to 'ah'.

As with actual words, so with whole books; once they have given him the initial impulse to compose they carry Delius little farther. He cannot lean comfortably on them, far less (as minor composers are glad to do) allow them to carry him over his own bald patches. Sometimes they are even a little burdensome. Perhaps that acknowledgment is the highest tribute one may offer a musician.

1929

XXIX—THE BARTÓK OF THE QUARTETS

Writing some time ago in 'another place' on Bartók's Sixth String Quartet, I remarked that it was 'the latest of what is arguably the most important series of string quartets since Beethoven'. I promptly qualified that apparently extravagant claim by pointing out that

there have not been many 'series' of quartets since Beethoven at all; so many musicians—Franck, Debussy, Ravel, Elgar, Sibelius, for instance—have thrown off single quartets of great value and then failed to return to the medium. Brahms's three quartets and Schumann's set of three, again, hardly represent their composers at the height of their powers; one certainly cannot trace in them their composer's musical autobiographies. It is rare indeed to find, as we do in Bartók, a composer who has turned to the string quartet at every stage of his creative career and put into his quartets the very best of himself.

Bartók is said to have written his earliest string quartet in 1899, but this work, like most of his early compositions, has never been published. The published quartets are dated as follows:

No. 1 (Op. 7)	1908
No. 2 (Op. 17)	1915–17
No. 3 (without opus-number)	September 1927
No. 4 (,, ,,)	July–September 1928
No. 5 (,, ,,)	6 August–6 September, 1934
No. 6 (,, ,,)	August–November 1939

and thus give a fairly complete cross-section of Bartók's development. Edwin von der Null has traced that development, up to the First Piano Concerto,[1] through the piano music; but although the piano compositions are much more numerous, they are marked by such vagaries of style —many being folk-song arrangements or pieces for children—that they do not collectively give such a clear impression as the six quartets. Moreover the quartets represent Bartók's best or at any rate most serious work at each period—which can hardly be said of many of the piano pieces. The Bartók revealed by the quartets (we may put it) is the greater part of Bartók, though by no means the whole Bartók.

The earliest work in which Bartók showed his real mettle was the set of fourteen *Bagatelles* for piano, Op. 6. The *Bagatelles* might serve almost

[1] *Béla Bartók*, Halle, 1930.

as a dictionary of modern music; each is a study in one or more of the devices that were just being added to the musician's vocabulary: poly-tonality, added-note chords, fourth-chords and melodies derived from them, appoggiaturas used instead of 'real' notes of the harmony, and so on. There are some charming things among the *Bagatelles*, but a good many dry things. One gets the impression that some of them are rather cold-blooded, cerebral experiments; indeed Bartók himself admitted as much to von der Nüll. As a set they are less immediately attractive than the *Ten Easy Piano Pieces* written in the same year: 1908. The First Quartet also dates from 1908, and bears the opus-number following that of the *Bagatelles*; it also bears traces of the same delight in new-found resources. But it has none of the naked experimentalism of the *Bagatelles*; it is live music. It is essentially, perhaps, not so very different from the earlier Bartók, though the thought is now expressed in more difficult idioms. The middle section of the slow first movement, for instance:

is of the early, not the mature Bartók. And the expressive canon, first for the violins, then for viola and cello (with the violins continuing in free parts), which opens the movement and, in a curtailed form, closes it, has really very little in common with Bartók's later uncompromisingly linear style; the chromatic polyphony should be no more, if no less, worrying to modern ears than the polyphony of the Prelude to Act III of *Parsifal* was to Victorian ears, and it analyses out, harmonically, in something the same way. Nor does the *allegretto* second movement, which follows without a break, offer any special difficulty; the thirds in which the transition-theme is stated are curiously un-Bartókian. (I call it the transition-theme because it is so used, although it is later woven firmly into the movement proper.)

There is a break after this second movement, and with the introduction to the third we at last reach music that bears the quite unmistakable hall-mark of Bartók, 'stamping' chords for the three upper strings, the only outlet for his tendency to percussiveness that he had yet found through this medium, and the rhapsodic cello recitative that answers them. Two points in particular attract attention in the recitative: the ♪ ♩. rhythmic figure, from Hungarian folk-song, and a motive obviously derived from an accompaniment figure that has played an important part in the *allegretto*:

But it is only with the opening of the finale proper that the importance of this motive becomes fully manifest:

(The chafing seconds of the violin parts are, of course, very characteristic of Bartók; but their uncharacteristic resolution suggests that the movement dates from before the piano *Bagatelles*.) Ex. 3 turns out to be the first subject of a movement conceived broadly on the lines of sonata form. However bold his melodic, rhythmic and harmonic experiments, Bartók has seldom revealed revolutionary views of form, though the Third Quartet is boldly experimental; indeed he has often appeared definitely conservative in this respect. In this movement the formal outline is easily recognisable despite the organic fusion of sections and the blurring of tonality and cadences. The key is A minor—a very Bartókian A minor, of course—and the exposition consists mostly of development (the motive *a*, worked imitationally, *b* more lyrically); a second subject duly turns up, *adagio*, in what Bartók probably regarded as B flat minor; and there is a development 'proper', beginning with a declamatory octave passage and proceeding by way of a lengthy *fugato* on a theme evolved from Ex. 3. The evolving process includes the growth of a new motive with a triplet kink, which plays some part in the recapitulation, but the recapitulation is no freer than many classical examples, and the *adagio* second subject even recurs in the tonic. Bartók was still clinging to shreds of the tonal principle when he wrote his First Quartet.

In the interval between this and the Second Quartet he wrote, among other things, the *Dirges* for piano, *Bluebeard's Castle*, the *Deux Images* and *Four Pieces*, Op. 12, for orchestra, and *The Woodcut Prince*, works in which he showed himself a complete master of the new resources that had been only partly assimilated in 1908. The Second Quartet is thoroughly characteristic in a way that the First, as a whole, is not. It is by no means as difficult to grasp as the next two quartets of ten years or so later; but, standing back from the quartets as a series and trying to consider them in perspective, one feels that perhaps Nos. 3 and 4 are in one

sense only complications and subtilisations of an essence that is already
fully present in No. 2. The simplicity and intimacy of No. 2, as compared
with No. 1, are very noticeable, and the chief second-subject theme of
the first movement is remarkable for its euphony (admittedly a rare
quality in Bartók), particularly when it returns in the recapitulation:

For the first movement of No. 2, like the finale of No. 1, is in sonata
form, and the two movements have this further point in common that
one of the transition themes here has precisely the same triplet 'kink'
that we noticed in the earlier work. To speak of 'themes' in the ordinary
sense, however, becomes a little misleading in dealing with music of this
type. There are motives of four or five notes, and there are thoughts
spread over many bars; but the motives by no means constitute the true
substance of the thoughts: they are not so much the bricks in the musical
structure as the mortar. The subtlety with which motive grows from
motive, and with which a motive gradually assumes a new form, is well
worth close study (there are striking parallels to Sibelius's methods),
but could be shown here only with the help of abundant music-type
examples. However, two shorter examples must be used to illustrate one
other characteristic of Bartók's handling of sonata form: his conception
of reprise. In his recapitulation themes are liable to return in strongly
modified forms; as a rule in simpler or at any rate more easily apprehended
forms and in a purer harmonic atmosphere. I quote the opening of this
movement and the parallel passage, the opening of the recapitulation:

Both the scherzo and the *lento* finale present peculiar puzzles and attractions. The puzzle of the scherzo is its form, which appears at first hearing or reading to be hardly existent—or at any rate to be conditioned simply by the heading, *allegro molto capricioso* (sic), and held together by nothing more than its persistent minor-third motive. But if it be considered as a suite of miniature dances connected by lyrical interludes, on exactly the same lines as the much more extended *Dance Suite* for orchestra (written in 1923), everything becomes clear. Like the dances that make up this later *Suite*, those of the middle movement of the Quartet are attractive and strongly rhythmical; not (I should say) actual folk dances or imitations of them, but impregnated, like the vast bulk of Bartók's music, with influences from Hungarian folk music. The gradual—and to the unaided ear quite imperceptible—transition from the 2/4 of the *sostenuto* interlude to the 3/4 of the *allegro molto* dance is typical of Bartók's plastic conception of rhythm and tempo.

The final *lento* is harder to accept. Its painful brooding tries the ear's patience much more than the lively clashes of the middle movement. Bartók seems here to be experimenting a little too self-consciously with his fourths-harmony; near the end he builds up a chord of five perfect fourths (A sharp, D sharp, G sharp, C sharp, F sharp, B). But the muted passage, *lento assai*, is a beautiful demonstration of the expressive possibilities of this generally rather hard and unyielding harmonic idiom:

The finale of Op. 17 is to me the only really 'difficult' movement of the first two quartets, but in Nos. 3 and 4 the difficulties thicken. No. 3 is a particularly hard nut to crack; it came as the climax to a whole series of 'difficult' works including the two violin sonatas, the Piano Sonata and the First Piano Concerto. To the customary harmonic difficulties of Bartók's music and the difficulty of a melodic idiom of which one parent is a particularly remote folk-music, the other intellectual modernism, are added special difficulties of structure: of both inner, detailed structure and outer, general structure. Bartók's motive-logic is nowhere tighter than in the Third Quartet, but it is also nowhere more elliptical than in its *prima parte*. To grasp all the links in the chain of musical reasoning is impossible to the unaided ear, difficult to the score-reading eye. Yet one feels with absolute conviction that this is not mere paper music, like so much of Schönberg; the ingenuities of motive-logic constitute the structural principle, the organic tissue, of the music—not its real sense. That has to be apprehended in longer periods. One may put it that Bartók's Third Quartet occupies the same place in his whole work as Sibelius's Fourth Symphony in his. The gradual growth of one motive-form into another, the constructive functions of certain intervals (particularly the perfect fourth), and on the other hand the alteration of intervals to provide new melodic forms: all demand bar-by-bar study. But, short of critical exegesis on that scale, one can still point out the best ways of penetrating to the heart of the music. For Bartók is consistent in his personal development; one can generally find clues to his new works in his earlier music; he even opens this Third Quartet, after the five introductory bars, with a canon for the violins—a very Bartókian canon with inessential notes:

Ex. 7

precisely as he had opened the First Quartet with a canon for the violins. And, as I have said, Bartók's themes are liable to return, in recapitulations, in more easily apprehended forms and in a purer harmonic atmosphere. So we shall do well to look for the thematic clue to the Quartet on some later page. And accordingly we shall find it, not in the part of the Quartet actually marked *ricapitulazione della prima parte*, but towards the end of the *prima parte* itself:

Ex. 8

That passage, played by second violin and viola in octaves, contains the thematic germ of the whole movement.

But in this Quartet it is perhaps wrong to speak of movements. It plays without a break and, like so many older and newer experiments in single-movement cyclic form (Sibelius's Seventh Symphony is one of the few exceptions), fails to convince one that it is wholly successful. In the later quartets Bartók returned to a more normal plan. But here he gives us a *prima parte*, an exposition of the hard sayings just discussed, followed by a *seconda parte* which is best described as incessant variations on a seven-bar theme of folk-dance character:

Ex. 9

The variations, all very typical of Bartók's method of moulding his material plastically, grow very naturally, each from its predecessor, and —with all their use of transformation and inversion, canon and fugue— are easy to follow. But having towards the end reminded us in a *meno mosso, martellato* passage of a point in the first movement, they break into what the composer calls a *ricapitulazione della prima parte*. Needless to say, it is a recapitulation only in the Pickwickian sense, not only much condensed but with the material altered generally beyond aural recognition. And the work ends with a coda that is essentially a brilliant and exuberant continuation of the *seconda parte*.

The Third Quartet is 'on', but not 'in', C sharp. That is to say, there is no trace of major or minor tonality and C sharp cannot be called a tonic, but the note C sharp acts as a centre of gravity, an artificial tonic. Similarly the Fourth Quartet is 'on' C and the Fifth 'on' B flat. Written at an interval of six years, with the Second Piano Concerto half-way between them, they represent successive stages of descent from the asperity of No. 3. Each is in five movements, of which the first and fifth, and second and fourth, in each case balance each other:

No. 4	No. 5
Allegro	*Allegro*
Prestissimo	*Adagio molto*
Non troppo lento	*Scherzo (alla bulgarese)*
Allegretto pizzicato	*Andante*
Allegro molto	*Finale (presto)*

z

In both Quartets the first movements are in easily recognisable sonata form, though in No. 4 some of the material, and in No. 5 all the material, is inverted in the recapitulation. And in No. 5, the second subject returns before the first (for which, of course, there are precedents in the nineteenth century romantics), so that not only the whole Quartet but also its first movement is in this 'arch' form, A B C B A, which may well have been suggested to Bartók by Alfred Lorenz's monumental *Geheimnis der Form bei Richard Wagner*, of which the first volume was published in 1924 and which has much to say about *Bogenform*. I should explain that the first and fifth, and second and fourth, movements correspond to some extent in substance as well as in general tempo. The finale of No. 4 is based on material from the first movement, and the endings of both movements are practically identical. Again, as Alexander Jemnitz was the first to point out,[1] the rondo-finale of No. 5 is based on a free inversion of the chief theme of the first movement; while the two slow movements are not only linked by common motive-particles, both have the same expressive melody as their central feature—though the *adagio* melody:

Ex. 10

is naturally varied in the *andante*:

Ex. 11

The central *alla bulgarese*, again, is cast in the classical scherzo-trio-scherzo pattern, the scherzo material being inverted the second time.

As sheer sound that shimmering *alla bulgarese* (which repays comparison with the last six pieces, the Bulgarian dances, of *Mikrokosmos*) is delicious. Indeed the whole of the Fifth Quartet is less trying to the unaccustomed ear than the Fourth, much less than the Third. The two slow movements are easily appreciable; so too is the rondo-finale with its odd grimace in A major, *con indifferenza* and *meccanico*, just before the coda, though I personally find less in it than in the powerful dancing finale of No. 4. The opening theme of the first movement represents a remarkable adaptation of Bartók's innate percussive tendency to the quartet medium:

[1] In his long and detailed study of the Fifth Quartet in *Musica Viva* (April 1936).

Ex. 12

Once more a canonic exposition! (Though my quotation is necessarily too short to show more than the beginning of the long-breathed canon.) Very characteristic of Bartók's motive-technique is the way the quintuplet kink inserted in the viola-cello line in bars 8, 10 and 11:

Ex. 13

is beheaded and given a new tail to become the coda theme:

Ex. 14

Its shadow, *cancrizans* (*x*), had already fallen across the second subject:

Ex. 15

Or is that too fanciful? But such thematic subtleties are intensely characteristic of Bartók. He moulds and remoulds his motive-particles, resolving one shape into another until it is quite impossible to determine whether such subtleties are deliberate or accidental. But (it cannot be too often repeated) this motive technique is simply a device for forming musical tissue, a means to an end, not the end itself. It must be admitted, however, that in beauty of sound the central movement of No. 4—lacking these subtleties, but with sonorous long-held and repeated chords, against which the cello sings a very Hungarian rhapsody—and the two slow movements of No. 5 surpass the much more finely woven quick movements of either quartet. Amateurs often approach Beethoven, too, most easily through his slow movements.

From the Third Quartet onward Bartók began to experiment with new sound-effects. In No. 3, in addition to all the customary colour-devices of *ponticello* and so on, including passages *col legno*, he introduces long *glissandi* on all four instruments simultaneously and double-stops *glissando*; in the coda he employs quadruple stopping on the cello, played downward or down-and-up. In No. 4 he not only gives this new up-and-down arpeggio effect to the other instruments as well, but experiments with a new type of percussive pizzicato: 'a strong pizzicato making the string rebound off the fingerboard'. The latter is used again, though for one note only, at the end of the scherzo of No. 5; and in the *adagio* of No. 5 the second violin, accompanying Ex. 10, is asked to play four notes 'pizzicato with the nail of the first finger of the left hand, at the extreme end of the string'. But I must emphasise that all these tricks are used very sparingly.

They are used again, though very little, in the Sixth Quartet—separated from the Fifth by a group of works that includes the Sonata for two pianos and percussion, the *Music for Strings, Percussion and Celesta* and the Violin Concerto. Like the Concerto, the Sixth Quartet represents yet a further stage in Bartók's progress towards classic simplicity. Texture, form, rhythm: all are crystal-clear, especially in the two outside movements. Nearest to the earlier Bartók are the second and third movements: a march (akin, but far superior, to the 'Verbunkos', first of the three *Contrasts* for violin, clarinet and piano written the year before) and a 'Burletta'. For in No. 6 the composer abandons the five-movement 'arch' of its two predecessors and tackles the problem of over-all formal unity in a new way, or rather by a new application of that favourite nineteenth-century device, the motto theme. The motto here is the mournful, Hungarian-folksongish strain played by the viola unaccompanied at the very beginning. Played by the cello against a shimmering, muted background, it also introduces the march; worked polyphonically, it provides the prelude to the 'Burletta'. But in none of these three movements does it play any but a preludial part. It is an *idée fixe* three times shaken off. In the short, sad finale it returns and refuses to be shaken off. It dominates the whole movement, and though two of the main themes of the first movement proper make a transitory appearance—the usual Bartókian link between first and last movements—they are now heard in slow tempo, subdued to the mood of the motto theme. And with the first part of the motto, again on the viola, in its original form and at the original pitch, the Quartet ends in a mood of profound and mournful resignation which may have been inspired by contemporary events. (The score, it will be remembered, is dated 'August–November 1939'.)

Most of the familiar characteristics of Bartók's technical procedure reappear in the Sixth Quartet, e.g. when the march proper is repeated after the trio, some of the material returns in free inversion. But everything sounds clearer, easier, less aggressively individual. The first movement is in absolutely classical sonata form with a return to something very like tonality: a first subject in D minor–major and a second subject in a contrasted key in the exposition, in a reconciled key in the recapitulation. And there is more than one point where one is reminded of Beethoven's last quartets: at the beginning, for instance, directly after the viola motto, all four instruments in *pesante* octaves announce the real first subject of the movement in rhythmic augmentation—a passage precisely parallel to the opening of the *Grosse Fuge*—while the main theme of the march awakens echoes of the *alla marcia* in Op. 132. Such similarities are only superficial, musically of no importance. Yet somehow they do not seem insignificant. It is not insignificant that one can mention Beethoven's last quartets and Bartók's in the same sentence without appearing ridiculous.

1945

INDEX